Michael Shepler
1/1/98

The Radical Novel Reconsidered

A series of paperback reissues of mid-twentieth-century U.S. left-wing fiction, with new biographical and critical introductions by contemporary scholars.

Series Editor
Alan Wald, University of Michigan

D1554469

Books in the Series

To Make My Bread
Grace Lumpkin

Moscow Yankee
Myra Page

The People from Heaven
John Sanford

Salome of the Tenements
Anzia Yezierska

The Great Midland
Alexander Saxton

Tucker's People
Ira Wolfert

TUCKER'S PEOPLE

TUCKER'S
PEOPLE

IRA WOLFERT

Foreword by Angus Cameron

Introduction by Alan Filreis

University of Illinois Press • Urbana and Chicago

© 1943, 1997 by Ira Wolfert
Reprinted by arrangement with the author
Foreword and Introduction © 1997 by the
Board of Trustees of the University of Illinois
Manufactured in the United States of America
P 5 4 3 2 1

This book is printed on acid-free paper.

Library of Congress Cataloging-in-Publication Data
Wolfert, Ira, 1908–
Tucker's people / Ira Wolfert ; foreword by Angus Cameron;
introduction by Alan Filreis.
p.   cm. — (The radical novel reconsidered)
Includes bibliographical references.
ISBN 0-252-06598-0 (pbk. : acid-free paper)
I. Title. II. Series.
PS3545.03453T83   1997
813'.52—dc21   97-4100
                                              CIP

To Helen

CONTENTS

Foreword
Angus Cameron xi

Introduction
Alan Filreis xv

BOOK ONE — A PROLOGUE
The Power of Samson 3

BOOK TWO
Within the Walls of the Rich 73

BOOK THREE
An American Hero's Son 147

BOOK FOUR
The Forgotten 209

BOOK FIVE
The Law Business 233

BOOK SIX
A Gleichschaltung 299

BOOK SEVEN
The Victims 373

BOOK EIGHT
An Epilogue 495

FOREWORD

Angus Cameron

It has been fifty-four years since I first read *Tucker's People*. It was in manuscript form then and I had been waiting three years and two months to read it in its entirety. I had read it *ad seriatim,* as its author handed me portions in progress, for Little, Brown & Company, the publisher that had taken an option on the novel at my urging as its New York editor. When the contract was made we had agreed to give Ira Wolfert a small advance to see the finished novel and then an additional advance against royalties if we decided to accept it. When I carried the completed manuscript home to read, I took it as a devoted friend and admirer of the author but with serious concerns about its eventual fate in Boston. The option contract had been issued with some misgivings by my colleagues. Alfred McIntyre, a remarkable man and publisher who could recognize a best-seller clear across his spacious office at 34 Beacon Street, had clearly been indulging his New York editor. He was the kind of executive who believed in hiring staff people and then trusting their judgments to the limits of their positions and responsibility. Alfred knew at once that I had great expectations for *Tucker's People,* not necessarily as a best-selling novel, but as a social and literary achievement of prestigious force. He therefore responded carefully to my strong editorial report by demurring.

Disclaiming any editorial *superiority* ("I'm not an editor, and you are, but I can give, I think, a useful opinion about how well the book will sell"), he paid due respect to my judgment and said, "At this late stage I frankly do not believe another 'gangster novel' can find any kind of an audience, but I see you believe that it will be a novel of such quality that no good publisher can turn it down for commercial reason. Therefore I propose that we give

Mr. Wolfert an option contract and make a final judgment when
he delivers the entire manuscript."

Now, three years later, the entire manuscript had been delivered and the editorial chips were down, as it were. The novel was
subject to the readers of the house. Among the young editors it
found real support, but the best I could extract as a young editor without much editorial muscle was the proposal by Alfred
that we send the manuscript to an outside literary critic of stat-
ure and reputation and let that report settle the matter. I was
exultant, for I believed that the man they had selected would
render a report that would place the novel in proper historical
and literary perspective. I agreed to the proposal with enthusiasm.

I will not denigrate our editorial arbiter, because his report was
respectful enough, but he did not put it alongside *Sister Carrie* or
An American Tragedy, as I had. Unhappily, he even used Alfred's
term "gangster novel." When I encountered that passage I realized that I had lost the battle. During this process, Raymond
Everitt, executive vice president and my good friend, elected to
remain neutral. I guess he knew a losing cause when he saw one.
I was naive then, I suppose, for although I was a politically aware
person I did not believe (as he did) that a novel, Balzacian in
concept and method, that dealt with the Mafia as a mirror of
capitalism in its method and morals might be rejected on political grounds. The author even evinced surprise once that a critic
should ask about the politics of the book. In the end, for this
reason or perhaps others, thirty-two American publishers declined
what some critics consider one of the best novels of the thirties.
Without sociologizing, without politicizing, *Tucker's People* was
a literary work of pure fiction whose social import lay hidden in
the play of deeply revealed characters.

It remained for a refugee publisher, L. B. Fischer, himself a
political victim of Nazism, to recognize that this novel must be
published on its literary merits. He made up for the shortcom-
ings of thirty-two American houses.

My rewards were the chance to see and read the novel in
progress and to see Ira Wolfert's skills develop a social novel

about the lives of average human beings caught up in the irrationality of their social contexts. Alan Filreis in his introduction handles this with great skill and reveals the critical appreciation of the handful of critics who recognized the author's genius at the time.

INTRODUCTION

Alan Filreis

More Political Than Criminal

"*Tucker's People* remains one of the most distinguished American novels of the whole forties." So wrote Walter Rideout in *The Radical Novel in the United States* (1956).[1] His assessment not only commends Ira Wolfert's achievement but also complexly places this 1943 novel, and indeed the question of its literary value, in the context of a period—as a "forties novel," which is perhaps distinct from a "thirties novel." Such placement goes against the grain of most conventional as well as some otherwise outstanding "revisionist" scholarship focusing on the radical novel—such as that of Paula Rabinowitz and Barbara Foley[2]—because it implies that the 1940s was a major moment in the development of the genre.

The 1930s has been generally deemed the single most significant period in which radical novelistic themes and forms were both devised and set for a number of reasons. One is that forties works like those of Willard Motley, Nelson Algren, Norman Mailer, Chester Himes (especially *Lonely Crusade* of 1947), Wolfert, and others[3] seem to have emerged from a more or less independent radicalism, profoundly influenced by but (as Rideout puts it) "not committed to the [Communist] Party as the sole repository of the faith,"[4] and thus tend to be missed by those tracing a direct lineage from the thirties. (Alan Wald's call for studies in "the 'other' thirties" is in part a response to this disconnection.)[5] Another reason is that some Communist novels of the forties, such as Alexander Saxton's *The Great Midland* (1948), elaborately develop nuances of individuals' daily lives, including, in the case of Saxton, minute social and psychological details of a marriage in which the priorities of love are often checks against the demands of the Party—the full consideration of which might well have caused radical reviewers in the early thirties to have criticized the work as digressive, psychoanalytical, negative, or merely personal. Another reason for thirties exceptionalism is the persistence of the cold war–era tendency to relegate—in some instances a better word is *quarantine*—the depression decade as *the* single period in which such writing could have taken place. The result is a conveniently periodized target for repudiation, an occasion for ignorance about the many other modes and aspects of radical expression. Some scholarship on this period, consciously eschewing cold war criticism by celebrating the thirties, in a way (and in this way only) unwittingly furthers a cold war construction of the "Red Decade," unintentionally narrowing the focus of radical writing. When Rideout suggested that "Wolfert has increased the dimensions of the social novel"[6] he obviously meant an ideological broadening of this genre. But he also meant that the social novel has "dimensions" greater than the depression. To the extent that readers understand *Tucker's People* as a forties novel—indeed, I will argue, as a wartime novel—Wolfert's work can help enrich and complicate the received legacy of radical literature.

The radicalism of *Tucker's People* lies in Wolfert's approach toward the endemic gangsterism of corporate organizations. Two brothers, Joe and Leo Minch, apparently stand at opposite ends of the numbers (or "policy") corporation managed by Ben Tucker and his attorney, Henry Wheelock. The novel explores the pain and humiliation of the brothers' mutual discovery that they actually occupy much the same space in the continuum of profit, personal abuse, guilt, and complicity, despite their every effort to retain a distance created by angry separation in boyhood. Readers of *Tucker's People,* perhaps expecting that the Minch brothers would draw off the greatest share of the novel's energy for examining such a personal crisis, discover that nearly all of Tucker's many people face something of the same crisis. It is in seeing the Minches' dilemma written across the lives of all the people in the novel that enables its critique of the social organization to be so devastating.

Wolfert first conceived of *Tucker's People* with the help of the radical editor Angus Cameron as a response to the 1938 racket-busting trials prosecuted by New York's feisty Republican district attorney, Thomas E. Dewey. Wolfert covered the trial as a newspaper journalist, taking special reportorial aim at Dewey, whose ambitions already seemed to be moving toward a run for the U.S. presidency (he did run in 1944 and 1948). By the time the novel was finished and finally published, five years later in 1943, Wolfert had already achieved what the *New York Times* adjudged as "national recognition"[7] in 1941 for his exclusive report of the French recapture of Saint Pierre and Miquelon in his work for the North American Newspaper Alliance (NANA); indeed, he had been the only reporter traveling with the Free French forces.[8] For six harrowing weeks in 1942, he wrote about the battle for the Solomon Islands, and through part of 1943 he covered the many parts of the war in the Pacific. The experience that led to his best-selling *Battle for the Solomons* represented, according to the *Times,* an innovation of reportorial perspective—"the first time a major sea battle could be seen from beginning to end while the onlooker had his feet firmly planted on solid earth."[9] Soon after *Battle* Wolfert published *Torpedo 8, the Story of Swede Larsen's Bomber Squadron,* and, a bit later, *American Guerrilla in the Philippines* (a Book-of-the-Month-Club selection). During this hectic season he managed to see *Tucker's People* through press. Its 496 pages were finally released in April 1943. And in many ways, Wolfert's wartime reports and *Tucker's People* are of a piece.

Born in Manhattan to Jewish working-class parents, both immigrants from Latvia, Wolfert at fourteen began working as a copyboy in the real estate department of the Hearst-owned *Brooklyn American.* He entered Columbia's journalism program in 1926, married Helen Herschdorfer, a poet, in 1928 at nineteen, and left Columbia in 1930. Beginning in 1929, he "felt the Communists had the right answer."[10] A short story he published about a strike-breaker who became enraged with himself for beating up pickets drew the favorable attention of Communist writers, and he was invited the join the Party. He declined but attended classes at the Communist Workers School ("I wanted to read Marx," he later recalled),[11] as did Helen. A year of travel and then work at the Berlin office of the *New York Post*, in the early thirties, convinced him and Helen that "the Germans were insane," and his anti-fascism intensified. He came to know Ring Lardner's four sons through his work for NANA, closely followed events of the Spanish Civil War—including James Lardner's death there—and wrote a story about the grenade-caused blinding (at Jarama) of the Lincoln Battalion's Robert Raven.[12]

Given this attraction to political radicalism, it is no surprise that at the criminal trial of James "Jimmy" Hines, leader of New York's most extensive illegal betting organization, Wolfert would come to "dislike Dewey intensely."[13] The ambitious district attorney was then seeking the political prize of Hines, whom Wolfert, while covering the story, came to see as "a helluva nice guy."[14] The arrest "was more a political than criminal sensation"—so *Time* reported the obvious.[15] After most parts of the Tammany machine had turned against Roosevelt, Hines had remained an allegiant New Dealer, distributing federal patronage across Manhattan more or less straightforwardly (though, to be sure, in return for political influence), while providing protection for Harlem's $20 million-per-year numbers racket. Even the moderate and conservative press created a radical parallelism from an obvious metaphor: *Dewey* was "on trial" as well—"for his political life."[16]

The people brought before the public eye through this prosecution Wolfert found compelling. Samson Candee, whom we meet in the novel's opening chapter, "The Power of Samson," is based on the West Indian witness Wilfred Brunder,[17] while Henry Wheelock is modeled on Julius Richard "Dixie" Davis, Hines's attorney, whom Wolfert greatly appreciated. Davis was known as "the racket's smooth young mouthpiece."[18] Wolfert remembers that when Davis was indicted he was "mad as hell at Dewey": "He got on the stand," Wolfert recalled, "and as a lawyer, when you're under cross-examination you never volunteer anything. But he went out of his way to be loquacious, giving Dewey a chance to trip him up—which Dewey never succeeded in doing. I admired that guy." The events of Thanksgiving 1934 in the novel (told in the chapter "The Forgotten") were written straight out of the trial—from testimony about "Black Wednesday," November 23, 1931, a day of integration and consolidation for the corporate bosses, when the favorite holiday combination, 5-2-7, actually won (in a fix). The fixed big win drove out of business many of Harlem's smaller "bankers," who were suddenly unable to pay the many who hit the lucky number, at which point precisely Hines's (and Tucker's) people bought out the bigger independents.[19] As he witnessed the trial, as his hatred of Dewey's motives increased, and as his interest in Davis, Brunder, and others among Hines's people intensified, Wolfert began to see in his work as a writer possibilities for political commentary. When *The Nation*'s editorialists viewed the situation, they concluded that "one of the keys to [the presidential election of] 1940 may lie hidden in the policy slips that provide the background for New York City's current rackets trial."[20] Even in such generalizing these editorialists saw the larger significance of the Hines trial to be electoral, which was still too limited a view for Wolfert; he and Angus Cameron, however, meeting at Cameron's request at the Ritz Hotel to talk about ideas for a novel, were beginning to understand that this story of competing yet overlapping vertically organized "corporations" was well explained by their own radical analyses; Cameron was certain that Wolfert's writing would fully convey the personal consequences faced by the people within those organizations.

At the trial, Wolfert was impressed by an almost insanely apprehensive witness, a rackets middle manager, a "crushed clerk" as Wolfert later recalled[21]—a figure that became the paranoid character Frederick Bauer in the novel. Bauer is timid yet unforgettably resistant. When one of Joe Minch's drivers comes to Bauer's home to deliver him to the new site of Leo Minch's numbers office, Bauer hears the man say, "I got a car downstairs, . . . and I can give you a ride." Bauer overreacts. His "head flung upward. The word 'ride' had smashed through his ears. He had heard it too often in the movies. 'You tell your Joe Minch,' he said in a small, screaming voice, 'if he wants to kill me, he'll have to come here and do it" (226). As Bauer stiffens behind his sense of Americanism ("I'm a free American and I'm not taking orders from anybody in my own house" [226]), it in turn forces Leo, who is otherwise sympathetic to Bauer's poverty and general desperation, to reckon with his own increasingly undemocratic ways. Once Bauer has announced his intention to quit the bank and Leo realizes he cannot afford to lose his accountant, the two argue, but both men are aware that the topic of conversation is really Leo's overall loss of control and thus his increased need to control Bauer.

> "Honest, Mr. Minch," he said. . . . "I guess I'm not cut out to be . . . I mean, to be where . . . No, no matter how much I tell myself, still I feel sick in the head."
> "Take some pills then, a physic or something. You got to make up your mind that you're going to stay three, four more weeks until I break someone else in. That's final."
> "No! cried Bauer. "You can't stop me quitting. You're not my slave."
> "I'm telling you," said Leo. He walked out of the accounting room and up a small hall into the sorters' room.
> Bauer followed. "What do you mean?" he asked.
> "Never mind what I mean. . . . I told you." . . .
> "What do you mean!" cried Bauer. "Tell me what you mean!"
> "You got eyes. You can see yourself. I'm not alone in the business any more."
> "Oh my God!" (212–13)

Here Bauer tries to respond further but cannot utter a word and instead makes a "sudden movement as if to flee." Leo stops him, saying, "Just wait a few weeks," whereupon Bauer tries to pull himself together. "Mr. Minch," Bauer says, "What did you put me into, Mr. Minch?" The question has become, Who actually did what to whom? And What does doing constitute? Leo replies, "I didn't put you in nothing," and Bauer then says: "Did you put me in this without my knowing or saying? Did you do a thing like this to me?" Leo's answer is: "Who put you? Did I ask for it?" "What kind of thing is this, to do this to me, without my knowing or saying!" Bauer screams as he holds out both hands toward Leo, at which point Leo concedes to himself as much as to Bauer that *what* he has done (by joining Tucker's people) has made it impossible to discern the doer from the done-to. "What did I do?" he asks. "I didn't do anything. What do you think you're in, anyway?" Bauer walks away, placated for the moment, and Leo thinks: "I put him? They put me" (213–14).

Exchanges like these are characteristic of the writing in *Tucker's People* and led the Communist literary theorist Charles Humboldt, in a major statement on radical fiction published in 1947, to use Wolfert's book as a prime example of how the radical novel might successfully "part company" with naturalism, which of course had been the dominant tradition in U.S. proletarian fiction to that time.[22] Humboldt (the pseudonym for Clarence Weinstock) called for a postnaturalist radical novel that fully discloses conflicts as they are being enacted contrapuntally.[23] Bauer's and Leo's exchange on who "puts" whom is an instance of such dialectical "action." So is an opening passage of the novel that Humboldt quotes:

> Which shall be the user and which shall be used? Is the world a cloth that may be cut to fit its people? Or, are people cloth that must be cut to fit the world?
> So this story is of people cutting the world to measure where they can and cutting themselves to measure where they have to, and of the two, world and people, rolling through the universe embraced in battle and altered by battle.
> What was the beginning of this? Where is the end, since altered people alter their children, and altered children must likewise subdue themselves to this way of life? They must join the battle and cut the world and be cut by it. (3)

Crucial to Wolfert's idea about the social and economic origins of the situation in which all of Tucker's people find themselves— Bauer most dramatically—is that it is not personal in any sufficiently explanatory sense. Notwithstanding the novel's psychological acuities, found on nearly every page, Wolfert does not mean that in Leo's and Joe's youths as parentless brothers readers can locate sources of their adult dilemmas. Indeed, Wolfert's point, I take it, is that Leo and Joe finally share a propensity to gangsterism despite very radically different responses to the crisis of their early years. Without a trace of psychological determinism—yet with strong hints of his sense of inevitable political development (what Humboldt called the "pressure" that leads to "crystallization" and then further conflict)[24]—Wolfert describes Bauer's visit to his emotionally paralyzed and horribly rheumatic father, a former motorman and trolley car conductor, now keeping himself warm by tying burlap bags around his ankles while he throws Broadway line switches that could be thrown electrically from control boxes on trolleys. This final station was the "result of a 'good' act by a benevolent company" for which the elder Bauer had once scabbed during a big railroad strike, at which time the company had used this scab's "life story in an advertisement to show how square it was with its employees" (323). Indeed, the paragraph-long biography of Bauer's father that follows is presented through the language of that anti-union ad. We see the motorman from the double distance of Bauer's unfaithful emotional dissociation from his father and the company's self-serving symbolic reduction of its "faithful" employee.

Yet, interestingly, Wolfert's own experience comes closest to that of Bauer's father—or, rather, what we as readers are to think is the kind of work of which Bauer's father was once capable, before the company appropriated him. Wolfert had himself been a trolley motorman, working a shift that began at 1:30 P.M. and kept him from home until 2:15 A.M. (he had to arise at 7:30 to attend classes at Columbia)—with one break. He was eventually fired for running the line too fast (thirty-two minutes between South Ferry and 59th Street) after a start delayed by a drinking party. (He learned afterward that he had been blacklisted by the railroads, and he took to driving a taxi.) But for Wolfert the experience as a motorman continued (and continues) to be a source of deep pride in idealized hard physical work. It is not a coincidence that Bauer's visit to his father along Broadway occasions prose that comes closest to proletarian writing characteristic of Communist novels of the thirties. It is powerful here because by diction and tone it is *unlike* other writing in the book and because it puts Bauer's father's failure—and Bauer's, as a rackets accountant—in the clear context of aesthetic pleasure and revolutionary optimism that might otherwise be derived from labor. As Bauer turns away from his father he happens to see a young man robustly mopping a floor. Positive description of the work gives way to a generalization in which work as depicted in the novel as a whole stands as a negative example. Such idealized labor enables one to "shut out . . . the whole structure of business." The young man's

> trouser legs were rolled up to his knees and the white flesh of his round, hairy legs glinted. . . . He swung the mop huskily and cheerfully, with spacious, smooth strokes. . . . His leg muscles bulged in rhythm. His body swayed in rhythm and his face hung down and his young, plump cheeks bellied and swung back and forth in rhythm with the mop. For a moment he looked like the whole race of man living in a cheerful rhythm of work. He was experiencing, briefly, the joy of a man doing work from which the mind could be shut out and, with the mind, the whole structure of business. (333)

The passage, meant I think as a pure instance of social realism, a set piece, is designed to be framed, even to some degree ironized, by prose significantly different—that of the postnaturalist radical novel Humboldt later argued *Tucker's People* exemplified. Indeed, the ideal is not the novel that finds language and action simply in order to "*shut* out . . . business" or that which presents business, and other controlling agencies, as wholly determining, but one in which people, in Wolfert's terms, cut and are being cut. It can be said that the proletarian portrait appears as a thirties text set against the developments of the forties.

Ripened by History

When Wolfert watched the parade of witnesses at the Hines trial in the thirties, he already wanted to write something about what one really knew about these people—and *how* one knew. It was not until the war that he fully learned this technique. Indeed, the Ira Wolfert who wrote *Tucker's People* in part because he stubbornly "hates the bosses" (as he still likes to put it)[25] was precisely the writer who covered the war. The war seemed a massive—sometimes horrifying, often boring[26]—organizational project undertaken by essentially powerless and mostly uninformed "little guys" (another favorite phrase) and was to be best understood through the details of the everyday.

Taken as a whole, the collected dispatches of Ira Wolfert suggest a tragic idea at the heart of *Tucker's People:* people do not know entirely why they do what they are doing, yet they continue to do it and do it well. "This is not the men's fault, nor is the fault of the war," Wolfert argued in an essay published in January 1943. "It is our fault that the men don't know what the shooting is all about, the fault of everybody—teachers, journalists, politicians—who tries to put the emotions that shape men's lives into forms they can understand and accept."[27] Neither in his dispatches nor in his first novel did Wolfert feel that he was achieving anything other than the making of "forms" people involved in a human community "can understand and accept." It is that particular kind of "acceptance," the power and pressing need of it, that makes it possible to read *Tucker's People,* with its sense of pressure and of what today would be called structural violence, and to observe such acceptance partly won—won even by Tucker's lawyer Henry Wheelock, whose demise is otherwise nearly complete in the novel's final pages. "As it is," Wolfert wrote, "nobody shows him anything in a way that he can accept, and he goes on thinking only that he is fighting for his life against exploding steel."[28] Although this was written about the war in the Pacific, it might have served as Wolfert's gloss on the large problem faced in the novel by Wheelock—and by Frederick Bauer, Joe Minch, the policeman Egan, and, indeed, by Ben Tucker himself.

Wolfert's wartime journalism was widely commended for its unusual rhythmic prose, seemingly straightforward but in fact having the modernist quality—influenced by the Hemingway of *In Our Time* [29] who had been influenced by Stein and Picasso— of conveying a subject, or a state of mind, through the deliberate, even halting, verbal accretion of perspectives and surface perceptions. Readers of a NANA story run by the *New York Times* and other papers in June 1943 could have sensed in this language about Guadalcanal a very great difference from that used conventionally by war correspondents. Here were words that in themselves help report the exhausting, anxious, repetitious, three-steps-forward-and-two-steps-back sense of the battle:

> When the raiders come close, searchlights go up. When the searchlights find something, the guns go off. The guns are the most expensive part of the show. The fuse alone on each of these shells cost more than an expensive watch. . . . The Japanese do not come low enough for the guns to hit them. They stay up where our gunners have to use as much as a forty-second fuse and lead their target by as far as a mile and a quarter. Although the guns do not hit anything, they keep the Japanese so high that they do not hit anything either.[30]

Presented as a repetitive structure or syntactical spine, the seemingly simple passage might look like this:

When . . . come close . . .	*searchlights go up.*
When find . . .	*guns go off.*
Guns . . .	*expensive.*
Fuse . . .	*expensive.*
Japanese do not come low . . .	*guns.*
Our gunners . . .	*fuse.*
as much as . . .	*as far as . . .*
Guns . . .	*do not hit anything,*
Japanese so high . . .	*do not hit anything.*

Wolfert won a Pulitzer Prize[31] for such prose—muscular and confident at the level of the sentence, irresolute and halting at the level of the passage, disclosing through its obvious cracks how close to the surface lay great stress and desperation.[32] Although Humboldt does not especially laud the modernist influences working on Wolfert, he does praise *Tucker's People* for its real complication of human reaction to social and economic pressure as a check against straight-ahead naturalist characterization, noting that Tucker's people's responses entail "no trigger-fingered, oversimplified and unmotivated ferocity." Thus Humboldt makes a somewhat separate peace with Wolfert's prose ("he is forced to devise a kind of lyrical discourse which is independent of and to some degree destructive of his dramatic form"), for indeed it augments the dialectic quality of the conflict.[33]

It is obvious that Wolfert had little interest in conveying a standard narrative of *what happened* in war by means of transparent prose with no attention-getting character of its own. For readers of *Tucker's People* a half century later it is surely instructive to understand the novelistic qualities he sensed in the stories of battles otherwise incompletely reported by the news service. He expressed this anxiety by speaking in and of metanarratives, without ever parading them around as such. He took on, for instance, the story of how war stories were coming to be war stories. He examined the details of the convenience-seeking behavior of war correspondents and its effect on battle narratives mediated by unverified official U.S. Army memos. *Tucker's People,* too, was in a significant sense about what Wolfert retrospectively did not see in news coverage (including his own) of the organized crime trials of the late thirties.

Yet in the particular novel form he chose—what might awkwardly be called hard-boiled postnaturalist proletarian modernism—Wolfert found a way to tell about a psychological or emotional community he read between the lines of the trial record. For this reason alone *Tucker's People* is remarkable. Perhaps just as remarkable is that Wolfert could write essays during the war in which he wondered aloud if it was ever possible to *know* the war. Later this vexing question of medium and form would guide his response to Mailer's *The Naked and the Dead* (1948), an intrepid attempt to convey the war Wolfert found to have "a will of its own" that presents writer and reader "not with truth, but with the echoes of it. Thus what correspondents of the day produced while breaking the trail which Mr. Mailer follows was a description that was accurate on its surface but false—or least only temporarily true—internally."[34] During the war itself this apt introversion produced, for instance, not simply Wolfert's story about the battle of almost total destruction in the small Normandy town La Haye-du-Puits (1944) but *"What Do You Know About* La-Haye-du-Puits?"[35]

> The war correspondents who write "the news," as it is called, meaning the progress of the war, were licked at the start. . . . The "news" writers sitting tiredly at their typewriters that evening wrote, "American troops stormed into La-Haye-du-Puits this afternoon and tonight were digging in beyond the town" etc. etc., for their 200 or 600 or 1,000 words, as required by their editors. It was a waste of their time and of newsprint and of the time of their readers.
>
> The feature writers did whatever their temperament beckoned them to. I remember my own story of the day. It had nothing of importance in it. The animal ridge was not in it nor was the calm, barefooted German killer, putting on his socks and shoes while his enemies advanced on him. The Intelligence officer folding his maps and papers like a lawyer before crawling under the tank, the soldier too sad to get up to look any more at his wounded friend, the war correspondent elatedly discovering someone from Iowa—they were not in it. . . .
>
> No one learned from me what the fighting had been like that day at La-Haye-du-Puits.[36]

Reaching the limits of journalistic conventions and forms, Wolfert looked to the novel to convey what wartime "feature" writing failed to convey. "If you tell one story truly enough," he wrote later, "you tell them all. If you examine one problem thoroughly enough, you touch upon them all."[37] He has also said, "I wanted the book [*Tucker's People*] to go beyond its story."[38] The story beyond the story—the larger problem touched upon in the telling of the one story of Tucker's organization—is evidently that of fascism. The novel's success greatly depends on the persuasiveness of this large claim. Perhaps Wolfert has sensed this risk. When asked if he considers *Tucker's People* the culmination of his political thinking from the 1930s through World War II, he has responded, with disarming independence, "I never thought of it as a political book at all."[39] Yet when he described his aim as taking the story of the policy racket "beyond its story," he said he viewed Tucker's criminal organization—as well as the police, prosecutorial, and judicial figures implicated through political protection schemes—as part of "a fascist enterprise: gangsters with their henchmen, stormtroopers, bullies, sadists."[40]

The point is not hidden. In the novel, the one explicit reference to fascism is unambiguous in its suggestion that Bauer was the victim of fascism but also represents its popular base: "The little man had a heritage of insecurity. . . . He was born in a world given over to business played as a game with profit as the goal and man staking his life on reaching it. . . . Insecurity had made him into a certain kind of infant and had aggravated him into a certain kind of man. That man could see no way out of insecurity except death." In a long chapter titled "A Gleichschaltung," Wolfert embeds into the detailed description of Bauer's death-obsessed wanderings a link between the policy racket and "so great a thing as history": "Towards the end, fear was becoming strong enough to make everything that happened its food. . . . Already a nation of Germans, ripened by history, as the little man had been, and then flung into economic crisis, as the little man had been, had invented enemies, as he had, and stirred hatreds and nursed and fueled and fanned fear" (369–70). In this climate people "asked questions with the mouth and not with the brain": "The Nazi idea . . . was a climax to the modern world and its business game. . . . All of Tucker's people, and, of course, Tucker himself, were climax men of the modern world. Some were riper than others, but each was ripening" (372).[41] Wolfert's ability to insert such a political generalization into the course of narrating Bauer's collapse under organizational pressure, and to get away with it novelistically, is dependent on persuading readers of the fiction that "people" as far apart on the spectrum of social control as Tucker and Bauer were distinct only in the degree of their "ripening." The wartime context in which the novel appeared and gathered its first critical responses shaped the introduction of fascism as a "tragedy of insecurity" akin to what Bauer experiences. "In Bauer," wrote Thomas Lyle Collins, reviewing the novel for the *New York Times,* "Wolfert sets forth an explanation of Germany's Nazi insanity, a much more plausible one than any theory of a centuries-old Teutonic conspiracy."[42]

A critic as distrustful of radical novels as Diana Trilling by 1943 was convinced that Wolfert had "of course written a 'radical' novel" but one that uses "the method neither of pamphleteering nor or rabble-rousing" and "cuts through the whole bleary notion that all you have to do is drop the 'Communist Manifesto' in the social slot machine and out will come a society of smiling Workers and Peasants." She credited his view of "gangsterism as an aspect of our whole predatory economic structure," commending the book by calling it "as much a novel of legitimate American business as it is of racketeering" and of a society in which "the distinction between right and wrong is at last a legalism."[43] Because it is cast as an argument *against* radical writing as a form of proletarianism, Trilling's contemporaneous praise is more instructive to readers of the novel today, I think, than is Chester E. Eisinger's otherwise valuable later summary of the book as generally *befitting* thirties "fiction written in the ambience of Marxism" (to Eisinger, Wolfert "handles the problem of society and the self more effectively" than Albert Maltz, Tess Slesinger, Albert Halper, Leane Zugsmith, Josephine Johnson, and Meyer Levin).[44] What is especially revealing is Trilling's own blindness to the obvious fact that in Wolfert's antifascist set piece he was surely making *Tucker's People* the "thesis novel" Trilling claims it is not. She also believes that "there is no mention of economic or political theory," although the *theory* that "gangsters are little different from their legitimate brothers" (in her words) is what supports her sense that "this is no Damon Runyonesque novel of the underworld" because "Mr. Wolfert talks *out of his head,* not out of the corner of his mouth."[45]

Ira Wolfert is doubtless right to have savored praise from Diana Trilling at a time when radicals and radical novels were not much applauded in her reviews. He has never been a party or organization man anyway or, for the most part, an organizer, feeling that American leftists can become as "bossy" as managers and owners. Angus Cameron has stood for him as an exemplary exception because, even when deeply involved in the Progressive party campaign for Henry Wallace in 1948, his friend "never got bossy."[46] Wolfert's own radical views, however independent of the Communist Party, USA, were always at issue. Diana Trilling and other reviewers of *Tucker's People* simply began with the assumption. And there is substantial evidence of his commitments. Wolfert at least privately spoke of favoring distribution of wealth for equal opportunity. ("The primary function of the American society," he wrote in a letter to the blacklisted teacher and writer Joseph Barnes, "is to provide equal opportunity and if it costs money to provide it that money should come out of the public funds.")[47] He felt that manufacturers took merely one risk—that of the marketplace—and, even so, were "now well along . . . by means of establishing monopolies . . . in eliminating even *that* one." In preparing his long essay about dryland wheat farmers in the 1950s,[48] he sadly observed no such lessening of risk and argued that "if the American society is to fulfill its primary function"—"to provide equal opportunity"—"I believe that he [the farmer] should have *no* risk."[49]

By the time Wolfert and Barnes were discussing the farmers' plight, the House Un-American Activities Committee (HUAC) had branded Wolfert a Communist by association, listing him among the "sponsors" of the anti-anticommunist Scientific and Cultural Conference for World Peace held at the Waldorf Hotel (the list was drawn from one authorized by the organizing committee for the 1949 event, the National Council of the Arts, Sciences, and Professions).[50] And in two HUAC reports on the Waldorf conference, Wolfert was listed, correctly, as a "panel speaker," along with W. E. B. Du Bois, Howard Fast, Shirley Graham, Louis Untermeyer, F. O. Matthiessen, and others friendly to the Communist party.[51] He indeed spoke at the conference—about his opposition to anticommunist passport restrictions. HUAC also listed Wolfert as "affiliated with from five to ten Communist front organizations"[52] and put him among those suspect because they supported individual Communists in various elections, hearings, or trials.[53] He is among just twelve writers and artists listed as "supported by Soviet Agencies, press or radio."[54] The poet Aaron Kramer remembers that he, Shirley Graham, and Howard Fast met at Wolfert's home to plan "our roles as Waldorf Conference hosts."[55] (Wolfert does not remember this.) During the time of the blacklisting, Wolfert, Barnes, occasionally Arthur Miller, the brilliant Simon and Schuster editor Jack Goodman,[56] and several other anti-anticommunists met weekly at Goodman's house in Greenwich Village to see what could be done to defend their political friends against McCarthyism.[57]

Afraid in Your Heart

As Ira Wolfert visited the fronts of Europe and Asia in 1942 and 1943, he was skeptically quizzed by soldiers and sailors. They asked about strikes among workers in homefront war factories. Wolfert responded by strongly defending wartime unionism as part of "the battle for a peace that will give the workingman a square shake." The "military phase" of the fighting, he contended, was part of the successful "total war" against fascism that necessarily included workers "unwilling to give up the rights they had won," people who were "helping to win the war by the production of war materials and helping to win the peace by trying to make a world into which the soldier would want to fit when he went home and took off his uniform."[58] These contentious views he published in the *Nation*. Almost immediately an editorial in the *New York Times* replied directly, claiming to recognize in Ira Wolfert the sort of irresponsible radical who "ha[s] not learned to put first things first." The *Times* offered editorially that "Mr. Wolfert's talk is quite familiar . . . [as] the talk of the Popular Front in France . . . that in the end led to the French collapse." Wolfert was "unwittingly contribut[ing] not only to the loss of the workers' rights, but of France itself"—and "we do not want to lose America."[59] It is hard to know what to make of Wolfert's views in this case, especially in relation to the Communist party policy after the invasion of the Soviet Union in 1941, at which point Communists joined other parties, though not all, in supporting a no-strike pledge; it may be an indication of Wolfert's conscious independence from Communist positions or, then again, of his entirely undogmatic or "commonsense" approach to expressing his political views.[60]

In any case Wolfert was arguing for something larger and even more controversial than wartime unionism. He did feel the war to be "a good one," which, if it succeeded "in establishing the democratic process as a world's way of life, . . . will not have to be fought over again." The important thing was the ultimate freedom of individual citizens, workers, or soldiers to be "solider, better-integrated" people, "made so by the democratic process." The key to the morale of the wartime citizen, Wolfert was carefully arguing, was that "he hates fascism in much the way he hates to get up in the morning and loves democracy as if it were something he had been told at home he ought to love.[61]

Tucker's People must be seen in the light of the argument the *Times* felt to be unremarkably leftist—about hating fascism as so naturally and fundamentally part of the everyday that one can fully convey antifascism by telling about people getting up in the morning and about what one was or was not taught at home to love. Leo Minch, whom Wolfert is at pains to say was never taught at home to love, nonetheless survives through half the novel with his anti-organization instincts intact. He understands that "big business, fighting within itself, turned the industry into a lottery with yard goods as mere tickets in it" (9). Lawful, honest entrants in this economic lottery, as Leo had been when working in the woolen business before World War I, saw new organized practices transform lawlessness into the necessary condition for any kind of control. The novel depends on our view of Leo Minch as "a timid man" victimized by economic nonchoice (9):

a man at times unable, and at times able but unwilling, to accept conditions that would give him control, yet dependent on the pride of having a measure of control over the employees whom he knows he has entrapped. When first faced with the option of lawless business, Leo conceives of the metaphor that drives the novel: business in general is like the business of *giving chances* in particular. Yet it is a form of chance-giving largely controlled by the chance-takers. "The woolen men down the line," Leo remembered from his earlier experience with business, "bet on how the woolen men up the line would bet on how consumers would bet on how woolen men would bet. Prices moved up and down violently without regard to value. It created a false market for materials and disturbed the operations of the true market" (9).

While Leo struggles with loss of pride in his ability to make a "true" or "legitimate" profit, some of Tucker's other people act as the controllers of the process by which measures of both value and control are dispensed. Leo, only ever partly in control but never reaching a full realization of its limits at any point, continues working with his policy office staff, a strikingly diverse group—surely meant by Wolfert to be a representative ethnic and social sampling of the American working class—on the mistaken assumption that no business practice is so corrupt that it cannot be sufficiently transformed by good work: "Policy was truly a business like anything else and Leo, who was a 'good' man, could make it a 'good' business" (65).

At times Joe serves to prevent Leo from concluding that good business is distinct from bad. The brothers discuss the need for "discipline in any organization" (Joe's phrase), which means firing people in Leo's policy bank after the integration of Leo's once-independent office into Tucker's vertically integrated system:

> "I haven't got the stomach for this kind of business."
> "What do you mean this kind of business," cried Joe. "In any business, you got to face what is a fact."
> "Yes, but how you're going to do it, I mean."
> "I don't get you at all. 'This kind of business.' Every business has got to work with what it's got. . . . Whatever a busi-

ness has got, that's what it has to use the best way it can. Isn't
that true?"
    "Don't ask me what's true," Leo said. "I can't tell no more
what's true." (221–22)

Yet again, Joe epitomizes the strange confusion of agency: "He
had never tried to find out what business had done to him. Who
says business does something to a man? A man does something
to it. That would have been his attitude if he had ever bothered
to adopt one" (303).
    Henry Wheelock, in far deeper than he ever fully realizes, has
a biography Wolfert dramatically calls (in a section title) "An
American Hero's Son," in which a father knew "the end" of his
own small business "the minute the big lumber companies started working on the forests" (153). Typical of nearly every character in this novel, Wheelock's father senses a great economic
change coming, knows it is in effect a social change, and acts to
resist it sufficiently to create a still more painful consciousness of
the change—and then stands by, in recognition of failure, as the
change overtakes him. "He saw the day and he tried to prepare
for it" (153). Here, as in many other passages in the novel, Ira
Wolfert's style—which the *New Yorker* reviewer deemed mistak-
enly to be "no style"[62]—conveys something rhythmically of the
way business decline, concurrent with the demise of discrete
human identity, is less the event of a moment than a matter of
taking a progressive step for every several stumblingly back. For
Henry Wheelock's solid midwestern father, "the rock began to
sink and he had to fight to hold the rock up. It was a hopeless
fight. He was a man holding up something that was holding up
him. The old man must have known it would be hopeless and
must have known it was hopeless, but he kept right on with it.
It was heroic. It was a life to which music should be played"
(153). Heroism, unironized here but making Henry's later success
with Tucker in New York richly ironic—and setting the loquacious Democrat "Dixie" Davis battling Republican District Attorney Dewey in stark radical political relief—is founded on a basic American resistance to business that is *not* at the same time a

restatement merely of the durability of the individual will. We are left with the unlikely image of "an old, cranky-looking guy in a frock coat, sitting out in a town, trying to help set right the wrongs of the big fellows" (153). Somewhat unexpectedly here, Ira Wolfert's radical sentiments lie in the heart of the heart of the country.

This may be a nod to his editor and friend Cameron, Wolfert's favorite midwesterner, tough and principled. ("I Will Not Cooperate!" was the title given Cameron's statement before a hearing of the Senate Internal Security Subcommittee when it was later published.)[63] Although his own editorial elders at Little, Brown finally rejected *Tucker's People,* Cameron worked hard with Wolfert to place the novel; after twenty-six rejections,[64] the publisher L. B. Fischer was persuaded. But not before Cameron "sweated and bled over that book . . . for a long time." Rejections came on the basis that, as Cameron has put it, "gangster novels were old hat" by then.[65] This angered Cameron, who, in a career publishing many of the great Little, Brown authors, considered *Tucker's People* "one of the best novels I had to do with." Cameron prized Wolfert's devotion to the project: "the guy wrote that book from five 'til seven in the morning" while working for NANA.[66]

Wolfert's hard work, and Cameron's enormous editorial faith, paid off. *Tucker's People* received the critical attention and acclaim the two felt it deserved. Later, as Wolfert was completing what would turn out to be the first version of his next novel, *An Act of Love* (1948), Abraham Polonsky approached him with a plan that would bring the story of Joe and Leo to the shadowy screen— the remarkable *noir* film *Force of Evil* (1948), with Thomas Gomez as Leo, Howland Chamberlain as Bauer, and Roy Roberts as Tucker. John Garfield is Joe playing a version of Wheeler (the convergence of the two characters was Wolfert's idea).[67] *Force of Evil* is the only film Polonsky directed before he was blacklisted as an uncooperative HUAC witness in 1951. Although Polonsky, according to his own account (which Wolfert confirms), "eliminated the discursive power of the book and substituted for it so to speak centers of suggestion," the general impression has been of a film beautiful for its heavy reliance on language—even of (to several reviewers) a kind of urban blank verse. "The impression of that language," a film critic later wrote, "is of for the first time really hearing, on the screen, the sound of city speech, with its special repetitions and elisions, cadences and inflection, inarticulateness and crypto poetry."[68] Typical is Joe's lament to Doris as Tucker's enemies tighten their hold toward the end of the film:

> JOE
> (he is listening to his own heart)
> You don't know what it is to wake up in the morning and go to sleep at night and eat your lunch and read the paper and hear the horns blowing in the street or the horns blow in clubs and all the time whatever you're doing, whatever you're hearing, whatever you're seeing or wherever you are, you're afraid in your heart.[69]

Wolfert remembers that he and Polonsky worked "closely together" on the screenplay, but does not feel an especial attachment to the result. Nonetheless, the screenplay bears ample evidence of a debt to Wolfert's sense of his characters' desperate words.

Wolfert was not happy with *An Act of Love* from the moment it was published. Nor were the critics, for the most part. Diana Trilling, who so admired *Tucker's People,* found this second novel "operat[ing] in the realm of our most deeply hidden moves" but containing "not a single perception . . . which has the ring of validity."[70] Wolfert took the unusual next step of rewriting the already published novel from start to finish for the next several years and then of having Simon and Schuster publish the entirely revised new edition with the subtitle "A Completely Retold Version of the Novel" (1954). Granville Hicks's personal (unpublished) reading notes compared the book passage by passage and element by element. He and other readers found that the first chapter of the first version was now chapter 26 in the new—that Wolfert had "gone a long way back to get his start," lending some greater "validity," to use Trilling's term, to the main character's response to the crisis of the story (a wartime plane wreck). Hicks was awed by the revised version, persuaded that Wolfert's process of rewriting itself "deserves careful study."[71]

A third novel, *Married Men* (1953), a massive tale of 1,007 pages, won some critical praise but also led John Aldridge grumpily to declare "the failure of a form" in his book *In Search of Heresy* (1956).[72] Later, in 1960, Wolfert published his stunning collection of essays, *An Epidemic of Genius.* He has been working ever since on a new novel, which is still in manuscript form that only a few have seen (Cameron among them).

Aldridge's criticism of *Married Men* is withering. Wolfert is accused of "a mediocrity of taste, and an obviousness of feeling," among other sins. Yet in surveying "American Literature in the Age of Conformity" (his book's subtitle), Aldridge did see in Wolfert significant talents for clearly perceiving "environmental details" and "exploit[ing] to great dramatic effect the shade of difference between a fictional account and its constantly intruding factual basis." In *Tucker's People* this served him especially well, "for it made it virtually impossible for the average reader to see the fiction except through the haze of his emotional response to the social condition against which the fiction was a protest." *Married Man* failed because it could not accomplish the goal we can take to be that of all Wolfert's work: "to analyze on a major scale the politics of the relationship . . . between the structures of economic class and the structures of the self."[73] This momentarily allied the supposedly "heretical" Aldridge with the Communist Humboldt, who recommended Wolfert by way of calling for a new kind of radical novel that "presupposes an equal interchange between the individual and society, a constant welling-up of ideas and emotions in the midst of contradiction and conflict."[74] Finally, though, for Aldridge, in his "deplor[ing] the passing of the 'independent' writer," Wolfert failed because he engaged forms of intellectual dependence.[75] For Humboldt, on the other hand, the conflicts entailed in Wolfert's novelistic choices were a means by which, indeed, "social realism comes of age."[76]

NOTES

1. Rideout, *The Radical Novel,* 270.
2. Barbara Foley, *Radical Representations: Politics and Form in U.S. Proletarian Fiction, 1929–1941* (Durham: Duke University Press, 1993); Paula Rabinowitz, *Labor and Desire: Women's Revolutionary Fiction in Depression America* (Chapel Hill: University of North Carolina Press, 1991). For a full consideration of this question, see Wald, *Writing from the Left.* Wald generally seeks to redraw categories of radical writing and to suggest continuities across periods (as well as genres). Laura Hapke's informative book, *Daughters of the Great Depression: Women, Work, and Fiction in the American 1930s* (Athens: University of Georgia Press, 1995), doubtless delimiting the period as a necessary function of scope, briefly looks toward the successive eras as entailing a break with the depression "moment" of women's radical writing ("the nation would be swiftly reconciled—at least for a time—to the women at work" [223]). Yet there are strong continuities from the thirties to writing of the forties by Ruth McKenney, Margaret Walker, Alice Childress, Shirley Graham, and others.
3. Alan Wald urges study of "the broader Communist 'movement' beyond the Party" and warns of a "membership fixation" in describing an "Agenda for Research" that includes writers named here as well as many others. "Culture and Commitment: U.S. Communist Writers Reconsidered," *Writing from the Left* 74 (movement beyond the Party), 75 (membership fixation), 77–81 ("Agenda").
4. Rideout, *The Radical Novel,* 270.
5. The argument is implicit throughout *Writing from the Left* and much of Wald's later work. See, in particular, "The 1930s Left in U.S. Literature Reconsidered," *Writing from the Left,* 100–113.
6. Rideout, *The Radical Novel,* 273.
7. "Ira Wolfert," *New York Times,* May 4, 1943, 12.
8. "News Beat Tossed NANA's Way when Free French Seized Isles," *Newsweek,* Jan. 5, 1942, 50.
9. "Ira Wolfert," 12.
10. Interview of Ira Wolfert by Alan Filreis and Alan Wald, June 21, 1993, Lake Hill, N.Y.
11. Ibid.
12. Ibid. See Peter N. Carroll, *The Odyssey of the Abraham Lin-*

coln Brigade: Americans in the Spanish Civil War (Stanford: Stanford University Press, 1994), 105.

13. Wolfert interview.

14. Ibid.

15. "'Almost an Angel,'" *Time,* June 6, 1938, 13.

16. "Safety Play," *Time,* Mar. 6, 1939, 15.

17. In "'The Numbers': Scope of Racket Overshadows Interest in Fate of Hines" *(Newsweek,* Aug. 20, 1938, 9), Brunder's testimony and the Harlem numbers racket are described as "dominated by dusky West Indians."

18. "New Style Trial," *Time,* Sept. 12, 1938, 24.

19. "Black Wednesday" is described in "'The Numbers,'" 10.

20. "Policy and Politics," 236. Incidentally, another radical writer was compelled by the rackets trials prosecuted by Dewey. Robert Rossen had Warners collect the transcripts of the March 1937 trials; Rossen drew closely on these documents in writing an original story that, in December 1937, became the treatment entitled "The Market" for the film *Racket Busters,* which opened in July 1938.

21. Wolfert interview.

22. Humboldt, "The Novel of Action," 395.

23. Ibid., 400.

24. Ibid.

25. Wolfert interview.

26. Wolfert wrote: "Loneliness and boredom and anticipating Japs are much more terrible enemies for a man than bullets." Quoted by Roger Pippett in "Vivid Writing about Our Men on Guadalcanal . . . ," *PM,* Jan. 24, 1943, 27.

27. Wolfert, "Talk on Guadalcanal," 117–19.

28. Ibid., 119.

29. Wolfert interview.

30. Ira Wolfert, "Japanese Radio Attacks Morale of Men on Guadalcanal with Tales of Home Folk," *New York Times,* June 24, 1943, 8.

31. He won the award in the category "telegraphic reporting of international affairs."

32. "Wilder Play, Sinclair Novel, Are Pulitzer Prize Winners," *New York Times,* May 4, 1943, 1.

33. Humboldt, "The Novel of Action," 404.

34. Wolfert, "War Novelist," 23.

35. La-Haye-du-Puits is located in the western part of Normandy, about fifty kilometers south of Cherbourg. During the fierce fighting that followed the Normandy invasion, some 80 percent of the town was destroyed.

36. Wolfert, "What Do You Know about La-Haye-du-Puits?" 71.

37. Letter dated "Feb. 28" (no year), "Wolfert" file, box 40, Joseph Barnes Papers, Rare Books and Manuscripts Library, Columbia University.

38. Wolfert interview.

39. Ibid.

40. Ibid.

41. See also 71.

42. Thomas Lyle Collins, "New York Underworld," *New York Times,* Apr. 25, 1943, 7.

43. Trilling, "Fiction in Review," 45–47. Trilling found it "the most thoughtful and talented novel I have read this year" (45).

44. Chester E. Eisinger, "Character and Self in Fiction on the Left," in *Proletarian Writers of the Thirties,* ed. Dave Madden (Carbondale: Southern Illinois University Press, 1968), 177.

45. Trilling, "Fiction in Review," 45–47.

46. See, e.g., Curtis D. Macdougall, *Gideon's Army* (New York: Marzani and Munsell, 1965), 202, 248, 301, 811; Wolfert interview.

47. Wolfert to Joseph Barnes, Feb. 27, "Wolfert" file.

48. "A Hundred Years' War," *An Epidemic of Genius,* 1–100.

49. Characteristically disinclined to prescribe programs, Wolfert did not care how one achieved "the methods by which [the farmer's] guaranteed market is being devised," but he insisted, "leave the principle alone." Wolfert to Joseph Barnes, Feb. 25, [1959], "Wolfert" file. To which Barnes replied: "Maybe the dust bowl is now inside the hearts of Republicans." Barnes to Wolfert, Feb. 27, 1959, "Wolfert" file.

50. House Committee on Un-American Activities, *Report on the Communist "Peace" Offensive—A Campaign to Disarm and Defeat the United States,* 82d Cong., 1st sess., H. Rept. 378, Apr. 1, 1951, 107.

51. Ibid., 110; House Committee on Un-American Activities, *Review of the Scientific and Cultural Conference for World Peace, Arranged by the National Council of the Arts, Sciences, and Professions, and Held in New York City, March 25, 26, and 27, 1949,* 81st Cong., 2d sess., 1950 (originally released, Apr. 19, 1949), 61.

52. HUAC, *"Peace" Offensive,* 108

53. Ibid., 40.

54. Ibid., 48.

55. I am grateful to Alan Wald for this information.

56. Wolfert was among the writers with whom Goodman worked as editor; others were Meyer Levin, Norman Corwin, Ben Hecht, and Paddy Chayefsky. "Jack Goodman, A Book Executive," *New York Times,* July 23, 1957, 27.

57. Wolfert interview.

58. Wolfert, "Talk on Guadalcanal, " 117.

59. "Unity in War Aims," *New York Times,* Jan. 25, 1943, 12.

60. See Maurice Isserman, *Which Side Were You On?: The American Communist Party during the Second World War* (Middletown, Conn.: Wesleyan University Press, 1982; reprint, Urbana: University of Illinois Press, 1993).

61. Wolfert, "Talk on Guadalcanal," 119.

62. "Briefly Noted," *New Yorker,* May 1, 1943, 74.

63. "I Will Not Cooperate!" *Masses and Mainstream* 6.6 (June 1953): 3–4. The hearing, one of many to which Cameron was subpoenaed, took place on May 7, 1953.

64. Interview of Angus Cameron by Louis Scheaffer, Feb. 8, 1977, Columbia University Oral History Collection, interview 4, Rare Books and Manuscripts Library, Columbia University, 177–78. Wolfert's agent showed Cameron twenty-six rejection cards.

65. Ibid., 178.

66. Ibid., 179.

67. Wolfert interview.

68. William Pechter, "Abraham Polonsky and *Force of Evil,*" *Film Quarterly* 15.3 (Spring 1962): 48. Polonsky's statement about changes made to the novel in the film comes from a correspondence interview Pechter conducted for the same article (51).

69. Wolfert and Polonsky, *Force of Evil,* 109.

70. Trilling, "Fiction in Review," 49.

71. "Ira Wolfert," typescript notes, Box 69, Granville Hicks Papers, Department of Special Collections/Syracuse University Library.

72. Aldridge, *In Search of Heresy,* 177–85.

73. Ibid., 179.

74. Humboldt, "The Novel of Action," 395.

75. Dustjacket copy, Aldridge, *In Search of Heresy,* McGraw-Hill hardcover first edition, 1956.
76. Humboldt, "The Novel of Action," 407.

BIBLIOGRAPHY

Works by Ira Wolfert

An Act of Love. New York: Simon and Schuster, 1948.

An Act of Love: A Completely Retold Version of the Novel. New York: Simon and Schuster, 1954.

American Guerrilla in the Philippines. New York: Simon and Schuster, 1945.

Battle for the Solomons. Boston: Houghton Mifflin, 1943.

An Epidemic of Genius. New York: Simon and Schuster, 1960.

"Finally Harriet." *Harper's,* Nov. 1938, 528–37.

Force of Evil (with Abraham Polonsky). Shooting script dated May 25, 1948. Roberts Productions, Inc. 1948.

"From a South Pacific Notebook." *American Mercury* 48 (Feb. 1944): 165–71.

"In the Black Morning." *American Mercury* 47 (Aug. 1939): 451–58.

Married Men. New York: Simon and Schuster, 1953.

"Mr. Wolfert States Position." *New York Times,* Jan. 27, 1943, 20.

"Song Hits, and Misses." *New York Times,* Jan. 19, 1941, 11.

"Spearhead." *Collier's,* Jan. 6, 1945, 16, 24.

"Talk on Guadalcanal." *The Nation,* Jan. 23, 1943, 117–19.

"That's How It Is, Brother." *Collier's,* Sept. 22, 1945, 14.

Tucker's People. New York: L. B. Fischer, 1943. Republished as *The Underworld.* New York: Bantam Books, 1950.

"War Novelist" (review of Mailer's *The Naked and the Dead*). *The Nation,* June 26, 1948, 22–23.

"The Way the Luck Runs." *Harper's Magazine,* Nov. 1938, 637–45.

"What Do You Know about La-Haye-du-Puits?" *Saturday Review of Literature,* Apr. 14, 1945, 9–10, 12, 71.

"Winners." *Collier's,* July 10, 1943, 13.

Reviews of *Tucker's People*

Collins, Thomas Lyle. "New York Underworld." *New York Times Book Review,* Apr. 25, 1943, 7.

Derleth, August. Untitled. *Book Week,* May 2, 1943, 4.

Feld, Rose. "Tucker's People." *New York Herald Tribune Weekly Book Review,* Apr. 25, 1943, 10.

Geismar, Maxwell. "Tucker's People." *New York Herald Tribune,* May 2, 1943, 17.

L., J. C. "Ira Wolfert Pens Potent First Novel." *Springfield Republican,* May 20, 1943, 8.

Levy, Newman. "Wolfert's People." *Saturday Review,* May 15, 1943, 10–11.

Mayberry, George. "Persons and Place." *New Republic,* May 3, 1943, 602.

Trilling, Diana. "Fiction in Review." *The Nation,* June 26, 1943, 899–900. Reprinted in *Reviewing the Forties.* New York: Harcourt Brace Jovanovich, 1978. 45–47.

"Tucker's People." *Atlantic Monthly,* June 1943, 129.

Unsigned. *New Yorker,* May 1, 1943, 74.

Other Sources

Aldridge, John W. *In Search of Heresy: American Literature in an Age of Conformity.* New York: McGraw-Hill, 1956.

Eisinger, Chester E. *Fiction of the Forties.* Chicago: University of Chicago Press, 1963.

Grella, George. "The Gangster Novel: The Urban Pastoral." In *Proletarian Writers of the Thirties,* ed. David Madden. Carbondale: Southern Illinois University Press, 1968. 186–98.

Humboldt, Charles [Clarence Weinstock]. "Fiction on the Left." *Masses and Mainstream* 10 (Mar. 1957): 48–50.

———. "The Novel of Action." *Mainsteam* 1.4 (Fall 1947): 389–407.

"Ira Wolfert: NG as Motorman, OK as War Correspondent." *PM,* Feb. 7, 1943, 4.

Joseph Barnes Papers. Rare Book and Manuscript Library. Columbia University.

Madden, David, ed. *Proletarian Writers of the Thirties.* Carbondale: Southern Illinois University Press, 1968.

Mandel, Ernest. *Delightful Murder: A Social History of the Crime Story.* Minneapolis: University of Minnesota Press, 1984.

Moley, Raymond. "Dewey the Prosecutor." *Newsweek,* Aug. 8, 1938, 40.

"Policy and Politics." *The Nation,* Sept. 10, 1938, 236.

Rideout, Walter B. *The Radical Novel in the United States, 1900–54.* 1956. New York: Columbia University Press, 1992.

"Unity in War Aims." *New York Times,* Jan. 25, 1943, 12.

Wald, Alan. *Writing from the Left: New Essays on Radical Culture and Politics.* London: Verso, 1994.

TUCKER'S PEOPLE

Q. Were you asked if you wanted to join this combination?

A. We wasn't asked yes or no if we want.

Q. Well, how was the deal made? That's what we'd like to hear, just how it was done?

A. He said, "Your business, you got one-third of it left from here on. Two-thirds is mine."

Q. Who said?

A. Tucker. That's the way it was.

Q. That's all?

A. Well, he said. . . .

Q. Who said?

A. Tucker. He said he'd break my bones, beat me all up if I don't.

Q. Were those Tucker's exact words, "beat you up"?

A. No. He said he'd put me on the spot so where did I come off arguing?

Q. Now were those his exact words, "put you on the spot"?

A. Words? He didn't have to say words. He was Tucker.

Q. You want to change your testimony now and tell us now he didn't say anything?

A. I didn't testimony he said anything. No sir, why should he say words? He was Tucker. All he does is bend his little finger and everybody comes running.

Q. So the truth is, as you testify to it, that he didn't say anything to you?

A. No sir, that's the truth. I never even seen him to point out in my life.

> . . . . an excerpt from the record,
> trial of People vs. Bunte.

THE POWER OF SAMSON

I

THIS STORY has no beginning and, as you will discover if you read to the last page, no real ending either.

It is a story of our own modern world, and of what the world does to its people and of how a question has been laid upon both the world and its people, for each to answer as it can:

Which shall be the user and which shall be used? Is the world a cloth that may be cut to fit its people? Or, are people cloth that must be cut to fit the world?

So this story is of people cutting the world to measure where they can and cutting themselves to measure where they have to, and of the two, world and people, rolling through the universe embraced in battle and altered by battle.

What was the beginning of this? Where is the end, since altered people alter their children, and altered children must likewise subdue themselves to this way of life? They must join the battle and cut the world and be cut by it. Then the children are further altered by the battle and must alter further, in their turn, their own children.

As there is no proper beginning, the story can be begun anywhere and it is begun in the autumn of the year 1930. A white man and a mulatto were talking business in the office of a garage in the colored section of New York City. The white man's name was Leo Minch. He had been in business in the garage, but the landlords had seen an opportunity to get more rent in the fact that Leo's success with his business had increased the value of their property. They had brought suit, broken the lease, thrown Leo out of business and rented to a new tenant. The new tenant was a little embarrassed. There had been no immediate profit for him in the transaction and the emotion stirred by a future profit that he would have to scramble for was not acute enough to subdue his embarrassment. He let Leo use the office during the slack hours of the afternoon to clear up old accounts receivable and outstanding bills. The mulatto was Samson Candee, a big, fleshy West Indian of some prominence in Harlem as a real estate operator and promoter. He was putting a proposition to Leo and now, suddenly and unexpectedly, as the story begins, he began to worry about how Leo was taking it.

It had not occurred to Samson Candee to worry about that part of the deal before. His proposition involved the lottery business. It included running a lottery and so was against the law. But it did not seem exactly against the law to Candee. He had grown up where lotteries were licensed by the government and run as a regular business. The law against lotteries in New York couldn't seem anything more to him than a part of the local setup, one of the conditions under which the business had to operate, a sort of extra risk and tax. But, abruptly and without any reason he could describe to himself in words, he began to think Leo might feel otherwise. The thought made Candee uncertain. The meaning of his words became more and more general and vaguer and vaguer.

Leo Minch sat still. He seemed to be listening. His small, heavy face appeared gray with thought and his eyes were dark with thought. Since his eyes bulged a little and looked wet, they always seemed to be brimming over with whatever emotion was on his face. But Candee wasn't sure whether Leo was listening to what he was being told or to things going on inside himself. "Or maybe," Candee thought, "he is a broken-up man and has got the habit for liking his sleep." Candee had noticed people like that, particularly since the depression. They looked all right but they couldn't concentrate. When they just had to concentrate, they got excited and were no good or went to sleep and were no good.

"If it's anything, it's that," Candee thought. But he couldn't be sure it was anything. The man listened all right and now and then he said something, and whatever he said showed he had been listening to what he was told; but he always spoke just a little bit late. He spoke only into silence and only after there had been time to feel the presence of silence.

"Or maybe," thought Candee, "he's sitting there feeling sorry for himself." Because it couldn't be, Candee decided, the man was trying to make himself out so big, such a big shot that he didn't have to cut a corner now and then to pick up a dollar like everybody else. It had said in the paper Leo's brother was "Guinea Joe" Minch who, everybody knew, was one of Tucker's people, one of the real boss people Tucker had working for him and the landlords had broken Leo's lease because the police had found Tucker's beer trucks in the garage on dead storage, hidden away there for Tucker. "Where does he come off," Candee thought, "sitting there with a pride on him like that, that I'm not good enough for him, the business I got to talk is not good enough for him."

At the moment, Leo sat thinking of nothing. Soon after he had realized Candee was not calling to pass the time of day, but to outline a proposition he would have to consider, thoughts had begun swarming in Leo's head. Candee's words came to him through the noise of his own thoughts. Sometimes the words were muffled by the noise. Sometimes they were entirely smothered. They never became compelling enough to rise free of the noise.

He was out of business, Leo had told himself at the beginning, and had come back to that again and again. "Yes, sure, plain," he had told himself, "everything going out, nothing coming in. Certainly my friend, old friend of mine, fifty-year-old, life-long friend and best and only friend you'll ever have, you are out on the street and eating yourself up with expenses like a dog eating his tail."

Then a picture of the dog had come clearly into his mind. While Candee talked uncertainly and vaguely, Leo sat watching the dog go around in a circle after its tail. It was a starving dog. It wasn't playing. It wanted to eat its tail. As he watched the dog, Leo thought of himself eating breakfast and going around doing nothing until lunch, eating lunch and going around doing nothing until supper, and eating supper and going around and around in his mind in bed. He thought of this and kept seeing the dog and got himself all mixed up with the dog and began to feel dizzy. He closed his eyes. The dog vanished. The dizziness ended slowly. When it stopped, he opened his eyes and looked at Candee.

He saw an effortful, rather wheedling smile of ingratiation on Candee's face. The man was saying nobody could lose, there were some pretty low grade operators in the business but not even they had yet found a way to lose in it. The smile assured Leo. Candee had not got to the point yet and he had not missed anything important by not listening, and he thought, yes, it certainly was sure he had to do something with the few dollars he had left. But what? Where was there hope for a man with not enough money to get along at a time when everything in the whole world was going down? He had $23,000 invested in apartment houses. Rub it out. Wash it out. Kiss it goodbye. He might as well. He could stall the bank for the interest on the balance owed for another month, another two months, then. . . .

Although Leo did not move, he felt himself draw his finger across his throat and grimace.

He had some stocks and bonds left over from trying to get rich on Wall Street after being finagled out of his garage. He couldn't buy peanuts with them now. He had borrowed on his insurance policies to hold on to his apartment properties, so there was only small change left there. He had about $4,000 in cash in the bank. That was all really, that was his last cent in the world between him and being an old man on a park bench. And if he took his last cent and put it into a proposition and lost it as everybody was losing everything? Then where was he? And if he didn't, he'd be at the same place. It would take a little longer, that was all. He'd eat himself up instead of letting a proposition eat him up. That was the only difference.

"And you don't have to put nothing in it," said Candee. "That's the beauty of it. Just cigar money to start and after that you work with their money." He smiled wheedlingly into Leo's face and waited for a response.

The silence glared in Leo's head. He became aware that Candee required an answer from him, a nod of understanding, a smile of approval, something. He leaned forward to smile. Then he felt well up in him a desire to do something at once before he ate up all the money he had left. "Why don't you come to the point and not waste so much time," he said urgently.

Candee was startled, more by the urgency than by the words. "I thought I'd give you a general outline of the lay of the land, what it is," he said.

"No, straight to the point, that's what I want. What you want out of me, how much money, straight out, that's all, like a business-man, without going around the mulberry bush all the time."

"It's not that kind of a proposition, to put down money and get chips and start to play, as I'll show you if you give me a chance."

The glare of silence dimmed in Leo's head. He remembered he had a long time to wait before supper and a long time to wait after that before going to bed, and then there would be a long time before he could fall asleep. There would be no hurry about falling asleep because he had nothing to get up for, no reason at all to get out of bed except that he had been an active man all his life and had the habit of being up and doing something to earn a dollar.

"I'll give you all the chance you want," said Leo. He sat back placidly. "I'm not doing anything anyway just at this moment." Candee regarded him uneasily. He could not decide whether he was dealing with a man whose mind was too quick for him or whose mind was disconnected and incoherent. In any case, he began to feel, it was not going to work out too good for him.

Leo knew something about the lottery known as policy. It was a popular game in Harlem, where it was called "the numbers." A player chose three numbers. If he picked the right numbers in the right order, or "hit" as they said, he was paid six hundred to one. If he had paid five cents for his three numbers, he got back $30. If he had paid $1, he got back $600. The winning numbers were arrived at daily in various ways. At this period in the history of the game, the pari-mutuel odds at a race track determined what they would be.

The men who took the bets from the customers were called col-lectors. Some of them had hung around the garage when Leo

was operating it, and three of the game's bankers had stored their
automobiles with him. Everybody in the garage had played the
numbers every day and even Leo had put up a nickel or a dime
once in a while "to help the boys out." Also, to win if possible.
Leo knew the collector worked under a controller on a commission
basis and turned over to the controller whatever money he took
in, less his commission. A controller might have several hundred
collectors working for him. He took his commission from the money
turned in to him by the collectors and handed the balance to a
banker. The banker paid off the hits and ran the business, and
whatever was left over was his.

Leo had never thought of policy as a business. To him it was
just something being done for a living by people who were not
in business. But Candee said it was plenty of a business. He said
he could name by name quite a few bankers who were making
$1,000 or $1,500 a week net for themselves as their end of the take.
He paused to make his statement dramatic. "Some of those I could
name the names of to you," he continued, "are taking in their
$50,000 a year net for themselves every day in the week like clock-
work," and he paused again for dramatic effect. But this time he
paused a shade too long. Leo heard the silence in the room and
roused himself from his thoughts.

"That's lots of pork chops," said Leo.

Candee felt he was being insulted. Leo read the feeling in the
man's face. "That's plenty lots of pork chops," he said, "from having
men with holes in their pants run around collecting a nickel and
dime here and two cents there."

Candee always carried a fat, twenty-cent cigar in his mouth.
This and his horseshoe stickpin with its small diamonds and
rubies, his two diamond rings, and his imitation silk shirts and
the gabardine suit he wore winter and summer composed his
"front." When he was short of money, he did not light the cigar
until just before going home for the night. Now he rolled the
unlit cigar in his mouth carefully, to keep from fraying it, and then
took it out and held it between his fingers, delicately, to preserve
the wrapper, and looked at it to avoid seeing the sneer on Leo's

face. Leo sat still. He sneered angrily at the top of Candee's sloped head, but he was listening so intently to his own thoughts that he was not aware of Candee at all.

The thoughts ran, nagged, tickled and prickled on Leo's mind like bugs on a ball. Just as bugs always seem to be searching for a way to reach the center of the ball, so Leo's thoughts flocked and swarmed over the surface of his mind and seemed to seek the center. In the center, within the wall of the ball of his mind, he was afraid, not over whether he would make money, but of how he would make it. He was a lawful man and his need of money was lawless.

Leo had been lawful in business all his life. He had started in the woolen business as an errand boy and had built a substantial firm for himself. But the war and the boom after it, and the big businessmen woolens attracted and made, and the tactics they used against each other, all this changed Leo's business into something he couldn't manage. Big business, fighting within itself, turned the industry into a lottery with yard goods as mere tickets in it. The woolen men down the line bet on how the woolen men up the line would bet on how consumers would bet on how woolen men would bet. Prices moved up and down violently without regard to value. It created a false market for materials and disturbed the operations of the true market. Leo was a timid man. His mind could not breathe well in an atmosphere of insecurity. There was nothing secure about betting on a market like this, but he had to do it to stay in business and he did it unhappily and fearfully, fear unbalancing his judgment, until a steeply falling market caught him with shelves loaded and, before the market could recover, his creditors ganged up on him for their money and put him out of business.

Although Leo had credit enough left to make a new start in woolens, he couldn't bring himself to do it. His experience had been frightening enough to create in him a real revulsion for the business. Instead, he saw an opening for himself in butter-and-egg routes in the suburbs. The construction industry had left the open-

ing. It had not been able to keep up efficiently with the spread of
the city during the boom and there were not enough stores for the
houses on the outskirts.

Leo made money out of door-to-door selling of butter and eggs
and staples, but he was not satisfied. The business, somehow, did
not seem useful to him. He had been a merchant all his life, providing goods—not merely service. To sell service, somehow, seemed
false. Leo had to feel useful. If he didn't feel useful, he felt insecure.
And, anyway, the whole business was too risky for him. He could
see the end of it. Big business had left a hole for him, but only
because they were busy with other things and they would soon fill
up the hole—with him inside it, if he remained. The construction
industry would get around to putting up stores. As soon as it did,
he would not be able to compete. He would be selling a delivery
service to people who would not need it.

"I'm a mouse eating when the cat is away," he told himself and
sold out his routes at a profit and bought a store in a newly constructed neighborhood. He had a notion of developing the store
into a chain, but the chain-store business was too big against him
and a single store seemed too small to him. The money he could
make out of a single store forced him too far down in the scale.
He sold out his store, again at a profit, and then went into the
business of buying stores in new neighborhoods, building them up
and selling his lease at a profit.

This was scratching for feed among the backyards of the large
new world the big men of business were building for themselves.
Leo scratched hard, with claws. He used the approved method for
building up his stores—loss leaders and premiums, doing things for
good will that a man who was there to make a living out of running the store itself could not have afforded to do. Get the customers
in, then sell them to a man who could not make a profit out of
keeping them, especially when the chain stores would start to
compete—it did not seem exactly honest to Leo and he felt dis-
satisfied and insecure.

Between stores, Leo scratched in other backyards. He bought
real estate and sold it when he could and filled in some of his time

with gambling on Wall Street. He operated his real estate speculations on a shoe-string, investing as little as he could in a property and then milking it. He stalled off the payments on the mortgages and taxes and bribed inspectors to overlook "temporarily" the repairs required by law. When he had collected enough rent to make back his investment and a profit, he stepped out and let his creditors foreclose.

Then, suddenly, he was through with all this. He flung it from him and there was an emotion of violence in him and of relief as if he had broken some foul and loathsome hold on himself. He felt that way. Inside him there lay a feeling of escape and inside that feeling lay a revulsion against what he had escaped from. He made a large investment in two apartment houses, planning eventually to pay off the mortgages and own them outright. He leased a garage and determined to run it as a business, not as a mere squeeze-box for squeezing out profits.

But, however he tried to hide, the world in which he lived hunted him down. Whatever barricade he tried to erect for himself, the world tore it down and got at him. When the depression cut the income on Leo's apartment houses, the money he had put into these properties became valueless, and only the money that remained owing on them had value. When he tried to do a favor for a brother he had not seen in many years, he lost his garage business. Tucker's business rivals found the trucks and had them confiscated and the garage padlocked. Leo's landlords saw their opportunity to profit from Leo's work and get more rent from a new tenant. And again Leo was loose in the world, with no place in it, feeling naked and insecure against it.

Money was not enough to keep his feeling of insecurity under control. He did need money. His mind needed money to breathe, exactly as his lungs needed air. But money itself was insecure. He required "position," too, a commendable place in society, one in which he need not feel vulnerable to his enemies. Money was only the first need. Money was for survival. "Position" was to make survival endurable. It was for existence, and what he feared in these latest, hunted days of his was the existence his need for survival could compel him to lead. He had an example of what this could mean in his brother, the dreaded "Guinea Joe" Minch, and the living presence of his danger sat before him in Samson Candee, gingerly making a proposition about the policy business.

But Leo could not recognize his danger with his conscious mind. If he did, it would mean he would have to examine it and understand it and understand how small his chance for escape from it had become. Then his feeling of insecurity might dishevel his mind. He might become apathetic or erratic, one of the cases of "shock" so common in the depression. So, instead, whenever the danger became unbearably plain, his conscious mind took to lapsing into blankness. It struggled to keep unknown and unthought his unknown thoughts and his unthought thoughts. And Candee sat in the cloud of the struggle, puzzling over its shadow, while Leo sat in the middle of the struggle, "day-dreaming," he thought, and finding it difficult to concentrate, and finding himself unaccountably contemptuous at times towards the man before him and unaccountably irritable at other times, as one is in the face of a danger whose existence one refuses to admit.

The unlit, twenty-cent cigar was twiddled a moment gently in long, thick fingers as Candee wondered whether it would be useful for him to go on. He knew a policy banker who was in trouble. The banker had had bad luck and had been hit for more than he could pay out. The man was trying to pay off the hits in instalments. In the meantime, people did not place bets with a banker they knew was too hard up to pay his hits so the commissions of the bank's controllers and collectors had fallen off. If they could hear of a desirable new banker, they would willingly leave their present banker to his debts. Candee knew all seven of the controllers concerned. He knew they could take their collectors—maybe 1,500 collectors all told, or maybe even more—with them wherever they went and Mr. Minch would be a great temptation for them to go. The garage had made Mr. Minch a substantial figure in Harlem. It had been the largest in that part of the city. The association of his name with Ben Tucker and "Guinea Joe" was even more attractive for the policy business. Tucker meant big money, hits being paid off with Bank of England solidity and promptness, and meant freedom from police interference. It was true that, occasionally, the police did arrest a collector for being in possession of policy slips—the slips on which the numbers selected and the amounts bet were written. When this happened, the slips were confiscated and the players concerned lost, not only their chance to win, but the money they had paid in. An arrest like that wouldn't happen to a collector working for Mr. Tucker or for Mr. Minch, whose name meant Tucker in Harlem now. Anyway, what was just as good, the customers would feel sure it wouldn't happen, and they'd be happy to bet with Mr. Minch's collectors. But if Mr. Minch was going to make out like this, thought Candee, put on the dog and give him the ritz like this, make out he's too good to cut a corner for a dollar, then what was the use of giving away the information he had?

The cigar was twiddled in silence. Samson Candee's head was stooped in silence. Leo sneered angrily into the silence until at last he became aware of the silence and strove to remember what Candee had been saying and couldn't and saw he was looking at the unlit cigar.

"Here!" Leo took matches out of his pocket. "Have a light for that cigar of yours."

Samson Candee lifted his head in surprise. "No thanks," he said.

Leo knew that the index to Samson's financial position was whether his cigar was lit. But this was a moment when he was contemptuous of Samson. His contempt was bodied with a hatred that was at once inexplicable to him and irresistible. He struck one of the matches and held it towards the cigar. "Go ahead, Sam," he said, "and see if it'll burn."

Samson pulled his cigar back and leaned forward and blew out the match. He blew slowly and thoughtfully. "You want to hurt my cigar with that thing?" he said at last and laughed with embarrassment.

Leo laughed, too, in an eager way. For a moment he had a sense of power over Samson. Then, with the volatility that afflicts a mind trying to struggle away from what is inside itself, a feeling of misery came into Leo and sank drowning in him. He realized it was not he who had the power, but Samson. Samson had come to him to make the deal and he had not wanted to make it. Yet he would make it all the same. He would associate with riffraff and run a riffraff gambling game and pay police to keep him out of jail. All because he had no power against Samson. The real power had been Samson's and had been exerted irresistibly ever since he had mentioned that Leo need risk very little of his money to get the profits offered.

Then a curious thing happened in Leo's mind. Almost separately from him, without his being clearly aware of what it was making him do, it roused him tiredly to fight against making the deal. "What happens to the banker when I take away his controllers?" he asked.

Candee had been saying this thing was so good he would like to handle it himself without Leo, only he had so many other promotions to attend to he could not spare the time "at this junction." Leo's question interrupted him. "Who?" he said, puzzled.

"The banker with his debts. When I take away his business."

"Oh him. He's out, that's all. Scratched. He goes right out of the picture altogether."

For a moment Leo was sorry for the banker and tried to feel that he couldn't do to another what had been done to him, couldn't drive a man into the street out of business at such a time. But his emotion was only momentary and he began to think that, after all, the man's assets were safe. If a policy banker ever had to pay out more than he took in, all he need do was go out of business. His creditors were powerless. There was no law on their side. Whatever the banker had to leave behind in going out of business was chicken feed. There was no plant, just an office for the bank with a few sticks of furniture in it. There was no stock of merchandise. The stock was cash. It lay in the banker's pocket. It came in every day and hits did not have to be paid until the following day. There was not even a payroll, except for a few clerical employees in the office and the police. Everybody else worked on commission and took his commission in advance.

So Leo's capital would be safe. He would not have to put his last cent on the line. He thought of this a long time. There was a feeling of fright in him that he mistook for excitement. Then he was roused once again by something deep in him to a new attack against making the deal.

"Why do you pick me out for this?" he cried. "Why not go take your deal to somebody who's already in the business?"

"Well . . ." Samson smiled uneasily. He believed if he revealed to Leo everything that made Leo the right man for the job, then Leo would feel he no longer needed Samson and would squeeze him out. "I thought we were kind of friends," he said, "know each other for a long time now and I know, heard you were looking around for a little action somewhere and thought I'd help you out if I could."

"Yes, but how can I help you? I'd like to help, you know that, Sam. I like to help everybody. That's my trouble, all my life. But why should these controllers go to work for me when they can walk across the street to another bank that is already a going concern?"

"You got a name, Mr. Minch."

Leo looked at Candee suspiciously. This was what he had wanted to bring out in the open, the name of Tucker and his connection with Tucker so that he could become frightened of it and revolt against it with the strength of fear. "I'm through here, you know," he said and raised his hand slightly to indicate the office and the garage.

"No, but you got a real high-class name for the business, Mr. Minch, just what they need."

"Name for what? I'm through here, I told you, washed up. I'm not in the garage any more. It's not mine. I'm just sitting in the office to have a place to sit. I ain't got a button in this place that's mine."

"That's all right. That's good. You won't need a garage to tie you down once you get in the policy business with your name."

"What name? I told you. . . . Name for what?"

"A name for just what's needed to the business."

"What do you mean? What are you talking about?"

"What we all heard about, Mr. Minch, read in the papers that time."

"Tucker?"

"It's just the name what's needed to the business and will make a big business for you in a month's time, just sitting still in a month's time."

"You mean," cried Leo in a high, panicky voice, "you want me to go in this business with Tucker?"

"No, no," Candee said. "Oh no, just the name, because of you and him being in the public eye together, connected there, by this thing that happened."

"I got no connection with Tucker," said Leo. His voice rose. "I never saw him in my life. I wouldn't know him if I saw him. I never heard of him from a hole in the ground." He stood up. "And that so-called brother of mine who works for him!" he shouted. "You know what's the truth? I've seen him maybe two times since I'm a boy. I don't want to see him. He's as good as dead with me, you hear, as far as I'm concerned!"

Samson had risen, too. Leo took a few angry, excited steps away from him. Then he turned and began to search Samson's face. The fleshy, leather-colored folds told Leo nothing except that Samson was startled. There was no longer any panic in Leo. Something in him had expected the mention of his name with Tucker's to drive him into an outburst of strength over Samson, but it had not happened. Instead his mind was working rapidly and coherently. Samson had not believed him. Nobody would believe him. They would all expect him to keep a connection with Tucker secret. But, if it ever came to the point where the truth had to be proved in a way that everybody could believe, then he had his own words to fall back on. He had told them. Was it his fault they hadn't believed him? In the meantime, Tucker's name could be the capital in his business. It would be like a gold reserve. It need not be there to fulfill its function. The only thing necessary was belief that it was there.

The surprise faded like light in Samson's face and left his face emotionless. He watched the angry fear give way in Leo to thought and then to an easy, pleased kind of cunning.

"You mean *you* don't talk to them," said Samson, "and *they* don't answer?"

He smiled a little. Then his smile broadened and his teeth thrust through the smile. Leo looked into Candee's smile for a moment with the blankness of thought. After that, he, too, began cunningly to smile.

II

SAMSON DID not understand the reason for his power over Leo, nor did Leo. It was hopeless for Samson ever to expect to understand it and nearly hopeless for Leo. The reasons were too complicated. Not only were things Leo himself had lived through involved, but also other things of which he had no knowledge, obscure events, some of them going back to before he was born, others taking place out of his sight. One of these occurred in his parents' bedroom in the tenement flat on the upper east side of Manhattan where he and his brother had been born. He was twelve at the time, Joe was eight and they slept side by side in their own bedroom while the incident took place.

The boys slept and Sara Minch, their mother who had been sick a long time, now lay in her own room nearly dead. Her husband fussed in the room without looking at her. It seemed to him so still there that to walk in it was like walking in a cloud. Jacob, too, was sick. For several years he had had the feeling his own body was decaying around him. It was too much for him to watch

his wife now, lying inside her exhausted, shut-eyed body as in a
coffin. While Jacob fussed, the blood gushed in his downcast head
and the windy sound of the blood blew through the cloud of quiet.

When there was nothing further he could pretend he was doing,
he pulled the smooth bedclothes smoother over his wife's motionless body, still without looking at her face. After that he stood still.
He looked at the floor and looked along the floor to the wall and
along the wall to the corner and down the corner to the floor and
then stopped looking. He stood with his eyes open and empty.
Finally he saw Sara's hand below his. He began to wonder why
he could not look at his wife's face. A force held him. His head
was rigid on his rigidly held neck and would not raise. He felt
ashamed. But, how could that be? How had he wronged her?
He must be afraid that, if he looked at her, he would see she was
dead. His face crinkled at the thought, but he could not raise his
head. He touched her hand with one finger, shyly and pleadingly.
She did not move. He lifted his eyes in fear and saw that she had
died.

"She is out of it," he thought.

The thought was unexpected and he did not understand it. He
struggled to understand it. The words of the thought clung to his
mind, but fear creamed in him like a wave. Fear went down
through him and up through him and then it shook the flesh of
his brain.

"She has ended it," he screamed. The cloud of emptiness in the
room took in his words and was silent. He looked at the door
beyond which his sons lay sleeping. "Boys," he shouted, standing
stock still and staring at the door, "your mother has ended it."

Leo and Joe stirred along each other, but did not wake and were
not awakened.

It had been possible to afford only a young doctor for Sara, and
he turned out to be what is known as a nice boy. He was still
impressed with, and not yet coarsened by, the aspects of doctoring.
He assumed responsibilities with serious intentions and had few
and weak defenses against the responsibilities he did assume.

Therefore it became inevitable, during the treatment of Sara in her last illness, for the Doctor to feel it was important that Jacob should understand exactly the reason for his wife's death. If Jacob understood that Sara had died, fundamentally, because she had wanted to, he might refrain from going the same way for the sake of his sons. It did not occur to him that the mother and father had engaged privately and without words in a plot to end their lives and that Jacob's shame over his wife's death was due to shame over their plot.

The Doctor began gently, as soon as the two boys were out of the way. The talk must be as delicate as surgery, he thought, and he picked among many words before uttering any. Jacob, he thought, no doubt was blaming himself already for the death. "If I had not done this or had done that or had or had not done any one of a hundred thousand little things, then . . ." that sort of thing. In that case, irremediable harm could be done by telling the man plainly and immediately, "It is true; in a way you are to blame; you did not make her want to live." No, this was surgery. The truth had to be laid open, but skillfully and without shock.

Then the Doctor discovered Jacob did not seem to understand, or perhaps did not want to understand, that such an event was possible, a person could induce illness and succumb to illness, all because of a thought in his mind. The Doctor felt overcome with helplessness at the size of his task. It was not so much that he was a busy man as a young man, with the feeling in him always that, beyond whatever he was doing, there was his life waiting for him to live it. He decided the whole thing would have to be done for Jacob by a friend whose knowledge Jacob respected. Yet, where was such a friend to be found? Jacob seemed somewhat above his surroundings and there had been only neighbor men and their women at the funeral. The Doctor thought for a moment of making himself into such a friend. But he did not have the time. No, no time. And then, whenever he would come calling, there would be tension about whether to pay and what to pay for. And who, actually, would pay him for the visits and for treatment in a field in which he was not qualified, not entirely qualified, only in fact an amateur? No, no, he could not do everything for everybody.

But he had begun, so he continued—somewhat less delicately now. "It was just a case of one thing after another," he said. "She had no resistance. She kept going down, like a snowball—you know, things piling on. That's the way it was."

"But why just her should get it?" cried Jacob.

"I told you, no resistance. That's the way those things work. You have no resistance so you get sick. The more you get sick, the less resistance."

"But why just her should have no resistance? She was a big, strapping woman."

The Doctor looked embarrassed. "The body gets worn out," he said at last.

"From children?"

"No! Now don't think a thing like that, not in this case!" The Doctor had spoken sharply. He knew what mischief such an idea in a widower could cause. He would not have undertaken the conversation at all if it had not been for Jacob's two sons, particularly Joe, the younger, especially attractive one.

Now the Doctor became embarrassed again and impatient. His sharp tone had jarred the mood he had been constructing to make Jacob understand what had happened to his wife without feeling guilty or ashamed. He wanted Jacob to feel moved instead, to cure his own susceptibility to that kind of death. It would take too long to restore the mood and too many words. The Doctor was not a man for words and really there was no time, no time.

"I'm going to tell you something that will be hard for you to understand what they mean, where they fit in in this case," the Doctor said and halted, startled, because he had not intended anything so abrupt and businesslike. Then, even more embarrassed and more impatient, he floundered on with, "I want you to think about what I'm going to tell you, think all around it and about everything it means and where they fit in. It's very complicated, so think about it and don't make up your mind what the truth is about where it fits in for a long time, not until you've thought about it for a long, long time, I mean months and years."

Jacob nodded and hunched forward in his chair. He liked this. He was fond of making his life sound great with words.

"All right," said the Doctor, "so here it is: there are things in the mind that no one knows. It's a mystery like everything else. Now you think of that, what goes on in the mind, things in your own mind that you don't even dream are there, that you don't know, you never heard of. And if you yourself tell yourself they're there in your own mind, you'll say to yourself, it's a lie. But they're there just the same, your own thoughts."

The Doctor paused and Jacob, although he still sat forward, seemed disappointed. "Do you see what that means?" the Doctor cried and added with exasperation, because now he was condemning himself for ever having begun, "No, you can't see all at once, it's not possible. But think about it. Keep it in your mind. Here are your thoughts. They are in your own mind and you don't know it, you never heard of them, you don't care. But they live there and they got electricity to play with and chemicals to play with, all this power to work with on the body and try to do to your body what they want, when you don't even know what it is yourself, although it's your body and your mind."

Jacob sat staring. He was no longer disappointed. Electricity and chemicals, power. His surprised brain fumbled with the Doctor's unexpected words. The way that Sara had taken was plain to him now. He had understood it all along. The accusation had even come unexpectedly into his mouth as he saw her dead. "She has ended it," he had cried. But it had not been clear to him then, as it was now, in the way a path is lighted for a man to follow.

"That's really some mystery I tell you," he said and remained staring with mouth open.

"Yes, but you must think about it and just keep thinking about it and you will know it is true, that there is a mystery in the mind, what it's thinking about and what it's doing to you. Then, when you know it's true, you will see where it fits in in your case. Don't believe that you will get it the first time. Say no, that's not it. The truth where it fits in is something else. And the second time and the third time and so on, so forth, like that, until at last, years maybe, it fits in perfectly, every little detail fits in just perfect like a glove."

"That's really some mystery to me altogether I tell you," said Jacob.

The Doctor had a sudden feeling of fear, as if he had made an injection and had forgotten what he had put into the hypodermic. Frightened, he stared at Jacob's face to discover whether he had injected a fluid that would heal or destroy. The face told him nothing of what he wanted to know. It was covered with surprise and grief and worry.

"The trouble with me is," the Doctor told himself as he left, "I take everything too serious."

The boys did not return to the house until the Doctor had gone.

Jacob forgot the Doctor's words more quickly than the Doctor did. At least, he put them out of his conscious thoughts more quickly. Yet the words remained underneath the surface of his mind, for they had been what was needed.

Jacob was always tired now. He believed his tiredness came from grief, but his grief passed rather quickly and his feeling of exhaustion did not. It became chronic. "I am a very sick man myself," he told himself.

The struggle to die was begun in him. It went on below the surface of his mind. Sara and the Doctor had shown him the way out of the life he was leading. Part of him was afraid to take it and part of him knew he would take it. Part of him refused to take it for his sons' sake and for the sake of self-preservation and part of him insisted on taking it. Fear and the struggle itself sucked his tissues empty of strength. He could not sleep well or eat well, but he was not aware of the fear or the struggle, only of an exhaustion he believed must be caused by grief.

"How can I get sick?" he cried to himself. "What will become of my boys?"

Then he felt he was going to die soon. That was his fate. He was an unlucky man and fate had always been against him. If it were not for the boys, he would not be sorry. No, he was tired and would not be sorry to die.

There were tubercle bacilli in him, as in all city dwellers. They became the harpies of his death. His mind worked nerves to work glands to secrete juices to stir reactions. A symphony became loose in him. Electrics and chemicals and the forces of nature thundered unheard up and down him and waked the harpies. A wall that had sealed the harpies in a corner of a lung wore thin and split and crumbled.

"I have not long to live," Jacob told himself.

The harpies stretched awake and reached for food. They ate Jacob and fattened and ate more of him and fattened more.

"I got no resistance," he thought. "The wind goes through me like my chest is paper."

Then Jacob was sick with tuberculosis. After that, he died.

Before dying, Jacob set his household in order as well as a money-less tailor could. He had that much sense of responsibility towards Leo and Joe. He moved his sons into a three-room flat, small enough for them to manage, and trained them to manage it—all of it, cooking, cleaning, marketing, laundering and even sewing.

Up to that time, Leo had been overshadowed by his younger brother and ignored. As a baby, Leo had been not merely unexpected to his parents, but unwelcome as well. Sara and Jacob were then still fighting against the poverty that thronged their lives. A child made their struggle seem hopeless.

They did their best for Leo. They talked love for him into themselves and cooed over him and fondled him. But all the sum of each of them was flung into a fight against the life each was being compelled to live. The baby was one of the enemies in the fight. No matter how unnatural they would call their feeling for their baby, no matter how repelled they were by their feeling, no matter how they tried to alter it and destroy it, the feeling lived on.

They buried it and it lived on. They assured the world they loved their baby and assured each other and assured the baby and even, in the privacy of their own minds, assured themselves. But the fact that poverty had made their baby their enemy lived on and there could be no love in them for Leo.

By the time Joe came, four years after Leo, Sara and Jacob stopped fighting and gave in to poverty as their way of life. But it was too late for Leo now. It would be forever too late.

The parents turned from fighting poverty to escaping from its effects. Everything in their lives was turned by them into a means of escape. They fastened on Joe as a new baby, one they had never hated. He became to them a way out of the life to which they were bound. They loved him. His spirit was nourished by their love. His nourished spirit fed his body. He became a sound, burly boy. Health sunned his face and made him good looking. His mind, free of the fears that can numb minds, unfolded boldly and grasped and grappled and conquered.

"A regular little genius," he was called, "smart like a whip."

Since it is natural for pure man to love all men, it was natural that Joe and Leo should love each other. Their love went deep and was lodged securely. But their love had no chance to grow straight. It grew as they grew, in poverty. That was their foe, poverty. Poverty was their cultural heritage, the endless chain of life by which the past manacles itself to the future. Because poverty had made his parents ignore Leo and love Joe, the love in each little boy for the other developed strange growths. Leo's love for his baby brother grew into admiration and then envy. Joe's love for Leo grew into pity. Leo responded to Joe's pity with gratitude. Joe responded to Leo's gratitude with more pity.

Yet the two boys remained fixed in each other. Love had no room to grow correctly and give off good fruits in the lives they were made to live. Soon, indeed, there was little to show they loved each other, and then there was nothing to show it and they could not know it themselves. There was no sign of love except, somehow, they were not able to let each other alone. That was the wonder. Poverty and life in poverty could twist their love, but could not destroy it. Their love had become part of them and part of their fate.

It was Leo who took to his father's housekeeping training. Joe became the one who was slow to learn and indifferent and sullen and "lazy."

"The ugly duckling grows up," thought Jacob. Leo puzzled him. Joe worried him.

This sudden change-over between the two boys was not mysterious except perhaps to those around them. Leo was now happy. He had his own home to manage and he could feel that the job he had in the shipping department of a woolen goods firm was keeping it up. He no longer had parents to ignore him. He no longer need feel helpless in his gratitude towards Joe and thus resentful of his gratitude. Now it was he who was helping Joe. So he was settled in the tenement flat and became good at managing it and was settled in his job and became good at that, too.

But Joe's experience had been exactly opposite. The death of his mother and his father's preoccupation with his own oncoming end moved Leo out from under a cloud, but it took away from Joe all the source of his strength. Before Joe could find a source of strength in something else, he had been put in the charge of one he had long pitied and now must feel guilty towards for ever having pitied.

Leo planned on keeping Joe in school until Joe had learned a profession or had become, as he put it, "at least an educated man with a high school diploma." His emotion was logical, based as it was on love. Until the change-over happened, Joe was successful in school. Leo, on the other hand, was conscious of his own lack of schooling. He felt inferior to people and, not knowing enough to blame it on the insecurity his parents had given him, he believed in his inferiority and blamed it on his lack of schooling. Joe, he determined, would be given an education.

But Joe did not cooperate. What father and brother thought of as "the stage" he was going through did not end. It became worse.

Neither Jacob nor Leo knew what to do. No one knew Joe had pitied Leo. Joe himself was no longer conscious of it. No one could understand, not even Joe, Joe could only feel, what it meant to a human mind robbed of security to be placed in the power of one who had been pitied and now no longer need be or could be.

Joe understood merely that any success Leo had or even any effort at success Leo made was something that stirred hate in him. Not hate for Leo. Nothing so cleansing as that. Love stood in the way of anything like that. Not even necessarily hate for what Leo was doing. Just futile, pus-bearing hate for whatever there was around. And Joe began to feel inferior to Leo. Soon he became inferior to Leo.

Still the affair of love between the brothers went on its sick, sickening, crooked and crippling way.

The way Joe lived after his father died, it was only a question of time until he got himself into a jam there was no getting out of, and now one came that seemed to be it. He was fifteen. He had been lucky steadily for years. Now his luck was turning against him.

Joe had just been living along in Leo's home. He tried hard to be as he had been and was expected to be, but he couldn't seem to try hard long enough. He wanted to make enough money to become independent of Leo. That was his ambition. It filled him full. Sometimes, even, he had a sensation that, if he put his teeth together, he would bite into it.

Yet, whatever he tried in order to get money seemed to go against a grain in him. He'd get a job and be fired or quit and then loaf around with nothing to do and break out to get hold of some money or maybe just to be doing something. Then he'd wind up scared at what he'd done. He'd be frightened of the risk he'd run, and also ashamed at what he was becoming, and find another job and keep it for a few days or a week—once for four months and it looked, that time, as though he really were going to settle down —and then be without a job and start his restless loafing again.

Joe shined shoes and sold newspapers and became an errand boy and then a messenger boy for the telegraph company and a helper on a truck and an apprentice in a hat factory and an apprentice to a furrier and delivery boy in a fruit market and helper in a bicycle repair store—thirty-four jobs altogether in three years. He was fired more often than he quit. He was fired generally because of the way he acted when he was told to do something and because, whenever he worked, he was sullen and hard to get along with.

"You got a weakness in your character," the exasperated Leo told him. "You fly apart because there's nobody around who's boss to lick you."

When his restless loafing had ended in trouble, Joe had always managed to think a way out before Leo could learn of it. But, he felt now, he was not going to think a way out of this one. He had owed a boy called Shortie $5 for two months as a result of a bet and had always told the boy he'd pay him when he got down to his name on the list of creditors because Shortie was soft and easy to push around. Now, as they were standing in a candy store, where the boys hung out when tired of the pool room, Shortie was telling him the money had to be paid right away, before eight o'clock that night, and Joe had the feeling he was listening to what he had been expecting to hear for a long time. He had no money. He didn't know a place to get any.

"The rabbit jumped up and bit me in the heart," said Joe to himself.

Shortie knew Joe had sneaked into a Lexington Avenue saloon about five blocks away and had crouched along the bar until a customer had put down a dollar bill and then had grabbed up the dollar bill and run. Now Shortie was saying, if he didn't get his fi' bucks before the bartender went to work at eight o'clock, he was going to go over to the saloon and tell the bartender where Joe lived.

The boy was skinny and small. He was sixteen, but he looked twelve and always felt put upon and always was put upon. By God, he told Joe, he was going to get his five or the pleasure of it and, if Joe beat him up and sent him to the hospital, it didn't make any difference. He wouldn't forget, no matter how long he had to stay in the hospital, and as soon as he could walk again, he'd go over to the saloon and tell the bartender where Joe lived.

"Okay, Shortie," said Joe. He held up his fist and pointed to it with one finger. "What are you going to do about this five after you get your fi' bucks?"

"I don't care," Shortie told him. "I'm right. I've let you guys kick me around long enough and use me and throw me around long enough and now I'm finished, that's all. You got till eight and not another minute, that's all."

Shortie was drawn so tall his body trembled. Joe could tell by the boy's face just what Shortie was feeling and he thought, suddenly, that must be the way he himself looked sometimes when arguing with Leo. Just the same, he moved on Shortie slowly, holding his fist up and tapping it with one finger. He moved scowling, but as in a dream, with the sensation of walking through his own thoughts and through the image of Shortie's white, stiffened face.

He came to a slow halt. He realized there was no use trying to do anything with Shortie. It would only make everything worse. He had been the way Shortie was now often enough to understand that the boy was beyond being argued out of what he had made up his mind to do, no matter how unreasonable it was and no matter how unreasonable he knew it was, and was beyond being scared out of it or beaten out of it.

For an instant, Joe pitied Shortie and, with the pity, came a feeling that he wanted Leo to know he had stolen money off a bar. The feeling was violent. It had pleasure in it, too, but it seemed crazy to him and he stopped thinking of it.

"You know what's coming to a squealer," he said to Shortie. He lowered his fist and spit at the floor near Shortie's feet.

"I know what's coming eight o'clock," Shortie said.

Joe was shaking as he walked out of the candy store. He stood in the street, hands in pockets, and thought, "This is it all right. Here's the one I'll not get out of."

It was an afternoon in early autumn. The doors to all the stores were hinged open. He walked along slowly. At fifteen, he looked nearly as mature as Leo, then nineteen. Leo was a dumpy young man. Joe was taller and broader and more solidly built. He had his parents' big frame with well-muscled flesh on it. A tough-guy look had been laid over his face and there was a tough swing to his walk and to his talk. Yet, although Joe looked much more the man than Leo, he did not feel the better for it. Leo's slightness made him feel too big and clumsy.

Now he thought it was funny a five-dollar bet with Shortie should come to be the blowoff when there had been so many other more important things. He told himself he was glad, anyway, that the thing Leo was going to find out was a little thing and thought, "Christ, fi' bucks! There's plenty of places to get hold of fi' bucks." He discovered he was looking into the stores as he passed them and thinking of the money that lay in cash drawers and looking at women and their pocketbooks and thinking how easy it would be to slip up behind one of them and grab her pocketbook and run, run, run like hell on legs, down the block, around the corner, into a doorway before the woman had time to take in enough breath to scream.

"No," he thought, "I'm in this and I'm just going to sit in it and take what's coming to me."

His brain felt tired. He stood staring into a butcher store. It was empty. The butcher had gone into the big icebox in back of the store. A grab-and-run steal would be easy. Joe turned around abruptly and went home.

"All my life I've been worrying about getting out of trouble," he thought. "This time I'm tired. I'm going to sit in it and not move and the hell with it."

The alarm clock in the kitchen showed four o'clock when Joe reached home. Leo wasn't due before 7:30. Joe sat around the house for a while trying to think of something to do. He began looking for an object to fool around with, maybe something to repair, and while he was opening drawers he discovered he really was looking for money. He didn't expect to find any, but he hunted and thought of asking Leo for $5. "What for?" he heard Leo say and heard himself answer, "To pay a bet," and heard himself laugh at himself. If Leo knew Joe was doing any betting, he'd think Joe was on the way to prison.

Joe looked in all the drawers in the house and in all the dishes and pots and pans. "That guy don't leave a dime nowhere that's not nailed down," he told himself and looked behind the pictures and in the tank of the toilet and in Leo's shoes. It occurred to him suddenly Leo must have money somewhere. He had never thought of Leo's money before but now, thinking of it, he knew Leo would not spend all he earned no matter how little that was. Leo had all the virtues, every single lousy virtue there was in the good book. Joe almost pulled Leo's shoes inside out digging into them. He searched the linings of Leo's clothes and even the linings of his own old clothes, thinking Leo might have hidden it there because he knew Joe wouldn't go near old clothes and they were kept only because Leo never threw anything out.

On the windowsill there was a flower pot full of dirt but without any plant in it. Joe poked the dirt with a pencil and got excited when the pencil hit something hard. It was only a stone. He dug the stone out and hefted it and snickered. The snicker seemed to float in him on a vast hopelessness. He leafed through some of Leo's books and some of his own old schoolbooks and the books their father had left. Then he went to the closet and got out the trunk where Leo kept embroidered linen that had belonged to their mother's trousseau. He went through all the things and even ran his fingers over the lining of the trunk, looking for lumps, thinking every lump was money.

He got down on his hands and knees and searched under the furniture and looked behind the wall moldings and ran his fingers along all the floor boards, looking for a loose one, and sat a while on the floor, staring at the floor aimlessly and at his hands and at the legs of chairs. Then he got up to look into the one place he had been saving for last because he knew it was in there, it must be in there and was in there all right and all the rest was just monkeying around, drawing it out, piling it up, saving the best for the end, making the end good, making the end happy.

This last place was a cardboard box in which Leo had stored mementoes of his mother and father—a photograph, his wallet, her last pocketbook, the dress she had been married in, her shoes and his shoes and a complete outfit of his, including underwear and shirt and tie. Among the folds of the garments, Joe found a savings bank book made out in Leo's name. No withdrawals were recorded, only deposits—most of them for $3, some for as little as fifteen cents. The total was $267.35.

"Jesus!" said Joe. He was stunned and somewhat frightened. The word had been torn out of him. He looked around him. "Why," his voice was loud and surprised and fearful and angry, "wouldn't you just know it with a guy like that!" The words dropped into silence. He heard them echo and became aware of the quiet and the feeling of loneliness in the empty flat. He put the bank book into his pocket and put away the trunk and the cardboard box and spent a long time tidying up wherever he had searched.

He went into the kitchen and put some water up to boil. He had decided to make a soup for supper with thick pieces of meat in it and beans and barley and with what was called in the neighborhood "soupen greens." The feeling of surprise and fright would not leave him. He put in the meat and salted the water and sat down to wait for it to boil.

The fire in the coal stove was silent. Darkness grew silent. He sat in it for a long time, hardly thinking. Then he took out the bank book and opened it and looked at the last figure in it—$267.35. His tongue licked along his lips. It was a rapid, involuntary gesture. A very hungry man might have made it at the thought of food.

Joe didn't know what he was going to do when Leo came home. He knew only that this was important. It was a crisis. Something was going to happen and whatever happened was going to decide a lot of things. He wasn't aware that he had made a decision long before, while standing in the candy store facing Shortie, and had decided he had been driven far enough down by his emotions towards Leo and now was going to make a stop. He didn't think of how he was going to do it or that he was going to do it. He thought only of how Leo had saved all this money out of nothing, out of the $12 a week he was now getting since his promotion in the shipping department, and had saved it in three years.

No, less than three years. Because, when their father had died, there had been $20 left over from his funeral, and they had opened a joint savings account with it. A few months later, four, five months later, when the account got up to $31, he had had a fight with Leo and had run out of the house and had run to the bank and had drawn out all the money without telling Leo, because he was going to run away from home and make his own way that time sure. But he hadn't run away. Instead, he had hung around with the money in his pocket and had bought a gold watch for $20 and a jackknife for $1 and had lost the rest of the money on cards and horses and pool. He had told Leo the watch cost $31 and was a good investment. "It's something we can hock in an emergency," he had explained and Leo had said to keep the watch out of his sight because, if he ever got his hands on it, he'd smash it to pieces even though it cost a fortune of money. So Leo must have started this new account after that and had saved all this money in two, two and a half years.

Joe didn't envy Leo the money. He didn't take any satisfaction in learning that the family was comparatively well off and did not have to worry any longer about emergencies. To him, the figures in the bank book were a map on which he could trace the whole course of their future life together—Leo going ahead in business and becoming a solid, prosperous figure, Joe in the shadow as the no-good brother, the family bum, succumbing more and more to the life of a street loafer until he was lost in it forever. Maybe he was lost already. The thought was cloudy in him. It was hardly more than fear. He sat still in his fear and tasted it and did not know why he was afraid.

"If I start all over again somewhere," he told himself at last, "it will be better. The trouble with me is I'm too weak. If I got Leo to lean on, I lean on him and don't want to work. But if it was work or starve to death, I'd get along all right."

He knew what was true about himself, that he was smart and resourceful.

When Leo came home, Joe waited only for him to take off his hat and then told him he had something important to say and said he had heard of a good opportunity for a job in Kansas City. Joe had picked Kansas City as the place to go because it sounded far away and like a city. He took a chance and added, "in a meat-packing place," and studied Leo's face and saw only suspicion on it and said, "That's a real good business to get into with plenty of millionaires in it."

Joe's voice quavered as he said it and he thought, "Oh, if only something wonderful like that would happen to me once in my life, just only the one time," and imagined Leo handing over the money without fuss and imagined himself sitting on a train to Kansas City. He knew it couldn't happen, not that way anyway, and thought, "If only he'd feel how good it would be to do it—to do it now, now, just the minute when I need it most and it would be the most wonderful, to do it without asking a single question, to do it just right out, 'here, here's the money, good luck.'"

Leo was still frowning at him suspiciously. "Meat packing's Chicago," he said.

"This one what I was told about is hiring people is in Kansas City."

Leo knew Joe was lying, but he did not care a great deal. He thought for a moment of driving this foolish new notion out of Joe's head by questioning him and making him admit he had not heard about any job there. And Joe felt Leo was going to do this. He stood braced for the questions and tried nervously to think of where Kansas City was and what meat-packing was and who among his friends might have told him about meat-packing. But Leo didn't think the matter was important enough to waste time over.

"How do you expect to get there," Leo asked bluntly, "walk?"

The unexpected question threw Joe off guard. "That's what I was going to ask you, for some money," he said.

"Ask me?"

Leo's tone was sharp and Joe floundered on. "Yes," he said, "about seventy-five or a hundred, so I can get there and get a real start, the real right kind of a start, say with a hundred or so or whatever you can spare."

The pleading moved Leo. "Joe," he said and looked into his brother's flushed face and hungering eyes and stopped. "All right," he said, "I'm not against it, you know that, if you want to go out and make an opportunity for yourself in business. But, why not the right way? Get a job here. I'll help you. Get a job and put a few dollars together and then go wherever you want."

Joe looked up unhappily. "This job isn't going to stay open all my life," he said in a low tone.

"Well, I know, if you had been in a position to take advantage of it, but . . . well, what can I do if you're not in a position?"

"You can give me the money if you want."

"Who me? Where'll I get it?"

"You got it."

"Who? What? Where should I get it? A hundred dollars."

"Don't give me that," said Joe. He lifted his face. He wasn't embarrassed any more at having had to lie. He was no longer afraid to be caught lying. Leo had driven him to lie and had driven him to be afraid to lie and had driven him to beg and had driven him to be ashamed of begging. But he forgot all that now because Leo had lied. "You got the money," he cried. "You took it from me."

"That's a new one," said Leo.

"Yes," said Joe, "maybe it's new to you, but you've been taking money from me four, five years now and I want it back, what's mine."

"The money I took for the house before you could throw it down the sewer?"

"That's what your story was—for the house!" Joe pulled Leo's bank book out of his pocket and waved it in the air. "This is a hell of a fine how-do-you-do!" He slammed the bank book on the kitchen table and stood tall with rage.

Leo looked at the bank book earnestly. Then he turned towards Joe. "Where did you find it?" he asked.

Joe remembered suddenly how he had hunted in silence like a thief. "What's the difference," he cried. "I want my money you stole."

Leo looked steadily at his brother for a moment and then walked to the stove and lifted the lid of the soup pot and peered in.

"I'm not playing," said Joe. He thrust out his lower lip and narrowed his eyes and clenched his fists. "I want my money back."

Leo faced around quickly, throwing himself. "You think you're a big clumsy ox you can beat me up for it?" he sneered. It was unfair. He knew it was unfair. He realized Joe felt awkward because of his size, but he was a short man with his own sense of inadequacy, and, like all short men, he hit big men where he could reach them, below the belt.

"I don't know what I'm going to do," said Joe, and was gnawed into a shout. "I'm not responsible. A thing like this, to do a thing like this to me! I'll break your head open, you hear, if you don't give me my money back."

Leo was angry now, too. He ducked his head and thrust it towards Joe and tapped it with the fingers of one hand. "Go ahead," he said. "I'm not big enough to stop you."

"I will!" The words broke from Joe. "Don't drive me on like this! I will! I will!" He swung his fists through the air. His fists struck the air and thrashed it.

Leo, his head still ducked, stood waiting and watching and sneering. "I expect it from you," he said finally.

"You took my money," cried Joe. "I got a chance now and it's bad enough you take my money and hide it so I got to look for it like a thief without spoiling my chances, too."

"All right. Tell me. What's in Kansas City? Cowboys? You want to be a cowboy?"

"Never mind. I got a right to my money."

"If you think it's your money," said Leo, "go ahead to the bank and draw it out. Go to Kansas City and be a cowboy. Go ahead. Go to the Yukon and dig up gold. Go ahead. Go! Go!"

"You got to go with me to the bank. They won't give it to me without you."

"Why not, if it's your money, what you say."

"You know they won't give it to me alone."

"So you want me to go and hand it over to you for a present?" Leo said. "Swell chance. You got a better chance to be Queen of England."

"It's my money."

"How do you figure that? I took that money out of my stomach and put it in the bank and off my back. That's my lunch money and going without a piece of fruit for breakfast and my clothes money in there. I walked to work when it was snowing, raining, when there was ice in the holes in my shoes, to save a nickel carfare and put a nickel more in the bank. Did you do it? Not that I remember. Not once! You wouldn't even keep a job."

"Part of that money comes from me. I know it. I didn't have fruit either."

"What comes from you? The three, four dollars you made before Columbus came to America? That's in there? The two cents you made when you could spare the time from hanging out in God knows where, saloons or what? That paid for your eating for six years? That gave you clothes and a bed to sleep in with a roof over it, a gold watch . . . where's your gold watch?"

Leo had noticed suddenly it was gone and had remembered suddenly he hadn't seen it in a long time. Joe had sold the twenty-dollar watch for four dollars a month before.

Joe looked around the room helplessly and saw the kitchen clock. It showed five minutes after eight and he thought of Shortie and the bartender.

"It's being fixed," he said.

He picked up the bank book and opened it and looked hurriedly down the row of deposits—3.00, 3.00, 3.00, 0.20, 3.00, 3.00, 3.10, 0.25, 0.95, 2.15, 3.00, 3.00, 3.00, 3.00. He was trying to find one amount he could remember giving Leo and could claim now as his own.

There wasn't any. He slapped the book shut between his two hands.

"I gave you all the money I ever made for the house," he said, "and it didn't go into the house. It went in here." He threw the book on the table. "I want it," he cried. "You're not going to spoil my life the way you always do. That's my money and I want it."

"Spoil your life? That was me who did it?"

"Yes, you! You! Who else, making me do what I don't want to do; and whatever I want to do, who else stops me! I want my money right this minute without arguments."

Joe looked again at the alarm clock and thought of the bartender calling the policeman on the beat.

"You live like a bum and I did it?" said Leo. "You won't go to school. You won't settle down with a job, and I did it? You fly around the streets in the day, in the night—and that's me doing it?"

"Yes, you, you, nobody else but you. I'd be all right if you'd give me a chance to breathe. Look, look!" He pointed to the clock. "The time is going!"

Leo did not turn his head to follow his brother's finger. "Where is it going?" he asked, so angrily he did not know what he had said.

"Give me my money back, that's all. If you'd only let me alone, I'll be all right. Give it to me, give it to me back!"

Leo glared at his brother. "A fine all right you'd be," he cried. The truth in Joe's blame had stung deeply and he cried from the bottom of him. "You think I'm blind? You think I don't know what you're up to, Mr. Streetguy? Reeve's grocery and Mettner's shoe store and that girl, that whore bum, putting your mouth on that piece of, God knows, that piece of filth, germs, sickness like it crawls, and you with your filthy, dirty laying with her in her disease and grabbing pocketbooks. You think I don't know? You're going to get yourself locked up in prison, Mr. Streetguy, and you'll sit there and say I did it."

"What do you mean?" faltered Joe. "What are you talking about, me or you or what?"

"I mean I know more than you think I know. I never said anything before, that's all. Go ahead. What's it my business! Hang yourself. Grow up to be in the pimp business. Become a jailbird. What's it to me? Every time I say anything to you, what do I get out of it? I get my head bitten off, I'm butting in."

"You're talking you don't know what you're saying."

"All right, I don't know. I can't see what's in front of my eyes. But I'm telling you for the last time: I didn't do nothing but good to you; I never did nothing but good to you. And if you get me excited once more, I'm going to throw you the hell right out of this house and into the street where you belong. You're a plain bum, that's all."

Leo's arms flew into the air and he flung them downward and turned and looked into the pot for a long moment, struggling to control himself, and said, "I'm going to eat my supper," and walked to the closet to get a plate.

The alarm clock stared at Joe. He looked away from it hastily and quivered. He couldn't think. He could only feel. The things he had done in his restless loafing, added up like this, spoken out clearly like this, shocked him. They had seemed different when he had done them and, later, when he had thought about them. He felt now that the way those things had seemed to him was not reality, and the way they seemed to Leo was the way they really were. Leo saw them as the world saw them, and what the world saw must be the truth. If he had thought of these crimes, these shocking, repulsive, smothering crimes as being not quite crimes, as being things he had done unwillingly and not with himself and thus as things for which he could not be blamed, then, Joe felt now, it must be because he was not part of the world. He was shut out of the world.

He wanted to run. He wanted to run from the terror of being an outcast and from being hated and hating. He wanted to run from the terror and hate of Leo knowing about him and run from the policeman and the bartender and Shortie. His whole body battled to get loose from the floor on which it stood. But the clutter of his thoughts paralyzed him. He was held fast by the separate terrors and separate hates and also by a new fear of what crimes lay waiting outside for an outlaw who was without money.

So he stood shaking in his emotions. His gaze was on Leo and his ears strained to catch footsteps on the stairs that might be the policeman, and his brain felt as though it were fainting and falling through his head. It fainted and fell and struggled back and fainted and fell. Words came out of his mouth. He didn't know what he was saying. He couldn't even hear what he had said after he said it. He knew only that he was shouting and should not shout. He should be down on his knees begging Leo for money to run away from the policeman.

"No," Joe shouted. "You're not going to get out of it by calling me names this time. No, no, no!"

Leo had not yet taken down the plate. He sprang around. "I warned you," he said violently.

"No, no! You hear? No!" The skin of Joe's face rose and fell and shuddered as he shouted, but his gaze remained fastened on Leo. "You're not going to get away by making me in the wrong. You're the one in the wrong. You stole my money. I want it. I want it, you hear! You hear you! I'll get it if I have to kill you." His hand reached out and picked a heavy porcelain sugar bowl from the table.

"I warned you not to get me excited," said Leo.

"You see this?" Joe raised the sugar bowl and looked at it and saw what he had in his hand and then looked at Leo. "Give me my money, that's all. Give me my money or I'll kill you dead."

Leo was afraid now. He drew himself up and stretched out one hand and pointed to the door. "Get out of my house," he said.

"No, never, never, you can't make me!" Joe lifted the sugar bowl high over his head. "Give me the money! The last time! Give me the money!"

Joe wanted to kill. The bowl jittered in his grasp as if gathering to leap. Leo thought he would throw it and crouched. His whole face curled with fear. Joe saw Leo's face and saw his brother's darting eyes and felt a wail burst inside him and slammed the sugar bowl on the floor. He jumped into the air and came down on both feet with all his force. The room shook.

"Give me my money back," he screamed.

He ran to the stove. The sugar bowl had not broken. It had bounced and scattered sugar over the floor. Joe's shoes grated as he ran through it. The grating sounds were like nails in his ears. They were voices telling his guilt. He lifted the pot of soup from the stove and threw it as hard as he could against the wall. It crashed and splashed and fell to the floor and bumped and Joe looked at it without seeing it.

"I'll murder you," shouted Joe at the top of his voice and kicked the stove and felt pain rocket up his leg and through his body and kicked the stove again and screamed with pain and kicked it again and again and screamed again and again with pain.

Leo stood staring with open mouth. "What's the matter, Joe?" he asked. His voice was strained. He came forward slowly and there was a look of suffering on his face. "Joe, my Joe," he said, "are you in big trouble, Joe?"

"Don't come near!"

Leo stopped.

"Give me the money, that's all!"

"Tell me what it is if you're in trouble, Joe."

Joe glanced desperately around the room. He seemed to be looking for something else to destroy. He saw the clock showing fourteen minutes after eight and saw the bank book on the table and ran to it and grabbed it up. "I want what's mine," he shouted, "or I'll tear this bank book up in pieces."

"You behave yourself!" Leo tried to make his voice stern, but he was too overcome with concern for Joe.

Joe had set out knives and spoons on the table before Leo had come home. With a sudden gesture, he swept up as many as he could in one hand and threw them at the window. The window shattered with a crash and a hundred tinklings. The two brothers stood looking at each other. Their eyes were stained with fear. Some of the glass and cutlery landed on the fire escape and they heard it tinkle and clang and some slipped through and fell to the courtyard below and they heard it smash and tinkle and clink.

"Now," cried Joe, "maybe you're satisfied what you made me do." Leo began to answer, but he didn't have time. Joe sprang out the door, still clutching the bank book. Even as the words halted in Leo's throat, he heard the door bang and heard Joe's footsteps going down the stairs so quickly they sounded like heavy falling.

"That crazy kid," thought Leo, "he was going to kill me." He began to sweep up the broken glass and the spilled sugar. "What's going to become of a lunatic like that?" he asked himself and got out a mop to take up the soup.

While Leo was mopping, Joe hurried to the freight yards on the Harlem River. He was going to catch a freight, west-bound. "To Kansas City," he thought and wondered why and wondered what he would do when he got there and told himself, "there's nobody in the whole world, whatever they try, going to stop me from getting to Kansas City."

Leo felt weak with fear and thought, "He takes my supper and throws it on the floor and leaves me with nothing to eat and breaks up the house and says I did it. Is that a person or . . . or . . . a what?"

Joe skulked on the edge of the tracks, waiting. "Anybody stops me, they'll get what I give Leo," he told himself.

Leo washed off some of the meat and made a sandwich of it, but he didn't feel like eating. He stared at the sandwich for a while and fingered it unhappily and then he went downstairs to look for Joe.

Shortie was standing in a doorway nearby and, when he saw Leo, he came over and asked, "Is your brother upstairs, mister?"

"He went out," Leo told him.

Pieces of his bank book lay on the sidewalk and another part of it was in the gutter. All the pages had been torn out of it and had been crumpled and trampled and kicked. The cover of the book had been torn in half. Leo gathered up the parts carefully.

"When you see him," said Shortie, "tell him I'll give him another week. He'll know. Just say, 'Shortie says he'll wait another week, but not any longer than that.' "

"You keep away from him," said Leo. "He's a good boy and you and your other tramps, you leave him alone. I see you so much as look at him again, I'll lock you all up, you understand!"

Joe was in an empty coal car now. He sat with his head in his hands and rocked with the car and thought the policeman must be upstairs by now, arguing with Leo. He heard the sugar grate again under his shoes and the sound plunged into him. He heard the window break again and it seemed to smash inside himself. He saw himself standing on the sidewalk, tearing and stamping on the bank book.

Each time he remembered something else he had done to Leo, he cringed and struggled away from his cringing and told himself that, when he was rich, he would come back from Kansas City and show Leo what he had become—all by himself, without any of Leo's doing.

"I'll be all right," he thought, "once I get away from his bossing me."

Leo stood in the doorway of the flat. He had a presentiment Joe would not come back. The silence in the flat seemed to him to be alive and gathering.

As Joe sat with his head in his hands, his hands lay against his eyes, but his eyes were open and he saw Leo's face crouched before him, yellow and damp, the lips trembling and the eyes bouncing and running back and forth in the head like animals in a trap. Joe closed his eyes and held himself still against the rocking of the coal car and the face disappeared.

"I'll be all right," he told himself, "once I forget him."

❧

Loneliness was now the enemy for Leo. After a long time of waiting for Joe to return, he gave up his home and boarded with a family in the neighborhood.

They gave him the room their son, Harry, had vacated when he had married. Then, for two years, they waited for Leo to propose to their Sylvia, and Sylvia waited, too.

When Leo thought of Sylvia, he described her to himself as "the real home-maker type of beauty." She was round-faced and had small, round brown eyes and her hair was coiled in a round, brown mass around her head. Her housekeeping talents matched her beauty. They were stately, firm and attractive. But, while Leo was drawn by her, he did not feel a need for marriage or a need even to love her. His only need was to keep his insecurity under control. To be in a home where he was regarded as useful, to do useful things that won the respect or affection or, at least, neutrality of those around was enough for him. So he remained unaware that Sylvia wanted to marry him or that he might have wanted to marry her.

But the situation went beyond his control one evening when, in gratitude for a sensation of well-being after supper, he told Sylvia's mother, "I feel I'm not a boarder anymore, but like I'm ingrown in this place."

"Why not?" said Sylvia's father. "You got Harry's room, so you got Harry's place, too."

But Mrs. Kopper was more alert to the opportunity. "When time goes by," she said, "you'll see, I'll have trouble making you come for a visit."

"Where am I moving?" laughed Leo. "Unless you raise the rent, you got me here for life, a regular ingrown toenail."

"You can't tell me," said Mrs. Kopper. "I know my Sylvia. She will not be happy out of her own home."

The smile vanished from Leo's face.

"Mama!" cried Sylvia and then recovered herself. "What's that got to do with Leo?" she asked. She saw Leo bow in confusion and she tossed her head high and looked down her face angrily.

Mrs. Kopper ignored her. She leaned towards Leo. "You got to understand, if you want to be happy together," she said. "My Sylvia is not one of those fly-by-nights, put them in a furnished room, hup-hup with the dust cloth, with the broom, life is finished. She's a real, regular home-maker. She's got it in her heart."

"Stop it!" cried Sylvia. "What's it Leo's business what I am? Stop it!"

"Yes." Leo laughed, but with his mouth only. "What's going on here anyway . . . with shotguns, or what?"

"Look at *him!*" Mr. Kopper's voice and finger rose and pointed delightedly. "He's blushing like *he's* the bride."

Sylvia sprang to her feet. "You make me sick!" she shouted. Her head was held high. It trembled and her neck swelled with effort to hold it rigid. "All of you!" she shouted. "The whole bunch of you. You make me sick to my stomach." She flung out of the kitchen, where the family ate, into the parlor.

Leo got up miserably and stood looking after her a moment. Then he turned miserably to the table. Mr. Kopper was laughing and Mrs. Kopper looked disturbed. There was no help for him in their faces. They had no thought of him and he realized for the first time how quickly he could become their enemies by hurting Sylvia and knew it was impossible for him to remain in their house now unless he married Sylvia. "Where should I live?" he thought. "Where should I go home?" He remembered how his own home had felt after Joe left.

"You've spoiled everything," he said angrily to Mr. Kopper.

"Go 'way," said Mr. Kopper. "What's spoiled so bad?"

At night, after Joe had left, there had been darkness in Leo's house and Leo had lain small and open-eyed in it. He had not cried because he had been afraid of the sounds he would make. He remembered now how he had held back his weeping and caught up his tears before they could fall in the darkness.

"You made her cry," he said to Mr. Kopper. "What kind of way is this, like a clodhopper!"

"Crying washes out the eyes," Mr. Kopper said.

Leo went quickly into the parlor after Sylvia, before he had time to think, as if he were running from hostile faces and hostile loneliness. She was standing, wiping her eyes with a small handkerchief she had stitched and embroidered herself.

"I don't know what idea you must have of this, Mr. Minch," she said.

The name hit him. It made him feel that he had already become a stranger in her home and it brought the insecure past back to him again. The past was mingled now into one feeling, a feeling of large darkness that prowled and crouched around him and padded towards him and towards him and over him and towards him like an animal on paws.

"Mr. Minch was my father's name," he said. "I'm Leo."

As he breathed, loneliness thrust down his throat like a tongue. He felt smothered and felt the need for clinging and reached out abruptly for Sylvia's hand. As he took her hand, he realized tumultuously what he was doing and he felt it shouldn't be like this. There should be love. His face wrinkled and tears crushed in his eyes.

"See," he said, blinking, "when you cry, I cry."

She looked away from him and put her handkerchief to her nose and began to weep again. He pulled her to him gently.

"If you cry like that," he said, "my eyes will fall out."

"What must you think?" Her words faltered among sobs.

He kissed her. "What I think? I think, Sylvia . . . I think. . . ." He kissed her again. His kisses reached her cheek and searched along her cheek and found her lips.

She put her fists on his chest and tried to push away from him and wriggled her head back and away from his face. "I don't want your pity," she said. Her body squirmed in his arms. "Please, please now," she cried, "please let me go this instant, at once."

He held her so tightly that her fists dug into her breasts and hurt her. His face struggled towards hers and his body crushed against hers and bent over it. He put his hands on the back of her head and pushed her face into his. He kissed her so hard that he could feel her teeth as bones in her lips. The sense of darkness had left him now as fear leaves a man when he fights.

They were married and, even long after that, the thought would occur to Leo that it shouldn't have happened like that. There should have been love. "Yes, yes," he told himself, "it's not nonsense. There should have been love." He never believed he loved Sylvia.

He could not feel it under all his other emotions about her. The nearest he came was to believe he might have loved her if he had given himself a chance.

❧

Then Joe came back, after being away twenty-two years. This time it was Sylvia who put the brothers apart again.

Joe had knocked around quite a while, he said, without ever getting really started anywhere and then, in 1915, he had gone up to Canada because he had heard there were plenty of jobs up there and he woke up one morning in the army, one of His Majesty's soldier boys. He had been feeling down about being an outcast and had got drunk. That was how it was, although he didn't tell it that way. He just said he'd been a sucker like everybody else. But he'd got drunk and, even as he had been rolling around and blowing around and hollering around and feeling happy and feeling like fighting and talking the unhappiness out of himself and getting a girl, he had felt people's eyes on him and on his seedy clothes. He had joined the army to join the human race. He had taken a gun in his hand and had gone to the killing so that people would look at him as if he were a human being. But it hadn't worked out, because as soon as the killing had stopped and he had dropped his gun, he had seen people thinking of him once more as a dangerous animal who needed feeding.

So he had married in France and settled down in France with a war bride because there was nothing waiting for him in the United States and because he had thought the French would be grateful for what had been done for them and would give an ally a break. But that hadn't worked out, either. The French had been too canny with their money for Joe. The end of it was that he had used his wife's marriage portion to pay for a third class passage "home" for himself and her and their little daughter.

"And here I am," said Joe. "I come like Papa. You remember what Papa used to say how he came to America? 'My baggage is my ten fingers and a needle.' And what was the needle for? America couldn't stick him enough?"

Joe was thirty-seven now. He was a big, heavily-muscled man with thinning hair and, although his clothes were new, they were cheap and of a foreign cut and made him look down on his luck. Sylvia didn't like that. He had a habit of looking sly when he made a joke, and the slyness seemed so usual on his face it made him look even seedier. It made him look crafty and shabby. Sylvia did not like that either. Then, when Sylvia held out her hand to acknowledge Leo's introduction of him, Joe slapped her hand down with one finger and said, "I'm not allowed to kiss the bride?" She told him, "It's a little late to be a bride," but her words were smothered in his lips. He smacked her hard with his mouth. His red, hairy, rank-smelling face prickled against hers and she didn't like that.

But, most of all, she didn't like the fact that she had to put up her brother's family in her house. She had lost confidence in her talents as a "home-maker." She had not been able to have children, and Leo had not provided her life with anything that might take the place of children. Her empty, lonely life had emptied her. It annoyed her, she found, to have "strangers in the house." Then, she found that Joe's wife annoyed her and Joe's child annoyed her, too. Fannette was lonely for her home in France and could speak little English. The child could speak no English at all and neither Fannette nor Joe paid much attention to her.

Finally Leo, who had been thinking of taking Joe into his own woolen business, first as an employee and then, if that worked out, as a partner, changed his mind. It seemed to him that he and Joe were beginning to get on each other's nerves just the way they used to as boys. So, instead of making a place for Joe, he threw Joe back into the world to make his own place for himself and bought a cigar store for him for $1,300. "Honest to God," he told himself, "it's just to get him and his family out of the house." Yet he was surprised by what happened after that.

Joe took hold of the store and made it go. He thought up merchandising stunts, some of which paid off. For instance, he sent a two-for-a-quarter cigar in a gift box to every one of his dime-cigar customers with a note he composed himself:

> "My Baby (your store) Is One Tooth Old Today
> Watch Its Smoke(s)
> The Best At The Best Prices!"

The customers responded very well. Some of them even acquired a taste for two-for-a-quarter cigars. But more profitable than his merchandising stunts was a delivery route he worked up in downtown office buildings. It made the store into quite a sound business.

Leo was impressed. He saw that Joe had become absorbed in the game of expanding his little business and he decided now Joe was "safe." He still felt that business provided a man with a "normal" life and kept him out of trouble. Neither he nor Joe had ever found anything in their work but aggravation of the insecurity into which they had been born. Joe had found insecurity in failure and Leo had discovered that success did not end insecurity. In many ways, it sharpened it. Yet neither of the brothers ever thought about it except to accept it as inevitable. Both found fear in business and accepted it because, they thought, business could not be a kid's game where they give you back the marbles when you cry.

Then Leo discovered Joe was taking bets on horse races from his customers. "Have you gone crazy?" he cried. "The police'll put you out of business."

But Joe said making book on races was good for business and was a good business, too. "My cigar customers want to have a horse running for them now and then, so why shouldn't I put myself in a position to wash them with two hands," he told Leo. He couldn't be argued out of it.

After that, Leo never visited the store. He was afraid to. He was sure the store would be raided, and he felt it was going to be bad enough for him when it was discovered he had financed the business, without allowing himself to be caught on the premises as well.

Leo was not merely angry with Joe. He couldn't understand Joe at all or justify at all what Joe had done. It became a moral issue to Leo. Morality could not have stood up against the fact that taking bets from customers was good for business. But, the

1322133616348
LEY VETERINARY HOSPITAL
0 YGNACIO VALLEY BLVD
NUT CREEK, CA 94598
-932-2420

COUNT NUMBER	EXP.	AMOUNT
1587500558986	0400	$91.00
N CODE	AUTH.	REF #
	080690	001003

C _____

_____

Michael Shepler

JUARY 09, 2000 10:49AM   0

I AGREE TO PAY ABOVE TOTAL AMOUNT
ACCORDING TO CARD ISSUER AGREEMENT
(MERCHANT AGREEMENT IF CREDIT VOUCHER)

trouble was, book-making wasn't good enough for the business. It jeopardized the whole enterprise for a comparatively small profit and so it could become a moral issue in Leo's mind.

"Who would believe we're brothers?" Leo told himself. "We're altogether two different kinds of people."

He felt, as he had felt before, there must be some basic defect in Joe's character. To him, Joe was "bad" and he was "good." Actually Leo was a "good" man—"good" to people and "good" to the law. But he was "good" only because he was insecure and needed to be let alone. "I am friends with everybody up to money," he told himself, and meant that when being "good" aggravated his insecurity he stopped being "good."

And actually Joe was "bad." Like his brother, he was an insecure man and needed respect or kindness or to be let alone, but he had been an outcast too long and too steadily to be able to feel he could get security by being "good." So he did not bother. Instead he went straight to the point in business.

That was the difference between the two brothers.

When Leo's woolen business became bankrupt, Joe heard about it and paid his brother a visit.

"I brought five hundred of what I owe to help out," he said.

Leo had not expected anything like that from one he had given up as "bad." He blew out his breath noisily and looked at Sylvia. "You see," he cried and pointed at his brother. "You see what I told you what Joe is?" He realized he had given away what Sylvia thought of Joe and turned back to his brother. "It's a shock to me, believe me," he said. He got up and took Joe's hand and began to shake it. His face was working and he squeezed Joe's hand in both his hands and shook it up and down rapidly.

"After all, it's your money," said Joe.

"Believe me, believe me," Leo said. "You don't know how good it is, not the money, the money is a little thing, but to get help without asking."

When he became calmer, Leo asked if the cigar store had become strong enough to stand paying out so much money in a lump sum.

Joe said he had sold the store because it was tying him down too much. "I got a certain enterprise that I'm interested in and feeling my way there," he explained. When Leo began to question him suspiciously, he said, "I'll give you all the details if you want to come in with me."

Sylvia leaned forward abruptly. She had feared for a long time that Leo would become involved in some business with his no-good brother. "I wish you luck and prosperity in whatever it is," she said hastily to Joe and leaned back and lowered her head and smoothed her skirt, "you should get rich and not forget the balance of $800 what you owe."

"Keep out of this!" shouted Leo.

He had never spoken to her so roughly before. Her hands flew towards her face. "He . . ." she said, "Joe . . . owes . . ."

"I told you what I said, you." Leo smacked at her with his voice. "What do you know? Keep out." He turned to Joe. "Don't do this," he cried in the same violent, bullying tone. "Joe, I'm telling you not to do this!"

"Do what?" Joe tried to control his anger. "What did I do?" he asked Sylvia.

"You got a wife and baby," begged Leo. "You should cut out this kind of stuff."

The pleading tone took away Joe's anger and made him feel uneasy. "Maybe you know what you're talking about," he said and shrugged and laughed and turned again to Sylvia. "You're a witness," he cried to her. "What did I do all of a sudden?"

Sylvia looked away from him silently and looked at Leo and looked away from Leo.

"I'll beg him on my knees," thought Leo. "I'll order him. I'll cry to him. I'll break his neck and what'll it be? What I like? No! What he likes!"

Joe lowered his eyes. "I come here to do a favor, not get kicked around," he said sullenly.

Leo did not see his brother again in several years except for a flash once when Joe drove by as he was crossing a street. Joe was alone in a $3,000 automobile, a long, chocolate-colored straight-8 Packard with a tan top. The top was down and looked like a pretty girl's pretty parasol. Joe was smoking a cigar and wore an expensive-looking Panama hat with the brim turned down, and he drove carelessly, in a busy, comfortable way. There was no mistaking that he was a big shot in a big shot car and that he owned it. He wasn't there by invitation.

There were two more meetings between the brothers before the power of Samson could have its effect on Leo. The first of these meetings took place in the summer of 1929, and once more Joe came visiting to offer, as he believed, help. He had found out the top floor of Leo's garage was nearly empty, and he said he had enough beer trucks to put away on dead storage for a while to fill it up.

"I don't want you should go in blind," he told Leo. "They're trucks belonging to Tucker."

Leo wanted to know who Tucker was, and Joe did not believe at first that Leo had never heard of him. Finally he explained, "He's a man in the beer business, real beer and so forth."

Joe was in a hurry to get the trucks hidden away, but he didn't tell Leo that. He could have put the trucks into any garage at the regular dead storage price without paying a bonus, but he hadn't told Tucker that. He had decided to make this as nice a thing for Leo as could be, and now he said to his brother, "There's a bonus in it that I got out of it for you, two, two and a half."

"Two fifty on each truck?"

"On the lot of them, I mean. Two and a half on the lot of them, I mean. Two hundred and fifty dollars is what I mean, and furthermore it's between us that you can bill for live storage instead of dead storage. That's what I got out of Tucker for you because it's in the family."

Leo was not in a hurry to make the deal. He wanted to gossip. He asked about Fannette and their daughter, and Joe said they had gone back to France.

"On a visit?"

"Not exactly."

"What's this?" cried Leo.

"What do you think it is? We didn't get along like we should so she went home. Let's do business before pleasure. Is it a deal on the trucks?"

"A bootlegger's trucks?"

"That's right," said Joe, "if that's what you want to call it. But the trucks will be clean, no beer on them or anything like that, just trucks."

"I don't like to do business with such kind of people."

"You're doing business with me."

Leo was silent and Joe stood up. "I'm the only one you'll have to deal with," he said. He stood a moment nervously and then snapped his fingers. "Come on, what do you say!"

"Sit down," said Leo. "I don't see you or hear from you in seven, eight years. You stick your head in my office, hello, goodbye, then run away. I'd like to hear more, what this is about with Fanny and you."

"It's an old story already. She couldn't get used to the life here. She wouldn't talk anything but French to the kid."

"It's a nice language to know."

"A kid who lives here should talk United States. Then she kept playing that God damn violin of hers all the time that she had."

"It hurt your ears, a nice fine piece of music played beautiful?"

"I didn't marry a violin. You should have heard the way she got it in your ears all the time. It was like having somebody in the house crying—the kid yapping and crying all day, you couldn't oil that kid up to stop squeaking, she was just like Fanny. And the minute the kid's asleep she starts with her God damn violin."

After a while, Leo agreed to store the trucks to help Joe out.

"None of that," said Joe. "I'm helping you. There's no garage-man in the city of New York, I can walk in anywhere and make this deal for a lot less than I'm paying you."

Leo laughed indulgently. He thought of saying, "It's about time you helped me a little," but he didn't. He could be generous with Joe as long as he was able to pity him and feel above him.

"Okay," he laughed, "so you're helping me."

Tucker needed an outside garage for his trucks because he was having trouble with a beer syndicate headed by a man known as Big Raymond. When Tucker had trouble, his strategy was to go into hiding and try to settle things from his hiding place. Big Raymond's people knew this and were waiting for Joe to hide the trucks. As soon as the trucks reached Leo's garage, they told the prohibition agents with whom they had been doing business and the agents, as a favor to Big Raymond's syndicate, raided the garage.

The agents went through the place carefully. They found several pints of whiskey in chauffeurs' lockers and put a padlock on the garage and arrested Leo and fingerprinted him. Leo's name got into the newspapers as a brother of "Guinea Joe" and one newspaper, conducting a campaign against prohibition and gangsters, printed what it described as Joe's police record. Joe had never told Leo about any of it. The convictions had all come before the war. There was a one-year term in prison in Illinois for armed robbery. There was one arrest after the war, in 1925, for "felonious assault," but the case had been dismissed for lack of evidence. "As is customary in cases involving highly placed thugs," reported the newspaper, "the witnesses to the assault did not testify. They did not believe the police would or could protect them if they did testify."

Big Raymond's people waited for Joe to come out of hiding to help his brother. But Joe knew they were waiting and knew that, if he did come out, they might get a lead on where Tucker was, so he remained in hiding.

Leo tried to find Joe. But the lawyer representing the corporation that owned the trucks told Leo he had never heard of Joe, and the hotel where Joe had been living said he had checked out without leaving a forwarding address. Leo couldn't think of anything else to do except tell himself that if he ever got his hands on his brother again, he wouldn't let go until he had pulled him into pieces and had beaten the pieces into jelly and had burned the jelly and thrown what was left into a garbage pail and buried the garbage pail in manure, yes, manure, manure from diseased animals.

The government had no case against Leo, but it was dragged out as long as possible for Big Raymond's sake. It was dragged out for more than six months and then nolle prossed because Tucker and Big Raymond had made up their differences by that time. But, meanwhile, Leo had lost his garage and there was a new tenant in it.

A few days after the case was dropped, Joe called at Leo's home. He asked for Sylvia first and seemed relieved to learn she was out visiting her brother Harry in Brooklyn. Leo answered Joe's questions as briefly as he could, but when Joe started saying how sorry he was about what had happened, Leo didn't answer at all. He sat stiffly, with no expression on his face except stiffness.

Joe sat in the dining room. He had his suit coat and vest unbuttoned, but he did not take them off. "I'll tell you what I came up for," he said finally. "It wasn't our fault, you know that, but Tucker and me decided, I got him to decide to try and make it up to you anyway, what happened."

"No thanks," said Leo.

Joe pursed his lips and drummed on the table with his fingers. He had had to go through a dangerous series of quarrels to get Tucker to part with a good proposition for Leo.

"You ought to stop being like that," he told his brother.

"I don't want advice from you how to be." Leo did not raise his voice, but there was a quiver in it. "Frankly, we're finished together. You've sucked enough out of me in your lifetime and now you and your schemes and everything about you is finished with me, clean."

Joe frowned. He had risked his own place in the business to get something for Leo. Tucker hadn't seen any reason to be generous to a man who had made a fair, open deal and had been paid fairly and had lost out because of circumstances beyond Tucker's control. Joe hadn't seen any reason for Tucker to be generous either, but he had argued a long time and had become angry many times and had threatened and pleaded, and finally Tucker had consented, more to keep Joe working for him than anything else. Tucker wasn't a man to give anybody a fair shake unless there was a profit in it for him somewhere.

"I can't make you out," Joe said to Leo. His fingernails kept tapping nervously on the table. The sound was good for him. It was an outlet for the feeling of guilt and shame that mixed in him and turned to fear. "You knew what the deal was. I didn't keep anything back."

"Never mind. I'd rather not talk about it." Leo pressed his hand against his chest. "I get excited right in my heart when I think about it," he said.

"It wasn't anything we did."

"All right, I agree. I did it. If that's what you have on your mind, we'll talk about something else. Did you hear from your wife yet or what, something."

"I fought to get it for you—a bottle plant, glass works in Canada. It's good for a million dollars a year gross and you can have it, run it yourself, absolutely legitimate, not this much out of line." Joe put two fingers together and held them up. "Just making bottles in Canada, that's all," he cried.

"What's the use, Joe?"

"You can listen to what it is at least."

"No." Leo shook his head. "I'll tell you very frankly, I'm not cut out like you to be in a business where I have to hide under the bed."

"For Christ sake! Jesus! What a thing to say!"

Leo stood up. "Where did you leave your coat?" he asked. His voice was unnaturally quiet. "I'm sorry, but that's how it is. I don't want to talk about it and get all excited. I got blood pressure."

He walked to the closet in the hall and got Joe's hat and topcoat. When he returned, Joe was standing beside the dining room table, buttoning his vest. Joe's face was red and set and drops of perspiration stood among the strands of hair on his nearly bald head.

"I've made my living all my life," said Leo, "without doing things that I should be afraid."

"You did this once before." Joe pointed to his coat. "Maybe you're getting a habit to throw me out so often."

"I don't want your jokes. You cost me plenty. Don't forget that. It cost me $1,300 to buy you a cigar store and all I got back to this day was $500."

Joe had forgotten it completely. "Why didn't you remind me," he said excitedly. "I'll mail you a check as soon as I get to my office."

"Thanks, I'll appreciate it." Leo nodded stiffly. Then abruptly he burst out. "Remind you, yes, all right," he cried, "go ahead and remind you and, in the meantime, you and your big shot friend, Mr. Big Shot Tucker got me out of my garage and then ran away like rats. You cost me $20,000 equity in good will that I built up there, that the lease was worth. Are you going to send me a check for that, too, and for the nice little living expenses that I can't make no more?"

"That's what I was here for in the first place. You ask for peanuts and I got cake. It's good, Leo. Listen at least to what it is."

But Leo couldn't listen. He couldn't go into business with his brother, any kind of business, legal or illegal. If he did he would lose his hold over Joe and over himself, too. Their relationship would go back to what it had been in childhood before their mother had died. "Thanks," he said. "Here's your hat and coat." He dropped them on the table before Joe.

Joe put on his hat slowly. He pulled it low on his head and felt the brim to make sure it was snapped down. He threw his coat over his arm. "I don't know," he said and looked sullen and helpless. "Everywhere there's brothers who get along together. And when brothers get along, they're a big success. Wherever you look, it's true. What's Dupont? What's Gimbels? What's anything important? Brothers, fathers and sons, even cousins, just so long as it's family, all working together. And in this family all we can do is throw your brother out of the house."

"I hope the next time I hear from you, twenty years from now," Leo said, "it will be more sociable, Mr. Dupont."

So the events accumulated in Leo's life and put a weight on him to make him bend to the power of Samson. There was no coincidence in it. The Philistines will always find a Samson. Opportunity to commit a crime is not a coincidence, for the opportunity does not seem like an opportunity to the man who is not looking for it. Nor is the necessity to commit a crime a coincidence. They, the opportunity and necessity, are a climax. They are prepared for and they happen.

III

AT THE end of Leo's first day in the policy business, Sylvia heard his key in the lock. She came rapidly from the kitchen into the foyer and stood waiting for him. "Are your feet wet?" she asked.

Rain silvered his overcoat and stained his hat. He looked down at his feet. They were soaked. He remembered then that it had been raining all day and he had been going from place to place in the rain since morning. "Why should they be wet?" he said. "I left them home in bed all day."

Sylvia did not smile. She had not been told anything about the policy business yet, but she had begun to suspect her husband was involving himself in some kind of gambling game. "I put your slippers under the stove to warm up," she said.

"My slippers? What's this, a celebration?"

"I knew your feet would be wet the way you've been acting lately."

Leo looked away from her. He took his hat and coat off and put them in the closet. "Who makes a celebration over wet feet?" he said into the closet. "Unless," he turned and smiled nervously, "she's got some little scheme on her mind that she's scheming to ask for something."

"I got my husband's wet feet on my mind, he shouldn't catch cold." She went abruptly into the kitchen.

"That's very nice, very nice thank you," he called after her, "to have such a celebration when it's not even my birthday."

He went slowly down the hall into their bedroom and began heavily to take off his shoes and socks. He had small feet. They were white and sleek with cold. He pressed them flat against the warm, stubbly feel of the rug and sat looking at them. He knew now that Sylvia knew something and that he would have to tell her everything. He wondered why he hadn't told her before. "There was nothing really to tell," he said to himself. "This is the first day."

It had been a tiring day. It had been a tiring week, a tiring ten days. He had been tired ever since Samson Candee had first come to him with the proposition. Everything was so new and he got so excited over everything and he worried so much about everything and the people he had had to talk to and argue with and worry over and boss around and think about and deal with and kid with, the hundreds and hundreds of people, and the money coming in all the time and going out all the time, coming in like blood, going out like sweat, and the numbers. Who would imagine that numbers on a slip of dirty scratch paper could come into a man's eyes and make him cry vinegar tears? Yes, cry! That's what he had done until he had found out the number that had come out on his first day in business was not as bad as he had thought it was, in fact, was very good, although they told him it was just average, not even fair average. It left him with a net profit of better than $800 on the day, even after he had put aside $150 for legal fees because he had to figure, he had been told, on about $40,000 a year for bail bonds, lawyers and fines for his collectors who happened to get arrested.

That was standard practice. Everything about the business was a regular business, standardized inside and out. Players, collectors, controllers, office workers and bankers were standardized. The arrests of collectors were standardized. Lawyers' fees on policy cases, bail bonds, fines handed down by magistrates, even the police were standardized.

The police cost him $100 a week, $50 for Detective Captain Milletti of the local precinct and $50 for Police Captain Lecke. The payments meant that the bank and the banker and the controllers would not be bothered. It was business with Milletti and Lecke. They were willing to make a little extra profit as long as it did not jeopardize their regular business, which consisted of being officers of the law.

"Live and let live," Capt. Milletti had said. He was a friendly man and he had seen that Leo was nervous. "Playing the numbers is human nature."

"If it wasn't numbers with them, it'd be something worse," Leo had answered.

"That's right. So, there'll be no trouble from us unless, that is, we got to." Because, after all, he did have his regular business, and there would be no extra profits for him if he did not have his regular business, and his regular business was to pay attention to what was wanted by those who made a business out of taking care of the public interest. If these people thought there was a profit for them out of the public in getting Milletti to close up Leo's business and put Leo in jail, then Leo would go to jail. But that had never happened before and was not likely to happen and anyway, if it seemed on the way, Milletti would tip Leo off to it.

Leo sat staring at his small, sleek, white feet. They shone in the electric light. The words of all the people he had talked to ran up and down in his head on feet. The words tapped lightly and rapped and slapped and whickered lightly, and the faces of the people bulged and ran along the words like shadow. Collectors, controllers, clerical workers, lawyers, landlords, business people all, policemen, bondsmen, bondsmen's runners, Samson Candee.

He had been tough with Samson. He had had to be tough. He was worried and nervous and felt he was in a tough business and had to be tough, too, so he got dirty tough because he did not know how to be nice tough. Samson had wanted to be paid for the work he had done and Leo, ashamed at going into the policy business, couldn't even look him in the eyes, much less pay him.

"I never heard of nothing like this before in my life," Samson had said, "freezing a man right out of what is his own proposition."

"That's the way it works out."

A look of uncertainty had spread down Samson's face from his eyes. "You talk pretty rough for a little man," he had said and had made an effort and had looked rigidly into Leo's eyes, "but I don't frighten when I know what my rights are."

He means the boxers he's got, Leo had thought, his wrestlers and gamblers and pugs, his beat-up squad that he'll send after me. "If you want trouble," he had shouted, "you'll get it. I know where to find it for you."

Candee had understood Leo meant Tucker. "No sir, Mr. Minch," he had said. "Not from me. You're not going to have any trouble from me, Mr. Minch, except, I thought, because this was my proposition and the work I done getting the people together."

"I want to be fair on this thing." Leo knew he had won his victory. His need to be tough had been satisfied. "If you want to put some of your people to work as collectors, I'll fit you in that way. You can be a controller."

"Me?"

Leo had laughed. "You don't have to put on a show for me that you're not temporarily hard up." He had pointed, laughing, to the unlit cigar in Samson's hand. "You carry a sign around with you."

Samson had answered carefully. "I wasn't trying to hide that I can use a little extra money," he had said, "but, if you don't mind my telling you, the way I feel I'd rather not just as soon get mixed up with the people who are your downtown connections."

As he sat silent in his bedroom, Sylvia's face bulged in Leo's mind, too, and ran like shadow along the words. "What could I tell her?" he thought. "That this is the first day?" He had put off telling her and put it off and put it off and now . . . well, now he had something to tell her because it was after the first day. But he had kept quiet for more reasons than that. Was he ashamed?

No, what did he have to be ashamed about? And it was more than that. Did he think she would have stopped him from going into the business? Maybe, but it was more even than that. She would have tried to stop him and would have failed because his life had left nothing in him that could have stopped him from going into the policy business, and he didn't want to know that. He could feel it, all right, but feeling it wasn't knowing it.

He sighed and got up and walked, with bare feet, down the hall, through the dining room with the asbestos-covered steam pipe running under its ceiling, and into the kitchen. Sylvia was standing over the stove. She had kicked the slippers angrily from under the stove into the middle of the floor. He picked them up and sat at the kitchen table and began putting his feet into them.

"Why do you make fun of me all the time," Sylvia cried suddenly.

"I make fun?"

"Yes, you make it so hard when I try to do something for you." She threw a stirring spoon angrily into the sink. "You don't tell me anything what you're doing, as if I'm a stranger around here. What's happened to you, Leo, that you should be that way to me?"

"I don't know what I'm being."

"Yes you do, and it's lately, only lately, since you're up to something, I don't know what it is, you don't want to tell me."

"What am I up to?"

"You're up to something, I know it."

"How do you know it?"

"How *should* I know? I read it in the papers."

"In the papers?" he said in the same quiet, mocking tone. Then suddenly he had to hold himself down in the chair. He grinned. His face had been flushed by the heat of the kitchen and now it was drained gray and his wet eyes stood out in it, but he continued to force his lips into a grin. He put his hands on his knees. He could feel his knees tremble.

"Where should I know?" she continued. "You don't tell me nothing. What is it, are you in business with Joe?"

"You think I'm crazy?" It shook him to speak, but his voice was low and steady.

"Well, what is it? Why don't you tell me?"

"There's nothing to tell, just a little money I put down to see how it comes out in something that's like a raffle in a church."

"In a church?"

"Like a church or a club, bingo, like that, a raffle thing sort of. Well, the hell with it, I'll take a chance with a few dollars. What have I got to lose?"

"Is there a business like that?"

"It's a regular business, like everything else."

She was thoughtful a moment. Then she began to shake her head. "No," she said, "it sounds like Joe to me. It's not you, you know that, Leo. It's not like you."

"It's not like me because I've been everybody's sucker all my life. I went to Wall Street to pay for the numbers on the wall. Now, they got to come to me, buy my numbers."

She stared at him a long time. He tried to return her stare. It was harder than to control his fright over the thought that there had been a raid and his name was in the newspapers. He tried to put an amused look on his face. "What are you trying to do," he laughed at last, "be Sarah Bernhardt?" Then he looked away.

She kept staring at his averted head. Her lower lip fumbled nervously between her teeth. "I didn't marry Joe," she said. "I wouldn't marry a man like that . . . not in a million years."

"What Joe? Who Joe? I haven't seen him. I don't even know where he lives." He could return her stare boldly now.

She became thoughtful again and then again she shook her head. "I won't be married to a man like Joe," she said. Her voice quavered and rose. "I can't stand that kind of life. I won't either, Leo, not for a minute."

"You married me, not my family," mumbled Leo.

She began to serve supper.

Over supper and after supper and while she cleared the table and washed the dishes, Leo explained the policy business to her. He talked excitedly. He urged the business on her. He made it sound even better than it was.

"It's gambling," she insisted. "It's not a business."

And he cried: "What's a business? I've been a businessman all my life and, honest to God, I don't know what a business is."

"You were in the garage business. That was all right. Why don't you rent another garage instead of this?"

"All right, you think the garage was so nice? I had to steal there. On every gallon of gas there was an overcharge, three cents—two cents for the chauffeur, a penny for me for helping him steal from his boss."

"That's different. You had to do it for the business, but this . . . the whole business . . . it's not a business, the whole thing."

"Yes, and what was the whole thing in the garage business? A fake! A fake all the way through! Rent space, rent it to somebody else and sit there. That's the business. Fake! Fake! It's a fake I'm telling you, not a business."

"What are you talking about, Leo? People need a garage."

"They won't get it from me. I'm telling you. I used to sit there at night, remember, to give the night manager a day off? I used to sit there and think, what is this? Fake. The whole thing fake. I felt even I was a fake. I wasn't alive. Have I got legs? Have I got a face? Am I a person? What kind of business is it for a person to rent an empty space with walls around it from one person and rent it to somebody else? You call that being in business, to be a fake, to pay money for nothing and divide it up into nothing and sell it for something, to make a living from that, from renting out nothing, space, empty space?"

"You can't keep your car in the street all night. It hurts the paint. Somebody might steal it. It's against the law."

"It's against the law to steal. I did the stealing. I did the overcharging for the chauffeurs."

"That's different."

"Yes? How? Tell me how. And service. I gave them service in the garage business. Also in the policy business. People want to bet on the numbers. I don't make them. There's not even a law to make

them like the law you can't park in the street, have to use a garage.
No, people need the numbers to have a little hope in their lives."

Sylvia shook her head helplessly. "I don't know," she said.

"You don't know. But I know. Stealing. On anything the chauffeurs bought for their bosses—tires, tubes, oil, bulbs, grease, heaters,
anything, I had to overcharge on the bill, so much for the crook and
so much for me. That's business? Selling nothing and stealing pennies and nickels is business? Now at least, please God, I'm where I
don't have to steal any more."

Sylvia had dried the last dish. She hung up the towel and took a
broom out of the closet in the kitchen and began to sweep the floor.
Her movements were practiced and without thought. She knew the
apartment in the dark. She knew every lump in the linoleum. This
had been her home since she was a bride. In bride days she had
planned for a better home and had hunted busily and happily all
over the city to prepare for the day when they could afford and
would need an apartment near a park or playground and with
southern exposure and near a school and in a nice neighborhood
with nice children to play with and with an elevator on account of
the baby carriage. But children hadn't come and Leo hadn't wanted
to move. "Why move?" he had told Sylvia. "A home is not walls,
but the people in it. We can't move away from ourselves." And
Sylvia had agreed. Leo hadn't wanted to move because money wasn't
important enough to change him, and Sylvia had agreed because
she had lost confidence in herself as a home-maker and thus had lost
interest in the art.

She finished half the floor and then said abruptly, "You shouldn't
think I'm blaming you, Leo. I know how hard it is to make a
living." She stopped sweeping and rested on the broom. She felt
for the first time that whatever she thought didn't count with him.
He was lost to her. He had been the framework of her life. On him
her home was to be built. There had been no children and no home,
only the feeling in her that the framework remained. Now, even the
feeling was gone. She realized Leo was nothing to her; she was
nothing to him. Her face crinkled around her suddenly shut eyes
and she lowered her head. "Leo," she cried and could go no further.

The broom was shaking a little in her hands. He watched her uncomfortably. "If only we could have had children!" she said.

"What's that got to do with it?" Leo's voice lifted with surprise.

She turned her back and leaned the broom against the cupboard and put both hands on her face and stood with bowed head, crying into her hands. Leo sighed nervously. He walked towards her and stood before her and tried to look into her face. "You've got pride for me, Sylvia?" he asked. "That's why?"

She shook her head in her hands.

"A man can be proud when he does what's necessary for his wife and himself," he said. "That's when he's right to be proud."

"It's not that." She put her head on his shoulder and cried there.

"No?" he said helplessly. "No? Not that?" He put his arms around her and held her lightly. "If we're together in a nice way, what do we care?" he whispered into her ear. "As long as we're nice together, what should we care what else."

She continued to cry steadily and hopelessly, and he sighed hopelessly and hopelessly stroked her shoulders.

❦

But policy was truly a business like anything else and Leo, who was a "good" man, could make it a "good" business. And, after a while, word of Leo's methods got around and were copied by other bankers because the methods were profitable. Then it became easy to tell the home of a numbers player who had hit. A crowd waited in front to be in on the payoff. Even if it were raining, the crowd would be there, some standing in doorways and some looking out of windows.

When Leo drove up, twenty or thirty would come running. Generally, the kids saw Leo first and ran after the big green roadster he had bought "for business." When it stopped, they came up and touched it the way country kids touch a circus wagon. "Yeah man," some said and others said, "Hmmm-hunh!" After he left, they would argue about how much Leo could buy if he put all his money on the counter of a store. They believed he was the richest man that ever had been.

Edgar did the driving for Leo. Edgar was a bony, tar-colored young man, made serious by horn-rimmed glasses. In addition to being chauffeur for Leo, he went from drop station to drop station during the early afternoon, picking up the policy slips left by the controllers and bringing them to the bank, or office as it was called. He also served as secretary and general assistant.

During these payoff trips, Leo sat with Edgar in the car and the controller, whose collector had sold the winning policy slip, sat in the rumble seat. The collector usually would be upstairs with the winner, waiting to get his ten per cent of the payoff.

Nobody in the crowd paid much attention to the controller or to Edgar. They watched Leo. They watched every move he made as he got out of the car slowly and went slowly into the house, his wet eyes shining, a smile on his gray face. People at the back would call out, "Porter, boss?" or "Carry your cabbage, boss?" or "Give the money here, boss, save climbing the stairs." There would be laughing and pushing at the back of the crowd and a competition to get off remarks, but those in front remained silent. The smiles went out of the faces of those nearest Leo and their mouths opened a little. They looked at Leo the way hungry poor look at food.

The kids would scoot up the stairs ahead of Leo and some of the others would follow him. The crowd rose through the dingy building like a flock of birds, their talk and laughter and the sound of their feet chattering and fluttering in the dusky, musk-drenched air. The controller went along with Leo. Edgar remained downstairs to watch the car.

There was usually a bottle of whiskey waiting for Leo upstairs. It waited on a table alongside freshly polished glasses and a plate of cookies or cake. It was nickel-a-drink whiskey, the kind the Negroes called King Kong, and Leo never took any.

"Never touch it during business hours," he would say in a preacher's voice and look around to see if he had been heard and understood. If the effect were good, he would shake his finger at the bottle and say, "There's more misery come out of there than a cemetery."

A general murmur of "Amen" would follow and everybody would stare pensively at the bottle.

But if the effect of the sermon were not good and he was pressed to take a drink, he would change his tactics. "If I took a drink every place I paid off," he would say, "I wouldn't know what I'm paying." He liked people to remember that winning went on every day and that many won. Actually, however, Leo did not pay off in person unless the hit was for more than $100. All hits under $100 were paid off by the controllers, and Leo merely provided the money.

Leo paid the hit into the winner's hand bill by bill. "Best fresh lettuce money can buy," he said.

Anything he said made everybody laugh. They were in that kind of nervous mood. He tried to speak loudly so that even those who hadn't been able to push into the apartment and were out in the hall, craning on tiptoe, could hear. The audience waited for his words with twitching lips.

Leo played to them as if he were an actor. The payoff was the best place to advertise the business, and Leo tried to get all his controllers to put on a show when he himself wasn't making a personal appearance. He had bought a ruby ring which, like the big roadster, was to make the customers believe he was a moneyed man, and he wore the ring during the day on the little finger of his right hand where it looked largest. He had bought it from a bail bondsman who claimed to have got it from one of his clients. It didn't fit Leo. It was too small for his short, plump hand and, on his thick finger, it looked like a bone rubbed raw.

As Leo counted the money over to the player who had hit, he stuck out the ring finger stiffly and wiggled it before paying over each bill. The gesture got laughs and also it put a spotlight on the ruby.

"This is the kind of thing I hate to see going on," he said and shook his head. His short, round body seemed cocked. It sloped as stiffly as a bent ruler towards the man he was paying off and his behind stuck out like an old-fashioned dandy's. His gray face hung over the money in mock sorrow and his eyes bulged and rolled to take in the crowd and make it part of his act.

"Hot man!" the crowd said. "Pour it on, man!"

Leo had grown used to the expensive car, but he never did get used to the ring. He carried it in his vest pocket when he went home. However, in the interests of his business, he made it dance now and strut like a candied-up dandy on a stage.

When he had to make a payoff, Leo always stopped first at the bank to get a new $100 bill. This was for the climax of his show. The manager of the bank made a point of chatting with him. He had been trying for a long time to get Leo to keep his policy bank's cash reserve on deposit.

At the beginning, the manager had been tactful. "You know, Mr. Minch," he had said, "we are here to serve you. You can bank with us for all purposes, I mean anything at all you have in mind."

In those days, Leo was still uncertain how his business would be regarded. "That's really a good thing to know," he had replied and had done nothing about it.

Subsequently, Mr. Pierce abandoned tact and came to the point. "All the policy people use their neighborhood banks," he said.

Leo explained that, if he deposited the cash reserve, he would have to visit the bank every day to draw out money for the payoffs. "It's not a good idea to put around," he said, "that every time I walk out of here, I got a fortune of money in my pocket."

"We'll take care of that for you."

"With a bodyguard?"

"Then you won't have anything to worry about."

"Me? A policeman to be my bodyguard? For my money, my business?"

"Why not?"

"Why not? Well, if you ask me why not. . . . I don't know why not. But I don't think so. No, I hardly think so."

Pierce looked like a born banker. He was pale-lipped and wore rimless glasses and had sandy, colorless hair, and everything about his face seemed in order. "I want to tell you something, Mr. Minch," he said and looked directly into Leo's eyes. "I know something about this community. I've been up here fourteen years. They say a banker has no heart, but everybody puts his heart down on my desk and it gets written down in our ledgers and I can truthfully say I know something about what's in the hearts of this community."

"I wouldn't say that, a banker has no heart. Everybody is a person more or less no matter what he does for a living."

Pierce laughed and then became serious. "What I mean is," he said, "your business is a service needed in this community. It keeps people contented and looking forward. If everybody ran his business the way you run yours, things would be a whole lot better off in our little community up here and in the whole country, too, for that matter."

Leo flushed with pleasure. "Honesty is the best policy," he said.

Pierce laughed more heartily than necessary, but even so Leo did not deposit his cash reserve. He kept it in a metal box under the floor of a closet in his bedroom. Sometimes there was more than $45,000 in the box and, when he stood in the closet hanging up his $22.50 suit or eight-nine-cent pyjamas, he could feel the presence of the money under his feet. It was like standing on danger.

At the payoff, Leo saved the $100 bill for last. He made it crack before handing it over. It snapped before the eyes and ears of the crowd like a whip and what followed nearly always was the same:

The winner held the bill with two hands and people pushed around him to get a look. "Who's going to make little ones out of this?" he asked.

"That's the point," Leo told him.

"I can't use a big boy like this, boss. Scare the bartender to death if I flash this one on him."

"That's why I give it to you."

The room laughed and the winner laughed, too, uncertainly. The laugh was brief. It halted abruptly and dropped out of the air and left the people standing still and breathless.

That was what Leo waited for. As soon as the air was breathless, he began his speech. "You have to go to the bank to get it changed," he said. "My idea was maybe once you got in the bank you'd be tempted to use your brains for yourself." He looked around at his audience. "Listen, I want you all should hear me and pay attention for when you hit on the numbers. A man goes to a dance hall, what happens? The temptation is to dance. A man goes into a saloon, what happens that time? He eats a cheese sandwich? No. The temptation is to take a little something, a little beer. That is human nature and is not a bad thing. It's a good thing that makes the world go around. What is everything everybody does? Only temptation—to make money, have fun, whatever it is. Only a man should be smart, that's what he has to be, smart, use his noodle that he's got and go in the places where he is tempted good. A man goes into a bank, what is he tempted? To leave himself a little nest egg there for a rainy day."

The words went through the room like warmth. More often than not, they had an effect. Mr. Pierce told Leo that, in his first three years in the policy business, more than two hundred new savings accounts had been started with his $100 bills.

"Most of them don't last long," he said, "but that isn't your fault. I feel you ought to know that I think you are a very good influence in this community." He was still trying to get Leo to deposit the cash reserve.

But sometimes the winner knew his own mind and insisted on getting change for the $100 from Leo.

"It's your money," Leo told him, "and why should I argue with you? If everybody put their money in the bank instead of playing the numbers, how would I pay for this?"

He held his hand high and wriggled his fat little finger so that the ruby shone like a blot of blood.

The money came in daily and went out daily. There was flow as in all business and no one grumbled to any substantial effect. A law existed by which the community's businessmen might have rid themselves of the entire enterprise, but they weren't particularly interested. The enterprise did not compete materially with anything else in the community. The bulk of the money it made circulate remained in the community where everybody had a chance to get a piece of it. The only businessmen interested enough to use the law were in the business of law enforcement or in the business of looking out for the public interest. But, since there was not much profit for them in doing business where the grumblings were weak or artificial, not many even of these concerned themselves. Scattered arrests in easy cases—in the cases of collectors who carried the evidence (policy slips) with them—were enough to satisfy the few who did concern themselves.

So the policy business turned out to be as happy a thing for Leo as he had ever found. It made money for him and it gave him the chance to be "good" to a lot of people and feel safe in the world. He might have spent the rest of his days that way, safe, his sense of insecurity kept in check, except that he lived in an unlucky time. He had been born in the time of Rockefeller. He had spent his business life being hounded from the woolen business to butter-and-egg routes to real estate to the garage business to policy. He had run from place to place, looking for one place where he could hole up and be overlooked and at peace in a world of expanding big business. But all his running had done was advance him towards the time of Hitler, when big business and its creatures, when trusts and monopolies and their methods, having grown powerful and hungry in the hunt, were foraging even among the rabbit holes.

BOOK TWO

WITHIN THE WALLS OF THE RICH

IV

ON THE Friday before Thanksgiving, 1934, Edgar came into Leo's private office. "There's a man outside to see you who says he is your brother," he said. He seemed excited. He had heard of "Guinea Joe" Minch, but had never talked with Leo about him.

"My brother?" Leo frowned. "What does he look like?"

"Like a turkey with feathers," said Joe. He stood in the doorway, smiling. He wore a dark green topcoat with a green velvet collar and a dark green suit. His shirt was yellow. His tie was a light brown, and a brown silk handkerchief was folded in his breastpocket. "I got fatter, didn't I?" he asked.

"Maybe. How do I know? I don't know." Leo didn't get up. He sat frowning.

Edgar took a long, troubled look at Joe and then slipped out and closed the door. He worked in an outer room of the two-room office. This was an office Leo maintained apart from the bank's office.

Joe was fatter. He was fifty now. There was a small belly on him and his red face was softer and fuller and more lined. When Joe took off his hat, Leo was shocked to see that his brother was nearly bald and that what hair he had left was gray. He had always thought of Joe as a young man.

Business had brought Joe. The business was a mixed pleasure. The proposition he had to make was going to be good for Leo. It would make Leo a rich man. But Joe knew Leo would be hard to convince and knew, too, that if Leo did not go along with the deal voluntarily, he would be forced. In the process of forcing there was a good chance he would be hurt.

Tucker had learned about policy and had decided to merge all the banks in the business into a single combination. His method was simple and had a long tradition among monopolists. He was going to break them and then take them over. He had found out, that, during Thanksgiving week, there was a superstition about the number 527. A great many played it and its combinations— 257, 275, 572, 725, 752. If any of these numbers hit, most of the banks would go broke. Tucker planned to pay a pari-mutuel man $25,000 to make sure one of them hit on the Wednesday before Thanksgiving.

So the banks were to be busted Wednesday and, when they started looking for money to carry on their business, Tucker would be waiting for them. He intended to lend money for a two-thirds interest in the bank.

Tucker sent Joe up to Harlem to lay the groundwork for the deal. Joe had been picked because of Leo. Tucker wanted somebody he could trust and who knew the business. He felt he could trust Joe and that Leo would teach his brother the business. Besides, Tucker needed Leo. Leo was one of the biggest bankers in the business. Tucker felt that, after what had happened on the garage deal, Joe was the only man who could sell his brother on working along now. But Tucker didn't tell Joe any of this. He just said he was cutting Joe in on the thing as a favor.

An office was opened for Joe in Harlem and Joe went through the motions of trying to start a bank of his own with the help of a man called Herbert Ruddy, who was the regular bondsman for a number of policy banks. This was to make sure that, when the break came, the bankers would know where to look for money.

Tucker insisted that the whole deal and what came after was to be kept clean. He had decided he would have to work with the bankers after he took two-thirds of their businesses and he didn't want them sore at him. This was the only time the number was to be fixed. Only three people knew exactly what Tucker was up to—himself, Henry C. Wheelock, who was his attorney, and Joe. Tucker told his two associates that if a single word got out in advance or if they played 527 themselves in combination to make a little extra money and people could say there must have been something phony, they must have known the number was going to hit or they wouldn't have bet, then that was the end.

"The both of you will be through in every way I know how to make you be through," he said.

They knew what he meant. Tucker had been a regular killer in his day. He and his men hadn't been responsible for the death of as many as people said, or as many as some automobile manufacturers and steel barons had been with their fight against the unions, but Tucker had got his start in the world that way and had kept going.

There were going to be banks that would not be busted and other banks that would be able to borrow money elsewhere to stay in business. But Tucker had that situation covered, too. The combination would be strong enough and secure enough to attract customers away from any rivals. If that weren't enough, he would get the police to raid the competing banks and drive them out of business.

So it looked rosy all the way up and down the line and Joe had worked out a nice thing for Leo with Tucker. Leo's bank was to be made No. 1 in the combination. Where a bank needed too much money to re-open after the break came Wednesday, no money would be loaned it. The bank was to be allowed to die. Its controllers and collectors were to be put to work in Leo's bank.

Then Joe tried to get permission to argue Leo into joining the combination before the break came so Leo could save his money. Wheelock was against it and Tucker was, too, at first.

"If we get him on our side first," Joe said, "we can use him in the negotiations with the others."

But Wheelock argued that Leo would know then, or guess anyway, that the number had been fixed and, if one knew, everybody knew. Joe said Leo wouldn't guess a thing until the combination was forming and, by that time, he would be one of the top men and wouldn't talk against himself.

When Tucker still said no, Joe told him he'd have to get another boy. He said he wasn't going to be put into the position of taking away his brother's money without giving him a chance to save it, not for Wheelock, not for Tucker, not for anybody he ever heard of. Wheelock said all right, to count Joe out and Tucker said Joe ought to look at this thing sensibly.

"I'm sensible, but I'm a person, too," Joe told Tucker.

"We're going to do him good in the long run."

"Do you think I'd touch this at all if I didn't know that?"

"Well, what then?"

"I can't get it out of my head, that's all, it's in my heart that the poor slob worked like a son of a bitch all his life for the few dollars he's got."

Joe's head was lowered. His face was working in embarrassment. Tucker looked at Wheelock and Wheelock compressed his lips and shook his head, no. However, Tucker finally told Joe to go ahead, but to be careful what he said to Leo. Joe promised that he wouldn't tell Leo anything except a combination was to be formed and he could get in on the ground floor.

"If he still holds out," said Joe, "I'll have his bank raided. Then he'll come to me to have the raid thrown out and I'll tell him, if he's in the combination, the raid is out."

Tucker shrugged. "If you want to shoot off popcorn at your brother, it's okay with me," he said. "He'll be in the combination after Wednesday anyway."

That was what Joe started to tell Leo about now, the combination, and how it was going to save everybody money on expenses and operate the business more efficiently and how Leo could get in on the ground floor.

After listening to it for a while, Leo said suddenly, "This is blackmail," and Joe stopped talking. "You know it is," said Leo. It hadn't seemed that way to Joe at any time before, but now, with Leo sitting before him, it did seem like blackmail. Joe looked down at his hands. "I thought it was a good idea," he said.

"You and those friends of yours taking over my business that I worked to build up is a good idea to you?"

"We're not taking over, just a merger."

"You call it a merger, I call it a blackmail."

Joe looked helpless.

"What did I ever do that you should act like this to me?" cried Leo.

Joe looked into a corner of the room sullenly. "I'm trying to do good for you," he said.

"A man like you knows what's good for me? If you want to do me a favor, take your proposition and yourself and get out of here."

This is the third time he's throwing me out, thought Joe angrily. Anger conquered his feeling of guilt. He stared at Leo with unwavering eyes. "I have a good mind to do it," he said.

"Go ahead!" Leo flung his hand in the direction of the door. "Get the hell out of here with your blackmail and stealing my business."

Joe calmed himself with an effort. "The trouble with you is," he said, "you're so busy hollering you didn't listen to me."

"I heard enough." Leo stood up and looked around his office. While his head was turning, he cried, "My own brother acts to me like someone he should hold up on a street corner."

Joe jumped to his feet. "If I weren't your brother," he shouted, "I wouldn't be here trying to help you, let you in on the ground floor. Don't you know what that means, you damn dumb fool!"

"Yes? Like it was a second-storey burglar you're letting me in on the ground floor."

"Cut it out."

"No, I'm not cutting it out. You're a crook and you want I should be a crook too."

"Cut it out. I warn you. Cut it out now."

"No, it's true!"

"God damn it! I'm telling you. Cut it out!" Joe took a threatening step towards his brother.

"If you don't like what I'm saying, then get the hell out of here, you won't hear it."

Joe stopped. His fists unclenched and he laughed suddenly. "You're as crazy as you ever was," he said. "It reminds me of home." He turned around and pulled his chair back close to Leo's desk. "I'll wait till you cool off," he told Leo and sat down. "Then I'll begin where we left off when you went crazy."

He crossed his legs and searched leisurely in his pockets for a cigar. He bit off the end of the cigar and held the spot of tobacco on his lips and looked around slowly for a place to spit it. Finally he removed it with arched fingers and dropped it into an ash tray on the desk. Then he fumbled in his vest pocket for a match and ran the match through the mouth end of the cigar. He jabbed gingerly and twiddled the frayed hole clean. He dropped the match into the ash tray and took a silver lighter from another pocket and lit the cigar. He sucked deep and turned up the lighted end of the cigar to see that it burned evenly and, while he inspected it, a gust of smoke blew from his lips like a sigh of pleasure.

Leo watched him for a moment and then went back to his desk and took up a letter describing an apartment house he had already looked over and decided not to buy. He concentrated on the letter carefully.

"Now listen to me," said Joe, "and I'll try to make this clear to you. Listen to me without interrupting or I'll walk out."

Leo's head darted towards him. "I interrupt already," he said. "Get out."

"Now, Leo, for God sakes."

"I'm busy. Can't you take a hint or should I tell you plain I'm busy?"

"Well, you got that hot one off your chest, now listen. You said something you think is smart, now you can listen. There's going to be a combination made whatever you say or don't say. We're going to every policy bank in the city and put the same proposition to come in on the combination. I'm putting it to you first because you're my brother."

"Not interested."

"I got the combination to agree in advance that you would be the top man for the whole thing and you and I could run the banks, the whole combination, every bank in the city of New York."

"Not interested, not one bit."

"No? Not at all? You act as if I didn't know what you did up here with the name Tucker to build up your business. I know that three years already, four years."

"Show me one thing I did," cried Leo. "I didn't do one thing, not one word. I told them I wasn't with Tucker. They didn't believe me."

"You don't have to worry if I know. The point is, if you can build up a business because you're supposed to be connected with Tucker, then what do you think is going to happen when Tucker comes up here himself with a big band playing?"

"It's nothing to me what he does."

"I'm telling you, you can't stand up against him. He'll throw everything into one pot and there will be only one payroll on the legal fees for the whole combination and only one payroll for the ice, the okay to operate. You can't stand up against an outfit like that with your expenses."

"You want to hear my answer now?" said Leo. "It's no."

"For Christ sakes, will you get wise to yourself a minute! You know what will happen to your business when the combination starts working? It'll dry up under your nose. You won't have any business and you won't be worth a God damn. I'm telling you. You're fifty-two, what is it, fifty-three . . "

"Fifty-four already."

"Fifty-four years old and you'll be out on the street and not worth a God damn. And don't come to me because I won't be able to help you. I'm not boss. Tucker is boss."

"I got my own little business and I'll keep it and Tucker can keep his," blustered Leo. "When you rob it away, all right. That's the end of it."

"Leo, please. Nobody is going to rob you."

"And I'm not going to take any threats from you. Did you ever hear of this in your life? My own brother comes in here and holds a gun over my head. No. No. That's my answer. My answer is no. No. No. You hear what I'm saying? I'm saying no."

"How do you spell it?" asked Joe.

Leo glared at him. His face was puffed with emotion. "Why do you do this to me, Joe?" he said. His voice shook. It almost broke and he lowered his head quickly.

It's an agony, thought Joe. But if he didn't go on with it, worse would come to Leo, worse and worse and Joe would have to blame himself for it. The least he could do was try to save Leo. "I see you don't understand one word I'm saying," he said. "All you do is holler." Joe did not show the pain he was suffering. He was sweating a little, but he did not show his pain in any other way. "Here it is. Now listen to me, listen and don't holler. A corporation gets together . . ."

"I'm not listening."

". . . gets together and they decide they're going to merge all you banks together, buy you out and make you all one combination to be run economical, big time, on a big time business basis. I know about the deal and I say to the corporation. . . ."

"You're talking to yourself."

". . . say to them I got just the man for you to run the combination when it's ready. My brother, my big, quiet, sensible, level-headed brother, Leo. He knows the business. He knows everybody in Harlem. He's liked all over Harlem. After you come to terms with him and make a deal for his business, he will help you make the deals for the other businesses and then run the whole combination. Isn't that nice? What more do you want for yourself?"

"Just you should leave me alone."

"You don't understand. There are big men in this city who'd sell their mothers' teeth to get what I'm giving you."

"I understand all right," Leo said. "A bunch of gangsters get together and they call themselves a corporation. You call that a corporation, Mr. brother of mine, with dirty necks and guns in their pockets and everybody a jailbird?"

"You don't know nothing, if you're alive or what. Big men I'm telling you, the biggest men in the city of New York."

"I don't do business with people like that."

"Is that final? I want to give you every chance, so think before you say if it is or it isn't."

"It's final. It's my final answer. Finally no."

"Okay."

Joe stood up and put on his coat and pulled his jacket smooth under it. He set his hat carefully on his head.

"I suppose you know," he said, "that your no don't stop the combination. There's going to be a combination and those that are not in it, that we don't want in it, will have their business dried up and will be on the street crying. Don't come crying to me then. It will be too late. The minute I walk out of this door, it will be too late for you. You'll be out."

"Goodbye," said Leo.

He picked up the letter describing the apartment house he had rejected and began to read it again.

Joe put both hands on the desk and leaned over until his face was on a level with Leo's. "Can't you see?" he said. His words fell swiftly and heavily from his mouth. "Us two will have the keys. Can't you see what I'm putting in your lap? Do I have to make blueprints? You've been scratching for chicken feed all your life and now I've got it for you. I've got something, pearls on a plate, Leo. You'll be a big man."

"You want to make a gangster out of me, too. That's what I see."

"Oh Jesus!" Joe stood up straight and cried into the air. "Jesus! Jesus Christ!" He kicked the foot of the desk.

"You want to make me a big shot gangster with horns coming out of my head," said Leo.

Joe stood suffering. His face was raised towards the ceiling. His eyes were closed and his fists strained the seams of his coat pockets. Then he shook his head and walked towards the door and turned and went back to Leo. "Tell me this," he said. "Tell me, before you make up your mind yes or no you'll study the proposition. You'll come down to Wheelock's office and look at the figures."

"I don't know who Wheelock is and where his office is and I'm not looking at figures for what's my business."

"Henry C. Wheelock. Henry Clay Wheelock, like the cigar, Henry Clay. He's the lawyer for the combination. He's got the whole thing down in black and white, everything, what he'll give you for your business, what your cut will be on the combination, the whole story."

"Nothing doing."

"Your mind is made up definitely?"

"Yes, final. My final answer is finally no. That's what it was when I first heard it. That's what it'll be if you and your shyster crook lawyer talk till you're blue in the face. The answer is no. No. Absolutely and finally, positively no."

Joe looked at his brother speculatively. Emotion had blotched his ruddy face. His face was stained with strain. There were white blotches on it under the ruddiness.

"You're dumber than I ever thought you were," he said.

"Fine. Now that you know, maybe you'll leave me alone."

"The trouble with you is," said Joe, "you're a small man. If it's a small thing, you're all right. But if it's a big thing, you piss in your pants." He twisted his body and began to mince and pout. "No, no," he simpered. "Oh no, so much for me? All that for poor little Leo? Oh no, it can't be. It must be some mistake. It must be for somebody else."

"You're so funny you ought to go in the movies."

"Funny? You think it's funny? It's the saddest thing in your life. If you hold out your hands, it's yours. I'll give it to you. You can trust me, your own brother, to give it to you. But you can't hold out your hands. You haven't got the guts to take what is yours, what's there waiting for you. That's why you've been a small man all your life and you will be small to the day you are dead."

"You're better when you're funny," said Leo.

Joe walked to Leo slowly. He held out his two hands pleadingly. "Come downtown with me," he begged. "Not right now. Tomorrow morning. Look at what Wheelock's got in his office. You will see the possibilities. A blind man will see the possibilities. You'll become a really big man."

He saw a stubborn look come over Leo's face. "Just, for Christ sake, put a nickel in the subway," he cried. He took a nickel out of his pocket and threw it violently on the floor. "Here," he shouted.

"Here's a nickel. Put it in the subway. It will make your fortune."

"I don't want a fortune," said Leo. "All I want is not to have headaches from the way you yell like that."

"Through!" Joe spit out the word. "You want it, you're going to get it, you God damn dumb son of a bitch!"

He walked out and slammed the door behind him, and Leo took up the letter about the apartment house he had decided not to buy and sat holding it without seeing it.

❧

Joe walked to a telephone in a cigar store around the corner from his brother's office and tried to reach Tucker. He knew what he had to do next to Leo. It had been his own idea. But he was ashamed and wanted to be told to do it.

He called seven numbers. The first one said he had heard something about Tucker going downtown to see Wheelock some time in the afternoon. After that, there were five numbers that did not answer and the last one said he did not know where Tucker was. Then Joe tried Wheelock, and Wheelock was out, too, and nobody knew where he was or when he was expected back. "A fine hell of a lawyer that is," he said to himself.

He walked out of the store and stood a moment on the sidewalk aimlessly with his hands in his pockets. One moment he felt tired and the next moment anger began spinning around in his head. When the anger stopped spinning, he became tired. Then the anger started up again and this time it spun around in his head and went down through him like a crash so that he tingled all over. He walked to the corner and, as he walked, he took his hands out of his pockets and hit his palm with his fist. He did it three or four times, each time harder. The anger kept getting bigger and bigger in his head and then it crashed all over him. He found that his hand was tingling and there was pain in his knuckles and he was so tired everything in him seemed to droop. He saw a taxi in the corner and got into it.

"That's one stubborn mule of a brother I got," he thought. "He'll have to be kicked, that's all, for his own good." Joe gave the taxi-driver the address of his new office on Lenox Avenue. "The barn is burning, you dumb mule," he said to himself. "Get the hell out." The office was one flight up over a drug store. The sign on the outside door said "A-Won Co." and under it was lettered, "H. Ruddy, bail bonds." There was one large room facing on the street and, in the back, two smaller, glass-doored rooms had been partitioned off. A smell of varnish and fresh plaster and shavings clung to the air in the office.

Some people were in the outer room talking to Ruddy. Joe saw Gonzago and Cordeles, who were bankers, and he guessed the others must be connected with them. He could tell without listening what they were talking about. They were trying to find out what Joe was really up to and to what extent Tucker figured in it. Ruddy, who was short and bald and very fat, was talking earnestly in a low tone and Cordeles and Gonzago were looking at him craftily.

Joe had known the moment he had met them they would be easy. They were afraid before he lifted his finger. When they found out exactly what kind of offer he was going to make them, they would be surprised and relieved and his friends for life, or at least until they could make a safe dollar out of cutting his throat. Joe walked past them without stopping or nodding, and Gonzago and Cordeles looked at him out of the corners of their eyes.

There was one telephone on Joe's desk connected with a switchboard outside and another private telephone that he had installed secretly. The telephone wasn't listed and he had taken the number off the dial. He had asked the telephone company to mail the bill for it to his home so that no one in the office would know he had it. He kept the instrument in the bottom drawer of his desk, and the wire came through a hole bored under the desk. No one could see it was there unless he got down on the floor and looked. Joe planned to use it when he wouldn't want to take a chance on someone listening in from the switchboard. There was no need for it yet. No one had been hired for the switchboard. No one could overhear him. But he used the private telephone now anyway.

First Joe tried Tucker's seven numbers. Then he tried Wheelock again. He couldn't locate either of them. He sat still a moment, holding the telephone. It was warm and wet in his hand. He was very tired suddenly. He hadn't taken off his hat and it felt heavy on his head. His head sagged and the flesh of his face slid down from the bones. He sat looking at his hand and feeling the sweat on it and the warm sweat on the telephone. The veins in his hand were thick as twigs. If there had been time to argue more with Leo, he would have waited before having Leo's bank raided and argued more. He would have argued a month if there had been time. But there was no time. This was Friday, and Wednesday was the end of it and maybe it was too late, even now. He began sluggishly to dial for Bunte. His head twisted so violently with each turn of the dial that his hat almost fell off.

Ed Bunte was a district leader who had been put on the combination's payroll to take care of all the details of protection. He wasn't at the clubhouse or at home or at his lawyer's office downtown where he kept desk space or at Tammany Hall or at his own office in midtown. Joe finally reached him at an Italian restaurant named Theo's, where he hung out sometimes.

"I'm sorry to bother you," said Joe, "but I'd like to get word to Capt. Milletti about a bank at 92-53 Edgecombe Avenue."

"A bank?" Bunte had a habit of talking over the telephone in a whispery voice. It made everything he said sound confidential and important.

"It's operating right under his nose," said Joe, "and I thought he'd like to know about it."

"Well yes," Bunte said. "Milletti certainly ought to do something about a thing like that. Whose bank is it?"

"It's in Apartment 2F, going wide open every day. It would be a good thing if it were knocked over right away." Joe looked at his wrist watch. It was too late today. "Tomorrow, tomorrow afternoon." Leo wasn't likely to be at the bank then.

"That's Saturday."

"All right. Monday then, the latest."

"I'll tell Milletti right away," said Bunte. "He'll appreciate the tip

I know. Oh say, Wheelock's with me now if you want to have a word with him."

"No," said Joe, "I guess not."

He had said it while thinking he had nothing to tell Wheelock now. The job was done. He didn't need anyone any more to tell him to do it. A feeling of shame came into him, so sharp it seemed to wail. He put away the telephone and locked it up and walked out of the door. He knew Wheelock was going to call up to make sure it was Leo's bank being raided and no one else's. He couldn't tell Wheelock out plain. Not just now. He couldn't tell anybody he had put the police on his own brother, even if it were for his brother's good.

"Wheelock may call me in a little while," he called across to Ruddy. "Tell him I couldn't wait and that I'll be down to his office tomorrow morning anyway."

Gonzago and Cordeles turned their tan, smiling, meaty faces towards him and nodded in greeting. He couldn't bring himself to return their nod. He wanted to spit at the greaser bastards. He walked quickly out of the office.

As he was going down the stairs, he heard the office telephone ring. "Wheelock!" he thought. He dropped down the stairs almost at a run, going lightly on tiptoe so that he should not be heard. When he reached the bottom, he didn't go out into the street but ducked behind the stairs and stood there in the damp, cellar-smelling gloom. He heard the door to the office open and Ruddy call, "Joe, hey Joe, oh Joe!"

He didn't answer. The fat voice seethed in his head and he began to tremble. "What the hell am I being afraid of Wheelock for?" he said to himself. He fixed his eyes on the door leading to the cellar and he felt the gloom close around him and his trembling subsided. He heard the upstairs door close. The paint on the cellar door, he noticed, was cracked and lumpy and was flaking. It reminded him of the steam pipe that ran under the ceiling in Leo's apartment. He knew from the telephone book that Leo still lived in the same place.

"He'll thank me some day," he thought. "I'll tell him this and he'll take my hand and thank me for what I went through."

Joe waited until Ruddy had had a chance to look out the window and see that he wasn't on the street and tell Wheelock he had just missed him. Then he walked out.

V

SIXTEEN PEOPLE worked regularly in Apartment 2F at 92-53 Edgecombe Avenue. Ten were sorters. They were paid $17 a week for arranging the policy slips according to the numbers and amounts. Five were bookkeepers. The sixteenth man was head bookkeeper and office manager.

The proportion of bookkeepers was so high because each controller was a separate account. Three of the bookkeepers were paid $21 a week and two, who had learned to operate adding machines as well as keep books, were paid $23. They kept the controllers' accounts and recorded, on a master sheet, the day's business and the day's hits. All the other records of the business—legal fees, bonding fees, protection money, the steady outgo of presents, touches, and bribes for policemen—were kept by Edgar in Leo's own office. Leo and the accountants and lawyer who helped prepare his income tax report were the only ones who ever saw both sets of books.

Seven of the ten sorters were women—Italians, Spaniards, and Negroes. They were all at least middle-aged and all had families. Before going to work for Leo, they had been domestic servants or charwomen in offices and hotels. The job in the policy bank gave them their mornings for their own housework and children and got them home in time to see their families off to bed. Working in an office at a white-collar job seemed wonderful to them and the hours were a blessing.

A dark, jolly, hairy sorter named Giuseppe Rizzizzi was called Juice. He was a big man, padded evenly in front and back and on the sides with hard fat. He had been a taxi driver until a rainy winter evening when his cab had skidded off a pier end. It had been cold and he had closed all the windows. Then, when the car settled in the black water, he was unable to open a door. The pressure of the water kept the doors sealed.

He flung his bulk against the door many times, butting it with his head and shoulders and fists, but it wouldn't give. It was like hitting a wall and it made him feel powerless. He lunged again and again and ended up against the door each time with a smash. A grunt came sweating out of his mouth. He could feel the muscles quivering up and down his back.

The cab was nearly silent. The only sounds were the thud of his body hitting the door and his grunts and, when he drew himself back for another lunge, his breath scratching in his throat. He heard that and heard the squirting of black water, skirted with black foam, as it spouted out from under the dashboard and up from the flooring in narrow, hard streams. Juice remembered those sounds afterward and how there was a roar in his head that seemed to burst outward. It never stopped bursting outward. He thought suddenly about the window. He put his back flat on the seat and lifted his foot and kicked out the glass with his heel. In a moment he was free of the car and a moment later he was swimming safely on the surface.

When Juice tried to go back to work, he found he couldn't. He could force himself to go into an automobile, but he couldn't keep himself in it. He was puzzled. The accident hadn't hurt him much. One shoulder was a little sore and the skin on his two big, hard-padded hands was broken from hitting against the door. But, aside from that, there was nothing. He hadn't even caught cold. He was still the man he had been, never a sick day in his life. Yet, every time he got into a car, and sometimes it happened in an elevator or when he came home late at night to a dark house, he began to tremble and he couldn't breathe. He didn't think about the accident he had had, but there was a feeling of blackness in his eyes and drowning through his body. He had to get away to shake it out. He would jump out of the car and stand shaking his wet, white face and then he would feel foolish and laugh and think, "I'm a real woman."

Another sorter was an old Mexican Indian, with white blood and black blood and red blood and brown blood and yellow blood, too, to muddy him. His name was Pedro Molinas. He was all the races of man, from Nordic to Malay. It seemed to make him incoherent. He was tall and thin with high cheekbones and had a sandy moustache and a copper tint in his black skin. He did not know much English, but he was talkative and liked to tell long stories about himself. He became very excited and hissed and spit among his words because no one could understand him.

He said he had a wife with "fi', sizza chillo" in Mexico and another wife with "fi', sizza chillo" in a place he pointed out on the map. It proved to be Galveston. He also said he had a third wife with "fi', sizza chillo" in Kansas City and that he was lonely for them in New York and was looking around for a fourth wife to give him five or six more children. He proposed to all the women in the place frequently. He would point across the table to his choice of the day and, with all the others listening, would say, "You me big slap slap in bed fun chillo."

Nobody believed he was serious, but he was serious. However, when they laughed, he would laugh, too, in a delighted way, looking from one laughing face to the other with black eyes that shone like sunned water. He had a habit of saying, "Ai-Yai," when anything unexpected happened and because of this and because his name was Pedro and because of his many wives and children, everybody called him Pie-Eye.

The third male sorter was named William Xavier Middleton. He was called Mr. Middleton. He was a placid-looking, elderly man with a comfortable laugh and a slow-moving, twangy, comfortable voice. His talk sounded like notes from an idling guitar. With his gray hair and pink skin and firm, slow walk, he looked to be about fifty years old, but he was actually sixty-one.

Mr. Middleton had spent most of his life as a telegraph operator and, although he had never been good enough to handle one of the boom-time, $100-a-week jobs in the brokerage offices, he had enjoyed his work and taken pride in it. When the teletype machines with their $25 boy and girl operators began coming into greater and greater use and the other men started worrying about Morse telegraphy being abandoned entirely, he refused to worry. "Worry is bad for your stomach and kidneys," he said and he said, "What's the use your thinking about it? You won't help or hurt by thinking. You'll just wear out your brains."

Instead of worrying about teletype machines putting him out of work, he began to worry about his sending hand going bad on him. This was something he had seen happen to other Morse operators. Nobody seemed to know exactly what it was, but the hand suddenly lost its sensitivity and couldn't send messages any more. The hand looked just the same as before. There was no pain or swelling and it could do any other kind of work. It just lost its ability to feel out the dots and dashes on the bug fast enough. Mr. Middleton had been sending with his right hand and he began practicing on his bug with his left hand.

To learn to send with the left hand after a lifetime of using the right hand was difficult for a man Mr. Middleton's age. He was fifty-nine at that time. He gave up his Friday night poker game and Saturday night movies and Wednesday night game of pool at Boyle's Billiard Parlor near his home in the Bronx and spent the time sending with his left hand. In six months he had done it. He was as expert with one hand as with the other. Then, suddenly, his right hand went bad. If he had been told he had worried it into going bad, he would have said that was crazy talk. He just thought his hunch had proved correct. He wasn't upset. His feeling was that he had seen it coming and had prepared for it and he was even a little pleased that his long, trying hours of preparation had not been wasted.

The men in the office didn't understand, either, that if Mr. Middleton had not been worried about his hand going bad, it would not have gone bad. They said he sure was a smart old duck all right to be ready when it came and some of them followed his example and began practicing with their left hands. They, too, had a chance, after a while, to be pleased with their foresight. Their right hands, too, went bad.

Mr. Middleton believed his left hand couldn't be expected to last as long as his right hand had. His right hand had lasted forty-two years. The left hand was not so strong, but it would surely last twenty years and that would be about long enough. However, his left hand went as dead as his right before the end of the year.

He held up the two hands before him. They were old hands. They had done a lot of work in their time, but they still looked pink and fleshy. They were not like some of those claws you see around. "I never knew there was that much difference between a right hand and a left hand," he thought.

Two of the bookkeepers were Negro women. The name of one had been picked by her parents for its music and was as soft as herself. It was Delilah Lowrie. She was a graduate of college and was trained as a teacher, but there was no teaching job for her. She was studying mornings for a master's degree. She thought if she had another degree, a really overwhelming degree, she would have a better chance when the Board of Education decided to appoint more teachers. The other woman bookkeeper was named Corinne Anderson. She was a dumpy-trunked woman, dark and flashy, and had been a waitress and restaurant cashier before going to work for Leo.

Of the other bookkeepers, two were Cubans, small, hot-looking men with tarry hair and tar-colored eyes. They both were musicians, put out of work by music that was delivered in cans. They looked enough alike to be brothers, but they had not met before getting jobs with Leo. What they wanted was to work up a vaudeville act together and, during slack moments, they'd go into a corner and figure out turns and falls and funny bits of business. They would get so excited and happy they'd forget there wasn't any vaudeville any more.

The fifth bookkeeper was a cocky Irishman, short, red-haired and freckled and rather plump. His name was Francis Murray. He was in his late twenties and, since leaving high school, had had a career of odd jobs, the longest of which was as a bellhop at sea for two years. He liked the sea, particularly the sense it gave of the ship being home and home being unattached to the world and its troubles. Every time he got on land, he felt overcome by the problems of living, but he could go home to his ship and his ship would take him away. So he might have stuck to the sea, but he had a temper. He got sore and quit when another boy was chosen, instead of himself, as bell captain.

Leo liked Murray. He talked to him about learning a trade or finding something to do that had a future to it. Murray had decided finally on the police force. Leo had advanced the money for courses at a civil service school and now, by the Monday on which Thanksgiving week, 1934, began, Murray had passed the examination and was on the list awaiting appointment.

It had been good business for Leo to pick servants and char-women as his sorters. They were grateful for their jobs and happy in them. But he hadn't done it because it was good business. He liked the idea of their being grateful and happy and having more time to spend with their children.

They told him about their families and sometimes, when there was sickness at home, he would give one an extra five dollars and ask her not to tell anyone about it because, if she did, everybody would want five dollars. However, the present invariably became common knowledge at once. Even if she said nothing, the look on her face was enough. Yet none ever came to Leo with a story of trouble unless it was true.

One Italian woman had fallen to her knees before Leo and had pressed kisses against his hand because he had helped her with five dollars. He jumped as if bitten, but it pleased him nevertheless. He felt they all loved him that way and, actually, they did.

Leo admired the placid way in which Mr. Middleton took his hard luck and used to give him a cigar once in a while. He listened to Juice's story sympathetically several times and once had Edgar take the door off his car to see if that would help Juice stay in it. It didn't. He was sorry for Delilah and secretly proud to have a college graduate working for him. He found her some pupils to tutor on Saturday mornings when she did not go to school and told her that if she got enough private pupils, then she would not have to work for him.

"I like to work for you," she said.

"A beautiful girl like you? With a college education like you? It's a real shame on everybody that there's no job for her that's worth what she is."

Delilah looked so glad he felt uncomfortable.

But whenever anything went wrong in the bank, Leo would tell himself it came from hiring cripples. "I do good for everybody but myself," he thought. Since he had gone into the policy business, he had become even more high-strung and he would go into fits of rage.

Once it had actually seemed for a moment as if he were standing in front of himself, yelling at himself and jabbing one finger at himself. A mistake had been made that cost him more than $100. "You want to be Santa Claus?" he heard himself scream at himself. "Go ahead and break your neck and be Santa Claus for the cripples!" He even saw the ruby ring on the small, fat little finger of his hand as it jabbed at him.

It was a startling apparition. He stared shocked. Anger bolted out of him like a frightened horse, with a kick and plunge that left him breathless. He decided finally his anger must have caused a heart attack. He must actually have been dead for a moment and the apparition standing in front of him and screaming at him must have been his soul. He must have been standing there dead and looking at his soul for a moment until his heart kicked over into life and began pumping again.

After that, Leo tried to control his anger. He walked up steps slowly to nurse his heart.

There was one man in the office who did not go out to Leo and was not loyal to him. This was Frederick E. Bauer, the head bookkeeper and manager of the bank at $25 a week. It was not in him to go out to anyone or to be loyal to anything. He was like Leo, an insecure man, but he had not had the kind of life in business Leo had had. So he was rather disliked by those who knew him. They said he kept too much to himself and was no fun and anyway had nothing to offer. The trouble was he had become too certain of rebuff to venture his emotions on anyone.

In 1934, Bauer was thirty years old. He was a tall man with an uneasy, mottled color that, at a casual glance, made his skin seem pimpled. His blond hair was thick and wet-looking and cut sharp along the edges of his head. It lay on top of his head like a mat. He had blue eyes, but square, gold-rimmed glasses made them seem colorless. His body was bony. He looked, more than anything else, like a German mechanic on a day off. However, he had never worked in overalls in his life. He had held only one job before going with Leo and that, too, had been in an office. Leo had found him where he had found Mr. Middleton, in Boyle's Billiard Parlor.

The depression had cost Bauer his job in the office of a hardware company. Bauer knew Leo by sight as one of Boyle's clientele and, although people treated Leo as a "businessman," Bauer was aware that Leo actually was someone "in the rackets." Bauer was there when Leo hired Mr. Middleton. He felt sure he could get a job from Leo, too. But he waited. He couldn't bring himself to go into "the rackets." He waited until his money was all gone and he couldn't borrow any more and he couldn't find any more odd jobs and the only thing left was charity. The way Bauer felt, it was more degrading for a family man to accept charity than to be a thief. At least, he thought, the thief had a noble motive and people could respect his motive. So he went up to Leo and asked him for a job. "I'll do anything," he said. He was trembling a little bit. "Ask me and I'll do it."

This was at a time when Leo was still uneasy about the policy business. Whenever he had noticed Bauer before, the man had been looking at him furtively, and when Leo had caught his eye, Bauer had turned away hastily like a boy caught sticking out his tongue. So Leo had asked who he was and had found out Bauer was a high-school graduate and an unemployed office worker and had told himself, "You be legitimate and I'll make a living in these hard times."

Bauer's abrupt approach now had startled Leo. "What do you

mean you'll do anything!" he cried. "What kind of a business do you think I'm running, you'll do anything!"

Bauer colored with confusion, but he was a slow-minded man. An idea had filled his mind. He couldn't change it quickly and he felt he had to say something right away, so he continued with what he had intended to say. "I don't care what kind of a business," he said. "There's no food in the house and four mouths there, five with mine." He knew he was saying the wrong thing. His voice fell to a mumble. "Just ask me anything and I'll do it," he mumbled.

"Maybe you think I'll give you a job making a stickup for me?" cried Leo. "Have you got experience?" People from other tables looked up.

"My kids are hungry," mumbled Bauer helplessly.

But Leo was too excited to hear him. "How would you like I'll give you a gun to shoot up some business for me?" shouted Leo.

The manager-owner of Boyle's came up quickly. He was a big man, named George Palumbo. He had once been a prize fighter. He put his arm around Bauer's shoulders. "Everybody is very upset nowadays," he said.

Bauer turned to Palumbo gratefully. "I was just asking him for a job when he jumped on me," he told him. Palumbo picked Bauer's hat and coat off a hook with his free hand and walked him to the door. Bauer began to struggle a little and Palumbo's arm tightened around his shoulders.

"Are you throwing me out for a man like that?" Bauer cried.

"You're excited." Palumbo did not relax his grip until he had Bauer on the sidewalk. "Everybody is got a temper these days on account of the hard times. You go home and you'll cool down and feel better."

If it hadn't been for Palumbo throwing him out, Bauer might not have taken the job when Leo came around to his house to offer it. Leo's conscience made him offer Bauer a job. His feeling of guilt made him enlarge on the incident and made him talk himself into regarding Bauer as "a real high type boy," clean-cut, steady and honest. But it was Palumbo choosing Leo over him when the showdown came that made Bauer decide to go in "the rackets."

They were all there working in the bank—the servants and charwomen, Juice, Mr. Middleton, the musicians, Delilah Lowrie, the restaurant cashier, the young man waiting to become a policeman, Bauer and Pie-Eye—when Milletti's raiders, ordered by Joe, came in. Leo was there, too. He hadn't wanted to remain in his own private office. He had been afraid Joe would come around there and argue some more.

There were two men in plainclothes for the raid and about half a dozen in uniform. One of them knocked on the door and Bauer, who happened to be nearby, went to answer.

"Who is it?" he asked, opening the door, and the men poured in.

They overflowed Bauer, and Bauer jumped into the air and came down on stiff legs. Then he ran into a corner and stood there watching them. Silence swept the room and, in the silence, everybody had heard Bauer run. He had made small, light, scratching sounds as if he were running on paws.

"Nobody move," said a detective. "Keep your hands as they were."

Leo was in an alcove with Delilah, trying to straighten out a complaint from a controller by checking back on old policy slips. He had some of them in his hand when the detective came in. His surprise carried him out of the alcove and towards the police, frowning and squinting. He realized suddenly he had the policy slips in his hands and the policy slips were evidence. He threw them to the floor.

"I'm sorry, Mr. Minch," said one of the detectives. "You done that too late."

The detective picked up the slips and put them into an envelope and wrote Leo's name on the envelope.

"Come here a minute," said Leo. He did not recognize the man, but that was not unusual. He had given presents to too many detectives to recognize them all.

The detective followed Leo slowly to the outside hall. There were already two policemen at either end, one at the head of the stairs going down, the other at the foot of the stairs going up. Leo knew these men and he nodded to them. They looked at him with embarrassment.

"I think we ought to be able to do business on this, don't you?" said Leo to the detective. He put his hand into his pocket. He knew that every once in a while, when a detective was hard up for money, he would make an arrest just to be bribed out of it.

The detective shook his head.

"Did Milletti go crazy all of a sudden," cried Leo, "or what is this?"

"He looked healthy to me when I left him," said the detective.

People who lived on the same floor were opening the doors to their apartments and coming out in the hall.

"Keep back out of this," the detective shouted. He turned to the patrolman at the head of the stairs. "Keep the hall clear," he ordered. He seemed nervous.

Leo went back into the bank.

The other detective, helped by some of the policemen, had finished collecting the evidence and had called for the patrol wagon. The policy slips before each sorter and bookkeeper had been put into separate envelopes and marked. Tags had been tied to the adding machines, the half finished master sheets, the tape off the machines and the other bookkeeping records and a bundle had been made of the lot.

The women were together near the alcove. Some were frightened, but most of them, after their first fear, seemed almost to welcome the break in the routine. Delilah sat a little apart from them. Her face was pensive. Her hands were folded quietly in her lap. Pie-Eye was standing over the women, talking incoherently in a happy, excited way, the spit flying like spray from his lips.

"That must be what God hears when He listens to the world," thought Delilah. A policeman was listening to Pie-Eye attentively.

The cop was young and ambitious and hoped he would overhear evidence.

"Sometimes I think he's talking pig latin," the policeman said at last, "and then again it sounds like double talk. Do you get it?" He didn't take his eyes from Pie-Eye, but he seemed to be addressing Murray who was standing nearest him.

Murray had been watching the work of the detectives and patrolmen with professional curiosity. He wanted to see if they actually did everything he had been taught to do in police school. "He's a high-class kidder," Murray said. "He talks double talk in pig latin."

Bauer sat facing the wall with his back to the room. Near Murray sat Juice and the two Cuban musicians. The Cubans were talking to each other in Spanish, and Juice was listening although he did not understand a word. His face was white and set and his big hands were closed into fists as they rested on his knees. He was trying not to think about the ride in the patrol wagon. Mr. Middleton was standing placidly on the other side of the group. He was smoking a cigarette and his vest was unbuttoned and his hands were resting on his white shirt over his belly. He looked as if he had just risen from a good dinner and was trying to decide what would be nice to do next.

Leo went to the telephone and called his lawyer and told him to have Ruddy, who was his regular bondsman, at magistrate's court prepared to bail out seventeen. He also asked him to send Edgar down to court with his car. Then he went over to Juice. "How do you feel?" he asked.

Juice looked up at him and Leo could see white balls of sweat on the man's thick, white face. "I'm not so good off," Juice said.

"It won't be bad," Leo told him. "It's a short ride, four, five minutes and we'll all be in there with you, right around you. We'll hold you down." He tried to laugh, but it didn't come out well.

"I guess I can stand it, I hope," said Juice.

"A big guy like you." Leo patted him on the shoulder. "It won't be anything to do."

"I'll try my best."

Leo decided he'd get the women to surround Juice. They'd shame him into keeping quiet. He went over to the alcove and, on the way, Murray reached out and pulled at his sleeve and asked to talk to him for a minute.

"Right away," said Leo irritably.

Leo whispered to two of the Italian women to sit on either side of Juice when they got into the patrol wagon. The women began to look motherly. "There's no use having a big fuss," he said and they nodded sympathetically. He turned to Delilah. "There's nothing to worry about," he told her. She didn't answer. She didn't turn her head to look at him. She just sat quietly and he stood over her a moment, wondering what he could do for her. Then he noticed Murray standing at his side, waiting to talk, and he turned away and walked quickly over to Mr. Middleton. "I'm sorry about this," he said.

Mr. Middleton took the cigarette out of his mouth carefully. He had been thinking that, when his hands had gone bad, he could have learned teletyping—or Mux, as it was called. But it had seemed too much of a come-down. He had preferred to tell the company he would find something elsewhere that was more suitable for a man of his age and position.

"Worrying isn't going to do any good," he told Leo. "It just wears out the brains." He looked at Leo and smiled and put the cigarette back into his mouth carefully.

Leo walked quickly into the hall. He felt he had to get away from them. He had enough worries of his own. He walked up and down the hall until a policeman came up the stairs to say the patrol wagon had arrived. Then Leo went back into the bank and got his hat and coat.

"Get going everybody," said the detective. "Come on! One at a time and follow me. Don't anybody try to get ahead or hold back. Just keep your place in line."

He kept shouting and the line formed slowly and shambled into the hall. A detective and a patrolman remained in the room to bring up the rear and they saw Bauer sitting motionless, facing the wall, his back to them. The detective walked over to him and Bauer cringed away awkwardly. His long, bony body twisted in the chair.

"What's the matter with you?" asked the detective. "Can't you walk?"

"No," said Bauer. His head was lowered and his eyes were closed. He shook his head several times quickly. "No," he said, "no, no, no, no." He spoke in a mutter.

The detective laughed. He was a family man and Bauer had looked exactly like a stubborn child. "No-no-no-nnnnnnn-o," said the detective in a sing-song. He put his hand on his hip and tossed his head in the air and stamped his foot. "No-no-no-nnnnnnnnnn-o!" He laughed again.

Bauer became silent. He didn't open his eyes or raise his head. He gripped the seat of the chair so hard his knuckles turned yellow. With a frantic, scrambling motion, he wrapped his legs around the rungs.

"Come on!" the detective said. "Stand up!"

Bauer sat silently. His hands shook with the intensity of his grip.

The policeman at the door called to the detective in front to hold up the line and everybody stopped and turned and listened. Fear sprang up in all of them. Even Mr. Middleton's fists clenched.

The patrolman inside the room walked slowly toward Bauer.

"Look at the bastard, will you," said the detective. He stared slowly around the room. Then suddenly he lunged forward and grabbed Bauer by the hair. "Stand up!" he bellowed and yanked Bauer's hair.

"No!" shouted Bauer. Then he screamed. He opened his mouth wide and screamed with all his strength. "No!" he shouted and screamed and then shouted, "No! No! No!" and then screamed again. His eyes remained closed and he kept his quivering legs and arms wrapped around the chair.

The people in the hall stirred. The screams passed over them like wind over high grass. Corinne Anderson began to giggle and Juice stepped out of line.

"Come on," said the detective shepherding them. He saw his flock was in danger of getting out of hand. "Downstairs! Get going!"

"Excuse me," said Leo.

He started to push his way past the others to get back to the bank. A policeman stopped him.

"It's me," Leo said.

The policeman was undecided for a moment. Then he turned to the crowd. "Come on, you heard!" he yelled. "Get going!" He pushed Mr. Middleton in the back with his nightstick. "Step on it, grandpa," he said.

Bauer's hair was wet with sweat and the detective couldn't get a grip on it. It was too short and too wet. The detective's hand slipped and he held it up and looked at it with disgust and then flicked it. "Give me a hand with this shit," he said to the policeman at his side.

The policeman got behind Bauer and put his arm around Bauer's neck and squeezed and hauled upward. Bauer's eyes bulged beneath their lids. He tried to bite the policeman's arm, but he couldn't reach it with his teeth. The arm was under his chin. At the policeman's pull, he rose clear of the floor, but he still clung to the chair and the chair rose with him.

The detective stooped and clawed to loosen Bauer's feet. He couldn't budge them. "All right," he said, "put him down a minute." He was breathing heavily. He unbuttoned the bottom of his coat and reached into his back pocket and pulled out a short lead bar covered with black leather. He swung it before Bauer's closed eyes. "You see this?" he said in a slow, loud voice. "If you don't let go of that chair, so help me Christ, I'll break your fingers and I'll break your legs." He lowered the billy and straightened up. "All right," he said, "stand up now!"

Bauer's eyes remained closed. Tears began to run down his lumpy, high-boned face. The policeman kept his hand loosely about Bauer's neck. Bauer opened his mouth wide. He didn't say anything for a moment. Then suddenly he screamed, "Help!" His voice blotted out his next words. Then he shrieked, "They're killing me!"

Leo had come into the room and had been watching. "Wait a minute, boys," he said. He walked forward slowly, looking worried. "Go away, I'll handle him for you."

The policeman and the detective stepped back. They seemed glad

to have help. "Do it fast," the detective said. "We ain't got all day."
"That son of a bitch is crazy," said the policeman. Leo stooped
and put his arm around Bauer's shoulder. "Freddy," he whispered.
"Listen to me. You got to listen to reason, Freddy."
"No," said Bauer, "no, no, no, no." His voice shook and the
words spilled out of him as if they were broken.
"This is Leo telling you this. Nothing is going to happen to you.
I'll take care of you. What can happen to a man earning his living
running an office? I promise you. Did you ever go wrong on Leo's
promises?"
Bauer remained silent for a moment. Then his eyes opened for
the first time. They looked glazed. "I can't walk, Mr. Minch," he
said. His head swayed and came to rest tiredly against Leo's chest.
"It's all right," said Leo. "Just lean on me." He put his hand on
the side of Bauer's head and pressed him against his chest. "Leo
will help you along." He spoke in a low voice that sounded like
crying.

❧

The raid had been made in mid-afternoon. When they got out
of the house, the sun still lay cold yellow on the gray street. A
mob had bustled together and children stood in silence and men
and women craned around them, making shuffling, whispered
noises.
The patrol wagon was high and dark. It had a board grate on
the floor between the two benches that were attached to the walls.
Leo sat deep in the dark with Bauer and across from him sat Juice.
Their knees almost touched. Bauer leaned his head against the
wall at his left, the wall behind the chauffeur. He couldn't seem
to stop whimpering.
"I can't stand it," said Juice. The van was loading and had not
yet begun to move, but he was already trembling.
"We'll be there in a minute," Leo told him. He patted Juice on
the knee. "A big guy like you," he said.
There was a prison smell in the dark air of the van. As they
drove slowly through the streets, automobiles would loiter behind

and people in them would look eagerly at the prisoners through the iron mesh of the door in back.

Leo stared around at the clutter of people whispering in the darkness, at the dark, creaking walls, at the two detectives and the two policemen standing at the end, at the cars crowding up behind to get a look and for a moment he thought it wasn't he who was sitting there. He sat thinking of himself as if he were somebody else.

"It's a funny way to make a living," he thought finally.

Bauer's whimpering kept on and Juice leaned forward abruptly. "If he don't stop, Mr. Minch," he said, "I'll clip him." His heavy, white, sweat-wet face was working.

"Isn't there enough trouble already without that?" cried Leo.

"Tell him to stop his noise. Honest, Mr. Minch, I can't stand it."

"He wants to let it out. Can't you let him let it out?"

Leo saw that Juice's face was quaking and his bulky body was swelling. He looked like an animal bunching to spring. Leo turned hastily to Bauer. "He means it, Freddy," he cried. He shook Bauer's shoulder and Bauer twisted away. "Please," said Leo, "we have enough trouble without this."

Bauer drew in his breath and held it a long time. His head remained leaning against the wall. A gray light came through a small circle over his head. The light was as frail as shadow and it fell on Bauer's shining face and put a watery blue film on his glasses. His breath slid out in a quavering sigh and he sucked it back with loud, deep gulps. He held his breath for a long time again and then he let it go and began whimpering once more.

Juice had been watching him. He lurched forward as the whimpering began, and the women on either side of him clutched his arms and pleaded with him in Italian.

"I don't care," Juice told them. "I'm going to clip him."

One of the women turned to Leo. Her dark face was straining. Italian words burst from her mouth.

"No spikka," said Leo. "What did she say, Juice? I can't spikka her talk." He leaned forward and pushed Juice in the chest. "Hey," he cried, "I don't kapisha. What did she say?"

Juice didn't answer. The patrol wagon had bumped up a driveway and stopped and he began pushing to get out. "Please," he murmured, as he climbed over legs, "please, please, please." His voice was loose as wind.

They all knew what was in his mind and leaned back to give him a chance to get out first. When he got into the air, he stood breathing deeply. "Regular woman," he said aloud, shaking his head slowly and trembling. Then he laughed and added, "That Bauer is."

Leo came out last with Bauer. The prison smell was crawling and tickling in his nose. The station house yard, where the van had unloaded them, was walled in with buildings and no sunlight reached it. Leo walked through the bodiless gray daylight, thinking of Juice and Bauer and how, if Bauer hadn't been whimpering, Juice would have had nothing to think about except himself and would have blown up.

It occurred to Leo suddenly that a few years ago he wouldn't have been able to stand what he had gone through and was about to go through. He would have blown up, too.

VI

DETECTIVE CAPTAIN MILLETTI lived in a small, new brick house in the Bronx. Leo found him there the next morning after breakfast. He had gone around to the back of the house because he didn't think Milletti would like the neighbors to see him. The Detective Captain was in the kitchen having breakfast. There were grown-up children at the table with Milletti. His wife was standing serving in a kimono.

Milletti invited Leo to have a cup of coffee and Leo said, "No thanks. What happened between us yesterday?" Milletti took him into the living room and closed the door and asked him if he meant the raid. "Yes, the raid," said Leo, and Milletti said he didn't know a thing about it except the order had come through the police commissioner's office and there was nothing he could have done about it.

"That's unusual?" asked Leo.

"There's no statute against it. The commissioner's office has the right."

"I know, but what about the other two banks in the building?"

"I got no word on them."

"You mean then, you don't bother anything unless you have to—now, just like before?"

"Yes," Milletti said, "I don't make trouble unless I got to."

Leo went out the back door and walked around the block to where Edgar was waiting in the car and drove to his office. Until his talk with Milletti, Leo had felt there was a chance the raid had not been aimed at him by Tucker, but was the beginning of a police drive against policy. Now he knew there was no chance. It was Tucker all right. "You are going to have a fight that you don't expect, Mr. Tucker," thought Leo.

The fight was already on. Leo had gone ahead on the theory that the raid was Tucker's idea to force him into the combination and on the day of the arrest, even while waiting for arraignment with the others in the bullpen adjoining the courtroom, he had planned and begun his campaign. The major thing was to keep the business going. The first step was to get a new place for the bank. Police had put a guard on the old one until the case could be disposed of. Leo sent his lawyer to rent another apartment and sent Edgar to round up the controllers and bring them to his office because the next step was to tie the controllers tightly to him, so tightly they would not run to work for Tucker's combination as soon as they learned it was being formed.

This was not a simple thing to do. The controllers worked on commissions and the raid was going to hurt them in the money pocket. The players who had hit the day of the raid and could not be paid now because the police had confiscated the policy slips that showed who had hit—these customers were going to be sore, and their families and friends were going to be sore, and they all could be counted from now until memory failed them as so much lost commission. Then everybody who heard about the raid would figure the Minch bank had lost its okay to operate and these, too, these thousands of customers could be counted as so much lost commission. But if he were given time to operate, he could get all these customers back again and put his bank on its feet again. The point was: time. One of the points, anyway. And to gain time he had to make sure Tucker could not take his controllers away from him.

As soon as pleas of not guilty had been entered and the magistrate had consented to postpone the hearing and admit them to bail, Leo had hurried off to his controllers. He had spent half the night arguing with them. The point he got across was that he was with Tucker, that he and his brother were together and that Tucker was a big man and would straighten everything out. The controllers had believed Leo was one of Tucker's people since the day they went to work for Leo, but he wanted to remind them of it so that when they heard of Tucker's combination they would decide, if Leo's okay to operate was no good, it was because Tucker's was no good. By the time they learned the truth, maybe Leo's business would be back on its feet and they would have no reason to leave him. "Maybe, maybe, maybe," thought Leo, "but, in the meantime, fight. Let Tucker know he's got something on his hands, not a pussy cat."

It was only a little after eight in the morning when Leo reached his private office, but already a number of people were waiting to see him—bankers who had come to express their sympathy and thus find out if they were in danger; collectors who wanted to know what to tell their customers and wanted to get it straight from the big boss himself, not just from their controllers; players who claimed to have hit the day before and wanted to be paid.

Leo insisted on seeing them all himself. That, he felt, would be fighting. He explained over and over again to customers who had hit, that he would like to pay, but there was no way to tell who had won what.

Some wanted to know if the police would return the slips after the case was over and they could get paid off then. "That's just the trouble," he pointed out patiently. "We have to claim the slips don't belong to us."

None of them could follow his reasoning. They had their own reasoning. They had paid for a number. The number had hit, maybe for the first time in their lives, and where was the money. Some got noisy and Leo had to stop thinking about Tucker and what Tucker was going to do next and think of the man in front of him because the man was saying, "It's my money and what I want to know is not this or that or if or but or what the police say or you say or he say, but where is my money."

"I'm sure you won," Leo told him. "You got a real honest face and I know you hit. But if I pay you without having a record, then everybody in Harlem will come up here and say they got hits and I'll have to pay them, too. Not everybody is as honest as you are in this world."

"That's a hell of an answer to where my money is," the man said and, after a while left, still sore, no longer a customer, very much no longer a customer.

They all came in sore and they all went out sore. So what was the use? It was a mistake to see any of them, a waste of time and a tiring thing to do. But it was fighting. Even if it was fighting the wrong people the wrong way, it was fighting.

But there was the case against Leo. He ought to be doing something about that. Tucker held the case in his hands. The complaint read: "Found with policy slips." That was the usual complaint in such a case. It was loose and almost any kind of evidence could be brought in under it. Possession of policy slips was usually proved under such a complaint and that was merely a misdemeanor and could be handled by the magistrate. Ruddy, the bondsman, and Leo's lawyer could be trusted to do business with the magistrate on that. But if the police decided to try to prove the contriving and operating of a lottery? That was a felony and the magistrate would have to send it downtown to the criminal courts. Leo had no "in" downtown. He knew no one who could do business for him there. Except Tucker. And Tucker was sitting with the police, telling them what to do, and sitting with the magistrate, telling him what to do, and he was sitting downtown, too!

"So now," thought Leo, "I go to jail." He remembered the prison smell in the patrol wagon. There had been the same smell in the bullpen. It had gone up Leo's nose as if it had feet. He had taken the tip of his nose between his two fingers and pulled it from side to side, but he hadn't been able to shake out the smell. He had tried to squeeze it out. He had put two fingers against the bridge of his nose and pulled the fingers down along the bone. It hadn't done any good. He had just felt as if he were squashing something. The squashed smell had been even worse.

His memory of the smell was so clear that he felt it crawl up his nose again on feet. "All right," he thought, "I'll live in dirt, in damp, on cement. Bugs and rats will run over my face with their legs when I sleep. The mattress will smell like they washed it in bug blood. But, Tucker will know something from me. He'll know what a fight is."

And anyway, Leo had decided, Tucker wasn't out to get all Leo's people. Tucker would make a felony case only against Leo, so that Leo would come running to him to square it. The others would get off with misdemeanor charges and Ruddy and the lawyer could take care of those. That would leave some kind of organization. The controllers were tied tight and Edgar could run them, and Bauer could run the office and, if the worst happened, he would still have some business left when he got out, something to start with and build up.

No, thought Leo suddenly, it's no good. There would be more raids and more and more raids and more and more and more raids. If he were held on a felony charge this time, he surely would be fingerprinted. Maybe he could do business downtown and get the case against him dismissed, but the fingerprints would stay on file waiting for him. He would have a record and how long could a judge, even a judge he was able to buy away from Tucker, go on dismissing cases against him? No! It was crazy even to think of it!

They already had his fingerprints from the beer trucks. According to those fingerprints, he was a bootlegger. The lottery case would make people believe he had been guilty as a bootlegger and just had got away with it, and the bootlegging case would make people think he was guilty in the lottery case. Judges had to take all that into consideration, even if they were in the market to do business on a thing like this. And what would they have to take into consideration if there were a second lottery case against him and a third and a fourth and a fiftieth? No, he had no chance. He was on the way out of the picture.

Leo thought of going to see Joe. "I'll see him dead first," he told himself. "He done this to me. Let him come to me." Joe was waiting for Leo in his own office. He did not even go out to lunch for fear he would miss Leo's call. But Leo was sure Joe would come to him. "His conscience will bring him," he decided and then thought, "a man like that has no conscience," and thought, "anyway, I don't have to go before the magistrate for three weeks and, if he sends me downtown, that will be another three, four months." He felt there was time to see Joe at the last minute and, in the meantime, he could fight. If he had to go down in the fight, he'd cut flesh off Tucker before he did. Yes, he'd cut flesh and he'd hear Tucker scream like a baby. That was what, Tucker screaming like a baby, making music that would be a pleasure to hear.

Leo clenched his pudgy fists on the desk. "I am a little man," he told himself, his head shaking with the rhythm of his words, "and Tucker is a big man and feels he can't be hurt. But I will hurt him and his hurts will stick in his brains like boils and I will stick sticks in the boils. I will stick sticks with nails on them into the boils on his brains and wipe the nails first in germs that will rot his face so that when he looks into the mirror he will see what he really looks like and, with every breath he takes in, cracked glass will go into his lungs. You hear, Mr. Big Shot Ben Tucker? Cracked glass!" He looked around him with an expression on his face as if he thought the walls of his office would come tumbling down from the rage trumpeting in him. But the walls did not come

tumbling down and he stared at them a moment before realizing
he had known all along they wouldn't.

❧

Then Leo left an office-full of sullen people to make sure his
bank employees had checked in at the new address. He was confident of all but Bauer. The others had recovered from the raid
quickly and had accepted it. But Bauer had stood with stooped
head while being booked in the station house and had sat looking
at the floor in the bullpen and had not raised his head once, even
when being arraigned before the magistrate and entering his plea
of not guilty.

Leo had taken Bauer's arm and had walked out of the courtroom
with him to where Edgar was waiting in the large, green roadster.
He wanted to be careful with him since Bauer was the man he
was depending on to run the office for him if the worst happened.
"I know you don't feel so good now," he had said, "but you just
got to come to work tomorrow."

Bauer had tried to say something. His throat had been blocked
and he had made only a rasping sound. He had cleared his throat
several times, feebly, and then had become silent.

"You know what it is when a thing like this comes up," Leo
had said. "I've got so much to do tonight and tomorrow to get
everything straightened out and the next few days, I can't be inside
for you. So you'll be sure and come, won't you?"

"I'll try, Mr. Minch."

"No, make me your promise. If you're too sick to take the bus,
I'll send the car for you. But you got to be there."

"Would you?" Bauer had raised his head.

"Sick or no sick, I'm sending Edgar in the car for you tomorrow."
Bauer had taken on determination. He's thirty years old, Leo had
thought, and has children and you can twist him around like a
baby. "I'm not telling you to hear myself talk," Leo had said.
"The whole business depends on you tomorrow."

Bauer had raised his fists nearly to his chest and had jiggled them determinedly. "I surely will promise to try my best," he had said.

Edgar had opened the door of the car and Leo had gotten in heavily and had begun to think of what he would say to his controllers and had remembered he hadn't called Sylvia to say he would be late for dinner.

"You can rely on me not to let you down, Mr. Minch."

Leo had forgotten Bauer was still there. He had put his hand out the car and patted Bauer's shoulders. While Edgar had started the car and maneuvered it out of the parking place, Leo had watched Bauer walk down the street. The man had seemed so full of determination that a giggle had bubbled up in Leo. "He's like a girl," Leo had thought, "who gives from under her dress for a ride in a car."

But, as he sat looking at the street from the windowsill of the apartment where the bank was now located, Leo wasn't sure any more that a childish trick would work on a grown man and wondered what he would do if Bauer refused to come with Edgar.

"That Tucker!" he thought. His leg began to swing and his words swung in his head. "That stink, Tucker! That garbage, Tucker! That sewer, Tucker! His mother must have had iron guts to carry him, and not get sick to her stomach. His father must have had pus from a snake to father him. His wife must have a mouth like a shark to take his kisses. Why does he live? How does rot like that, filth like that stay alive without a heart, without a brain, without feelings, just alive, that's all, like a piece of poison is alive."

Then Leo saw his car pull up in front of the door. When Bauer stepped out of the car, he had a newspaper folded under his arm. He carried it like a cane and rushed crisply across the sidewalk, smacking his heels down hard. The man seemed to be trying to live up to the car and the chauffeur and be very much the young executive on his way to important business.

After that, Leo went back to his own office to wrestle the rest of the day with stubborn, sullen losers. He returned to the bank in the evening for the figures on the day's business. Business had dropped away like something going over a cliff. Leo went through the master sheet and the controllers' accounts with Murray and Delilah. He was so disturbed he did not notice Bauer wasn't helping. Bauer appeared to be working over a ledger book, but he didn't write anything. He just sat with head stooped over the book.

Bauer said good night to Leo with the others and got to the door with the others, but then he walked slowly back to Leo. "I have to talk to you a minute, Mr. Minch," he said.

Leo was putting on his hat and coat. "Give me a hand with this first," he told him. He gave Bauer his coat and turned his back and Bauer helped him on with it. "Thanks," said Leo. He pulled the sleeves straight. "Now, what's on your mind," he demanded harshly. He was exhausted and discouraged and didn't feel like babying Bauer any more.

Bauer lowered his eyes. He fingered the knot of his tie. "I'm sorry, Mr. Minch," he said at last, "I think I'll have to find something else."

Leo buttoned and smoothed his coat. He was on the edge of saying this was the best news he had had today, but he remembered that, if he did get the worst that was coming, there wouldn't be time to train anyone to take Bauer's place or maybe even find anyone to trust with the job. He kept fussing with his coat and thought yearningly of saying, "You, you at least, I can afford to tell to go to hell," and said finally, "What's the trouble? Don't you think you've been treated right?"

"Oh no," Bauer said. "It's not that. You've been the best to me there is."

"Well, if that's so, why don't you be the best to me at a time like this when I'm in a pinch?"

"I can't, Mr. Minch. I tell you . . . I'm not cut out . . . I mean, every time . . . what happened yesterday. . . ."

"I have taken care that it don't happen again."

"But all day, every time I heard a noise today, somebody walking on the stairs or something, it just got in me. I'm not cut out for it, I guess, and I can't. I really can't."

Leo listened patiently and waited a moment to hear more and

then sat on the edge of the sorters' table and swung one leg gently and looked at the embarrassed man. "What do you think you're going to do for a job in times like nowadays?" he asked.

"If I can't find something else, I'll go on the relief. They're giving out relief now, not like Hoover."

"So? They're giving out charity and you're ready to take it, throw away your job when you're needed most and take five dollars a week, whatever it is, and walk around the streets like you're a bum."

"Not charity. It's a job with the relief now, twenty-two a week, something, depending on the job."

Leo smiled mechanically. "You want a raise, is that it?"

"No, it's not the money," said Bauer. "A dollar here or there, that isn't the point. I don't care as long as I get enough to get along on."

"How much are we paying you now?"

"Twenty-five."

"All right, you can draw $27.50 from this week on."

"I told you," Bauer said, "it's not a question of money."

Leo sat still frowning. His leg swung back and forth for a moment and then stopped and hung stiffly. "Did you think of this," he said, "that if you're not working for me when the hearing comes up, how can I pay out money from the business to defend you?"

"Now that's not fair, Mr. Minch. You know that's not a bit fair. The hearing will be all of us together and, if one of us is guilty, then all of us are. It's not fair for you to try and trick around with me like that."

There was a knock on the door, but neither paid any attention to it. Leo rose to his feet. His tired face tightened and looked sulky. "I know it's not fair." He drew back his head to look into the taller man's eyes. "But, what's the reason I should be fair when you do a thing like this to me at this time?"

Bauer's hands rose into the air and then dropped helplessly. He turned from Leo and looked at the floor. "It's not fair," he said.

Another, louder knock came and Leo glanced at the door impatiently. "Go and see who it is," he said.

Bauer opened the door. It was Joe. He was rubbing his knuckles. "Your bell don't work," he explained.

Leo turned his back deliberately.

"I hope I'm not discombombulating you," said Joe.

"You'll excuse me a minute," said Leo angrily. "There's business here."

"Don t mind me, go right ahead, as the undertaker said to the dying man." Joe waved his hand and stepped back and began to wander around the apartment.

Leo turned to Bauer. "Well, what do you say?" he asked.

Bauer looked at Joe and then at Leo. "I can't." His tone was uncertain. "Really, there's no use. I try but . . . there's no use."

Leo clicked his tongue vexedly and took a step forward. "Listen, boy," he said. "I need you for two, three more weeks until that thing, you know," he glanced in the direction of his brother, "is over. You can stay at least until then, can't you?"

Bauer shook his head. He wanted to make Leo understand how afraid he had been all day and how he had been unable to work and had had to fight himself to keep at his desk, but he didn't know how to explain it and he was embarrassed before Joe.

"If you want a couple days to rest up, that's all right," Leo said. "But I have to rely on you to be here, at least until we're straightened out."

"Maybe that will do it." Bauer looked at Joe again uneasily. "Maybe that's all I need, a little rest."

"This is Tuesday. Thursday is Thanksgiving, anyway. Take the balance of the week off. Come in Monday. Here's your pay for the vacation." Leo counted out $27.50 from the money in his pocket. "I think maybe you're the first man in the history of the city of New York," he said, "who got a raise and a vacation at the same time."

Bauer took the money and held it in his hand. "That's just about right, I guess," he said. He looked sad and uneasy. "You've been very decent to me all the years I been with you. I got no kick coming about that."

Leo patted him on the shoulder. "Come back Monday with a sunburn," he cried, "and warm us up to look at you."

Bauer laughed awkwardly. "Well, goodnight, gentlemen." He included Joe in the wave of his hand, and Joe nodded.

As Bauer walked out, he folded the money neatly into his wallet.

❧

The two brothers watched Bauer go in silence.

"It's not much of a place you got here," said Joe. He picked up an unpainted kitchen chair, one of those used for the sorters, and shook his head.

"I'm not going to get sore," Leo told him. "I found out long ago what you are and what's the use getting sore at you. But this is really a surprise, that you should have the gall to show your face to me."

"Why? I heard you had a little trouble yesterday and I came over the minute I heard."

"You heard? Somebody had to run and tell you?"

"I didn't read it in the papers."

"Listen." Leo advanced on Joe, shaking his finger in the air. "Listen to me. You never heard in your life or read anywhere that one brother should send another to jail. Did you? No. No. You had to think it up yourself. Nobody else could think it up. It came out of your own brains. Fuie!" He wrinkled his face and spit on the floor. "You got brains that's not human. They were vomited out by a horse!"

Joe tried to look unconcerned. He tried to smile, but his eyelids quivered. "Nice talk," he said. His voice was strained. It shook with emotion and he shouted, "That's real nice, God damn talk all right. It certainly took something, gall, all right, to come see a God damn wild man lunatic like you."

"Yes? Well, you and your dirty neck corporation take this into consideration: You need me; you want me, don't you?"

"*I* want to help you, not the corporation. It's *me*."

"Listen to what I say. You want me? You'll never have me. Put me in jail. All right, I'll stay there. I'll rot there. Keep me there as long as you want. It won't do you any good."

"Leo, I'm telling you, it's me. . . ."

"No, now you listen and shut up. Take my business. All right, here, here's the business with a ribbon around it." He held out both his hands. "Beat me up with your hooligans. All right, I'll fall down. I'll bleed. My bones will break. But me you'll never have. Never, never, so long as you live. Not you, not this big shot hooligan of yours, whatever his name is, Tucker. Nobody else neither."

"Tan-ta-ta-ra."

"Get out of my place!" Leo pointed to the door with a trembling finger. "Get out!"

Joe sat down on the edge of the table. "Do you think it's going to help you to abuse me like that?" he asked.

Leo bounded toward the door. "A rat like that," he cried and wrung his hands, "with a heart like a snake!"

"You know one thing about this rat like that?" said Joe. "I've taken things from you because you're my brother that I wouldn't take from anybody. No, not from nobody, not even from you. Leo, have a little sense. For Christ sake, Leo, use your head a little bit." He stretched one hand out pleadingly. "You're in a situation where the combination can help you. It's got the right of way all the way down the line. If you're in the combination, they can take care of anything."

"No."

"But why? Why? Jesus, why? Tell me, what are you afraid of?"

"Who's afraid?" cried Leo. "I'm not afraid."

Yet, the fact was, Leo was fighting a fight he did not have to fight and one he knew he must lose. Only a man frightened out of his wits does that. And Leo was not frightened that badly, not yet, since he knew he could rely on his brother to repair whatever damage Tucker did him. Then, why did he fight so frantically? What reason forced him to keep fighting even after he had given up hope of winning and was already figuring out his retreat? Leo thought he was fighting for his business, but actually he had realized the impossibility of keeping it and was fighting now for something quite different. Although it remained unthought in him, he wanted to be able to feel, and he wanted Joe to feel, that when he did join the combination, he would have joined it, not as Joe had, but involuntarily, under the compulsion of force stronger than himself. Then he and Joe, although working in the same enterprise, with Joe perhaps having even greater authority in it, would remain on different levels, as they had ever since becoming orphans.

"No," said Leo, "the trouble with you is you can't understand a man like me. Rather than mix up with a dirty, lousy, criminal gangster like Tucker, I'd go to jail. I'd give him my business. I'd die first."

"Are you afraid you'll lose your money?"

"You don't know. It never occurs to you, but there's such a thing as honesty in this world and honest business and honest people and an honest way to act in business and do business."

"You won't lose your money," said Joe. "Listen, I shouldn't tell you this, but I go over the books of those coming into the combination. I don't know what you got, what cash reserve. Come in with anything, with two thousand, three thousand. You had bad luck. You got hit hard. Jesus, are you a schoolboy I have to spell out everything for you?"

Leo walked to the light switch and took his keys out of his pocket. "I'm locking up here," he said.

Joe stood thinking desperately. How could he tell Leo to refuse to take bets on the 527 combination tomorrow? What way was there to say it without letting Leo know one of the numbers in the combination was going to hit? How could he warn him unless he was merged and safely in with them? Take a chance on his gratitude for being warned? No. Leo would use the information against the syndicate. He'd fight the merger by going around telling everybody Tucker had fixed the number.

"Well," said Leo, "did you hear me?"

Joe went to the door and leaned heavily against it. His face twisted with pleading. "I'm asking you as a favor for your own good," he said. "Come in tonight so I can help you before it's too late."

"Too late for what?"

"For what?" cried Joe harshly. "For what? Too late, you fool, too late."

"For what, I'm asking? Too late for what?"

"You stubborn, dumb mule you. The barn is burning on your head. Too late! You hear? Before it's too late. Before your case goes too far. Too late for the merger. I'm not the corporation. You're my brother, but I'm not the corporation and I can't do everything for you that I want, only what I can do."

There was time, thought Leo. He'd wait to see how things worked out with his business and with the judge. He could always give in. With Joe there, he did not have to give in until the last minute. Leo didn't answer. He turned out the light and pulled open the door and waited for Joe to walk out. Then the two brothers went downstairs together without saying a word and parted on the sidewalk without saying a word.

❧

On Wednesday evening, a little before six o'clock, an enormous event was set in motion. The number 527 hit. A monopolist had made his first move. The consequences were incalculable.

There was nothing new about the move. It had a long, respected history in business. A monopolist had consulted with his lawyer and had decided on a plan for applying pressure in steadily increasing amounts until his objective was achieved. The number 527 was the first, gentlest application. It blew, cut, and smashed like exploded steel into the lives of the fourteen big policy bankers in Harlem and the forty or fifty small ones and into the lives of more than seven hundred controllers and into the lives of more than eight thousand collectors and into the lives of more than half a million players.

No one of all those involved in this vast explosion could say what would happen next, except to himself—not the policy player who had hit and was in danger of not being paid; not the collectors, controllers, and bankers who were in danger of losing their livelihood; not even the monopolist who had ordained the explosion without having more than a concept of one single aspect of what he was ordaining. Nor was there anyone, from monopolist down, from player up, who cared what would happen next, except to himself.

Because of Bauer's holiday, Leo was in the bank when the news came that 527 had hit. Murray got the number over the telephone and showed it to Leo, and Leo put his hand to the side of his face and said, "Ouch!" He couldn't take in the full meaning of it all at once.

"A bad one," said Murray.

Leo took the memorandum out of Murray's hand. He looked at it a long moment. "Are you sure?" he asked.

"I asked twice. I made him spell it."

"Call back and make sure. It's impossible."

Leo went over to Delilah who was beginning to tabulate the winning slips. He riffled through a pile of them. "Must be fifty, sixty thousand dollars' worth here," he said.

"Oh I don't think so." Delilah felt sorry for him. "It couldn't be that much."

"Forty, fifty thousand dollars." He riffled through the slips as if they were on a pad. The numbers flitted and twitched before him. There were a great many 1-cent bets. Each one meant a $6 payoff. "The chewing-gum business suffered, too, today," he said. "I'll send them a sympathy note."

Delilah laughed. "You are taking it very well," she said.

He looked at her quickly. "I'll tell you the truth." He smiled. "I feel like sitting in the middle of the floor and crying, but what's the use? It's only money." Only only, he thought, the only only there is. He saw Murray standing in front of him, nodding his head. "Well," he asked sharply, "what do you want now?"

"I checked back like you said. It's 527 all right."

"I know it. I know it." Leo's voice was as sharp as a cry. "You told me that already. Are you trying to rub it in?"

Leo was due at his office. He put on his hat and coat and told Murray to call him there or at home when the master sheet on the day's business was ready. He walked downstairs slowly. Delilah came into the hall to watch him. He did not see her. He was holding the bannister lightly. His hand trailed along it and fiddled with it playfully. He tapped it with one finger stiff, thumb cocked, as if shooting it and then drummed a snatch of rhythm on it. These were boy tricks and Leo wanted more than anything else at the moment to be free of himself and be a little boy again.

Delilah went back into the bank and told the others, "He's taking it like a real major."

Edgar was waiting with the car. Leo knew his office would be full of people wanting to see him. The controllers would be there wondering what to do about tomorrow. The bankers who had not yet met Joe on their own would be there, trying to make a deal through him with Joe. He thought of them with their tongues out for money and walked abruptly down the street. Edgar trotted after him. "Shall I put the car away?" he asked.

Leo didn't answer. He looked at Edgar's dark, earnest face and then he looked away. He had his hands in his coat pockets and he lifted his shoulders until they rose high over the sides of his face. He forgot what he had wanted to tell Edgar and then he forgot what Edgar had asked him. He remembered hearing it, but he couldn't remember what it was. He began to walk off. Edgar came after him. "There's people waiting in the office," he said. "Shall I tell them Friday?"

"Who? Oh, all right. What about Friday?"

"The people . . ."

"Sure, go ahead, tomorrow is a holiday to enjoy."

Edgar decided to let well enough alone. Getting off early was all right with him.

There was a tight feeling in Leo. He wanted to walk it out and he wanted to have the cold smell of the twilight air in his nose and he felt he needed time. Time for what? Time to think. Time to think of what? Of what to do. There wasn't anything to do. He was out of business. A feeling he had not had since the day, four years before, when Samson Candee had walked into his office in the garage came back in Leo. He thrust it down in him and walked on. He walked almost all the way home.

He followed a street car line down a long hill and across a bridge and past a baseball stadium and under elevated tracks. The air was purple with evening at the top of the hill. At the bottom it was black and then, past the elevated, there was a burst of shops that gave the air the color of gaiety.

Naked turkeys hung in a brightly lit butcher window, and cans of plum pudding were stacked in a delicatessen window and next was the Lucien bakery. It was a famous bakery in the Bronx. Sylvia came there for cream cakes on special occasions. Leo stopped before the bakery and looked in the window and thought of Sylvia and thought of buying her a favorite cake and thought of how for even such a simple thing as eating a man needed money. "Some day," he said to himself, "they'll think of a way to charge money for breathing, like for the plain water you drink."

There was a pumpkin among the pies in the window. The pumpkin was big and orange and the pies brown and the naked turkeys white and the cans of plum pudding blue, and red raw cranberries had been spread before them like a lawn.

He could throw away his business and live off his money. He could find something else to do with his money to occupy himself. Or he could stay in the policy business and use the cash reserve to pay off as much of the hits as he could and fight the combination as an independent. Or he could keep his cash reserve and go in with the combination. One of these it had to be.

Leo walked a little longer. Then he took a trolley car home. The trolley was nearly empty, and he decided it must be the dinner hour. He thought there would not be many bankers going home for dinner now and thought of players all over the city celebrating their "hits," spending their winnings in advance, and thought of Joe and of Joe's office filled with bankers, scrambling for Tucker's money with crafty voices, craftily signing away their businesses and their lives, ruining themselves cunningly.

A man seated across the aisle from Leo was holding a live turkey in his lap. The man's large, pink face was shining and his eyes were shining and his lips were wet and shining. He seemed to be a little drunk. He had won the turkey in a raffle in a saloon.

The turkey was tied in burlap sacking. Its proud head stuck out of one end comically. It looked fighting mad and exhausted and puzzled. Its beak opened wide every now and then, but it made no sound. It sat still and stared with bright eyes, looking straight ahead in a tired, angry, puzzled way and all around, but never up, never at the man who held it and held a monopoly on its life.

The man patted it when it moved its head. He had hard, stubby hands, but he patted it gently. His lips moved like slow, wet things. He looked as if he could already taste the tired, angry, bewildered bird. He saw Leo staring at the turkey and he patted it with pride. The turkey's proud head ducked. "Juicy eating there," the man said.

Leo looked away. He didn't think of anything for a moment. Then he thought, "What am I? I'm out of business." A wave of emotion rolled up in him. It shuddered up the length of his body and smashed against the walls of his head and fell back and drenched and smothered him.

"I get both his legs and his breast," said the man.

Leo smiled at him, but did not answer. "What am I so worried?" he asked himself. "I got money. I won't pay off, that's all." But it was the business that was important to him. The business was his property. It had given him security. If he tried to live off his money, he would have to go back to the way he had lived in 1930, looking for something safe, going crazy looking for something safe. No, Joe was the best. He'd go in with him. He knew how to handle Joe. Those others didn't. If it didn't work out, he always had time to quit. While he was adding to his money, he could be looking around for some other proposition. He would be up there making money, and propositions would come to him like honey to a hive.

The man with the turkey got up and walked down the aisle. He carried the bird waist high before him, as if it were on a platter. The bird's head was jutted forward and its angry eyes blinked. It seemed to be trying to see where it was going.

When Leo got home, Sylvia told him Joe had telephoned. "I said you were out and would be home for supper."

"All right," he said. "I was out and now I'm home for supper."

He hung up his hat and coat listlessly in the hall closet, and then the telephone rang. He thought it was Joe, but it was Murray reporting the day's losses. $39,374! Leo listened in silence.

"Quite a kick in the labonza," said Murray.

Leo did not answer and Murray listened to the stillness for a moment. "I'm sorry," he said in a low tone.

Leo clung to the telephone and the two remained listening to each other's silence for a while. Then Leo hung up.

While he was sitting in the kitchen, trying to eat, the door bell rang. "If that's my brother," he said, "tell him to wait in the foyer."

"What do you mean?" Sylvia cried in surprise.

"I said it plain. Tell him to wait in the foyer until I'm finished eating."

"What is this? Did you become all of a sudden a doctor?"

He was embarrassed. "I'll write you a book," he said angrily.

Sylvia closed the kitchen door behind her. Leo heard the outer door open. Then there was a mumble of voices. He picked slowly at his food. When Sylvia returned to the kitchen, she shut the door again and sat down opposite him. He did not look at her. After a while, he let his fork drop and leaned back. His head was lowered. When he raised it, he saw that Sylvia was staring at him. "Don't you feel well?" she asked.

"Not exactly." He looked around the room slowly and then lowered his head and looked at the table. He stretched out his hand and began to finger a crumb. "I lost all my money today," he said quietly.

"Leo!" Her cry leaped out of her mouth. It was boned with terror.

"That's right." His tone rose a little. "Every penny. More." His voice had begun to tremble and he stopped talking. He brushed his hand over the table and let the breath whistle through his opened lips. "Gone," he said. "Clean." He stood up.

Sylvia was sitting far back in her chair. Her head was raised and her mouth open and her face looked sunk in fear. Her eyes were wide and dark in her whitened face and pain was in them. She raised her two hands slowly and pressed them flat against her chest.

"Don't worry so much," he told her. He could hear the dry, crackling sound of her breathing. Her breath rustled past her dry lips like wind over dried leaves. "We've been there before, haven't we?"

"Not at our age," she whispered.

"That's right." He stood looking sadly at the table. "There aren't a whole lot of people left who are older than us."

"Don't say that."

"It's true, isn't it? There are millions younger, but, how many people do you know older than us?" He turned his eyes from the table and looked at her. She had her face in her hands. He put one hand on her shoulder and looked back at the table. He stood like that a long time, one hand on her shoulder, his gaze fixed on the half eaten food on the table.

Sylvia slid gently from under his hand and stood up. He didn't seem to notice. His hand fell to his side and he remained staring raptly at the table. She turned him towards her and pulled his vest smooth and brushed some crumbs off his trousers. "Is Joe here to help?" she asked.

"I don't want his help." He stepped nervously away from her and she followed him slowly and came around in front of him slowly and looked at him. Then she leaned forward and lifted her head and rested her cheek against his. He remained standing stiffly.

"Don't aggravate yourself so much, Leo," she whispered. She put her arms about his shoulders and he stood stiff and trembling. She stroked the back of his head. He began to weep. He turned a little away from her, but she clung to him. His short, round body shook. He made small, struggling sounds. White tears began to roll down his gray face.

"Sssssh, sssh," she whispered, "sssh, sssh, darling." She continued slowly to stroke the back of his head. After a few moments, he became quieter.

"I was a rich man this morning," he said.

"I know. Yes. I know, darling. Sssssh, sssh."

"A lifetime of work went like nothing, like air blew it away."

"That wasn't any business for you anyway. You'll find something nicer that's more for a man like you."

He walked away abruptly. She had been stroking the back of his head and her hands were left in midair. Her face flushed and she went hastily to the linen closet and came back with a clean towel and a washrag. He was standing exactly where she had left him, waiting like a little boy. She held the washrag under the faucet and rung it out and then touched it timidly to his face. He took it away from her. "You don't do it hard enough," he told her.

He scrubbed until his face became shiny. She knew he was going to Joe and going to make some deal with him. When he had dried himself, she pulled his vest straight again and brushed it with her hands and brushed the collar of his coat and tightened his tie. Then she followed him into the foyer.

Joe had been reading a newspaper. He put it away and stood up. He was wearing his hat and coat.

"Come on," said Leo harshly, "what do you want?" Joe looked at Sylvia. "I have no secrets from my wife," said Leo.

"Excuse me," interrupted Sylvia. "I have the dishes and to put away the food before it spoils." She went into the kitchen and again she closed the door tightly behind her. She didn't want to overhear anything. She didn't want to feel responsible for anything that would happen.

"Now, Leo, don't be stubborn," said Joe. "Put on your coat. We'll go somewhere we can talk. Cordeles and Gonzago were to see me already and Guaraldi. They were all to see me. I just left them."

"I'm glad to hear you're so-popular all of a sudden."

"Don't be like that. I want to help you. This is the luckiest day of your life, if you knew. Come on, get your coat."

"That's a ha-ha all right." Leo got his hat and coat. Then he went into the kitchen and told Sylvia he would be home late and she shouldn't wait up for him.

"Wait a minute," she said. Leo had left the kitchen door open. She closed it in Joe's face. "I don't know what he's got in mind." She tossed her head in the direction of the foyer. "But it's not for you."

"That much I know."

"You hear, Leo? It's not for you, whatever it looks like." She had decided she could not avoid a feeling of responsibility simply by pretending to herself she didn't know what was going on.

"I know, I know," he said. "Such advice I know already."

She came close to him and touched his arms. "I've been thinking," she told him. "We'll move into a smaller place. What do we need all these rooms for?"

"So instead of paying $55, we'll pay $30 in a tenement and have a toilet in the corner of the kitchen. How much can we save?"

"You'll find something, Leo. You're wonderful that way. I'm not a bit worried. You'll find something better, I'm sure. Maybe we can borrow from Harry. You can do something with it."

Her brother, Harry, was a post-office clerk at $1800 a year.

"What'll he do," asked Leo, "take money out of an envelope?"

"It's all right. We'll live economical. What do people like us need to get along? I'm not a bit worried with a man like you. You're not like the others, break in pieces when they get a wallop. You've been wonderful all your life that way. You'll still be wonderful."

"Aaah, you talk like a child."

Leo walked out of the kitchen and out of the house and Joe followed him, stepping quickly and eagerly. Sylvia gave a worried sigh. She had known that what she would say could have no effect, but she had said it and now she could feel she no longer had any responsibility.

VII

THE DEAL with Tucker was made the same Wednesday night in Henry C. Wheelock's home. The home was an apartment squarely among the rich in a high, massive building near Park Avenue. The high, massive building stood among others like it. But, just as each million has its distinction when piled up—one being held together, say, by rubber bands, another by string, a third by paper arms, a fourth by grime—so did this building have its distinction.

As its distinction, this building wore a hedge across its edge—a frail, dark, sapless hedge from which all the reality had been barbered carefully. The hedge stood in boxes chained to the sidewalk. The only unconcealed earth on the street was wrapped around its feet. In its frail, sapless way the hedge fenced in a strip of yard where a brightly polished hydrant bloomed like a bush. The yard's earth was covered with concrete.

So there was a stone-walled yard with a concrete lawn that bloomed a bush of brass and locked and chained boxes over which juiceless, frizzed hedges lay like wigs. All day long and most of the night, the sleepless rich and their sulky servants, deep in business, passed the hedge with hardly a glance. Only the children of the rich and the dogs of the rich included the hedge in their lives. The children used the hedge to throw each other into it. The dogs of the rich watered the hedge all day long. In the late afternoon, a man in uniform came out of the house and washed off their thoroughbred water and put the city's water in its place.

A Filipino in a white, brass-buttoned jacket opened the door to Wheelock's apartment for Leo and Joe and, as the two brothers stood in a foyer giving the man their coats, Wheelock came sensationally to greet them. His hand was outstretched. He entered the foyer like wind, uttering rapid cries of welcome, and stood with small, swirling movements. There was a feeling of flurry to each step he took and to his hands and face. The words tumbled out of his mouth. Smiles bounced on his face. His laughter bounded into the air.

In his tiredness, Leo did not fight Wheelock's nervous, unnerving energy. Instead he gave himself to it with an emotion of relaxation. He went sheeplike into the living room, relaxing in the sensation of being taken in charge as Wheelock nipped and coaxed at his edges with words and smiles and gleeful yelps and a darting, fluttering body. Wheelock was so unexpected to Leo. He had thought the man would be something like his own lawyer, loud-voiced, a little shabby, unhappy-looking and with a manner of naked greed. Or perhaps he might be nattier, a snappy man dressed snappily, but still loud and unhappy and greedy. But Wheelock was nothing like that. He was young. He had brown, curly hair fluffed up from his head, and large, light brown eyes. His full lips and soft, full, evenly rosy face made his smile charming, although a little girlish. Despite his youth and eager friendliness, he was commanding. For all the bustle of his manner, he had poise and what Leo called manners, and he lived in an apartment that was like a mansion in the movies. The living room, for instance, was filled with heavy old walnut furniture. The walls were panelled halfway to the ceiling with matching wood, and there was a fireplace in which logs were burning. The fire threw off furry sounds and a red light that added a feeling of warmth to the somber room.

However, the apartment had been subleased furnished by Wheelock. His air of self-assurance, too, had been, in a manner of speaking, subleased. It had been acquired in a small town hotel his father had run. Wheelock had been brought up in the hotel. For as long as he could remember, he had been meeting strangers every day and making conversation with them and learning to be at ease.

Leo drank infrequently. He did not drink at all this night. Joe took two drinks and then no more. Wheelock drank steadily all evening. He kept a Scotch highball on a table before the sofa with a decanter of whiskey alongside it and soda and a bowl of ice. Every time his glass became empty he filled it.

At the beginning of the evening, Joe said to make his rye. He held his elbow out straight and raised the glass slowly to his pursed lips, the elbow rising level with the glass. His hand shook a little bit. When the glass touched his lip, he tossed his head back and the whiskey flew down his throat in a single gulp. He let go of his breath heartily and, as he did, he held out his glass for more. He stood watching Wheelock pour the whiskey. Then he repeated the rite. His elbow protruded stiffly. His lips pursed. The trembling glass, the trembling hand that held it, and the elbow, all rose slowly in a line until the glass reached the lips. It seemed to touch a spring there. The head sprang backward, and the whiskey vanished in a gulp. "Hah!" said Joe and patted his chest and looked at the glass and then put it down and took a cigar from an ebony box on the table.

Wheelock seemed amused. "Wouldn't you like a chaser?" he asked.

Joe ran his tongue across his lips and shook his head and pointed with one finger to his cigar. The smoke would be chaser enough.

When they settled down to talk business, Wheelock put on horn-rimmed glasses. It seemed to quiet him a little. The words didn't tumble out of his mouth and he smiled less frequently. His drinking, too, seemed to help soothe him. The more he drank, the quieter he became. It was the only visible effect the liquor did have.

Wheelock kept a yellow foolscap pad on his knee for notes. He made Leo go through his whole business, and somewhere he had learned exactly what to ask. The more Wheelock drank, the gentler became his voice, until at last the furry sounds of the fire could be heard among his words.

The red light came like a wash of water over his black shoes. The shoes seemed to Leo the richest he had ever seen. His eyes clung to them. He had read of custom made shoes that cost $65 a pair, and he thought Wheelock's shoes must have cost thirty, forty dollars anyway. He had read, too, there were men who never resoled their shoes and had never been to a shoemaker in their lives, didn't know what one looked like. He hadn't actually believed it when he had read it, but now he thought suddenly Wheelock must be that kind. He looked up into Wheelock's round, young face with a feeling of wonder, and then his eyes dropped back to Wheelock's shoes.

A long time was spent going over Leo's expenses, his payroll and rent bills, legal fees, commissions, protection money, the presents and bribes he had to give policemen and district captains. The questioning became a cross-examination. It even got down to the allowance of $22 a month made for Edgar's apartment because the place was used as a drop station for policy slips. There were four drop stations altogether and the total rent allowance for them was

$37 a month. The other three were in collectors' apartments, and Leo said he allowed only $5 a month for them, but Edgar needed more.

Wheelock stopped at that and seemed about to say something. He took off his glasses and looked at Leo with blank eyes. Then he frowned and put the glasses back on.

"He's a boy who worked with me to put himself through college," explained Leo. "Now he's through college and can't find what's fit for him to do. But a college boy with a wife has to have a place that's nice to live, I think. I pay half his rent and that's what it is, that's all."

Wheelock smiled, as if in approval, and went on to something else. He made a note of Edgar. There were a lot of things like that, he thought, sloppy things, where expenses could be cut when the business would be managed properly. This man Leo didn't seem able to get used to paying people their wages and letting them alone.

When they got into the income from the business, Leo became nervous. He had $31,000 under the floor of his closet that belonged to the bank as cash reserve. But, if this were to be a deal where Tucker simply bought the business and put Leo in practically as a manager on a commission of one-third the profits, then Leo felt he was entitled to hold out the cash reserve. Tucker couldn't buy money. All he could buy was an organization and good will and a clientele. Leo began to try to conceal the cash reserve by exaggerating the shortages among the collectors and controllers.

There was always a little shortage. It was known, among policy people, as "overages." Occasionally, collectors would come to controllers with policy slips, but without the money for them. Sometimes the controller refused to accept the slips, but more often he decided to try to get the shortage back from the collector's future commissions. If he didn't, the collector would get sore and take his business to some other controller. The controller tried to make Leo share a part of these losses and Leo said it was his practice to do so "in moderation." He explained there was no rule about it. It depended on how he and the controller felt about the particular situation.

Wheelock was interested. "Where does the money for the slips go?" he asked.

"Crap games, things like that. They're funny people. You treat them right and, when they win in a crap game, sometimes they pay you back the whole thing all at once if they feel like it."

Leo saw that Wheelock suspected he had exaggerated the overages to hide the cash reserve and was going to hunt him down on it. "It's like bad loans in a bank," he explained. "If a bank gets all its loans paid back, then it isn't lending out all the money it should. It's being too careful and turning down too many people and really losing money by not having bad loans. That's the way I figure on overages. If I don't have overages to a certain extent, I'm not running my business right. Too many of my collectors are taking their slips across the street."

Wheelock tapped the foolscap pad gently with his pencil. "A bank allows a margin of two per cent for bad loans, not more," he said. Leo's margin was over eighteen per cent.

"That's the way it's done," cried Leo. "I never bothered to figure it out, black on white. What I felt like, that's the way it was done."

Wheelock was pressing the matter further when the bell rang. He put away the pad and looked at his wrist watch. The houseman came swiftly and softly out of the kitchen and crossed the living room and went into the foyer. Wheelock stood up and shifted restlessly. "Excuse me," he said and followed the servant.

Joe was standing up, too. He winked at Leo. "You're doing okay," he said.

Leo turned away.

"I think you got a good headstart tonight on your first million," Joe said.

"If I come out of this with my shirt, that's all I want."

"A gold shirt, I'm telling you, with diamond buttons."

Joe wandered off to the foyer, and Leo, left alone, walked to the window and looked out. The street lay far below. Empty, lifeless quiet rose up from it and stood in the air.

"It feels like midnight," he thought and looked at his watch. It was 11:18. He put back his watch and stared at the quiet that stood dead among the large, lifeless walls of the rich. "Plenty of money around here," he thought. "Millionaires sleeping everywhere you look." He stared ahead curiously and from right to left. He saw only darkness and stones and barren quiet. "It feels real dead outside," he thought.

There was a rumbling rush of voices in the foyer. Leo decided it must be Tucker. Then he heard a woman laugh and decided it couldn't be Tucker. Outside he saw Joe's car and, behind it, a large black sedan. A man wearing a felt hat rested against the front fender and chatted with the doorman. He held one hand to his mouth as if picking his teeth and occasionally turned his head aside to spit in the direction of the hedge. Leo stared absently at the two small figures and at the two expensive cars and at the lifelessness bought by the rich to surround their homes.

His head was crackling with figures. He had been lying steadily all evening. He couldn't keep it up. The way Wheelock had gone after the overages made Leo sure his lying had been found out. Suddenly he couldn't remember whether he had told Wheelock his $31,000 cash reserve was $2,300 or $2,700. A feeling of panic wrung him and he turned from the window and saw what appeared to be a crowd coming into the room.

It was Tucker. He had his wife with him and McGuinness, who had been a bodyguard in the old days and still acted as bodyguard. With Wheelock and Joe, they looked like a party.

Mrs. Tucker was a blonde woman, heavy, but graceful. She walked lightly and with a small, swift sway. Her eyes were blue and set high in her pink face. She was warm-looking. She dressed in bright colors, green and white now with brown shoes and brown stockings and an amber necklace. Although she was almost as tall as her husband, she combed her hair flat and wore low-heeled shoes to make herself seem shorter. She felt a man should be taller than a woman. There was a large diamond ring on the fourth finger of her left hand under a wedding ring. Tucker had bought it for her two years before to celebrate their fifteenth wedding anniversary. She had insisted on sawing the wedding band off her finger to get the diamond ring under it. She wanted people to believe she had got it for her betrothal.

McGuinness was a fragile man with a waxy skin. His hair was a solid gray, and his eyes were gray and wide and cheerful looking. He had attached himself to Tucker back when Tucker was on the way up and had never been shaken loose. He was like a dog that had found a home.

There were no signs of the life he had led on Tucker's face. He looked rather thoughtful in a bulky, burly way. He was a man of middle height, in his early forties now, pudgy-faced and with dark, gray, friendly eyes and a thin nose and a small, thick-lipped mouth. His hair made him look sedate. It was dense and well-grayed. He was a shy man and his shyness was noticeable when he laughed. When he laughed, he lifted his head a little, and his mouth shaped a long, nearly perfect, affected-looking oval.

Wheelock introduced Leo, and Tucker stepped forward and held out his hand. "We know each other a long time without meeting, don't we," he said.

Leo shrugged and shook hands briefly. He had turned pale. A heavy, exasperated breathing blew in and out of his nose and made his nostrils rise and fall.

Tucker thrust his head forward. Leo's attitude rasped his own shyness. "I don't look like such a terror, do I," he said. "You don't see horns growing out of my head, do you."

There was a slight sneer on Leo's face, but his eyes looked frightened. "I'm not afraid of you," he said.

He turned to the others and then he looked back at Tucker. "I didn't think my funeral was going to be a party," he cried.

"Well, my friend." Tucker's tone was harsh and threatening. "I think you got that wrong, don't you."

"All turned around!"

It was Wheelock. He stepped forward and put his arm around

Leo's shoulders and laughed. "What I see is," he said, "this party is getting to be as dull as a funeral. Why not a drink for everybody?" He squeezed Leo's shoulders, and Leo felt the swelling of terror in him halt and begin slowly to subside.

While both Wheelock and McGuinness were preparing the drinks, Mrs. Tucker began to talk. She, too, had understood the fear Leo felt for her husband. "We went to the movies tonight," she said, "but Mr. McGuinness did not get any laughs there." She looked at him tenderly. "Poor little Mickey Mac, his feet hurt him."

"These shoes is too new." McGuinness bent his ankles so that the shoes touched the floor only at the edges. "I can feel my feet cooking in them."

Mrs. Tucker smiled at Leo and looked at the others and smiled again at Leo. "Mr. McGuinness wanted to take off his shoes," she said, "but Ben kept changing his seat to get nearer the stage, so he made poor Mac keep his shoes on."

"That wasn't the only reason Ben made me keep them on," grumbled McGuinness. "They're his shoes. I'm breaking them in for him."

She exploded at that. She laughed for a long time almost hysterically and, at the end, words popped out among her laughter. "Ben," she cried and laughed, "Ben, Ben, Ben," and gasped, "My Ben's crazy," and choked, "wouldn't give Mac's feet," and drew in her breath violently, "an hour off at the movies." She put her hand to her side and looked pained and struggled to stop laughing and then began to laugh all over again. "I can't stop," she said helplessly and exploded once more, and wisps of her blonde hair fell loose and whisked about her warm, pink face.

The men looked at her and then at each other. They began to laugh, too. Even Leo smiled. When Mrs. Tucker saw that, she regained control of herself quickly. "You really should have seen it, Mr. Minch," she said to Leo.

She had a cozy voice. It settled around her listeners like something comfortable. When she wanted to, she could make it sound as if it were snuggling into one's ears, and she made it sound that way now as she looked at Leo and Leo felt himself go out to her.

"Whenever anybody in front got up," she continued, "Ben was down the aisle after the seat, honest to goodness, as if somebody had dropped a match in his pocket, back pocket." She gave Leo a knowing glance, almost as if she had said something wicked, and Leo burst into a laugh. " 'Whiiiis!' Ben would say and poke my ribs and down the aisle he'd go, smoking from the back pocket, with his ears laid back."

She waited for the laughter before resuming: "Well, there was me. I had my wrap and my purse and my whatall, gloves and a program, and down the aisle I'd go after him, catching up everything as I went." She made swift clutches and half rose from the chair. "I don't know what people must have thought except maybe, with all that fur sticking out behind me in the breeze, I was maybe the bearded lady running backwards."

Everybody laughed and, before the laugh died down, Tucker held up his hand excitedly and said, "The one I like best was what you said about that fellow, what was his name, the Italian fellow with the big hooked nose and no teeth. That was real clever. What was it you said, Edna?"

Edna put a vexed expression on her pleased face. She was very pink now and her blue eyes looked sunlit and she sat forward commandingly.

"What was it she said, Mac?" asked Tucker. "You was there."

McGuinness thought a moment. "Something about Ficco's nose looking in his mouth," he said and looked questioningly at Edna.

She waved her hand deprecatingly. "And his nostrils blew back in surprise at what they saw," she finished quickly.

Small laughter followed and she cried into it, "I don't see what's so funny about that." She shifted forward commandingly again, taking charge of the room and making the men in it into an audience.

"After the bearded lady running backwards," she said, "who should come but my little Mickey Mac in Ben's shoes walking like . . ." She clapped her hand to her mouth and rolled her eyes and tittered and they all leaned forward, their lips twitching expectantly. "It's not ladylike, but, excuse me, that's the way it was,

every step he took he gave a little hop up like somebody was . . ."
she prodded her thumb into the air with comical determination,
". . . giving him a goose for Thanksgiving." She sat back luxuriously
as they laughed and stared around with a look as of sunlight pouring from her eyes.

"My corns grew so big," McGuinness explained, "I had to hop
over them."

While they finished their drinks, Tucker took up the notes Wheelock had made and began studying them. Midway he waved the
pages at Mrs. Tucker and she stood up. Wheelock was the only one
to rise with her.

"Take Mac with you," Tucker told her.

Joe and Leo and Wheelock and Tucker followed her out of the
room with their eyes.

"That's one hell of a real fellow," said Tucker suddenly.

Edna heard, but she did not turn around. She kept walking with
a slight, swift, graceful sway, her head high.

"You know how the girls like to do," said Tucker with a pleased
laugh. "They like to make an exit."

Tucker had something of the actor in him, too. He laughed in a
fond way, as if he were pleased to have discovered his wife's weakness and to have exposed it.

Wheelock pressed a button near the fireplace. When the house-
man came, he ordered supper. "I'll ring when we're ready," he said
and turned to his guests. "Unless you fellows would like something
now?"

They all shook their heads and the houseman disappeared. Then
Tucker began to ask questions. He did not ask as many as Wheelock. Some of the questions Joe or Wheelock answered and, when
they did, Tucker checked quickly through the pages of notes
Wheelock had made.

Leo studied him furtively. He had expected his rugged bulk, but
not that he should dress more like himself than like Joe. Yet

Tucker's $22 suit and his $1 shirt and his $6 shoes did not seem to affect his air of authority. He was the boss, thought Leo, a real, regular, hard boss, like a millionaire. Not hard in the way Leo had expected him to be, in a tough-guy way, but hard in a business way —quick to fight to win the least point and unemotional between fights.

Tucker listened attentively to what he was told and took it in and moved on to the next thing with a quick gesture, sometimes of his hand and sometimes of his body. He never seemed to think of anything but money or things connected with making money and, once or twice when Wheelock tried to lighten the heavy going with a little joke, Tucker looked at him blankly as if he hadn't understood what he was saying. Everything about Tucker was businessman. He had a quick, shrewd mind, the power to concentrate with it, the determination to concentrate with it, a certain amount of confidence in himself, enough to make his fighting calculated and unemotional, but not enough to blunt the edge of his lust, his all-consuming need for money; and—best of all—he had what insecurity and its fears can give, an almost complete failure to feel that people were people or were anything at all except things he could use or must fight. It was this that had enabled him to do whatever he had to do to get where he was. Much to Leo's surprise, Tucker didn't seem concerned over the small amount of cash reserve reported. "How long have you been operating on a narrow margin like that?" he asked.

"Quite a few months," Leo told him. "I had more once, but . . ."

"Can you get along on such a reserve?"

"Not very well, but in one way and another, at least until today."

"All right." Tucker looked down at the pages of notes before him. "What I see is," he said, "that I'm buying a broken property, $38,000 worth of debts. Well, this is the way we go ahead. Two-thirds and one-third. Joe goes in there with you to look out for the organization's two-thirds." He held up his hand as Leo started to protest. "Get the whole picture before you say anything," he commanded. "I don't want to waste a lot of time arguing. The $38,000 I put into the business is to be paid back out of the profits. It's a prior lien on the business itself, with regular six per cent interest and a $2,000 bonus for making the loan, and it is to be amortized by the week, so much a week, we'll see what. From your figures and what we can do about cutting expenses, I'd say a thousand a week, but I'll be reasonable and see whether the business can stand it."

"Do you want me to speak frankly, Mr. Tucker?" said Leo.

"That's what I want, everything out."

"All right, I'll tell you then. I call that the worst lousiest partnership offer I ever heard in my life." He stopped and looked around, and Tucker asked him if that was all he had to say.

"No," said Leo. "In the first place, a two thousand dollar bonus for making a thirty-eight thousand dollar loan is bad enough, but amortization every week and six per cent interest? That means, twenty-four per cent, thirty per cent interest, God knows what, like these loan companies that lend to poor people, you got to pay back every week out of salary. Whoever heard of a businessman paying like out of salary? How can you do business like that?"

"Finished now?" asked Tucker as Leo paused.

"No, I'm not. Then, in the second place, what kind of a partnership offer is it to put in your capital to get hold of a business and then pull it out?"

Tucker looked at him indifferently. "I'm not putting capital into the business," he said. "I'm putting in my organization."

"All I can see," said Leo, "is that you're taking my business for nothing and feeling you're generous because you give me back one-third to work for you."

"Just a minute here." Wheelock leaned forward. "As far as I can tell, you haven't got a business."

Leo looked at him fearfully. "You're not going to bulldoze me into anything I don't want," he cried.

"No," said Tucker, "there's not going to be any talk like that around here, not from you," he pointed to Wheelock, "nor from you either." He pointed to Leo. "If you and I, Mr. Minch, are going to establish a monopoly up there in policy, we can't start off being small. My organization is going to cut the costs on the legal end—

what is it averaging you?" He looked at the notes. Leo had paid out a little more than $40,000 the year before for bail bonds and lawyer's fees for arrested collectors and almost $15,000 to policemen for protection. "You got a $55,000 bill here," said Tucker, "and that's the first place we cut. My organization pays its own way. It will have to pay its own way. The money isn't going to come out of your pocket, is it? No, the organization pays itself out of what it saves you.

"Now then, when we go in there, things is going to run up there on a businesslike basis. For instance, to take one thing, there is not going to be any more of that stuff about shortages, overages, whatever you call them. The controllers and collectors will all be working for one corporation and, if they can't shoot crap with their own money, they won't work. There won't be anybody waiting for them across the street to put them to work. I think, for another example, thirty per cent commission is too much for those fellows and they ought to be cut. Things like that. You can't do it by yourself. Maybe we can cut the payoff, too, down to 500-to-1, instead of 600-to-1 and give ourselves more spread. Things like that, but you got to have an organization for that. You got to have everybody in line and keep them there. That's what my organization will do to earn its share in the partnership, and if you take your own figures here and not figure in any increase in business, even though the business ought to increase if the players have confidence that everything is stabilized, but take your own figures on what we'll save for you and you'll see your one-third ought to be bigger than when you had the whole thing and ran it independent with a lot of other independents fighting you."

"We didn't need it before," said Leo. "We got along all right without a monopoly."

"Well, we'll get along better now. Until the $38,000 with six per cent and $2,000 bonus is paid off, there is not going to be much profits. I see that. You can have a drawing account as against the profits, $75 a week. We'll split up quarterly on the surplus."

"I need more than that to live on," cried Leo. "I need a hundred with my expenses, maybe a hundred and a quarter."

"You'll get it out of the profits on the quarterly split-up. In the meantime, seventy-five will have to do."

"No, Mr. Tucker, you're not going to pull a trick like that on me. I'm not a baby in negotiations, getting me to argue on some small point and then giving in and agreeing and that settles the whole thing. No sir, I've done negotiations before in my life."

"I don't have to try tricks on you," said Tucker. "If you don't want to join the combination, okay. Try and do business your way. That's up to you."

"I need a hundred and a quarter to live on," said Leo, "and I think you ought to put capital into the cash reserve."

They argued a long time. Wheelock was still drinking. He got up after a while and, a highball glass in his hand, walked with slow, short, loose steps into the room where Mrs. Tucker was sitting with McGuinness, listening to the radio. Tucker looked after him. He seemed worried. Joe was arguing for Leo, and Tucker suddenly shook his head.

"That boy is going to kill himself one day," he said in a low tone, "with all the booze he hits."

"It's his funeral," said Joe. "I'll send the flowers."

"I've noticed that before, that you don't like him," Tucker said.

"We get along all right."

"You'd better, if you're going to be in this thing together."

"We'll be all right. He sticks to the legal end and I stick to the business end and we get along fine."

Tucker shook his head again. "I want to see cooperation there." He turned to Leo. "Well, all right, a hundred. Make your drawing account a hundred. The hell with it." He lifted his head. "Henry," he shouted. "Hey, Henry."

Leo realized abruptly it had happened as he had expected. Perhaps he had wanted it to happen. Perhaps both he and Tucker had wanted it. Anyway, it had been done. They had argued on a small point. When Tucker had given in on that, the whole thing was over. Leo's business was in Tucker's hands.

"That's some high pressure merchant," thought Leo. The inside

of his head began to swirl as he tried excitedly to poke through
the maze of remembered snatches of their conversation.

Wheelock entered the room slowly. "Coming up," he said. "Coming up boiled on toast." He still had the highball glass in his
hand. He lifted it high. "Boiled on toasts. Here's to success, money,
plenty monies, all that jolly kind of old thing, success and plenty
monies, plenty womans." He smiled and his face looked soft and
relaxed from his talk with Edna. His glass was empty and he went
to the table and filled it.

"I want you to be in on this, Henry," said Tucker. "You three
are going to make the deals for the other banks."

"Three musketeers," said Wheelock, "with muskets."

Tucker didn't pay any attention to him. His mind was too fixed
on what he was going to say. He turned to Leo. "You, too, Mr.
Minch," he said, "because whatever is broken you get the pieces.
I want your bank to be built up to number one in the combination.
Now, this has to go this way: Everything goes on the same basis—
two-thirds and one-third and the same bonus and amortization as
with Mr. Minch here; the banker gets $60 a week drawing account
against the split-up of the surplus every three months; you can go
to $75 if necessary, but that's the roof and no exceptions; if they
haven't got confidence enough in the business to wait for their
money out of the profits, then we don't want them; I want all their
books audited and I want every penny of their cash reserve left
in the business; the cash reserves will be put into one pot for the
whole combination—that will make the bookkeeping simpler and
spread the strain in case one bank gets a sock on a certain day."

Tucker looked at Leo and Leo looked back at him steadily, feeling all the blood puddle in his face and all the nerves go tight in
him. Here it was. Here was when his $31,000 cash reserve was
taken from him.

"I think we can leave Mr. Minch to take care that they don't
cheat us on the cash reserves," said Tucker. "He seems to know all
the ways there are about that."

The nerves twanged loose in Leo. The puddle of blood swept out of his face. The $31,000 under the floor of the closet in his bedroom was safe. He understood now that Tucker knew about it, but was going to let him keep it.

"I'll get every penny out of them for you, Mr. Tucker," said Leo. His voice trembled with gratitude. "You can trust me."

"Trust you?" Tucker looked at Leo in a sly, nearly benevolent way. He felt satisfied that Leo would scratch deep to build back the cash reserve of his own unit and scratch deep for the cash reserves of the other units. "I never trust anybody. Now listen, if you decide against a bank, not to advance it money and let it fold up, the collectors and controllers are shifted over to the Minch unit. But before you do it, I want to hear about it, either from Joe or Wheelock. That's because I don't trust you, Mr. Minch, or your brother here."

"That's not fair, Ben," said Joe.

"No, maybe I was kidding. But I don't think we ought to be shortsighted in this and we ought to go slow about letting banks fold up. I don't want there to be a whole lot of hard feelings stirred up against me by putting too many people out of business."

"As a matter of fact," said Wheelock, "I've been thinking we ought to go further than that. There will be a lot of animosity anyway, at first at least, and we ought to have our own bank outside the combination operating independently."

"For Christ sake," said Joe, "what the hell good will that be?"

Wheelock didn't pay any attention to him. He looked at Tucker.

"Henry's right," decided Tucker. "It's the way to get the sorehead business from the customers who are sore at us. You should have thought of it yourself, Joe. That's the business end."

"I still think it's dumb," said Joe. He looked at Wheelock angrily.

"Whatever you think," Tucker told him, "I want it done. You and Leo look around for a banker that we can tie up like that. And remember what I said about being shortsighted. I don't want everybody out of business and only a Minch bank left up there."

❦

There were a few more details to be straightened out. One of them was the case against Leo and his bank. Wheelock made a note of it and said not to worry and that he would represent Leo at the hearing.

Then Leo said goodbye and Joe went with him to drive him home. They walked past the room in which Mrs. Tucker and McGuinness were sitting. McGuinness had his shoes off and his feet on the windowsill. The window was open and he held his feet against the cold night air. He turned around in his chair and waved. "Edna give me permission to knock off work on Ben's shoes," he said.

Edna Tucker rose and walked towards them.

"You got a real humor," Leo told her, "a real dry sense of humor, very dry. It's been an enjoyment to listen to you."

"What a nice thing to say!" She smiled. "I'm sure you're going to find my husband a fine man to do business with. He has a temper sometimes, but I suppose everybody has. You, too, Mr. Minch."

"Terrible," said Leo. "I'm ashamed of myself." Then he added earnestly, "I'm sure you wouldn't be his wife without he's a fine man."

"Oh my, oh my, oh my." She fluttered her eyes and pressed her hand faintly to her heart.

Joe and Leo had to wait a long time for the elevator. The hall was wide and its walls were papered green and, hung along it, were small, framed pictures of estate lawns and dogs with sad faces and horses jumping.

"You begin to see the possibilities now, don't you?" said Joe.

"I see that I had a business when I came up here and now I'm working for Tucker for salary."

"You'll see, when the combination has the field organized, your third will be . . . well, figure it out yourself and then maybe you'll kick your pants off, making me wait in the foyer, I'm not good enough to go in your house."

"Please," said Leo. "I'm tired. I'm falling down from sleep."

The elevator man looked sullen. He smelled sour from sleep. While the elevator sank slowly and soundlessly, Leo thought of all

he had talked about tonight. Phrases knocked in his head, and
Tucker's face and Wheelock's face and Mrs. Tucker and McGuinness sitting with ankles turned so that the edges of his shoes rested
against the floor. "It was funny," he thought, "but hard, too, not
to give that man's feet an hour off from work in the movies."

He saw the faces of the bankers who would be put out of business—Cordeles, certainly, Richards, maybe; maybe Carroll and
Williamson, too. They were people whose wives and children he
knew. There would be no more crap games with company money.
Edgar. What would Edgar think when they cut his $22 allowance?
And the people wouldn't smile any more when he came into the
room. He'd have to be a real hard man now, getting himself a
million dollars, and they'd all think he was one hell of a real,
regular big league son of a bitch.

"I don't want it," he cried to himself wearily and never told himself whether he didn't want the million dollars or didn't want the
people to stop smiling when they saw him.

The gilt, mirrored lobby was stale and airless and, when they
got into the street, Leo shuddered. "Getting to be regular winter,"
he thought, but he hadn't shuddered at the cold. He had shuddered at the feeling of death in the dark, stone-shrouded, expensive
quiet all about him. He didn't like what the rich had to go through
to get their money, and he didn't like what they bought with it
once they got it.

Joe pointed to a big, square, red-faced man in a felt hat sleeping
in the car behind his. It was Tucker's car. "That's Johnston," he
said. "He used to be in the navy and then he drove a speedboat
for Tucker from Windsor to Detroit for real high-class alcohol
during prohibition."

Johnston's head was far back so that it faced the roof of the car.
His mouth was open. Leo looked at him. "How long has Wheelock
been with Tucker?" he asked.

"About three years, something like that. Tucker made him rich
overnight."

Leo glanced up and down the street. There wasn't a single human being on it except themselves. "If I get a million," he thought, "this is where I'll live."

The street looked like a path through a petrified forest.

"All the things a man has to go through to get to live here," thought Leo, "the things, the things, thousands and millions and millions of dirty things to hurt people and hurt himself."

The street seemed drowned in stone. It looked narrow and drowned, a thing emptied of life and walled with swollen, stone bones. The feeling of costly desolation was heavy in Leo. This costly desolation was splendor, but Leo did not think of it as splendid. Yet he tried to be faithful to the rich. He tried to think of the costly desolation as good for sleep. Only the rich could afford to buy quiet like this in the heart of the city, he told himself. He felt suddenly that only a man who had made himself rich could become barren enough to want and be comfortable in this desolation.

As Leo stepped away from the walls of the rich, he noticed the little hedge. His eyes rested on it gratefully. "It's a pretty thing to have in front of your house," he told Joe.

He liked it partly because he felt he shouldn't have thought about the rich as he had. Rich was what everybody wanted to be, and everybody respected and envied the rich.

Joe looked at the hedge and was stirred as the dogs of the rich were stirred. "That reminds me," he said. "I need a leak."

AN AMERICAN HERO'S SON

VIII

LATER, HENRY C. WHEELOCK was to become known as a lurid man. Now he seemed merely unexpected. His mind was more talented than that of those around him, and the mind, of course, is not merely an instrument. It is itself alive. Just as man is shaped by the world and shapes it, so his mind is shaped by events and shapes them. Thus, although Henry's mind had endured approximately the same disasters as the minds of his associates, it had had the talent to work these disasters into something quite unexpected to those with whom he was in business.

Henry had been born and brought up in a small town in the western timber country. The big lumber companies had moved in before he was born and had prepared his world for him. They had made a lot of people happy with money that could build a village into a town, pave streets, put up stores and a factory and sawmills, a big brick depot and sidewalks. Like all who are so involved in the game of business that they can become big in it, the lumber magnates had no thought of people as people or as anything but tools or opponents. So they plundered the forests and got theirs out of it and, when the getting was no longer good, they moved to new timber country.

Their tools and opponents followed, but the village that had been built into a town could not follow. The town stayed along its sidewalks. The people whose day as tools or opponents of the lumber magnates was over walked along the sidewalks. The stores stood planted, and all around the people and the stores and the hotel and the big brick depot was the forest, gaped open like a looted safe.

Henry's father, Roger, owned the hotel. The elder Wheelock

had known what the big lumber people were up to, but he hadn't been able to figure out what to do about it. His object was to hold on to what he had. He had decided if he owned the hotel all free and clear, then he would be safe. So he had put everything he had earned back into the hotel and had got it free and clear of all mortgages. But that hadn't helped. After the lumber people went, he had had to borrow on the hotel to get enough money to keep it going.

Roger Wheelock spent more than twenty years of his life going backward in this way, the twenty years in which Henry remained with him. The old man kept getting pushed backward little by little, each year a little more, and, whenever he made a step back, he knew there was no chance to regain what he had lost. There wasn't even a chance that next year he wouldn't be pushed back some more. Just the same, he kept trying. He threw everything he could grab up into the fight to stand still and finally he began throwing his family into it—first his wife, then his daughter, then his two older sons and, at the end, his baby, his favorite, Henry.

From knowing what was going to happen and from watching it happen, the face of the senior Wheelock became pinched and cranky-looking. He wore a frock coat to work and rimless glasses and, as he walked around the hotel or stood behind the desk welcoming patrons, he had the appearance of a relaxed undertaker. It did not help business, nor did it hurt it. His was the only big hotel in town.

Mrs. Wheelock, Henry's mother, had a round, rather puffy face and colorless lips. She was an ailing woman, and a look of reproach seemed to be fixed on her face. She met all the events of the day with it. Even when she laughed, she seemed to be reproachful, as if she were thinking while laughing that her laughter was only temporary.

The old man had been a fun-loving hell-raiser once upon a time. But, for as far back as Henry could remember, there was hardly any juice left in him. What was left squirted out in little remarks that were more bitter than funny. After Roger had had to cut his staff and bring in his wife to help out, he said that he and Martha got to look the way they did from marching into occupied rooms armed with a bible instead of a house detective.

In passing, it might be noted that the remark had a career familiar to remarks made in small towns. The remark went around town. Then it was forgotten. But it gave the Wheelocks a name for being too holy. That was what remained in people's minds. However, the Wheelocks weren't religious at all. They went to church only to keep up the reputation of the hotel. They looked religious because they were worried.

Henry was the bright one of the family. He bit into learning the way an axe bites into yellow pine. Because of that and because he was the favorite, he was the one sent off to Madison to college. His father had met and been impressed by a lot of lumber company lawyers and had never talked anything but law to his boy. Roger was sure Henry would become quite a lawyer. None of the lumber company lawyers had a quicker mind than Henry. The boy got hold of a proposition and saw around it and was off to what followed before the proposition was all the way out of a person's mouth. Besides, practically everybody liked Henry right away, and the big lawyers had said this was more important than knowing law or being smart. They said you could buy law books and rent fellows who were law books, but you could not buy clients. The only way to get clients was to make them like you.

When even the sawmills nearest town started closing and the branch of the furniture company that advertised "From Forest To You" moved away and the railroad cut its passenger train schedules in half, Henry told his father he wanted to quit fooling around in school and begin earning some money. He had then finished his second year at Madison and was home for the summer vacation.

"I don't need your ten dollars a week or whatever you could make," Roger said. "You stay out of the way in school. We've been watching this thing come and we know just how to lick it."

The town had decided it could get along without trees. It was starting mink farming and fox farming and a lot of other businesses and was putting up a kitty for the state to run a tourist bureau that would talk up the wood country as a vacation land.

"There is plenty of fight left in this town," Roger told his boy. "When we have a fight on our hands, we don't want to be tripping over lads who should be out of the way in school."

Roger wanted Henry to have a chance. His daughter had married the assistant cashier of the bank that held the mortgage on the hotel, and he never could get over the feeling that he and Martha were more responsible for the marriage than his daughter had been. The girl hadn't been able to make up her mind one way or the other for a long time and then finally she said she guessed she might as well marry him. Roger wondered if she ever would have said that if there had been no mortgage on the hotel and he and Martha had not seemed so anxious for the marriage and hadn't worked so hard to give the couple chances to be together.

"I want you to be happy, girl," Roger told his daughter, "and not be in a rush to make up your mind."

"I'm not rushing."

That was true. Lucy had had plenty of time to think it over. She had known the man all her life and they had been keeping steady company for three years before they announced their engagement. Just because the marriage worked out to be a good thing for the whole family as well as for the one who did the marrying was no reason to think it had been arranged for the family's good.

So, following the wife, Martha, the daughter, Lucy, was thrown into the fight to keep the hotel. The two older brothers were trapped in the campaign to diversify the town's industries. They had taken part of the hotel's mortgage money and had borrowed some more from the bank and had started a mink farm together. The oldest boy, Andrew, did not like it. He was a fun-loving hell-raiser the way his father had been and he wanted city life. But, like his father, he had married and settled down, and the mink farm seemed to do him. Jefferson, the second son, didn't marry. However, he was like his mother, born settled, and wherever he was put was where he would stay.

Henry was kept out of the fight until the last. But, in the end, another portion of the mortgage money had been used to continue him at Madison and he was sucked in, too. After his second year at college, there wasn't any more mortgage money left. It was decided Henry would leave college and go to law school in New York. It was felt that, if he were studying in New York, he could start making the friendships that would be useful to him when he went into practice. Besides, it was easier to find a job there that would pay part of his expenses.

"Go where the honey is, my boy," said his father, "but be careful you don't get stung."

Soon after he arrived in New York, Henry got a letter from his father asking him to be sure to send home certified copies of his school marks.

"I like to brag around a bit," Roger wrote, "and you know how our estmd. fellow townsmen are. They are d—n (for darn, of course,) fools. They do not believe in Ingersoll and they do not believe in our Lord, Jesus Christ. They do not believe in the nose on their face until they catch cold there."

Roger took the certified copy of the marks down to Mr. Hyde, the banker who held the mortgage. He and Ellis Hyde were old friends and Roger knew that, if the worst came, his son-in-law would see to it somehow that the hotel wasn't foreclosed. But the country was dying in the bank's hands. Trying to get other businesses started in the community had loaded the bank up with commercial paper, most of it long term. Besides, the hotel's value had depreciated so steeply that, whenever the mortgage had to be renewed, it became more difficult to get it past the examiners. Roger brought in Henry's marks to cheer himself up and to cheer up Ellis. He wanted to show Ellis there was more collateral on the mortgage than just the hotel and, with all the things worrying him, it felt good to see Ellis study the results of his boy's work.

"He looks like a comer," said Ellis.

Roger felt suddenly that Henry was his last hope. His other boys were stuck on the mink farm. They would never do more than make a living for themselves. His son-in-law and daughter were fastened to a small, struggling bank that couldn't expect more than to survive, in Roger's lifetime at least.

"A real, humdinging comer," said Roger, "if I do say so myself."
Henry began to understand what his father felt when, after
suggesting once more, in a letter this time, that he quit school and
go to work, Roger replied: "These marks are worth more to me
than any ten or twenty dollars a week you could bring in. I want
to see your shingle flying in the breeze like a banner of gold and
that's all I ask out of what's left of my life. That's all any of us
back here in the sticks—or, to be specific, stumps—want out of you."

For as long as he could remember, Henry had had the feeling
of money being scarce with no chance of its ever getting anything
but scarcer. So he didn't resent the starved life he led in New York
to put himself through school. However, although he didn't react
badly, his mind did. It became hectic. He was working too hard
and he wasn't eating enough and he wasn't sleeping well. He
became more nervous. His mind felt frayed. He couldn't shake off
the idea that his father had mortgaged the hotel to give him a
schooling and that it was up to him to make good now.

When Henry looked back on this period, he laughed at the
strange trick his mind had played on him. It had made him race
his books. The hero had had to get through the books to foil old
villain Ellis Hyde with the papers and, when the hero turned the
last page of the last book, the villain must slink off foiled.

But, at the time it was happening, there was no laughter in it.
Henry fretted himself to sleep with thoughts of how, when the
last page of the last book was turned, he'd go out and do it,
do it sure. When he fell asleep, he dreamed of winning his first
case, a big one, with a big fee. The jury came in and announced
the judgment and the client, who had gray hair and a brown face
like Mr. Hyde, rushed up with the big fee and slammed it down
so hard right there on the table in the courtroom that the pile of
yellowbacks slapped like a whip and woke him up.

If Henry had entered one of the big Eastern law schools, there
might have been a chance for everything to work out. But these
schools required three years in their own colleges for admission
and four years if a student went to college elsewhere. Henry had
been able to complete only two years of college. If he had won

his honors in a big school instead of in night school, he would have been offered a good job the day he was graduated. But, when he was admitted to the bar, the best job he could find paid $30 a week. He turned it down. It wasn't enough money to help. To do any good, he had to get hold of a real lump of money.

He borrowed a few hundred dollars and opened an office for himself. This was another mistake his sensitive, fevered mind tricked him into. But his mind couldn't permit him to take a job and work up conventionally. It was too driven by the way things were at home.

Henry slept in his office to reduce expenses. It was against building regulations and he had to leave the office in the evening and stay out until late and then sneak back and go to sleep in a sleeping bag he had used before on camping trips. He kept the sleeping bag under his desk during the day and he used to get baths in the apartment of a friend.

Hardly anybody came into the office. He had a lot of time to look out the window and think. "Brains is not enough," he told himself, "but it's enough for this."

Henry sat there nearly a year, thinking about the dying town and the dying hotel and the long fight his father had made. Roger knew the end, his son thought, the minute the big lumber companies started working on the forests. He saw the day and he tried to prepare for it. He got his hotel all paid off and he thought that would be the rock he would stand on. Then the rock began to sink and he had to fight to hold the rock up. It was a hopeless fight. He was a man holding up something that was holding up him. The old man must have known it would be hopeless and must have known it was hopeless, but he kept right on with it. It was heroic. It was a life to which music should be played.

"There's the American hero all right," thought Henry, "an old, cranky-looking guy in a frock coat, sitting out in a town, trying to help set right the wrongs of the big fellows. And the hero's son sits here!"

This was boom time in New York. Henry sat looking out the window and the big, rich city hung before him, fat as a ham, smoky with juice, sweating money. The feel of money was spread all over the city like air. When he went into the street, he breathed the smell of money. He saw money on people's faces and, whenever they talked, he heard money. The whole world was a sack of money that had split open. Everybody was getting his face into it. Everybody was hogs plunging for the sack and rooting in it, grunting and crunching and slopping over it. Their feet on the pavement as they rushed about their business made a noise like snouts slapping into swill. When they went home at night, their faces looked pink as suckling pigs. They shone with money, and their bellies swung from their ribs like bags of gold. And there the hero's son sat, looking at them, unable to move. He sat still to feel the dust settle on him.

There were some clients, enough to pay the rent, but the most frequent interruptions were from salesmen and process servers looking for work and the mailman with advertisements and bills and letters from home.

"I don't want you to feel that you are being pushed by anyone or that anyone back here is getting impatient," his father wrote. "Slow and sure. That is still the quickest way there. I know what it is for a young man to find a place for himself in a crowded city. There is no one pushing you, boy. Be happy. It's adventure. To begin to realize on your future is the great adventure of a lifetime. No one in the world has a right to push you. Just go slow and sure and am sure you know that our hearts are with you. Our hearts are all with you, boy, and they are not pushing you, just being with you as you go along nice and easy and slow and sure."

Henry read the letter four times. He had a mind as sensitive and kind as his father's. Each time, the picture of his father writing the letter at the desk in the lobby became sharper.

"He must have just come back from the bank," thought Henry, "or he wouldn't have written a letter like this." He threw it down on the desk before him. "What the hell does he expect me to do?" he cried to himself. "I'm trying, trying, sitting here trying the best I can."

He took up the letter again and examined the writing. It was florid and firm, the ends all firmly curled in the style his father had been taught. "It would be," Henry told himself. "He would hold on to himself whatever happened."

Thick tears spurted into his eyes. They were thick as pulp from a squashed grape. With a furtive, quick motion, he lifted the letter to his face and brushed his lips against it and felt foolish and better.

A short while later, there was a letter from Andrew, the fun-loving brother. "Dear kid, Just a line," and so forth, and something about "the minks still feel like fur-inners in these parts," and then at the end: "We have raised every cent we can anywhere to keep the hotel and I thought maybe you could get your hands on a little money in New York to help out if you knew that it was really a serious situation. It is very serious. As you know, Dad is very set on keeping the hotel although it is only good as a place where the wind can go in to get warm. I don't want you to think that because there is a little joking around in this letter that I don't mean what I said. I mean it very seriously, because it is serious. But you know me. I have to have a laugh sometimes or go crazy and become a minkompoop, all minkompooped out, my minkom-poopsy."

When the bank finally took over the hotel, Roger was asked to stay on as manager. Ellis fought for that and got it for him.

"It's really very much better than I expected," Roger told his wife. "I've been managing for them, actually, for twenty years, for all the money I got out of it for myself, and now they have to pay me for doing it."

But he died soon after, one week and four days before his sixty-second birthday. Henry came home for the funeral. He was really surprised when his mother refused to allow Mr. Hyde to attend the services. "He is your father's murderer," she said. She was convinced Ellis wanted to come only to shed fake tears to hide his guilt.

Henry thought of the long friendship between his father and Mr. Hyde and how the banker, even though he was not at fault, must naturally feel guilty and must want some way to work the feeling off. He thought of his brother-in-law who still worked in the bank, as cashier now, and who, if he lost his job, would not be able to find another one in the town. How would a thing like this react on him? Henry explained to his mother that she must put aside her feelings for the sake of her daughter and grand-children and son-in-law.

"I've put aside my feelings all my life," Martha said. "If I ever lay eyes on your father's murderer again, I will go and get a gun and shoot him dead."

Mrs. Wheelock went to live with her sons on the mink farm. There was too much feeling against her in the house of her son-in-law.

"She'll be at home here," said Andrew, "with all the mortgages to preserve the atmosphere."

Andrew was beginning to get the cranky look that had marked his father's face. There wasn't any fun in him any more. He just liked to say things to show he was witty.

"I'm going to send all I can for mother," Henry told him, "and don't worry about the mortgages. I regard them as my responsibility."

The laughter dropped out of Andrew's face. He looked earnest in an uneasy way, as if he were ashamed of his earnestness. "It's only right that you should," he said, "you getting that money for college and all."

Henry was annoyed. He didn't have to be reminded that the mink farm had paid back the money it had borrowed from the hotel and then had gone deeper into debt for the hotel. Nor did he have to be reminded that he himself hadn't paid back anything. Henry found he didn't like the whole town and the people in it. Up close, it didn't seem heroic. It seemed crippled and full of hate and stupid. It was a sucker town. The people's energy seemed to be for hating and hurting each other. They spent all their time gouging dimes out of their neighbors. They lived like animals in a slaughterhouse—fighting, fornicating, tearing at each other for a place to stay, forgetful of what had happened to them, knowing only what they were doing. Henry was glad to get back to his empty office in New York.

After his return from the funeral, two members of a bakery union brought Henry a case involving the illegal election of the officers of a local. He knew the moment they walked in they couldn't pay anything. They were bread bakers who worked from midnight to late in the morning and had come to him directly from their work. The flour was stuck in their pores and in their eyelashes and their skin was so white they looked bled.

They said they knew they couldn't pay anything down as a retainer, but this was an open and shut case of crookedness and, if Henry won it, they'd be able to get a fee for him out of the union's treasury. Henry took the case because it was something to do. He didn't want to be a labor lawyer. There was no money in that. But, in the meantime, he had to be some kind of a lawyer.

The union, it turned out, was run by Ben Tucker. The officers who had stolen the election were some of Tucker's people.

Tucker was not made in one day either. Yet there was a single day when something happened to Tucker that made him decide what to do with himself. Up to then, he had been fooling around with one job and another, trying to find a place where he fitted and not finding it and not minding much, satisfied enough with being married to Edna and with paying his bills and staying out of trouble. But that day he learned what to do to make a place for himself where he could fit, and he didn't fool around any more.

This happened in a mill town in New Jersey a little before the war when Tucker was in his early twenties. On that day, the National Guard sat in the armory four blocks down the avenue, and the Mayor sat in his office a half mile away saying no, saying the strikers were behaving orderly and the police could handle them all right and he was not going to call out the soldier boys when it wasn't necessary. The Mayor had said that in the newspapers; and then the Company had said in the newspapers that the Mayor had sold out to the anarchist-socialists and the town was in the hands of bomb-throwing foreign agitators. The Company was a foreign agitator itself because the mill was only one of its branches and its main office was in New York, but it was throwing whatever it could find. It didn't think it could break the strike without the help of the National Guard.

The strikers knew all about what was going on. They were not making any trouble that could give the soldier boys an excuse to come out of the armory. Except that, during lunch hour, when the machines stopped, they piled up outside the fence a block deep—men and women, holding up their children, holding up their empty dinner pails with the covers off, banging their pails and stamping their feet and hollering, "Come out, scabs!" over and over again. The noise made Tucker weak.

The first time it happened, almost a quarter of the scabs picked up and walked out, saying they'd rather go hungry than be in the hospital. And the Company said it was going to get the National Guard out to protect the loyal workers if it had to take that I Won't Work down in the City Hall, that bomb-throwing red atheistic socialist-anarchist by the slack of his pants and bounce him on a bayonet.

All the hired specials had their orders for the big push. When it was twelve o'clock lunch time again and the strikers were starting their noise outside again, Tucker, who was one of the new specials, ran on back to McGrady's office. McGrady was vice president in charge of personnel for the Company. He had been an officer in the Cuba war and had come over from New York to hire the guards himself and run the show himself because it made him feel like the good old Cuba times.

Tucker ran through the mill room. The super was standing on a platform yelling, "There's going to be shots. Don't worry! There's going to be shots over the heads of the strikers. Don't worry! The shots's just to scare the strikers away. Don't worry! This company takes care of its loyal workers." Tucker ran without listening. He passed through the areaway leading to the stock room where the specials were collecting.

McGrady had decided against loading the place with city hard guys because that might get the Company in wrong. So he had hired college boys and some fellows like Tucker, workers temporarily out of work and ready to do what they could for eating purposes. But, to show the amateurs the ropes, McGrady had thrown in a few professionals. These were McGrady's sergeants and now he gave them vomit-gas grenades and gave the amateurs lengths of lead pipe and said, "Get going, men. Push the enemy the hell away from that gate."

The specials piled on back through the mill room, a little knot of them, running hard at the double past the white-faced scabs, and ran down the front steps of the building to the yard. "This is going to be a killing," thought Tucker and told himself he wasn't going to do it, he was going to quit right now. But he ran with the others. They all ran together, one pressing the other, the professionals pressing the amateurs and McGrady pressing the professionals. And in the back of Tucker's mind was the speech the boss had made and how he had said they were going to replace their staff with acceptable men from the group who helped win the strike for them. Tucker wanted a steady job at this time. He was crazy hungry for a job and this was in him, too, along with fear and the desire to quit, and all of it kept rolling over and over inside of him while he ran towards the ear-filling, pouring roar of the strikers.

"Come out, scabs!" the strikers were roaring. "Scabs! Scabs! Come on out, scabs! Scabs! Scabs, come on out of there!"

"We're coming," yelled McGrady from fifty feet away.

Then Tucker heard the shots, four of them, from a window on the second floor. He had never heard shots before in sunlight. Each one knocked like a rock inside his heart.

For a moment the noise of the crowd stopped. Then it began again, one man here and another there, a group here and a group there until everybody was swinging into it and giving all their throats to it.

One of the specials opened the big front gate. The gate swung inward, but the strikers did not come in with it. Instead, they

swayed back a little, quietly, passively, without resistance. Then the
specials were out among them, pushing. "Keep moving!" they said
and pushed. "Come on! Keep moving!"

Tucker saw a fat woman's face sweat before him and saw, above
her face, a child's hot, red, sweating face. Both their mouths were
open. He knew they were screaming, but he couldn't hear the
words. All he could hear was a bellow that crushed his ears. He
pushed at weak, yielding bodies and saw reddened eyes looking
at him frightened.

"Come on!" he said. "Break it up! Keep moving! Break it up!"

The crowd began to dissolve. The women and the kids and
some of their men were getting back out of the way and other men
were gathering in quiet little watchful groups. The roar was quiet-
ing down. Then Tucker heard a scuffle alongside him, slapping,
thudding noises, a woman shouting at the top of her voice, "George!
My George! You George! Don't! Don't! You George! Come out
of that!"

Tucker was afraid to turn his head to see what was happening.
He was afraid to lose sight of the red eyes in front of him and
of the frightened-looking, yielding men. He held the lead pipe in
one hand and pushed with the other. Sometimes the pipe felt heavy
and sometimes he didn't know he had it. His eyes hurt when he
moved them, but he couldn't stop moving them because he had
to see everything. Any little thing might be serious. He could feel
murder growing in the men in front of him. Any little thing
might mean it had broken loose and was out to get him. Then a
brick went through glass off somewhere in back of him and another brick clattered along the open space at his side. He didn't
turn his head. He was afraid to, but he was afraid not to, as well,
because it might be that right now, just at this minute, someone
back there or someone to the side was aiming to give it to him.

Something soft and flurried came up against him in back and
he pushed at it hard with his elbow, not looking, and felt as if the
top of his head was being blown off with sudden fear and then,
right at that moment, a little man standing in front of him, a
thin, big-nosed, yellow-faced man with steaming eyes, opened up.

He looked right at Tucker and started screaming. "Killers! Killers!" he screamed. Tucker couldn't take any more. He hit the man across the mouth with the lead pipe. The man's whole, thin, screaming face seemed to fall into his mouth. "Move on!" Tucker said. "Break it up! Keep moving!" There was pushing and shoving and the sound of feet trampling.

"Move on!" Tucker said. He felt a wiry, straining, thrashing, flopping-around fight go on inside himself to keep himself from breaking out and screaming and killing. He was holding the lead pipe high, ready to hit the man again if the man came for him. A brick knocked the pipe out of his hand. Pain shot down his arm and went stinging up through the side of his face and into his head. He stooped and fumbled around for the pipe, keeping an eye on the man he had hit.

The man came for Tucker as Tucker stooped. He came all thin and spread out and loose. He stuck his skinny knee into Tucker's face and hit the back of Tucker's neck with his thin fist, and Tucker backed up. He backed, crouching, still feeling for the lead pipe, and came against a car and turned desperately to see what it was and banged his head on the door handle. He felt screaming inside his head, as though his brain were screaming, and rolled sideways and got around the man. The man stood looking at Tucker. His feet were spread wide.

"You want to be dead?" screamed Tucker.

The man didn't say anything. He couldn't get words through the blood. He couldn't close his mouth. His jaw was broken. He started to come in. His arms were flailing. He landed a punch high on Tucker's face between the temples and the cheekbone. His fist was as soft as a splash of water. Tucker kicked the man in the groin with his shoe as hard as he could. The man popped like a grape and doubled up and Tucker slammed his knee into the man's face. The man twisted sideways and fell, twisting, and Tucker leaped and landed all over him. He hit until he felt the bones of the man's face wabble under his hands. The man did not move any more except as Tucker pulled him.

Somebody grabbed Tucker and pulled him to his feet. "Come

on," he said. "It's all over." Tucker heard McGrady yelling, "Get those cameras! Smash those cameras," and realized the cameras had been pointing at him. He looked away. He saw the body he had just been beating and knew by the peculiar way the legs lay that he had beaten it to death.

"He had it coming to him," he said. He turned and grabbed the arm of the special by his side. "I give him what he asked for," he cried. The special did not answer.

Tucker saw men standing in a little knot on a street corner. They were yelling at him. A hundred yards back of them was a straggly line of men and back of them were others and others and others, thickening into a vast mass. Bedlam went up from them and rolled swollen over the air.

"Go to hell," screamed Tucker. "Go kill yourself, you murdering bastards." He started for them alone, his empty fists raised. He wanted to die on them, but he was grabbed and pulled back and held.

Then the soldiers came riding up from the other direction. They bumped along under their tin hats, boys mostly, looking serious and frightened. Their officers held revolvers that they started to fire into the air and the boys had long riot sticks.

"They'll break it up," McGrady said. "They're trained troops."

Tucker wasn't struggling to break loose any more. He stood looking at the soldiers and the people scattering and eddying into small groups and dissolving under the horses' hoofs.

When the specials got back to the factory, there were basins of cold water waiting for them alongside clean little individual towels and clean little individual cakes of white soap. Tucker washed his face and hands and got the blood off, but he couldn't get the feel of fever out of his skin. The fever burned through the cold water even as he splashed it over his face.

"Here you, what's your name," McGrady said to him. "I want to talk to you."

"All right, Chief, a minute," Tucker answered.

McGrady went into his headquarters in back, believing Tucker would follow him, but Tucker couldn't get hold of himself. Instead of following, he went out through the mill room where the scabs were standing on tiptoe looking out the windows while the super and the floor bosses yelled for them to go back to work and walked up wide stone stairs to the main office. A group of men and girls were standing around a desk talking. They looked at Tucker and stopped talking and he was afraid suddenly of what they might say about him.

"They don't know yet," he told himself and put his chest out and frowned and swaggered past them, the way a soldier had a right to before people he had saved from the enemy.

"Here," one of the men said, "you can't go in there."

But the man was frightened and did not come near Tucker and Tucker swaggered right on through the open door onto a soft carpet and saw a man standing looking out the window. The man turned around slowly. Tucker had his hand on the telephone on the big desk. "What are you doing in here where you don't belong?" the man said and he was so surprised and so indignant and so scared that his voice squeaked.

"I'm using your phone," Tucker said and was surprised, too, because he had growled.

Tucker called long distance and gave his home number in New York and lost sight of the man and the man's round, pink, well-fed face with the scowl stuck into it in a funny way, like an apple in a roasted pig's mouth.

"Hello," Tucker said when he heard Edna's voice. "How are you?"

"I'm fine. Who's this? Is this, Ben? What's happening?"

"Nothing's happening, except I'm lonesome for you."

"Are you all right?" She thought maybe he had been fired.

"I'm very lonesome for you."

"I'm lonesome, too, darling, but are you all right?" She didn't like the sound of his voice. It was too soft. It seemed crushed with pleading.

"All right? Sure, I'm all right. What are you eating for lunch?"

"I'll eat you if you don't tell me why you called up."

"Because I'm lonesome, that's all. Can't I be lonesome for the only wife I got and ever will have?"

"When are you coming home?"

"Not for lunch."

She laughed. He liked to hear her laugh. He smiled into the telephone.

"I know not for lunch," she said, "but when, silly?" She still thought he had been fired.

"I don't know, not for some time."

"The job is still holding up?"

"Oh yes."

"Remember what I said," she tried to keep her voice from sounding urgent. "If you can get a regular job there, I don't care. I'll come to live." They had argued about that before. He had said she would be lonely outside New York, away from her friends. "I'll live anywhere as long as you're there, too."

He didn't answer for a long time. He stood smiling into the telephone. She always made him feel that way, tough, a man standing on his own feet against anything. "It's a regular paradise here," he said at last.

"So, for goodness sake, get a job there and let me come, too."

"You like me anyway?"

"No, of course not. I married you for your money."

She laughed and he laughed. They laughed into each other and then he hung up.

"Now you get the hell right out of here," the man said to him.

Tucker saw his face then for the first time. It was Newell Smith, the big shot himself, the big boss of all the works, of this mill and eleven others like it. Tucker became frightened and reckless. "Are you going to make me?" he said.

A gray moustache stood on edge on Smith's smooth, pink face. He looked as if he had never had much to worry about, and he didn't seem to be worried now, but actually the specials had him scared. He felt there was danger they would get out of hand. "You oughtn't to come here," he told Tucker. "Use the phone downstairs."

Suddenly, without thinking he was going to do it, Tucker said exactly what he thought. "I wanted to be out of it," he said, "and in some place quiet when I talked to my wife."

The girls and the men were standing in the open doorway listening. Tucker started to walk towards them and Smith hurried and caught up with him and touched his elbow. "Pretty rough out there?" he asked.

Tucker thought, it must be that he doesn't know yet either that it was me who did it. He broke up inside. He took two quick steps away from Smith towards the door, his legs shaking under his knees. Then his knees began to shake, too, and he couldn't stand up any more. He fell down on his hands and knees and grunted. His eyes seemed to roll along with the carpet as the carpet rolled out from under his shaking body.

Smith put his arms around Tucker to lift him up. Tucker smelled his rich, washed smell and heard him strain to lift and thought, "Jesus, the big boss of all the whole works," and thought, "Jesus, I'm glad Edna can't see me like this," and thought, "if this guy knew . . . if Edna knew . . ."

Smith was a small man. Tucker was too heavy for him. "Those killers!" screamed Smith. "Why don't the police throw all those killers in jail?"

The words fell on Tucker like blows. He thought Smith meant him. No, he told himself, Smith wouldn't be acting like this if he knew. He cringed away from himself violently and then he passed out. "Oh! Oh!" were the last words he heard and a girl saying, "He's just a boy."

When Tucker came to, he was lying on a couch. There was a cold towel on his forehead. He did not open his eyes. He was afraid of what he would see. Then, at last, he opened his eyes and saw clearly in a single flash the gray lead pipe as it lay across the man's mouth and saw the man's face crumble into his mouth. He closed his eyes and remained silent.

"I hadn't meant to do it," he thought. How often had the judge heard that one before? How many years would that take off the sentence? When Tucker had hired out as a special, all he had wanted was a job. He was afraid to be out of work. He had been an outcast like Joe and had always got in trouble before when he didn't have a job. Edna's love had changed him. She had made him feel he belonged among people. He didn't want to be in trouble any more, now that he was married to Edna. But, when he went around asking for work, the bosses didn't even see him. They sent out word that there was nothing or didn't look at him when they said, "Nothing." And he thought, "If only I could get one of those bosses to see me, just to look into my eyes for a minute and see that I'm a person, not just something pestering them, but a living human being."

When he took the job as a special, he told Edna, "Once I get on the inside of that plant I'll do something to make them know I'm there." He thought surely he'd be able to get one of the bosses to look at him. He'd run to open the door to the boss's car or tip his hat and say "good night" or "good morning" or "fine day" and get the boss to see into his eyes and say to himself, "Now that's a fine upstanding young man, what can he do, maybe we can fit him into the organization."

"If I'm in the inside," he said to Edna, "they'll never get me out."

Tucker had never been in a strike before or seen one. The first day, the Company couldn't get the scabs inside because the pickets were jammed around the gate. He heard Smith say to McGrady, "Make a fuss out there. We've got to get the National Guard to help." Then a little later, McGrady told the specials, "Go on and rough them trespassers up. Push them the hell where they belong, away from that gate. Use your pipes. You're deputies of the law now and act that way."

But the Company had only a few guards and mostly the wrong kind, too, college boys and amateurs like Tucker. So everything went smooth that first time. The strikers got back from the gate. The scabs ducked in. Nobody was hurt. But the strikers made the rounds of the scab houses that night, and a lot of scabs didn't check in the next morning and those that did were so scared they couldn't work much. When lunch time came and the noise started outside, many scabs just picked up and quit, and now Tucker knew there was bound to be trouble. The Company wasn't going to take a licking like that without a fight. So there was going to be a battle to get the army to clear the streets of pickets and their noise, and Tucker was not going to be in it. No sir, not he. No sirree, not he. Not at all. Never. Why should he put his heart into dirt for $8 a day, push around all those poor people and their women and kids who were just like the people he palled around with and who were just trying to keep a job the way he was. No sir, not for him. Never on this green earth. Why should he be the fish for the big guys and turn hoodlum for them when what he wanted was a job so that he didn't have to turn hood? There was no sense to it.

But he had been wild for a job. He had been afraid not to have a job. He had been afraid of old friends, old habits, old experiences and, most of all, of the old feeling of being an outcast.

The Company Doctor came and examined Tucker. Tucker kept his eyes closed. "Sound as a drum," the Doctor said.

Tucker opened his eyes then. "I was only tired," he said.

Smith was standing alongside him. "Get him a glass of water," he told one of the girls.

"God Almighty!" thought Tucker. He felt if he didn't have to go to jail now, he would have been able to get a steady job sure. "I'm in cushy here," he told himself, "except for murder." He drank the water in small swallows with his lips tight to look refined before the big boss.

"I better go downstairs," said Tucker.

"No." Smith shook his head. "You've done a day's work. You rest now."

Tucker did not trust himself to speak. He lay back a moment. Then he got up and started downstairs. He wanted to get it over with. He wanted to know right away what the judge was going to give him, maybe one to twenty for manslaughter, but maybe it was murder in the second degree, maybe it would be ten years or twenty years or the rest of his natural life. For a single panicky moment, Tucker thought of running away, ducking out and home, picking up Edna and going on the lam with her. Edna wouldn't do it. He knew that. Anyway, he couldn't appear like that before Edna, all soft and womanish from the willies. Tucker held himself together and walked steadily into McGrady's headquarters.

McGrady was talking to a soldier who wore gold-rimmed eyeglasses. He nodded to Tucker and went on talking quietly and Tucker stood there thinking, "If only I could get a break. If only just nobody saw it. If only it could be made self-defense." But more than a thousand people had seen him. He had had a lead pipe—"lethal weapon"—and the other fellow had had only his bare hands. But Tucker had been deputized. He was an officer of the law engaged in the performance of his duties. But there this fellow had been, not doing anything, just yelling, yelling and standing there with his bare hands.

"Where the hell have you been?" said McGrady. The Guard officer had gone away.

"I passed out."

"That's nice. That's the kind of men I have to work with. It's a miracle that I achieve any of the objectives around here."

Tucker looked away. "I suppose you want a report out of me or something," he said.

"Yes, that's right. But read this first." McGrady threw some papers across the desk to him. "It's affidavits from eye-witnesses who saw it happen. They'll clear the thing up in your mind so your report can be intelligent."

There were four affidavits. The first stated that Tucker was seen to have been attacked with a lead pipe by a striker and was seen to have disarmed the man and to have fended off the man's further attacks with the man's own weapon. It was signed by Newell Smith. The other affidavits were approximately similar. Tucker read each once carefully and in silence.

"That's the way it was, wasn't it?" said McGrady.

Tucker looked up. There were tears in his eyes. "You won't regret this," he said. "You won't be sorry what you done for me."

"For you?" said McGrady. "I did it for you? Listen you. If it was up to me, you'd be at the end of a rope right now. I don't hold with a man losing his head and killing when he's on duty."

Tucker lowered his head in confusion. He saw the affidavits. They were shaking in his hands. They even rattled a little bit. He began to wave them up and down to steady his hands. "—— you!" he thought. "—— you, my friend, up the brown with a wooden ——." He thought of saying it and then he thought, no, he was in right, why throw it away, why leave a little boss along the line sore at him and out to knife him in the back.

"I didn't lose my head," he told McGrady.

McGrady was silent.

"I saw what you wanted done and I done it," said Tucker.

"Done what? Did what?"

"I done this self-defense for you." Tucker waved the affidavits at him.

"All right. Get busy on your report. And hold yourself ready for the magistrate when they call you."

"Yes sir, chief." Tucker saluted solemnly.

When Mr. Smith came down to go home, he stopped to chat with Tucker. He asked Tucker how he was feeling and said he was glad to hear it and said he'd pick Tucker up in his car and they'd go down to the coroner's together to watch the case closed.

Yes sir, thanks sir, you're being mighty decent sir, said Tucker. His eyes did not waver from Mr. Smith's.

He went out into the yard with Mr. Smith and ran to open the door of Mr. Smith's car and stood looking as the limousine drove off noisily past the troops and past four pickets and past sullen men standing silently in small bunches. Tucker didn't pay any attention to the people. He saw only the car. There weren't any people left for Tucker on earth any more—only himself and human beings he could use or could ignore or must fight. Business and its law of self-defense had taught him that.

Tucker had always had the drive to make money, but now he knew what it was all about and knew how to handle the emotions that had impeded him. Everything clicked into place for him. He did not remain a trigger-man for business very long. He started his own business. Prohibition gave him the opportunity to expand it and, at the time when Henry Wheelock started to annoy him with a lawsuit, he was conducting numerous enterprises.

The particular local for which Wheelock had brought suit, and in fact the whole bakery union, was one of Tucker's lesser interests. He used it to blackmail a regular payroll out of shopkeepers. But his largest business was beer, and his next biggest money-maker was an association of electrical contractors.

This association made a monopoly out of the electrical contracting business in a whole borough of the city. It had not been Tucker's idea and he was not head man in it, but he was important because he policed the setup and kept the contractors in line. When a contracting job was available—for example, the wiring of a new office building—the association met and decided what price to charge for it and decided which member's turn it was to get the job. They all put in bids of their own, but the one whose turn it was made the low bid. Tucker's job was to make sure that the bids were all drawn up as per agreement and to see to it that, if some contractor outside the association, underbid and got the job, he would have trouble completing it—labor trouble, perhaps, or trouble getting materials or trouble trucking his material to the job, any kind of extra expense that would convince him he couldn't make a profit on work in the borough. Each association member's profits went into the association's treasury, and the sum was divided quarterly on a pro rata basis.

In the course of watching the split-up of the profits, Tucker developed considerable respect for the art of bookkeeping. He realized that a well-run enterprise with shareholders in it could make more money for its managers in the bookkeeping department than over the counter.

Tucker was interested in several other smaller enterprises, among them a taxicab union. But hack drivers were hard, starved men and he couldn't get far with them. Control of the union was an easy enough job, since there were many part-time drivers who were not interested in the union as long as it allowed them to work. But the union itself was not strong enough to keep hard, starved men in line. The system Tucker used to make a profit for himself out of the taxi union was the same he used with the bakers. He demanded pay rises from the owners of fleets of cabs. The owners paid Tucker to keep his demands reasonable or forget them if he could. But sometimes it was difficult to make the hack drivers take what Tucker got for them from the fleet owners.

When the bakery case Henry Wheelock was handling came to Tucker's attention, Tucker didn't trouble to fight it. He had a cheap way to bribe Wheelock into throwing the case after it came into court. He offered Wheelock the legal business for one of the locals in the taxi union. But Wheelock was stubborn and did not yet see the possibilities in working for Tucker. He held out for more. Finally Tucker contracted to give him the legal business for the whole union and, in addition, $900 cash. Henry sent the $900 to his brothers' mink farm.

Tucker believed he was getting rid of Wheelock by putting him into the taxi union. But all Henry needed was a start. He began to realize Tucker could be not merely a client, but a career. The moment Henry got a foot in the door to something big, his mind began to teem with schemes and, in a few weeks, he had Tucker deeply involved with him.

This was a gangster Wheelock was dealing with. It did not occur to him at first and, when it did, it did not seem to be important. This was a man who had been prepared to kill to get money or to get a chance to make money or to protect money he had made and a man who had even, it was said, actually killed for all those purposes.

McGuinness told Wheelock a story once about Tucker having dynamited a man to find out something that was important to him, something that would eliminate a competitor's organization from the field and move the competitor's business over to his own organization. Tucker had grabbed two men who, he believed, had the complicated information he needed—names, dates, places, terms, and had taken the two men out to a place he had in the country.

The men wouldn't tell Tucker what he wanted to know. They said they didn't have the information. Tucker had them beaten and burned a little and cut a little. Still, they said they didn't know. Tucker knew the best way to get the bravery out of them was to keep them standing up without sleep and without water. But that took time and he was in a hurry. If the information was to be any good to him, he had to act on it in the morning. If these fellows didn't know, he had to get hold of somebody else right away. But he had to make sure they didn't know. He couldn't afford to waste time looking for others. If he lost any more time, it might cost him the opportunity.

He took the two men down into the cellar and had them bound to chairs in opposite corners. Both men were gagged. One was young and the other was middle-aged. Tucker decided to play with the middle-aged man. He felt there was more chance that a man of his years would be sensible. He had dynamite left over from a tunnel job he had once policed. He never knew why he had stolen it except that it had seemed easy to do. Now he put a stick of dynamite into the young man's mouth behind the gag so that it couldn't be worked loose and ran the detonator wire through a cellar window to a tree a short distance from the house. He wasn't afraid of the noise. There were plenty of stills in the woods around there and every so often one of them went off.

After getting everything set, Tucker went back into the cellar and took the gag off the middle-aged man. "What about it?" he said. "You going to make me blow him up?"

"Ben, you're crazy, I'm telling you." Tucker let him run on. He was watching him speculatively. "We don't know it," the man said, "how should we know it, Ben, Ben, if we knew, Holy Mother, why shouldn't we tell, but my God, Holy Mother, Jesus, Ben, Ben, we don't, don't, honest to God, I tell you on the bible, sign a statement with my blood, mother's blood if you give me a chance."

Tucker thought probably the man was telling the truth. It wasn't human to hold back the truth at such a time. But he had to be sure.

Yes, he had to be absolutely sure. He had to be sure the way a jury was sure, beyond the shadow of a doubt, otherwise there would be an awful waste of time and the waste might be fatal to the whole deal. He went over to the young man and saw he had fainted. He made an impatient sound. So there was no getting anything out of that one for a while, he thought. There was no making sure with him for a while. He would have to be slapped awake. That would take time. In that time, he would get back his courage to lie and it would have to be taken out of him all over again. That would take more time and, in the end, with all that time wasted, they'd only be back to where they were now. Tucker ran impatiently to the other one.

"Maybe you'll remember to know after he blows up all over you," he told him.

"Ben, you lunatic, you hear, my God, lunatic, crazy, Ben, Ben, lunatic."

"Shut up and remember."

"Oh my God and saints." The man's mouth wabbled and his words became mangled and unintelligible.

"You'd better remember," said Tucker, "because after he blows up all over you, you're next."

The man went from babbling to screaming as Tucker stared at him searchingly. Then Tucker ran out of the cellar without looking at the other fellow, the fellow with the dynamite in his mouth. If they're telling the truth, I'll know now, he thought, without guess-work. Anyway, he thought, the both of them were better out of the way where they couldn't think up trouble from what they'd been through.

Tucker pulled the detonator himself and ran back into the cellar himself. Both were dead. The middle-aged man's heart simply had stopped beating.

Nobody watched Tucker come out of the cellar, McGuinness said, except McGuinness. There wasn't a muscle moving on Tucker's face, McGuinness said. He just looked as if he was thinking hard. He left it to the people he had brought with him to get rid of the evidence and drove back to the city alone. He was hot on the deal.

Nobody was going to stop him from making this deal. He was that kind of a man in those days. Nothing and nobody could stop him. Anything and anybody who got in his way was stepped on.

"A good man to run with," said McGuinness. "Not so good to run against."

"And you know what the son of a bitch done then?" said McGuinness. "He grabbed up another guy right that night and brought him back to where we was and told him what happened to the other two, only he made it worse, said he blew the two of them up, and showed him the pieces that was left, the broken up chair and the other pieces that was on the wall and the floor and against the wood bin where it was. Then this guy give Ben what he wanted to know and in the morning Ben was set to make the deal."

"Relentless," laughed Wheelock.

"Who? Yes, quite a guy really, I'm telling you."

"Big Ben, the demon dynamiter," said Wheelock and laughed.

He couldn't believe the story. He couldn't let himself believe it. He had to dismiss it from his mind as not important enough to think about or find out about. Anyway, Wheelock knew that business had often fought its people with guns and he understood from his own life how business—without thought of anything but money—could destroy the lives of great numbers of people. If death were dealt out personally instead of impersonally, quickly and directly instead of indirectly, that didn't make the murder any more personal to the men who committed it. The murderer was the same kind of personality in either case, whether he was a big man and sat in a corporation's office and evolved a policy over a conference table that resulted in death for steel workers or automobile workers or railroad workers or oil workers; or whether he was a small man and had to supervise everything himself, both the policy and its evolution. In either case, the victims never appeared as people in the mind of their murderer. They were merely an opposition.

And if Tucker had dealt in violence instead of subtler destruction, if he had ended lives instead of merely wrecking them, then that was a small difference, too, in deciding whether to do business with a man. The difference lay in the commodities dealt with, not in the men who dealt in them. One man, losing a strike, moved his factory to the south where labor was cheaper and left a whole town hungry behind him. He left desperate families behind and sweated, sickened, crippled and poisoned the lives of a whole new community. That was business to him, and to his stockholders. Another man decided to monopolize an industry. He drove out the independents. Some of them committed suicide. Some of them became the kind of men who make their wives or children commit suicide. But that was business, too. Well, Tucker's activity was business to Tucker and it became business to Wheelock. No, Wheelock could not think of Tucker as a gangster, not after having grown up among destruction in the wake of business and after having been made to feel it was only self-preservation to travel with the destroyers.

Wheelock began to involve Tucker with him by setting up a corporation to get the exclusive agency to sell a new, expensive kind of taxicab. Then he made a proposition to Tucker to take over the agency. He did not have to point out to Tucker that the taxi union could help in the sales campaign for the cabs.

Tucker and Henry quarreled immediately over the personnel for the agency. Henry wanted to use automobile men who knew the business. Tucker insisted the people from his own organization must be boss. They could use the trained automobile men all right, but not on the managing end.

Tucker's organization was like that of any many-sided management corporation geared to absorb new businesses. He had a staff of men who corresponded to executive vice presidents. They were the managers for his various enterprises. He had a "new business department," although it was not called that, or, in fact, called anything. The people in this department got new enterprises started and patched up trouble where it developed. Joe was one of them. He had worked his way up into this department and then had risen further to the rank if not the title of executive vice president.

This was the executive part of Tucker's organization. The trouble with it, from Henry's point of view, was that it was made up in part of men who had risen off the streets with Tucker and in part of men who had not been substantial enough to make their way in legitimate business. Legitimate business attracted men of a "better" type and so the competition there was stiffer.

Some of Tucker's executives had criminal records from the days before they could get what they wanted in business without a gun. When these men went into court in civil cases, their records beat them before they started. This made for trouble. When a business-man cannot use the courts to protect himself, his competitors take advantage of him, and he has to rely on himself for defense.

Tucker's executives were manipulators and promoters. They had no interest in building up anything enduring because they could not believe anything would endure for them. Their entire interest lay in making quick money for themselves. They always felt that whatever business they had would be taken away from them in one way or another anyway, and the best thing was to get money while the getting was good.

Henry wanted the taxi agency to be a permanent business. But Tucker said he had his organization and wasn't going to throw it away for any proposition. Henry got the idea that this wasn't a question of choice or loyalty. Tucker was afraid to break away from his people. So Henry yielded. He joined the men who did their get-ting while the getting was good. He looted his corporation the way Wall Street bankers and brokers had looted the automobile business or the motion picture business or a hundred other businesses.

The campaign to sell the cabs began in the union. The union leaders got across to the drivers the idea that, if they had this new limousine-type cab, they would book more money. That started a little agitation in the garages for the car and, before it had a chance to die down, Tucker's "new business department" arrived to do the actual selling.

The fleet owners could buy on terms that allowed them to pay out of the cabs' earnings. They all were aware that, if they didn't buy, they were going to have labor trouble. If they didn't have a boycott or a strike on their hands, they would lose their drivers to those who did buy the new cabs. There was nothing they could do about losing their drivers. The drivers were paid a percentage of their bookings, forty per cent at this time, and would naturally go where the bookings could be increased. Tucker's union was not going to prevent the drivers from shifting to garages where the new cabs were. It was going to encourage them to do it.

Wheelock knew what was going to happen eventually and he stayed clear of everything but the legal end. He formed other corporations to get the agencies for automobile supplies and parts, tires, oil, grease, gasoline, for financing and repossessing cars and, towards the end, he helped in the purchase of the company that made the taxicab with which the whole enterprise had begun. This company was an assembly plant. It bought parts from different truck manufacturers, ordered a body made to its own design and then put it all together.

These were wonderful days for Wheelock. He was getting a retainer from each corporation and special fees and bonuses for doing the work for which he was retained. He made $90,000 the first year, but he knew his income wasn't going to stay at that figure and he didn't let his brothers know how much money he was making. He was afraid they would quit their farm and start living off him. However, he assumed the task of paying off their mortgages and sent $20 every week to his mother. He always made out the check himself and enclosed a note with it in his own handwriting. He could easily have made the check larger, but $20 was more than enough to keep her comfortably, and he thought if he sent more the family would suspect he was rich. How could a lawyer explain to people who didn't know about such things he had built up a practice that wasn't going to last?

For a time, with the help of Wheelock's manipulations, Tucker had everything his own way. The big companies scrambled to get Tucker to take the agencies for their products. Tucker had almost a monopoly on the New York taxi market and, as counsel for the monopoly, the money poured over Wheelock.

There was something almost unwholesome about the way the money poured in. It was as if, in the years before, Wheelock had been struggling desperately with something he could not get a grip on. Then suddenly, somehow, by accident, he had found the vital spot and had dug in with all his might and now he could stand still for a moment and let the money gush over him. The year passed like a day of fever, filled with dream-like events, and, as the money piled in and spilled over him, Henry was repelled and exultant and he had in him a feeling of release and a sick feeling of being drenched and of draining.

The big companies sent their biggest men, and when Tucker's new boy, his round-faced, smiling, shining-eyed, shrewd attorney, spoke, the big men listened. They sat around a table with Henry and puffed cigar smoke at him and invited him to their homes in Westchester and on Long Island and listened to every word he said because he did not waste words. He said money or he said no money.

Henry kept the sleeping bag he had used in his first office under his new desk for luck. The first time his foot touched the bag while he was arguing a deal, he pressed down on it hard. "For luck," he said to himself. The new bag gave under his foot like flesh. He had the feeling, as he crushed it, that he was crushing flesh. But he continued to keep it under his desk. He decided every successful man was entitled to at least one superstition.

Then what Wheelock had been delaying by juggling contracts and by making half promises happened. The companies Tucker had frozen out of the New York market began to fight to break the monopoly. Their first move was to make good-looking cabs. This hit Tucker where he was weak. The executive vice president who had been put in charge of Tucker's assembly plant in Ohio was making fast money for himself by buying chasses and motors second-hand and billing his corporation for new ones.

Tucker did not permit the fleet owners to buy the new cabs. This was an automatic response to the situation, and the companies he had frozen out responded automatically, too, and exactly as Wheelock had foreseen they would. They operated their own cabs on the streets. Since the anti-trust laws were against this practice, they evaded the law by operating the cabs through dummy corporations.

This move was designed to weaken Tucker's union and force him into making a deal with them. Drivers, always seeking better cabs because better cabs meant better bookings, began to seek jobs among the dummy corporations. They had to quit the union to get a job. The dummy corporations met union terms, but said they believed unions were un-American and must therefore insist on an open shop.

Wheelock had thought about what would happen so often, he was surprised to see events take exactly the shape he had predicted for them. He knew Tucker was beaten. With an organization composed of such men as his, Tucker couldn't afford to fight against important money. It was now simply a question of giving in on the best terms possible. Wheelock knew the outside companies didn't want to break up the union or even throw Tucker out of it unless they had to. They wanted a man like Tucker in there to control labor for them. That was something for Tucker to take into the conference room. To get more arguing points for the time when the deal would be made, a series of strikes were started.

The strikes were ordered by Wheelock only for their nuisance value, only to hasten the big companies into compromise and to put Tucker into position to exact a price for restoring peace. They were supposed to be fake strikes. But a lot of drivers did not know that. They thought they were fighting for their jobs. Those who went out on strike thought they were battling for the idea of union. Those who refused to go out and became scabs thought they were battling against a union that was doing them no good. They picketed and roamed the city, smashing cabs, and fought murderously among themselves.

They seemed far away to Wheelock, but not to Tucker. To Wheelock the men were as far away as the people in his home town must have seemed to the big lumber men. Wheelock never thought about them. He was busy trying to get the tire and gasoline and accessory companies Tucker represented as agent to stand behind their agent when the time came to decide on peace terms.

However, Tucker was now older and more experienced. The feeling that people were not people, simply opponents, was not as new and shocking to him as to Wheelock and had become somewhat refined. He could live with it normally now. So he thought about the strikers. They were beginning to get out of control. Real labor men were coming in, outside agitators, and were taking over the strike in rump sessions and fighting it seriously. Only more violence or a settlement of the strike could stop that. But violence even then was threatening to involve the courts. Neither Tucker nor the officers of the dummy corporations could afford to go into court. So both sides hurried to the conference room to arrange a settlement. Both sides were afraid Tucker would lose his union to "the reds."

Wheelock felt he was in a position to win when he went into the conference room. The big companies for whom Tucker acted as agent were committed to his side. That was perhaps his most effective ammunition. The other side had money and comparatively clean hands. Now Tucker's side could have money, too, and equally clean hands. Wheelock had arranged more ammunition for Tucker. Calling off the strikes would be worth certain concessions. The enemy had disclosed it wanted Tucker to remain in charge of the union and throw out "the reds." This was worth more concessions.

But all the ammunition exploded in Wheelock's face. He had thought the big companies committed to Tucker's side would deal honestly. They didn't. Instead they took advantage of the fact that Tucker couldn't do a thing without them except get rough. They went over to the enemy and made their own rules and Tucker had to accept them. If he got rough, they would throw him out altogether. This way they allowed Tucker to work for them under their own rules.

It was done deviously and to work out at length. But, a few weeks after the deal was made, Tucker saw how it would develop eventually. The big companies were in control. Whatever money he worked to get would go to them. "It's a cheese sandwich," he told Wheelock, "and I'm the cheese."

"We'd have had a better chance, if we had gone into the fight with our own clean hands instead of having to line up clean hands outside," Wheelock pointed out. "We could have tied them up in the courts for the rest of their lives. I told you I wanted regular automobile men in there right away."

It wasn't the first time Tucker had thought the same thing. He had always wanted a big business that would be legal, with angles to it, naturally, but legal angles. For a time, this taxi enterprise had looked as if it might be it. But, when the crisis came, his organization had made him helpless. They weren't businessmen. They couldn't make or market a product properly. They couldn't get away with the kind of thing that had to be done to build a big business. The public wouldn't allow it. And they couldn't use the courts the way regular businessmen used them. Yet how was a man who had come up the way Tucker had to develop any other kind of organization?

"The real trouble was with me, not my organization," Tucker told Wheelock.

"There's nothing the matter with you if you're by yourself."

"Your figures ain't right," said Tucker. "I haven't been big long enough. If you're big long enough, then you can do something—the way these slick guys from the automobile companies did to us. If you're big long enough, then it don't make any difference where you started from or what you did to get there. That's my philosophy in life."

"It's the American philosophy," Wheelock told him, "the whole Anglo-Saxon shopkeeper philosophy."

"It don't make any difference to anybody what you did," Tucker said, "except maybe to those you hurt to get there and, if you hurt them good enough, they become just bums anyway and don't count."

Wheelock thought of his home town and of the gaped-open forests all around it. If you stood on a hill and looked down, the stumps stretched away like gravestones and, with the brush around them, the stumps looked like gravestones in a forgotten graveyard. The big lumber people moved in and then moved on and the only place they ever stayed put was on the society pages of the newspapers or in "Who's Who in America." They were loved and admired and envied by everybody except the people they left behind in assassinated towns. These people hated them, but what was their hate? They were just bums. They were alone. They had been made to feel alone by what business had done to them. They did not join each other to fight business. They abandoned themselves to their feeling of loneliness and fought each other instead.

Wheelock turned abruptly from his thoughts. "I am going to tell you straight up and down, whether you like it or not," he said to Tucker. "You are not going to get anywhere unless you become respectable."

Tucker colored. "You just said yourself there is nothing the matter with me," he argued. "The way I look at it, if a man has a monopoly off in a corner somewhere, then everybody takes a shot at him. He's not exactly popular is what I find. All these things said about me is because I'm not popular, that's all."

"You're saying just what I mean," replied Wheelock. "In the eyes of every little louse with a lousy little business and a few lousy dollars in the bank, monopoly is gangsterism, and if you want to get away with being a gangster right out in the open where everybody is going to see you, then you have to be respectable. You have to be big and be respectable."

"You use very rough words for a man who's been to college," said Tucker uncertainly. Nobody had ever come so close before to calling him a gangster to his face. He looked away. "The time has gone by for me anyway," he said in a low tone.

"No," said Wheelock. "You have to be big and you have to be respectable, that's all. You have to be big enough to make bums out of your enemies so they don't count any more and what they say don't count. And you have to be respectable enough so that even what is said by those you didn't make bums don't count."

What Henry feared was, when the taxi enterprises dried up, he would be out. To prevent this, he thought up a plan for pulling Tucker loose from his organization. He felt if he could start Tucker on such a long and complicated enterprise, he could win either way. If the plan failed, Wheelock would have had the opportunity to work his way into handling the legal business for the whole organization. If the plan succeeded, then Tucker would be his career.

Tucker didn't make up his mind to act on Wheelock's plan. His children made it up for him. Tucker's boy, John, was ten then, and Dorothy was fourteen. On a Sunday when he was going over the household bills and feeling good because the bills were lower than usual, he told his boy:

"You got a choice of the whole world. You can be a doctor, a lawyer or an engineer or an architect or a dentist maybe because we can use a dentist in the family with the teeth I got. But it's going to be one of those, so make up your mind about college. I got the insurance for your four years pretty well paid up already."

Dorothy put her arms around her father's neck. "I'm going into your business with you," she said.

"Me too," said John.

"You got to have money to be in business with me," Tucker told them.

"I'll start in the office," said Dorothy. "There's lots of girls work in their father's office."

"No," Tucker said. "So you get that out of your head right away."

"Well I want to!" She stamped her foot and her hair tossed back. She was very pretty. He looked at her a moment, smiling.

"You like to be around your old man?" he said. "You think your old man has got something to him?"

"I think he's mean," she pouted.

He laughed. "You got that from your mother," he told her. He meant the small, thick way in which she pouted.

"Yes, Mommy thinks you're mean, too."

"You just be as nice as your mother, that's all, and you won't have to work in any dirty old office."

"I want to! I will! I'm going to make Mommy make you give me a job in your office."

"No sirree. If you were around all the time, how could I get any work done? I'd be giving you pinches all day long, like this." He reached over and nipped her behind, and she screamed and slapped his hand and ran away a few steps.

"You're not supposed to do those things," she cried angrily. "I'm not a child any more."

He was startled. He hadn't realized it before, but it was true. She was growing up. He looked, startled, at his son. John was blushing. Even John was growing up.

"Daddy," said John suddenly, out of his embarrassment, "what do you make in your office?"

"Why," said Tucker, "I make money I guess. Anyway, I try to make it."

He saw that Dorothy was standing still and watching him. Her mouth was open slightly and her gaze was intent. "I'm what you call an investor," he said. "I put money in different things and then I watch to see that they work out all right."

Dorothy's gaze did not leave his face. She gave an abrupt sigh. Her whole chest lifted and dropped.

"What are you kids trying to do!" he said. He pointed to John. "You go to college and be a dentist, and Dorothy," he pointed to his daughter, "tries to stay as sweet as Mommy. That's my orders."

He called her Dossie when he was not annoyed with her.

Pulling away from his organization was a slow, dangerous business. Besides Wheelock, only Edna knew about it. McGuinness had had some hints and had developed a pretty good idea of what was going on, but Tucker wasn't afraid of him. Mac had attached himself to the whole family, and Ben knew he had nothing to fear from him as long as he was kept on a payroll.

Tucker could not make a clean break. The men Tucker was trying to get away from had to be left in a business that would feed them and keep them going. If they were left hungry, they would make trouble. In addition, he couldn't simply turn over the businesses to them. If he did that, they would realize what he was doing and try to stop it. They knew no business they were in was stable and they looked to Tucker to get new businesses for them.

So what Tucker had to do was give them a chance to steal the businesses from him little by little. He had always let his executives steal from him. He felt the more they stole, the more they had to make. He knew he could rely on his people to steal the whole business if given the opportunity. He knew also that the chance to steal an entire business was tempting enough to make them disregard the fact that he wouldn't be there to provide them with a new one. Finally, once this process was begun, Tucker had to make sure his people would feel there was no chance he would use his knowledge about them and their enterprises to hurt them or force his way back in.

This was the only way to get free. He had to make his organization self-supporting, or think it was self-supporting, and make himself helpless against it, and he had to do it slowly and secretly so that the men wouldn't suspect he was getting rid of them. That way they would leave him alone.

As the process took form, Wheelock grew to know the whole organization. Piece by piece, its legal work came into his office and his office expanded. Tucker was responsible for it all and Wheelock knew it, but he wasn't particularly grateful. The relationship between the two men was a common one among people in business, where all emotions tend to become stunted or distorted. Wheelock liked Tucker and knew there was nothing he could do with him except by getting the man to need him and like him and trust him, in that order. The knowledge made the fact of liking Tucker unimportant. Tucker liked Wheelock, but he used him in this work only because he needed him and felt he could handle him. Tucker required someone he could rely on to stop the process of leaving the organization, if necessary, and make it work in reverse to put him back in charge. This, too, made affection unimportant or, at least, impotent.

When Tucker first began to study the policy business, he was already well clear of his organization and looking for the spot to make his bid for a big, legal business. With the repeal of prohibition, he had turned his beer business into a legitimate one and now he was letting his organization and the politicians who had helped build the organization steal away the business. He was letting the same people steal his association of electrical contractors. He had felt that, whatever he did in the future, he would need politicians and this was the way to keep hold of them. The taxi enterprises and the bakery union were falling into the hands of the men who ran them. He was still drawing money from all these businesses and still nominally in control. He could still step back into actual control whenever he wanted.

To both Tucker and Wheelock, policy seemed a perfect setup. At the time they became interested, a number of prominent taxpayers and some newspapers were attempting to have lotteries legalized in order to reduce taxes. Tucker believed that, once he got hold of policy, he could throw his politicians behind this attempt and push it through.

Then, policy was a business that could be handled without having to fight anyone of importance and without having to borrow help from Tucker's organization. The managers required to run the banks were already running them. They were the owners. They could be taken over with their properties. Joe was the only executive brought over from the old organization.

Wheelock had been against taking Joe. He felt business ought not to be complicated with family problems. One or the other brother, he had told Tucker, ought to be left out. Since Leo's bank was one of the biggest and the combination would lose too much by leaving it out, then Joe should be the one to go. Tucker didn't agree. He had no brothers of his own and he thought of brothers in business together the way Joe did. Tucker also knew, from his previous experience with Leo, that Joe would be needed to get his brother into the combination. In the end, Tucker had his way. After all, it was his show.

"You think the whole thing is really going to work out the way you say?" asked Tucker. "I mean the whole thing, after it's legal and all? You think they really can get away with letting me run it after it's legal?"

"I've lived long enough to know this," said Wheelock. "If you have the money that goes with the job of being God Almighty, then you can be any kind of a son of a bitch you want. You'll still be God Almighty to everybody who counts."

Tucker grinned at him delightedly. "He's a kid," he thought. "He's smart, but still a kid. What does he know about the world really?"

But nothing had developed yet to change Wheelock's mind. The enterprise was taking shape exactly as he had thought it would, even down to the last little detail of him drinking himself drunk that Thanksgiving eve and Joe and Leo going home early and Tucker and Edna and McGuinness staying on to have supper with him. Only it was taking longer to get drunk than he had expected. He was more nervous than he had expected.

IX

As soon as Joe and Leo had left Wheelock's apartment, the house-man began to bring in the supper. There were scrambled eggs and bacon, cheese and biscuits and buns and two pots of jam and coffee. While he was setting it out, the telephone rang and Wheelock said he would get it and went into the bedroom. He took his highball glass with him.

A silence settled down behind him. Tucker and Edna kept look-ing at the soundless Filipino. They were hungry. Edna's eyes fol-lowed the yellow, spongy, steaming pile of eggs and cheese out of the servant's hands and onto the table and she began to wonder which meal she could cut down on tomorrow. She felt tired and decided it would be breakfast. She would stay in bed late and take only a cup of coffee before the big Thanksgiving dinner they were having for the children.

"We had better talk it up," said McGuinness suddenly, "so Edna can't hear."

Edna shifted her gaze from the coffee service that was being placed on the table. "Can't hear what?" she asked. She settled back in her chair and smoothed her skirt, as if preparing to take up the duties of entertainment.

"What the boy friend is saying to the girl friend." McGuinness nodded in the direction of the bedroom.

Edna pulled her face back a little, pretending she had been hit, and Tucker said: "What makes you think it's a girl?"

McGuinness held out his wrist watch and pointed to it. It was nearly three o'clock. "It's either a girl or the milkman," he said.

"This is something new from you," said Edna. "I never heard you put in a knock for anybody before."

"I'm not knocking. I'm just saying." McGuinness's wax-colored face had spotted with red. He squirmed a little as he talked. "He's a regular Broadway fellow. He's playing Broadway all the time and I'm just saying it, that's all, that he's regular Broadway and that kind don't talk so refined to girls at this time of the day."

"Come on, come on now!" said Tucker. "I'm getting damn sick of you and Joe snuffling around under your nose about Wheelock, always trying to knock his brains out when he ain't looking."

"I'm not . . ."

"I want to know straight and right now. What have you got against him?"

"Who me? What makes you think anything like that? I didn't say anything except that he's kind of Broadway. You know, well, you know as well as I do what that kind is like, the way they talk to girls."

Tucker kept frowning and waiting, and McGuinness turned his head towards the table on which the whiskies stood and then looked down at the fire. "As a matter of fact, Ben," he said, "if you want to know the truth, I think that college boy is getting to be a kind of a little bit, well, sort of a little high-strung I mean."

Tucker sprang to his feet and stepped away restlessly. "He's always been a bundle of nerves," he said.

McGuinness kept looking at the fire and Edna stared at her husband as he walked back and forth.

"I don't think it's a girl calling him," said Tucker. He walked across the room quickly and down a short hall and stopped in the doorway of the bedroom.

Henry was hunched on the edge of the bed, facing the telephone that stood on a small table against the wall. The receiver was on the hook. He looked as if he had been sitting that way a long time.

He had his elbow on his knee and he was resting on it heavily and staring at the telephone.

"The eggs is freezing over," said Tucker.

Henry jumped up. A smile bounced to his face. "I'm terribly sorry," he said.

His highball was on the table beside the telephone and he picked it up and took a drink and then started for the door with slow, loose, short steps. Tucker went a little way into the room towards him. "I thought maybe you had passed out," he said.

Henry halted and looked at him in mock astonishment. "Me?" he cried. He brought his glass to his chest with a wide sweep.

They stood several feet apart, staring at each other for a moment, and the astonishment faded slowly out of Henry's face. He had been smiling and the smile faded, too, and he stood still, looking tired and thoughtful. "What do you think, Ben?" he said. "Hall has put a tap on my phone."

Hall was a special prosecutor who had been appointed recently by the Governor to head a big "clean-up" drive. He was going to clean up the opposition politicians and give his side a turn in office.

"How do you know?" asked Tucker.

"Who else could it be?"

"I mean, how do you know there is a tap?"

"The fellow on the other end must have been asleep. I heard him take off the receiver."

Tucker's eyes searched Wheelock's face. He wasn't looking for anything. It was just that Henry happened to be standing in front of him. He was thinking of Hall and whether he could reach anyone who could do business with Hall. All Tucker's connections were on the other side. "Who called you up?" he asked.

"Some girl you don't know."

"Did you give it away that you heard the tap?"

"Now Ben, please."

"Well I'm just asking. A nervous fellow like you. There is a lot of talk going on about wire-tapping shouldn't be evidence. It's against the law."

"It's admissible in this state."

"Did you ever use this phone for anything?"

"I talked to you a couple times."

"From here? Oh yes, I remember. That was nothing."

"I called Ed Bunte once."

"Well, that's it. That ties it." Tucker looked angrily at the telephone.

"It was about getting some tickets for the fight for you."

"I don't care. You shouldn't have done it."

"I didn't know there was a tap. For all I know, maybe the tap was just put on tonight."

"With a no good son of a bitch like Hall there, you should have been more careful. I never in my life have talked over a phone without saying what I had to say like I thought somebody was listening in."

What makes you think I'm anything like you, thought Henry, or should be anything like you, or could be anything like you? "He's a son of a bitch all right," he told Tucker. "The trouble is he's not no good." He looked at his glass. All the ice had melted. "This one got drowned in water," he said and started to walk out of the room.

He passed Tucker and got to the doorway all right. Then his shoulder hit against the jamb and he spun backwards slowly and reached out his hand slowly and swayed forward and touched the jamb. He seemed to be trying to steady it with a pat. "It's a funny thing." He giggled. "It was standing up out of the way this morning." He turned to Tucker and laughed out loud. "Come on, big fellow," he said, "laugh, laugh it off!" He threw his fist upward as if he were cheering. "Hey, big fellow," he cried, "give us that great, big, wonderful golden smile."

Tucker took Wheelock by the arm and led him towards the others. Henry was trembling a little bit. Tucker could feel the small trembling deep in the young man's arm, deep below his clothes and below his flesh. It felt as if nerves were humming low and deep down.

❧

Wheelock kept on drinking. He put a highball in front of his plate of scrambled eggs and washed the eggs down with whiskey and then he floated some brandy on top of his coffee and lit a match to it. They all watched it burn with a blue flame. Edna said she would have some of that, too, because it looked so stylish and then McGuinness and Tucker asked for some.

"It looks so stylish it can't have any calories at all," said Edna.

But McGuinness decided to take his brandy straight after all. He said he was a plain man and did not like fancy mixed drinks.

Then Edna tried to talk Henry into marrying and settling down with some nice girl. She had already introduced him to several. She had others in mind, but she didn't mention them. Henry told her his trouble was there was only one girl he wanted and Ben had seen her first.

"I'm serious," she said.

Henry said he would be serious, too, if Ben weren't there to spy on him. Tucker laughed out loud at that. "I can see how you would be on a witness stand," he told Henry. "Nobody would get anything out of you."

Henry looked at him in a quick, frightened way. All the laughter had gone out of his face. "Can they put a tap on a switchboard?" he asked. He had thought of the switchboard in his office.

"No," Tucker said. "I don't think so. I'll have to find out."

"We're hunted all right, aren't we?" said Henry. "There's an open season on us, isn't there?"

"I guess you're right."

Edna had been leaning forward, trying to stare into her husband's eyes. She sat back suddenly. Her hand fell off the table and dropped into her lap, and her face settled down into stillness.

"This is a new one for me," said Henry. "I can't figure out how I ought to feel. Sore? Something like that? Sore, nervous, want to get up and throw a punch, things like that?"

"What do you mean ought to feel?" said McGuinness. An imaginative man's instinct to create with his sensations irritated him. "You ought to feel how you feel, that's what you ought."

Tucker wasn't listening. He was looking at his wife. "I think it

will be all right," he told her. "We're just up against a young
prosecutor fishing around, that's all, trying his luck."

"Smart, young, tough son of a bitch trying to get ahead in the
world," said Henry.

Tucker looked at him sharply. He didn't want Edna upset.

"Why can't people be nice and mind their own business and not
get in the way all the time," said Edna.

Henry poured another glass of brandy for himself. Nobody else
wanted any. He took a greedy, nervous, noisy gulp and then sipped
the rest slowly while Tucker told McGuinness to let everybody
know about Hall and tell everybody to be careful what they said
over the telephone and to do all their important telephoning from
public booths.

"I don't suppose there's any use trying to make a deal with Hall?"
Tucker asked Henry.

"What can we offer him? Hall wants Bunte, our little Ed. That's
the business he's in. Bunte's his capital. Remember what I told you
about monopoly and being respectable?"

"Never mind."

"All I was going to say is, Hall wants to break up Bunte's
monopoly through you. If he does, he's got the monopoly. What
can we offer to top that? You can't give him Bunte without giving
him yourself."

"Who said anything about giving him Bunte?"

Anyway, thought Tucker, it's an idea. He had had the idea
before. It seemed dangerous. Bunte knew more about him than
he knew about Bunte. If he delivered Bunte to Hall, there would
be a big trial and he would have to testify. Hall would insist on a
big trial. That was the way he advertised the business he was in.
And nobody could promise what evidence would or would not
come out in a trial.

While Tucker was turning this over in his mind, he watched
Wheelock. He was trying to decide whether Henry was drinking
because he was scared or simply because he liked to drink. Either
way, if the man didn't stop he'd have to get rid of him. He couldn't
afford to have a drunk handling important business for him. One

moment Tucker was sure Henry was drinking because he was scared and the next moment he couldn't tell.

"Edna's right," he told Henry. "You ought to settle down and get married and get some home life into your system."

"I've got too much home life now. I've got three apartments and a vacuum cleaner in each one."

"To clean the girls out of bed in the morning," McGuinness said, but no one heard him.

"Three?" Tucker was surprised. He knew only of two.

"Yes, I think that many," said Henry. He held up his hand and began to tick them off on his fingers. "One on 58th Street, east side. I go there when I want to playboy, playboyish. To play. This one here. I come here when I want to feel like a corporation lawyer. The one on Central Park West. I go there when I want to be a businessman." He looked around with a pleased smile. "I'm a man of many moods," he said, "and when I want to feel like a heel, I go to my mirror." He laughed, but no one joined him.

"You got booze in all of them, I suppose," said Tucker.

"Yes sir, and I get drunk in all of them and take off all my clothes and lay naked in the middle of the floor and feel wonderful, like a bottle of whiskey."

"You're talking drunk now," said Tucker, "but don't take off your clothes."

He looked suddenly at Edna. Nakedness had made the thought of her stir in him. When Edna was naked in bed, her big-bosomed, big-hipped body lay in snowy heaps and mounds. "I'm not kidding," said Tucker to Henry. "You ought to get married. It settles a man."

He smiled at Edna and she smiled at him. She seemed to know what he was thinking. What Wheelock had said, thought Tucker, must have started them both thinking the same thing. A warm feeling went through him. "I used to be like all the others, too," said Tucker, "greedy for money, couldn't make it fast enough, tomorrow they'll get you so get it today. But Edna changed me, sort of settled me down so I can wait for my money now and not worry while I'm waiting."

Tucker hadn't been able to relax in his marriage and enjoy Edna until he had had enough money, until the money need had lost its sharpness.

"It certainly took a long time," said Edna.

Edna's voice was slow and warm and pleased. It tickled against Tucker's ears. "I guess it did at that," he said. "You had lots of things to work against. A man like me, with the kind of life I had, living out of garbage pails and so forth, you know, everything, this and that, the old story, a man like me is born worrying."

"It took a long time for you to admit what I did," she said.

Tucker smiled at her. The sound of her voice lay in the air. It was like a flower. He felt he could smell the sound and touch it and see it. It crushed against his ears.

"Well, you know how it is," he said. "It took a long time for me to even know it. I just thought about it lately with the things I been going through, when the pressure was on again, the same old pressure as before, but I was different, felt different."

"I'll tell you what," said Henry. "If you can find me a big keg of whiskey with a private bung hole, I'll marry that."

Tucker went white. He drew back in his chair and his nostrils flared wide. He got up. "I think you ought to go to bed," he said.

Wheelock was laughing. He couldn't seem to stop. He laughed all by himself while Tucker and Edna went for their clothes and the breath came back slowly into McGuinness.

Mac had thought Tucker was going to blow up sure.

On Thanksgiving Day, when Wheelock felt he could not bear bed a moment longer, he had breakfast and dressed carefully and sat reading a newspaper and wondered what to do with the holiday. Holidays usually were a bad time for him, but this one seemed worse. His drinking had left him tired and hot and dry. Whatever he thought of doing didn't seem to be an improvement over being bored where he was.

It occurred to him finally to go to a musical revue. He had seen all the revues then showing, some of them twice. He telephoned his ticket broker to see what was available for the matinee. Then in the midst of the conversation, while the broker was going through the slender list, Wheelock impulsively insisted on a show called "Beat It!" This was one he had seen only a single time. He remembered a girl in it and remembered suddenly that she interested him.

The girl had been listed on the program as Doris Duvenal. She was used chiefly to stand around among those present during comedy skits and to dance in the back row during the chorus routines. She was a $40 item in a $90,000 show.

The first time Henry had noticed her, a few weeks before Thanksgiving, she was dancing. She did not seem to know how to dance at all. She tried too hard and all Henry could pay attention to was her trying. She smiled all the time, but Henry could not see her smile. All he could see was that she was trying hard to smile. She kicked higher than the others and threw herself into the twists and turns of the routine with more dash, but he could not see her kicks or turns or twists. All he could see was that she was trying to kick and trying to turn or twist. She seemed to realize she was no good and it made her try all the harder.

"If only she'd stop working so hard," thought Henry and looked around to see if others in the audience were noticing her. He was afraid suddenly, almost it seemed capriciously, the audience would become irritated with her awkwardness and act to show it. But the lifted faces around Henry all looked pleased. The audience's eyes rolled and roved with the dance.

When Doris stood still, her awkwardness did not leave her, but it became less obtrusive. The fury of her smile diminished. Henry began to wish she would remain still. "If only she wouldn't try so hard," he said to himself, "maybe she'd be all right."

Then the dancing began again and he turned his gaze from her to the rest of the show. He knew she could not stop trying. The harder Doris worked, the worse her work became. The worse her work became, the harder she had to work. It seemed to be a law of nature and Henry knew it well.

It became an evening of caprice for Henry. Fastening his attention on this painful, ludicrous creature seemed a caprice to him. Then, during intermission, he had another caprice. He sent her flowers. In enclosing his card, he was seized by one more caprice. He wrote on the back: "I enjoyed your *work* very much," underlining "work" twice heavily and with a feeling of scorn quite out of proportion to the smallness of the insult. His final caprice was that he paid no attention to Doris during the concluding act of the revue and made no attempt to see her afterwards and, indeed, forgot to think about her at all.

But this was a serious disturbance. It could not be put down forever with a small punishment, an insult and banishment from the mind. Doris, spoiling her work by trying too hard and so having to try all the harder and spoil her work all the more, stirred too deeply among Wheelock's secret, unthought thoughts. From now on, she must rise into his mind some time, in fact whenever his unthought thoughts would.

Wheelock was a man whose mind had been made blind and sick, also, by what business had done to his family and to him. So his mind had seen only and yielded only to a need for money. It had seen further that the way to get it was to hunt with the plunderers.

For a sensitive man who had loved his father and regarded his father's way of life as heroic, to hunt down money was exactly wrong. Yet he became frantic for money and frantic to hunt it, as Doris seemed frantic to dance well. The harder Henry tried for money, the more he degraded his natural self, just as the harder Doris danced the more she degraded her self. The more degraded Henry felt, the more money he must try to get. The more money he got, the more degraded he must feel. The harder Doris danced, the more degraded she felt. The more degraded she felt, the harder she danced. This was what Doris meant to Henry, although as yet it could not be clear to him. It could only be a troubled kind of stirring in him, breaking out in morose caprices.

But the situation in which Wheelock had blindly placed his life could not endure forever. A limit must be reached, a crisis, during which the situation must be resolved in some way. The first time Wheelock saw Doris, there had been no crisis. He could still get her out of his mind with a little, private insult, one she could not possibly understand.

Now, on this Thanksgiving afternoon, crisis was beginning in Wheelock. The small click that had warned him his telephone was being tapped had sounded in him like the first note of a hunter's horn. So Doris returned to his mind and, with her, caprices. She seemed as ridiculous as ever to him. But he had seen less of "Beat It!" than of any other show in town. All he had seen of the whole first act was her. So, why not! Why yes? Well, why not? Why not!

Wheelock's seat for the matinee was down front, but far to the side. He could see Doris even more plainly than before. She was still trying too hard. She seemed forlorn to him and as if she felt she were alone on the stage and everything around her—the audience, the people on stage with her, the show itself—was an opponent to be fought.

When she danced, Henry became embarrassed. He looked nervously at those around him, but they didn't seem to notice anything was wrong. They didn't seem to notice her at all. They all looked friendly and smiling and willing to be entertained. He turned back to Doris. She was throwing her whole body into kicks and twists. Her eyes were intent. Intensity covered half her face and below it was fastened a wide, mute, unhappy smile. He remembered actors felt an audience was an animal crouching in the dark. But the faces around him were lifted to the stage and, if the audience were an animal, then it was a cat waiting patiently to be tickled under the chin. "If only she'd stop trying to kick them in the jaw," he told himself.

She made him uncomfortable. She spoiled the whole show for him, but he could not stop looking at her when she was on the stage and looking for her when she was not. Once, when a song was being sung and the chorus was standing in the wings waiting to come on, he saw her giggling mechanically among the others and looking tired and nervous. He forgot to watch the girl singing and did not even hear the song.

After the performance was ended, he went to a bar near the theater. The afternoon had seemed dreary to him. The bar was crowded and the rapid, happy noises of people talking as they drank bubbled in his head. "The only thing about that show is," he said to himself, "it's a long time between drinks."

He drank slowly and remembered Doris, surrounded by the others, deep among the others, but looking as if she felt alone against the audience. It must be, he thought, a terrible thing to feel. The feeling of being alone is not natural. It makes a person peculiar and makes him do peculiar things, talk to himself, other things, worse things. But, who isn't alone in this dog-eat-dog world? No, he felt, everybody is alone. Everything is competition. Make a profit or waste your life. That's how it is from the minute you're born, because it comes to you in your home before you're out making your own profits. So how can anybody be anything to you? If you love somebody or like somebody, it's because they're useful to you in one way or another, they make you happy, give you what you want. Nobody can be anything important to you, not really important. You love them only when you can make them happy because that makes you happy or only when they can make you happy themselves. And all other people? They're nothing to you—things you work with, things you can put to one side and forget about or things you got to fight. But it's not natural. It can be seen everywhere, what people are like, what happens to them when they go on like that, that it's not natural.

Wheelock thought about that a long time and then he decided, "Who knows what natural is? That's the way the thing is. You have to be alone in life. You have to make a profit or waste your life."

He began abruptly to think Doris's audience had not been like his. It had not been against her. She had just felt it was against her. But his audience in life actually had been against him. It had been willing to ignore him and let him starve.

Wheelock stopped thinking then. His next thought became merely a disturbed emotion. For Doris's audience had been willing to ignore her, too, and let her starve. She had thrown her bones out of joint, trying to kick it to attention. He had thrown his life out of joint trying to kick his audience to attention.

And now that his audience was coming to attention, now that it was looking at his telephone, what did it see? What did it see when, at last, it looked?

The emotion was a clouded shape in Henry. He did not outline it, or give it words or meaning. Instead, he struggled to free himself of it. He leaned over the bar and looked along it brightly and listened to the rapid, happy bubbling and smiled a mute, unhappy, Doris smile, and in that moment decided to meet her.

When Wheelock finished his drink, he went around the corner to the stage entrance of the theater housing "Beat It!" and gave the doorman a dollar and his card and stood waiting in a small, dirty stone and steel vestibule painted battleship gray.

It was like the bar. There were the same rapid sounds. All the show people were young or trying to seem young and looked freshly bathed and, when they ran down or up stairs, the noise they made was like happy people talking. There was a time clock near Henry, and its bell banged continuously. The stage door kept opening and closing and the feet went up and down and across the stone like talk and snatches of high, bright messages and goodbyes and dates rang in the air. Henry stood smiling and motionless among the noises. He was like a man hip deep in a stream and watching water leap all about him.

When he heard a firm, slow step on the stairs, he knew it was Doris. That was the way he expected her to come down. She would want to be queen to her courtier. He looked up the stairs. From where he stood, he could see only her feet. There were other girl feet behind her and they twitched impatiently around her, impatient of her queenliness, and came hurrying down ahead of her. Shoes, legs, knees, upper legs plunging into a billow of pink-lined darkness. There were many of them, three or four pairs of them, and when he saw the faces of the owners, he noticed they were looking at him curiously. They hurried past him and then halted at the time clock and lingered over their time cards, glancing at him out of the corners of their eyes. He turned and smiled at them and they looked at him coldly for a moment.

"Oh come on," cried one of them loudly. "What's the matter with you?" She did not say it, but the words "Never see a man before?" trailed through her silence as a kind of unheard echo. She went out the door and the others followed, looking as if they were holding in laughter.

Doris paid no attention to them. She descended sedately and stood sedately, her face emotionless. She looked younger now than on the stage. She did not seem more than eighteen. Her face had a childish roundness and did not seem to have any fixed quality. Any quality on it appeared impermanent, as if it had been put on, like makeup or an expression. Her hair was a reddish blonde. Her eyes were remarkable. They were a woman's eyes, large, full of the color of gray and shaped like long grapes lying on their sides. The rest of her face was pretty. Her forehead was small and rather narrow, but it was smooth. Her nose was sharp and good on her face. Her mouth was small. Her lips were so heavily rouged they looked as if they were beginning to fold for a kiss. She wore a dark cloth coat with a fur collar. It appeared to be inexpensive.

"Mr. Wheelock?" Henry came towards her, smiling. She stood tall, with head high and back stiff, and she suddenly looked uncertain, almost frightened.

"I got your flowers last week," she said. "I thought they were so cute." Her voice was disappointing. It was a high, frail, nearly bodiless voice with a simpering note in it. But Henry hardly noticed his disappointment. He had not expected her to be so young and pretty.

"Fresh stuff," he thought, "fresh laid egg, if she's been laid at all." He let the thought lick his mind. He had to make himself want her so that he need not think of why actually he wanted to be near her.

"You don't know how we of the theater appreciate when our efforts go over like that and are appreciated," she said. "I thought your note was real nice, too." She seemed to be losing her nervousness. She smiled.

The smile was so transparently gracious. It was so transparently intended as a smile that would be friendly and yet keep him in his place. Henry could see through it with ease. He laughed delightedly. He had identified himself with her. In conquering her, he could feel he was conquering himself. Now he saw she was a not quite bright child and it would be no problem to conquer her. This was another thought that licked his mind as with a tongue.

"I guess I'm your fan all right," he said. "You could do a real fan dance with me." He laughed again, with eager, triumphant delight and looked at her and looked down her slowly, his eyes giving small, upward jerks towards her face while they roved downward. It made him appear to be seeking to lift her clothes with his eyes, but it was only that he wanted to keep her extraordinary eyes fresh before him as he took in the rest of her body. Her body, like her face, was young. It seemed freshly formed and so without any fixed quality. But her eyes had the agelessness of great beauty.

Doris became alert. For a moment his attitude made her think there was something lewd in what he had said. Then she decided it was just a joke and laughed.

"I thought perhaps we could go and have a drink somewhere," he suggested.

She had promised to meet two of the girls in the show for dinner at a nearby cafeteria, but she knew they would understand if she did not appear. Wheelock attracted her. He seemed to be dressed as expensively as a successful actor, except one had to look closely to see how well dressed he was. She felt that, when a man concealed the cost of expensive clothes in conservative patterns, then his clothes were really a luxury. He didn't mark them off as part of the costs of running his business. Wheelock was young, too, and good looking. He must be one of those rich young men, she thought, who give girls fur coats and cars and apartments with a servant. This was thrilling. Doris was new to Broadway. She had not met anyone yet of whom she knew positively that he was one of those rich young men who inherit their money.

"I never drink between shows," she said. "Besides, you know," she smiled and waved her hand gracefully and shrugged her shoulders, "I don't really know you, do I?"

"We can fix that all up." Henry turned to the doorman and cried, "Pop, please, a minute." The doorman was an old, thin-chested man with a round belly. He had once been a stage hand and had always wanted to be an actor. He looked up grumpily and Henry took a $5 bill out of his pocket and went over to him and shook his hand. Doris would not have seen the bill passed if she had not been looking closely.

"My name is Wheelock," he said, "but Miss Duvenal seems to have forgotten it. Would you mind refreshing her recollection?"

"Why, I think you're silly," cried Doris.

The doorman looked at the corner of the bill before he slipped it into his pocket. His grumpiness left him. He stepped forward and put his hand on his belly and bowed. "Miss Duvenal, Mr. Wheelock." He took his hand off his belly and made a flourish. Then he returned his hand, with another flourish, to his belly and bowed again. "Mr. Wheelock, Miss Duvenal," he concluded.

"Brahvah," cried Doris. She clapped her hands delicately and looked excited.

"How do you do," Henry said to her. "It's extraordinary meeting you here again."

Doris giggled. She was like a school girl now. She did not stand tall any more. Her head bent forward eagerly. "I think you're really terribly silly," she said.

They took a taxi to a bar he knew further downtown. While they were waiting on a corner for a red light to change, he saw a florist's and remembered the flowers he had sent her the week before and the insulting note.

"You need a bouquet," he said suddenly and leaped out.

He left the cab door open and disappeared into the store. A cold wind blew across the floor of the taxi. Doris drew her legs close to the seat. She stared through the side window anxiously, wondering if the store had another exit and he would take it and leave her with the taxi bill, because the whole thing was a joke he had been put up to by one of the girls in the show. They were always playing jokes on each other.

Henry came back in a moment with an armful of flowers. He had roses and African daisies and gardenias and three white orchids, and he dumped them all into her lap. He held pins in his other hand.

"Oh, for goodness sake," she said.

He sat on the edge of the seat and explained eagerly that he hadn't known what kind she would like to wear on her coat. As the taxi started forward, her hands stirred through the flowers. The orchids, she thought, must have cost as much as her coat.

"I never saw any like this before," she said and pointed to the African daisies. "What are they?"

"I don't know, they're flowers. They're pretty enough to be called Doris Duvenals."

She didn't smile. She stared at the flowers. "Silly," she said absently.

Gardenias, too, she thought, and roses with long stems. There must be $25 worth of flowers in her lap. Finally, she elected to wear the orchids. She couldn't resist them. She had never had any before.

Henry was disappointed. He felt she should have picked the roses. They would have gone better with her girl-graduate look. Then suddenly he realized why she must have selected the orchids. He felt glad at being able to see through her and so he found himself able to understand her emotion and sympathize with it and be touched by it. He took her hand and squeezed it impulsively. "You certainly have good taste," he told her.

She freed her hand and wagged one finger at him warningly and said, "Eh, eh, Mr. Wheelock," and saw that he was annoyed. She looked down proudly at the orchids.

"I've always had good taste if I do say so myself," she said. "Even when I was home, mother let me fix up my room myself, and all my friends wanted me to help them with theirs."

Henry's irritation at her wagging finger disappeared before she had finished speaking. Her dull, uncomprehending words had removed his fear that she might yet become a problem for him.

"I'll bet you were chairman of decorations for the prom," he said.

"I would have been." Her face looked proud in a formal way and then sad in a formal way. "Only I didn't stay that long in high school because my family couldn't afford it."

Now I'm going to hear the story of her life, thought Henry impatiently, and thought instantly of a way to stop her from telling it. "You look pretty enough to kiss," he said and smiled softly at her.

Her face stiffened. She moved away a bit. "Now, Mr. Wheelock."

"I mean with the orchids on and all those flowers in your lap." He laughed and her face relaxed. "And," he said, "with that small, little mouth of yours, like cake to bite."

"Now, now, Mr. Wheelock," she said and held up one finger warningly.

An hour went by and Henry still moved with his caprices. His mind twitched and twittered like a violin playing. The whole experience was odd for him and seemed rather medical, yet there was relaxation in yielding to each twitch and voicing each twitter. A caprice brought Doris a $15 box of candy. Another made her face fling high in anger. Still another brought her a wool monkey and a box of tarts from a Viennese coffee shop on Central Park South.

They sat quite a long time over coffee and whipped cream in the peculiar, foreign coffee shop and then another caprice grasped Henry and compelled him. He no longer tried to be something before Doris or do something to her. He simply watched her. He looked frankly at her face and steeped himself in its detail—its childishness, the childlike aloofness that rested on it lightly, uneasily, as an involuntary and undependable barrier against him, the disappointment beneath the aloofness, making her seem like a girl striving to prove she did not mind being ignored at a party, and the boredom beneath that, boredom of a child who has waited eagerly for an experience and has feared it would not happen and now prepares herself for the possibility that it may not happen by casting about among stale, usual experiences for one that might relieve her disappointment. That was her face. But it was her eyes that were really subtle. They seemed to have nothing to do with her face. They were works of art. "Made of jelly," he told himself violently, "slimy things, jellied flesh, snotty to the touch." Yet they were devious and profound and separate and seemed to have lives of their own and to have their own thoughts and were in authority over all they saw.

"You are a nice child," he said to her suddenly. "Why do you want me to be wicked to you?"

"For goodness sake," she cried, startled, "whatever gave you such an idea?"

"No, I didn't mean that. I meant, why do you want to see wickedness in me? Why would that give you a kick? Why are you disappointed that you can't see it?"

"So help me, I can't understand what gave you such an idea. You don't talk logical to me at all."

"You gave me the idea, what you're thinking. But you're a child and you don't know what wickedness is. Maybe that's why you want to see it, play with it, because you don't know what you're playing with."

"Mister, you're too deep for me. Where did you grow the whiskers all of a sudden?"

"No," he cried, fascinated with his idea. "You're too deep for me. You're a love song I can't understand and sometimes can't even hear, only feel it in my ears."

"A love song? Ta-rat-tat-te-dee?" Her stubby, child fingers twiddled in the air with playful glee.

"You're wicked." He leaned towards her. There was a small smile on his face. His eyes were rigid and glistened with fascination. "You're really wicked under you, aren't you, cruel and wicked, a poisoned female, aren't you, and poisoning, with lips like claws and juice in your mouth that kills."

"What in God's name are you talking about, so crazy for, Mr. Wheelock?"

"That you're wicked, that your flesh squirms for me to do something wicked to you, make a play for you, bowl you over, sweep you up, take the purity out of you and stuff the hole that's left with pearls, with money, with sin. And that's wickedness, that's real wickedness."

"You've got a dirty mind and you've got the wrong girl in mind," she said angrily. "You talk just like a dirty book. I think I better go."

"No, just a minute. Do you know what wickedness is? If I put my hand in my pocket and gave you a ruby, a million-dollar ruby, just like that, just because you're beautiful and a child and I wanted to give it to you without expecting anything for myself, would that be wicked?"

"Have you got one?"

He laughed. "No," he said, "but would you see wickedness in me if I did it, gave it to you without wanting you to give me anything back?"

"You've got some line, Mr. Wheelock. It doesn't land a girl. It hangs her up to dry on it."

She giggled, but he cried above her giggle. "You see," he cried, "you don't know. But that's wickedness, to do that, not to want something back. That's perversion. Don't you see what it is? Not natural, don't you see? You go to great expense, great hardship to put yourself in reach of something. That's natural. Then, then, to reach out and take it! That's natural. But to get your pleasure from not reaching out, from cheating yourself deliberately, from not getting, from doing without—don't you see what a black thing that is in a man, to make him do."

"This is very dried out stuff to me, your line is," said Doris and giggled again, but Henry did not hear her. He had thought of Tucker hurrying impatiently away from the young man who had fainted because of the dynamite in his mouth. Impatiently! That was something McGuinness didn't have the capacity to invent. The whole thing must actually have happened!

Henry sat motionless for a moment. Then both his eyelids shuddered uncontrollably. He shut his eyes tight. "No," he said in a jarring tone, his eyes shut, "you are a child. You don't know what black things there are, waiting to be brought out in you."

Doris glanced at him uneasily and then lowered her head. His face was so odd it embarrassed her to see it.

Wheelock decided curtly to rid himself of her. He told her he was sorry, he had an appointment for dinner and would drop her at home where she might leave her bundles. Doris gave The Randolph, a costly apartment hotel on 54th Street, as her address. One of the stars of "Beat It!" lived there, and she decided it must be impressive.

Henry watched her get out of the cab in silence. She was holding the sack of flowers in one hand and the chocolates and box of tarts in the other. The wool monkey was imprisoned under her arm. Three orchids were pinned to her coat. She looked like a child coming from a party cluttered with prize and grab-bag loot. He said goodbye without asking when he might see her again.

At the corner, another caprice seized him. He told the driver to go around the block. He knew Doris could not afford to live at The Randolph. He intended to catch her out, and humiliate her. He sat on the edge of the seat as the taxi worked slowly through traffic. Yes, he thought, he would pass her walking down the block and stick his head out the cab window and yell, "Boo!" at her. Traffic was so dense, he began even to be afraid she would get away before he could catch up with her.

Doris was near the corner when he saw her again. She was walking to the cafeteria to meet her two friends. She still was laden with her expensive bundles. The white orchids bobbed and dipped as she walked. They looked like cold light in the night air. People were turning to stare at them. She walked briskly and held her head high and her back stiff and her shoulders square. Her face was expressionless. She did not notice Henry looking out the window at her.

"That great big beautiful dope," he thought. A laugh came up in him wildly.

He sat poised before the door, fiddling with the door handle. Her face was volatile in its expressions. He could imagine how it would vault with surprise when she saw him and then crumble into shame. The taxi had halted in traffic. He could hear the evening wind move in the darkness. It drummed down the street and among the cars and along the buildings, making a noise like running feet.

The taxi moved forward again. It caught up with Doris and passed her and Henry sat back. He did not halt either the cab or Doris. The last of his morose caprices seemed to have been too much for him, or perhaps there had been satisfaction enough in thinking of it.

BOOK FOUR

THE FORGOTTEN

X

ON THANKSGIVING Thursday, Leo became crafty. He took Tucker's money and paid off on 527. On Friday, he made himself hard to find. Joe knew what his brother was up to. Each day the other bankers remained floundering among their customers without money to pay meant more customers for Leo. Leo just wanted to keep them floundering a while. Joe felt Leo was entitled to that much, since his bank had been so badly hurt by the raid. He did not press his brother. Wheelock said to get after Leo, and Joe said he couldn't find him, he must have gone out of town. Then Tucker got on the phone and told Joe that Leo was to be on the line Saturday morning and negotiations to absorb the other banks were to begin Saturday morning and he wouldn't be interested in excuses. Tucker, too, knew what Leo was up to.

So Leo's game ended. Negotiations began Saturday morning and went on all that day and all day Sunday and most of Monday, sometimes in Leo's offices and sometimes in Joe's and sometimes in Wheelock's or, at night, in Wheelock's apartment. Wherever they took place and whoever the actors were, the negotiations were always the same. The faces and the color of the faces changed. Some of the bankers and their bookkeepers had been friends of Leo. But whether the men were black, brown, white, red or mixed, whether they were friends, enemies or strangers, they all said the same things and had the same schemes and tried the same tactics. The men had become a road over which a machine of business was traveling. They swelled and wriggled and twisted and threw up bumps and fell into holes, but finally they all lay flat and submitted to being a road.

They came in with the attitude that they were willing to listen to the proposition if it were made interesting, but they clung to Leo with their eyes. When Leo told them Tucker's final offer, they always said, "no." They threw loudness over their voices, but the voices themselves blew the loudness aside and only naked pleading showed. Leo did not have to say anything after that. They got up to go. They closed their books and put their papers away and Leo watched them in silence. Then they walked to the door and came back or they walked out and came back. Wherever they walked, they came back. Whether they were old or young or in-between, whether they had been storekeepers before going into the policy business or salesmen or holdup men or real estate owners or promoters or merchants, the point about them all was that they did such and such and said and so and then said no and then came back. For, whatever they were in themselves and whatever they had made of themselves, a machine of business had made them all the same now.

The haggling exhausted Leo. Once, in the middle of it, he became dizzy. He had put his head back to stretch and, when he got his head all the way back, the inside of it began to spin around. He felt his brain turning behind his eyes. His eyes were fixed. The room and the people in front of him were fixed, but the inside of his head was turning. Then the room began to turn around the people and the people sat still looking at him. He had become so pale, they were frightened. They leaned forward and stared at him and their mouths were open as if they were about to say something. Then they, too, began to turn. Everything was turning a different way, the room one way and the people another way and the inside of his head still another way. He closed his eyes and the spinning was faster. He put his hands out and held on to his desk and sat there with his eyes closed.

"Leo," cried Joe, "what's the matter with you?" The words came through the turning in Leo's head. The turning was slower and then, slowly, it stopped. "Don't you feel well?" asked Joe.

Leo opened his eyes. Joe was standing over him, looking as if he were seeing death.

"I'm not eating right," Leo said. He pressed deep into his belly with one hand. The faces of the men staring at him all had the sight of death on them. One gave him a cup of water. He drank it noisily and wiped his lips with the back of his hand and shook his head. "No," he said, "I'm not eating and sleeping like I should." The thought of death went out of the room slowly. But, very soon business was going on as savagely as ever. Leo listened and talked. He undid the schemes of his opponents and launched schemes of his own and kept wondering whether, if he put his head back, the turning would start again. He held his head forward until his neck ached. Then he slid his head back a little, and a little bit more, more and more, until suddenly the turning began again and he dropped his head forward hastily.

"Who can live like this," he thought.

❧

The crisis continued to gather. Small clouds, in each a little storm, jostled together. One little storm swelled another. One complication complicated another.

"I give you a chance to rest up for the business," Leo said to Bauer at the start of Bauer's first day back at work, "and what happens? You waste your time getting more tired."

Bauer did not seem so much tired as sullen. "I couldn't sleep good," he said. "I was worried." Joe was standing by Leo's side, smiling sympathetically. Bauer glanced nervously at Joe. "Can I get a minute private?" he asked Leo.

"Go ahead, talk. My brother is in the business with me."

But Joe was being very friendly just now. He said he would wait for Leo downstairs in the car. He had come to the bank this Monday afternoon only to be friendly, only to give the people Thanksgiving baskets and to explain about the extra ledger sheet for the combination on the day's total business and to show the people that he was all right, that he was a fellow just like anybody else and they didn't have to be afraid to work for him. Joe was buying the baskets through a friend of Bunte, a city official who owned a wholesale butcher business. It was a favor for Bunte and for his city official, but they were incidental in this case to the people in the combination's banks. Joe knew there would be no trouble about keeping the bankers in line. They were tied tight, with much to lose if they broke loose. But the bankers' people— some of whom might not like the idea of working for Tucker—had only their jobs to lose. A policy job was a small handle on a man. So Joe gave out Thanksgiving baskets and smiled ingratiatingly and left Bauer alone with Leo.

"What's your trouble now?" asked Leo.

"The same thing," Bauer told him. "I've been thinking it over, but it doesn't change."

"You want to quit?"

"Yes sir. I don't want to, but I have to."

"You picked a fine time to talk about it when I got twenty people waiting for me in my office. Talk to me later." He turned to leave.

"I just told you," Bauer said, "so you could get somebody else for tomorrow."

Leo halted. "Tomorrow?" he cried. "You're a man in a responsible position. You got to give me time to break someone in."

"I can't. Honest. I can't. I can't stand it here."

"It's a poison here somewhere?"

"Yes."

"After the way I've been to you, you shouldn't treat me like this."

"I can't help it."

"I don't understand you, a clean-cut boy who's a father with children acting like this, acting like I don't know who, what, sick in the head."

Bauer lowered his eyes. He shifted nervously. His whole body shifted. His feet, his hands, even the tongue in his mouth shifted. "When I get in this place," he said, "I feel sick in the head and all over."

"What happened last week. the raid, can't happen again, not no more. It's taken care of."

Bauer shook his lowered head. He spoke to the floor. "Honest, Mr. Minch," he said, "I know that. I tell myself that. I prove it to myself, but still it's no good. I guess I'm not cut out to be . . . I mean, to be where . . . No, no matter how much I tell myself, still I feel sick in the head."

"Take some pills then, a physic or something. You got to make up your mind that you're going to stay three, four more weeks until I break someone else in. That's final."

"Three weeks!"

"Four, five weeks, as soon as I get. . . ."

"No!" cried Bauer. "You can't stop me quitting. I'm not your slave."

"I'm telling you," said Leo. He walked out of the accounting room and up a small hall into the sorters' room.

Bauer followed. "What do you mean?" he asked.

"Never mind what I mean," Leo said over his shoulder. "I told you." Leo kept walking, across the sorters' room to a long, narrow foyer where the door was.

"What do you mean!" cried Bauer. "Tell me what you mean!"

"You got eyes. You can see yourself. I'm not alone in the business any more."

"Oh my God!" Bauer said it so quickly it came out as one word. He had seen rackets in the movies. When Joe had walked in, Bauer had remembered the movies. Now he knew the movies were true. The gangsters never let anybody out of the rackets. He was in and caught and held for the rest of his life. Bauer's mouth opened, but he couldn't utter a sound.

"Now just be reasonable," said Leo, "and the new people will be reasonable. They're all right. They just don't want to have any trouble, mixups and so forth, you know, until the new setup gets going smooth." Bauer made a sudden movement as if to flee and Leo grabbed his arm. "Stop being a baby," he cried. "Grow up, for Christ sake. Do you want to quit? All right."

Bauer wrenched his arm free and stood breathing heavily.

"I'm telling you," said Leo, "just wait a few weeks and there will be no trouble. I'll arrange it for you as soon as possible. That's my promise."

"Mr. Minch," said Bauer. He tried to pull himself erect and face

Leo and keep his voice steady. "What did you put me into, Mr. Minch?" His voice was so thin it squeaked.

"I didn't put you in nothing."

"Did you put me in this without my knowing or saying?" cried Bauer. "Did you do a thing like this to me?"

"Who put you? Did I ask for it?"

"What kind of a thing is this, to do this to me, without my knowing or saying!" Bauer held out both his hands. "Mr. Minch, Mr. Minch," he pleaded, "what did you do to me without my knowing or saying?"

"What did I do?" Leo brushed down Bauer's pleading hands with his arm. "I didn't do anything. What do you think you're in, anyway? Go back to work like I said and I'll straighten it out, you can quit with a good reference from me, in a little while, when things shape up."

Leo opened the door and went out. As he closed the door, he looked back uneasily. Bauer was turning away. His tall, lumpy body was folded over. He walked slowly and uncertainly.

"I put him?" thought Leo. "They put me." Bauer's words knocked in his brain. "Why am I to blame?" he cried to himself.

On the way to the office, Joe asked Leo what Bauer had wanted.

"Nothing," said Leo. "It wasn't about the business."

Joe had been offended by Bauer's uneasiness before him. "I don't like that guy for some reason in case you don't mind," he said. "He's a goof. I think you ought to get rid of him."

"I'll go back and fire him now."

"No, not this minute." Joe looked at his brother suspiciously. "Just the same, as soon as we can, that goof goes, believe me!"

By that Monday afternoon, seven banks had been examined. It had been decided to lend money to five of them and accept them into the combination and—tentatively, subject to Tucker's approval

—to refuse loans to two and let Leo take over their controllers and collectors.

The two who were to be turned down were waiting in the anteroom when Leo returned from his own bank. One was a Negro named Burrell Spence. He had been in the policy business for more than ten years. The other was Homer Richards, a white man who had once owned a chain of gasoline stations and had been driven out by the big oil companies. He had chosen the locations of his stations too well. The oil people had ganged up on him and then had divided Mr. Richards' locations among themselves.

The two men had been waiting for Leo in the morning. He had told them then that he hadn't had time yet to decide. Burrell Spence had gone away, but Homer Richards had remained in the anteroom. Leo saw him when he went out to make the payoffs. The man scrambled to his feet apologetically as Leo hurried by and smiled after Leo. He had stiff, curly, gray hair, parted in the middle. As he smiled, he looked like a clerk trying not to offend his boss. When Leo returned from the payoffs, both Burrell Spence and Homer Richards were in the anteroom. He passed them in silence. He passed them in silence when he went out to lunch and now again, as he returned with Joe, he passed them in silence.

Leo went into his private office and telephoned Wheelock to ask if any word had come from Tucker on the Spence and Richards banks.

"I'm seeing him tonight," Henry said. "I'm sure it's all right, but just the same we got to do what Ben told us."

"Them two are sitting on my head here like tombstones," said Leo.

There was a long silence. Henry was thinking of the tombstone-like stumps left by the lumber companies in the plundered forests and how they made the forests look like a neglected graveyard and what they had meant to the town and to his father and to his family. An abrupt, capricious sadness sprang up in him and shrouded his mind. "The tombstones follow me around across the country like dogs," he thought and struggled to smile through his sadness.

"Hello," said Leo. He thought he had been disconnected. "Hello, hello! Wheelock?"

"Yes, all right," Henry said. "Tell the tombstones to go home and sit until morning."

Then Leo sent for Edgar and gave him a list he had drawn up of Spence's and Richards' controllers. He asked Edgar to tell these men to come to his home that evening. By the time Wheelock telephoned to say Tucker had agreed to close out the Spence and Richards banks, Leo had already completed taking over the controllers.

Leo was in his office earlier than usual the next morning, but Spence and Richards were there before him. They both looked freshly shaved. Their hair was still wet from bathing, but their eyes had the broken look of sleeplessness. They were wearing their best clothes, as if they both had felt neatness might change Leo's mind.

Spence was given the bad news first. Leo thought the Negro would take it better.

"Well sir," Spence said, "I'm not assuming to tell you your business, but you're making a mistake."

"If I am," Leo told him, "you will make me pay for it."

"I don't want to make you pay, but I will have to. That's business."

Leo wondered what Spence would do in the afternoon when he discovered he was out of business, his controllers were delivering his banks' policy slips to Leo's drop stations. The Negro's eyes were painful to look at. In his black face, they seemed to be bleeding a blood that had been burned brown.

"You're being Santa Claus for my controllers, that's all," said Spence. "I'll have to raise their commission for a while, a little while, anyway, to hold them back in case you got temptations for them in mind."

"I'd like to hear how you make out . . . or if there's anything I can do."

"You'll hear all right. As long as you're in the business, you'll feel my weight."

Where will I hear, thought Leo, in the newspapers? Yes, he thought, in the newspapers. Man falls under subway. Man hangs himself in bedroom closet. No, it was the other one he had to be afraid of, Richards, the white man, the one who had owned the chain of gas stations. White men took business more seriously. There was one thing about Negroes. Business didn't boss all of them. You could still rely on some of them not to kill themselves when they lost out in business.

"I hope I hear something good," said Leo. He stood up to end the interview. He did not shake hands with Spence. He was afraid in the way he would have been afraid to touch a dead man.

Leo waited a little while before summoning Richards. He had forgotten how unpleasant this part of the negotiations would be. Everybody had forgotten. Everybody had forgotten everything important. "That's what they do to me," he thought, "make the whole world want to cut my heart out!"

Richards came in smiling. Then he said what Spence had said—"You're making a mistake you will regret." Leo offered him a job as controller and the man began a long story about the fight he had made to hold his gas stations against the big companies.

"Where I had a lease and didn't own the property," he said, "they bought out the landlord and started demanding. I do this, do that, build this, this is a violation, until I felt I was going crazy. You know what those fellows did? They went into my toilets and criticized even my toilet paper. I felt like wiping the floor with them, that's how I felt, only not the floor, you understand, not wiping the floor, you understand, that's how bad I felt."

"It was their job, too," said Leo. "They were made, too, pushed, too."

"Yes, but small things! Such small, little things! Anything to pick on. If there was cocker-roaches in the toilet, that was my fault. It was against the lease. Where I owned the property, they made contracts to sell me gasoline, you never saw such contracts in your life. Deliveries were late. They left me with dry tanks two, three days at a time. Oil had dirt in it. Grease came with sand, barrels of grease with sand in them! Did you ever hear of such a thing? Never, never, I tell you! Never in the whole world was it heard of that people should do business in such a way." Richards' eyes filled with tears and he put his head down.

"If you want to be a controller," said Leo, "I'll see that you get a good territory and start you off with a few collectors."

"What's the use? I'm through. I used to be a businessman, but I'm finished now. I'm a finished up article. My brain shakes in my head when I got to think something or do something."

"I went through the same thing, four, five years ago, I hardly remember. You'll see, you'll pull out of it and hardly remember, too."

"No I won't." Richards raised his head and looked directly at Leo. "You have no idea what bad luck I got, the stations taken away from me, now 527 has to hit and my policy business is taken away from me. And I'm an older man, too. I can't take a beating like I used to. Bad luck. Bad luck. Some people are just born to have bad luck, is all."

"This is what," Leo said. "You tell your controllers from me I said they can work for me only if they make room for you. That's my orders. They're, each one, to turn over a few of their collectors to you so you can be a controller, too. Otherwise, they're out in the street and I say it."

Richards hung his head again and began to cry again. "Bad luck," he said in a low, trembling voice.

Leo stood up. Take chloroform! he thought, take your troubles to God! He's got no worries of His own!

Richards blew his nose. He pulled his clothes straight. He thanked Leo. When he got to the door of the office, he turned and said, "I'm a nervous cripple." Then he broke up again and ran out. He ran past Edgar silently, his throat stuffed with weeping.

❧

Early the same afternoon, Leo went to his bank. He had to adjust it to the new load of work brought in by Spence's and Richards' collectors and he wanted to make sure Bauer had come in.

Bauer was there. He seemed to have been waiting. The moment Leo let himself into the foyer, Bauer came out of the accounting room and walked rapidly up the small hall and into the sorters' room and across the sorters' room. "I'm quitting right now," he said loudly.

Leo made an exasperated sound with his tongue. "Will you give me a chance to take my hat off first," he said and walked past Bauer to a hat rack in the sorters' room.

Bauer followed at a short distance. "I'm quitting and there's no one can stop me," he shouted. He was crouched with rage. He looked as if he had been nerving himself for this moment and now expected to be hit and to have to hit back.

The sorters had all turned from their work. Delilah had come up the hall from the adding machines and was standing quietly, one hand folded around her throat. Juice was smiling. Murray was smiling, too, but his smile was uncomfortable. Pie-Eye kept shaking his head.

"No one can stop you from doing anything," Leo told Bauer, "from being foolish or jumping off a bridge or anything."

Bauer was trembling so much his eye-glasses seemed to jitter. He remained crouched. His lips worked back and forth over his dried mouth.

"I explained to you what you're doing," Leo said.

"You're not going to stop me," shouted Bauer. "You and nobody else. There's laws in this country. I quit." He stamped his foot. His whole body shook. "I quit! I quit!" he said and stamped his foot again. "I want to quit. I'm going to quit. Nobody can stop me from quitting right now."

He stood a moment glaring. The hate in his eyes came through his glasses. Suddenly he reached past Leo and Leo sprang away, but Bauer was only reaching for his hat and coat. He tore his hat and coat from the rack and ran from the room.

Bauer ran lightly. He was an awkward man, but he always ran

lightly, on his toes. As he ran, his feet made ticking, scratching sounds against the floor. They sounded like the claws of an animal in a cage. He slammed the door behind him and the echo of the slam was a shout in the still room.

"What did he come to work for at all!" called Leo at the closed door. He turned to the sorters and spread his hands outward, palms up. "That's some hot corn," he told them. No one answered. They were all looking at him. He laughed and pointed in the direction of the toilet. "He was in such a hurry," he said, "he ran the wrong way." No one laughed. "He was in such a hurry to go to the toilet," giggled Leo, "he ran the wrong way." He laughed. The room remained silent.

The people turned slowly back to their work. Leo felt they were not on his side any more, as they would have been had it happened a week before when Tucker was not in the business with him.

XI

LEO HAD had an appointment that afternoon with Joe to continue negotiations. Now he couldn't keep it. He couldn't leave Murray to run the office alone. In addition, he wanted to stay with his people and try to win them back to his side. So Joe had to be told about Bauer. Leo didn't want to tell. He sympathized with Bauer. He had felt the same way about going back into the woolen business after the shock of bankruptcy and about going back into all the other businesses he had been frightened out of. Horses couldn't have dragged him back. But now he had to tell about Bauer. He couldn't think of any other explanation for delaying so important an appointment.

The negotiations were set over until evening. After they had been concluded and the brothers were alone, Joe told Leo he would take care of the Bauer matter and see to it that Bauer went back to work tomorrow.

"I don't want that," Leo told him. "I think if we just let him go, goodbye and good luck, then my people would know it's just like the old days between me and them. If they want to quit, that's their privilege, their hard luck. They have nothing to be afraid of. That way, nobody will quit."

Joe said he had to consider the whole combination, not just one bank. "Your people like you," he explained. "But in most places, the banker's got no hold on his help. You know that. Any little excuse and they will quit. We got to hold them in line a while. You know that."

"I know, I know, but I don't like it."

"What do you think we're going to do?"

"I don't care what you're going to do. It's not my idea of business to do it."

"You got to have discipline in any organization."

"I know, I know, but . . ."

"You know yourself that if Bauer gets away with quitting, there will be people quitting in all the banks."

"It's got to be a way that . . . with friendliness . . . they should like . . ."

"If they don't like us, okay, the hell with them. We can fire them one at a time when we find people to take their place. But when we want, not when they want. Not all at once. Not right away when we got all this work to attend to and can't pay attention to the little details of how the banks is running."

Leo rubbed his forehead a moment. Then he rubbed his eyes. His fingers dragged down along his face, pulling and rubbing the flesh of his face. "I'll tell you the truth," he said. "I haven't got the stomach for this kind of business."

"What do you mean this kind of business," cried Joe. "In any business, you got to face what is a fact."

"Yes, but how you're going to do it, I mean."

"I don't get you at all. 'This kind of business.' Every business has got to work with what it's got, use its assets, good will, credit, reputation for this or that, make its reputation, whatever kind of reputation it's got, work for it. Whatever a business has got, that's what it has to use the best way it can. Isn't that true?"

"Don't ask me what's true," Leo said. "I can't tell no more what's true."

❧

Louis Johnston, Tucker's chauffeur, was picked to do the job on Bauer. Joe told the man to get Bauer to his office the next morning, Wednesday, ten o'clock. Johnston wanted to know if he should go alone.

"Oh yes," Joe said. "Just tell him it's important to come. I want to see him." Johnston hesitated. "If you have any trouble with him," said Joe, "don't do nothing, but call me up and tell me what it is."

Tucker's chauffeur was a big, square, heavy, easy-going man with an easy way of talking. He was still salty looking from his long years around boats in the navy and during prohibition. But he was middle-aged now and bald-headed and, when his hat was off, his bald head made him seem sheepish in a friendly sort of way.

Johnston drove to Bauer's house in Tucker's car. It was a tenement neighborhood in the east Bronx and, when the expensive car drove up, children flew toward it. They tumbled from all directions like sparrows gathering to dive for bread. Johnston called to the largest boy.

"Here's a nickel for you if you watch this car," he told him. "Do you think you can keep the kids off it?"

The boy was about nine years old. What he was doing out of school Johnston did not know. Sweaters bulged under his jacket, but his face and hands looked raw with cold.

"Yes sir," he said, "easy."

Johnston handed over the nickel. "If I come down," he said, "and see no kid has been on it and it's clean like now, you get another dime." He looked at his change. He had only pennies and quarters. "If you can change a quarter," he added.

"I'll get change in the candy store, mister."

"I won't be gone long, five or ten minutes. So it's an easy fifteen cents for you. Easy come, easy go."

"There won't be no kids get near the car. I'll see to that, mister."

"Don't go blowing it all in on the one girl."

"Not me."

The boy turned ferociously on his friends and playmates. "Come on you kids, beat it," he growled and scowled at them and clenched his fists at them. They were no longer friends to him, only something in the way of a dime.

Johnston saw the Bauer bell in the foyer downstairs, under the letter box. It was the only one with a printed business card to mark it. One other wore an illegibly pencilled name, but the nameplate slots on the rest were empty. "That's a Heinie for you," thought Johnston as he noticed the card. "Everything tidy and shipshape." The downstairs door was open, however, and he did not ring the bell.

The apartment was three flights up. The building's wooden stairs lay in brown, sour-smelling air. Johnston went up quickly and saw a door which had thumbtacked to it another printed business card with the name: "Frederick E. Bauer." The address and telephone number had been inked out neatly.

A woman opened the door to a crack when Johnston knocked. This was Catherine, Bauer's wife. She was young and quite fat. Her dark hair fell about her pale face like a loosely tied litter. She looked at Johnston suspiciously through the crack and he took a step backward and removed his hat to show his bald head. He had learned, from a house-to-house canvasser he knew, to step back to give people confidence and he felt that the sight of his bald head gave people even more confidence.

"Is Mr. Bauer in?" he asked.

"Who wants him?"

"I'm from the office."

Without a word, she opened the door wider and he followed her into the room, closing the door behind him. It was the kitchen. A dark-haired girl child was playing on the floor with a cracked doll and some rags she used as bedding. Clothes, long since dried, hung on a line stretched from wall to wall. Breakfast dishes stood on an oilcloth-covered table among crumbs and stains of spilled coffee. Some of the crumbs had got on the butter and stuck there like flies.

"Everything is such a mess." Catherine seemed flustered. "He'll be out in a minute."

"I know what it is in a home with children, ma'am," said Johnston. "A mother don't have to apologize for nothing as far as I'm concerned."

He laughed and she smiled at him. "Let me take your hat," she said. He gave it to her and she hung it on a hook in back of the door. She asked for his coat, but he said he wasn't staying long. Then she asked him if he would like some coffee. "It's all made," she said.

Johnston said he had been advised to cut down on his coffee. He began to smile at the child on the floor. He gave her the forced smile of an adult who isn't sure what to do about children. The child stopped playing and stared at him, and he asked her what her name was. She didn't answer. He noticed there were two other children standing in the doorway back of him—a boy who seemed to be about three years old and another girl who looked only a little older. The child on the floor was the eldest. She seemed to be six, but Johnston decided she must be younger or she would be in school now.

The two children came out of the doorway slowly and the girl got off the floor and they all grouped themselves silently behind their mother. Their clothes looked dirty and were torn in places. Their hair was uncombed.

"I let them play around the house in any old thing," Mrs. Bauer said.

"I know what children are on clothes," Johnston told her.

A toilet flushed with a long, loud yawp and then began trickling distinctly and a door in a corner of the kitchen nearest the sink opened and Bauer came out. He was dressed, except for shoes and a shirt. He wore slippers.

Johnston lifted his fixed smile from the children to Bauer. "I'm from the office," he explained. "I'd like to talk to you a minute."

"Go in the living room," said Mrs. Bauer. "Children, you hear?" Her voice rose and became bullying. "You're not to follow your father into the living room."

"You can talk to me here," Bauer said to Johnston. "I got no secrets with you." He had not told Catherine yet that he had quit his job in the bank. Johnston looked at him for a moment and Bauer dropped his eyes. "Everybody stay here," commanded Bauer, "there's no secrets in this." He had felt a sudden need for the presence of his family around him.

Bauer sat down at the kitchen table. He wanted to put himself at ease. He sought a tranquil attitude, an elbow-on-the-table attitude, but the breakfast dishes his wife had neglected to clear were in his way. His elbow remained poised over the dishes for a moment. Then he sat back. His hands dropped uneasily to his sides and then rose uneasily into his lap and folded there.

"I don't get it, what the excitement is about," said Johnston. "Mr. Minch told me to tell you he would like to see you 10 o'clock, that's all."

Mrs. Bauer walked around to the back of her husband's chair and leaned against it. The children followed slowly and clustered behind her and stared at Johnston solemnly. For a moment Bauer could feel nestled among them and could feel that they were family, people he had gathered around him and created and fed and sheltered to protect himself from all others. "Joe Minch?" he asked. His voice was bold.

"That's the one I refer to," said Johnston. "Is there another Mr. Minch in the business?"

Bauer squared himself. Joe Minch was what he had feared. He squared himself resolutely against his fear, but as he straightened and reared, the bare flesh of his shoulder, exposed by the undershirt, touched his wife's arm and he jumped forward in alarm and twisted around and cried, "Why don't you let me alone, will you please!" He looked angrily into her face and suddenly he was desperate. It was no good reaching out to her. She would not respond.

Catherine drew away from her husband's shout. The children jostled behind her.

Bauer stood up in his fear and faced Johnston. "You tell Mr. Joe Minch from me, I'm not coming," he said. "I'm a free American and I'll do what I like."

"Look, Bud," said Johnston. "I don't know anything about it except what I'm told to tell you, so don't get sore with me."

"I'll get sore all I want. I'm a free American and I'm not taking orders from anybody in my own house."

The little boy began to cry and tug at his mother's dress. She pulled away exasperatedly, anxious to understand her husband's emotion. The child's crying went swiftly, with a swift, grinding noise, into a wail. "Shut up," said Mrs. Bauer. She pushed him away with her leg. The boy screamed and flung himself forward and clung to his mother.

"Aaah, Jesus!" cried Bauer.

Mrs. Bauer swept up the boy in one arm and bounced him up and down and made hasty, tender sounds. Her frightened gaze did not leave Johnston. The boy hid his face in her neck and sobbed.

"I got a car downstairs," said Johnston, "and I can give you a ride to the office, or you can go by yourself, anyway you want."

Bauer's head flung upward. The word "ride" had smashed through his ears. He had heard it too often in the movies. "You tell your Joe Minch," he said in a small, screaming voice, "if he wants to kill me, he'll have to come here and do it."

"Say, what the hell is this!" Johnston turned indignantly to Mrs. Bauer. "Is your husband crazy or something?" he asked.

The two other children began suddenly to cry. Mrs. Bauer didn't answer Johnston. She turned on her children. "What's the matter with you?" she said to them. "Don't you see something important is going on?"

They buried their small heads in her skirt. She tried to fend them off and they fought to get deeper. She had to brace herself. She had only one hand free. The other still held her son. She pulled her daughters away by the backs of their necks, one at a time. "I don't like the man," wailed the eldest. Then they both flung themselves forward again and butted and fought each other with their shoulders to get deep into their mother between her legs. All three children were crying now.

"Shut up! Shut up!" shouted Bauer. "For Christ sakes, shut your damned traps up!" He turned to the table and lifted his fist high in the air and slammed it down. A cup leaped up and fell over and dregs of coffee spilled over the tablecloth. He became frantic. "Shut up! You hear!" he screamed at the table and then turned to the children and his wife. "Shut them up this minute!"

The two girls squirmed deeper into their mother. She felt their small bodies quivering and digging between her legs and her boy trying to bury his head in her neck. She looked at her husband helplessly. "I'll take them out of here," she said.

"No," said Bauer, "no such thing!" He could not yet abandon himself to the feeling that he was alone and had no family to defend him in his time of need, had never permitted his wife and children to become a family to him. "This is their house. The man'll have to go. I've said all I'm going to say."

"If you put your shirt on," said Johnston, "I'll wait for you. You can ride down with me."

"Yes?" said Bauer. His voice was lost in the howling of his children. He himself began to feel lost in the jungle of noise. "Yes?" he shouted despairingly. "Yes? You think so? Well, you can go to hell, you and your Joe Minch." He walked out of the room.

Johnston watched him go. Then he looked at the children. His mind was crushed with the noise of them. He smiled at Mrs. Bauer. "I'm not a family man," he said. "I guess I'm not used to all this kind of thing going on."

He went slowly after Bauer. He walked through one bedroom that was so narrow he had to turn sideways to pass between the length of the bed and the wall. Then there was another bedroom, just as narrow, and, after that, a slightly wider, seldom used room, supposed to be a dining room, and finally a living room.

Bauer was sitting in an easy chair in the corner, staring sullenly out the window at the fire escape. A sense of defenselessness rose and rolled and fell splashing like sea in him. He sat giving himself to it, breaking up in it, rising and rolling in it and then falling endlessly down into a blinding, mouth-stopping, nose-stopping sense of being bundled in swift-circling stranglers' arms. When he heard Johnston enter, he lunged away from his thoughts so violently he was carried to the edge of his seat.

"Where do you think you're going," he cried, "forcing yourself into my house."

But there was an instinct for victory in Johnston and he knew he had only to stand there and make conversation for Bauer to give in. "I don't know what you're making so much trouble for yourself for," he told Bauer. "Why don't you stop being foolish and go down and hear what Joe has to say? Is that going to hurt you to do that?"

"If he has something to say to me, he knows where I am. I don't take orders from him."

"Is it orders when a man wants to talk to you, tell you about something? What's the use of getting him sore for nothing?"

Bauer didn't answer. He looked out the window for a moment, his head high, his lips tightly shut. The sense of breaking up into a sea and rising and rolling and falling with a sea returned to him. It seemed suddenly he had always known a man would come to say Joe Minch wanted to see him and that he would fight against going and lose and go. "All right," he said at last, "I'll hear what he has to say. If he tries tricking around with me, he'll be sorry. Remember that."

Johnston stood in the doorway of the near bedroom and watched Bauer dress. When Bauer opened the door of his closet, Johnston was surprised. The closet was so tidy it looked out of place in the house. The ties were carefully folded and there were trees in the shoes. The hats were put away in boxes. All the shelves looked uncrowded and neatly stacked. It was an oasis of order amid the disorder of the rest of the house—a map of his aloneness within his family. The closet was Bauer's province. The rest of the house was Catherine's.

The two men went into the kitchen together. Johnston got his hat from the back of the door. The children had been quieted, but when they saw the men they ran to their mother's side.

"I'm going downtown," said Bauer.

Catherine stared first at one, then at the other, worriedly. Her gaze lingered longest on her husband. It was a disturbed gaze, full of worry and tenderness and humbleness and loneliness, a pleading, troubled gaze. Her husband did not notice it. He was busy keeping his eyes averted. "Well," she said uncertainly, "I think that's best."

"What you think is no business of mine," said Bauer. "I don't care what you think or don't think or if you think. So shut up."

A glare of rage filled her face. Yet Bauer's outburst did not seem to have startled her. She seemed almost to have expected it. She could not know, of course, what her failure to contrive a dignified setting for her husband, what her neglect of the dishes and failure with the children and failure, most of all, to step into the fight against Johnston commandingly and take it over from her husband, had done to Bauer. Her husband could not tell her because he did not understand it properly himself and she could not know. But, although she seldom knew why he cut at her and Bauer, too, seldom knew why, she always expected that he would.

Bauer went out before Catherine could find words to express her rage and Johnston glanced at her briefly. He saw the anger on her face and, also, fright. He wanted to say something to help her, but he couldn't think of anything and he turned away with an embarrassed smile and followed Bauer down the stairs.

While the boy ran off to change the quarter and get his dime for watching the auto, Bauer waited silently in the car, his face sunk into his coat collar. Johnston stood in the cold on the sidewalk, patiently, thinking nothing, wishing the kid would hurry up because the cold was getting to his ankles, but thinking nothing, or, rather, lost in unthought thoughts.

The boy, being crafty and hopeful, returned with five nickels. He took two nickels for himself and gave the rest to Johnston.

Then he stood smiling a brave-lad, loyal-lad, begging smile. Johnston looked at the fifteen cents a moment. He seemed about to close
his hand on the money and put it into his pocket when, suddenly,
he gave it to the boy. An emotion about Bauer's children upstairs
had entered his mind. He did not know enough to blame the plight
of Bauer's children, their motherlessness and fatherlessness and loneliness, on the business world in which the parents had to live, but
he felt sorry for all children.

"You found yourself a sucker, kid," he said.

The boy took the money and sprang jubilantly to open the door
for Johnston. He felt that working up a piece of change for himself
like that was a pretty good thing, good and okay all right, all the
way up and down. Even chasing his friends had worked out for
the best, he thought, because now he could spend the money on
stuff for himself and not have to share it with anybody.

Joe, too, had an instinct for victory. He sat listening to Bauer
earnestly and patiently and made a remark every once in a while
about how he would like to straighten out whatever trouble there
was in the office because he wanted everybody to be happy in his
work, and waited patiently for the man to talk his bluster out.
When he thought the time was right and all the toughness was out
of Bauer and there was nothing in Bauer but fear, Joe told him
abruptly he was making a lot of trouble for himself.

"We've gone out of our way to be nice to you, you know yourself," he said. "Now we're getting near the end where we say, if
you don't want to be nice, well, we can't be nice either."

"What are you going to do?" asked Bauer.

Joe hesitated. "We're in a spot right now," he said, "where we
need every man's loyalty, especially where they are important to the
business like you."

"You can't make me stay," cried Bauer. "How can you make me?
What are you going to do?"

There was another silence.

"I want to be friends with all you people," said Joe. "I'm looking ahead to where we can work together on a nice, friendly basis. I don't want to be a boss that says you got to. I want to be a boss where the people do things by theirself because they like to."

"If I get up now and walk out of here, how are you going to stop me? What are you going to do to stop me if I get up and say I won't stay and walk out of here?"

Joe looked thoughtful for a moment. "You got entirely the wrong attitude, Mr. Bauer," he said finally. "If you're having some trouble with Leo, I want to help straighten it out. My brother is a reasonable man and you two ought to be able to get together. You've worked for him so long."

"No! I refuse, that's all."

Joe looked at Bauer steadily. He was leaning forward a little bit and he remained that way a moment until Bauer's eyes fell. Then he said, speaking softly and clearly and carefully, "You do what I say, Mr. Bauer, or I will have to kill you."

Bauer turned away. His head remained stooped. He looked shy. He had expected to hear something like this ever since he had gone into "the rackets" by taking a job with Leo. He had thought that when it was said, right out plain, he would die. He would scream and fall down dead. But he wasn't even frightened now. He felt more embarrassed than anything else. His face was hot and flushed with embarrassment.

"You see," said Joe. "I'm being very frank with you. Now you go back to work today and stop making trouble and there won't be any trouble."

Bauer couldn't lift his head. There was a churning going on deep in his chest. He felt it. He felt his face hang loosely, hot and flushed. Then suddenly the skin of his legs and arms prickled with cold. He was prickling with cold all over. A shudder bounded up his spine and plunged into his head and spread seething toward the back of his head.

"Well," said Joe, "what do you say? Is it a deal?"

Bauer got up. His legs were flabby. He had to lift himself from the chair with his arms. Joe was holding out his hand and Bauer touched his fingers to it in a kind of handshake.

"We don't want there to be any trouble," said Joe. "If you have any trouble up there with Leo or anybody, just let me know and I'll see what I can do to straighten it out."

He patted Bauer on the shoulder and steered Bauer out the door and Bauer worked that day, Wednesday.

THE LAW BUSINESS

XII

AT A FEW minutes after ten o'clock, the following morning, Thursday, a man telephoned police headquarters and, speaking in a high, nervous voice, complained that a policy bank was being operated in the apartment below his on Edgecombe Avenue.

"Just a moment please," said the policeman at the switchboard. "Capt. Foggarty's line is busy. Will you hold on a minute, please?" He discovered he was talking into a dead telephone. The man at the other end had hung up.

About twenty minutes later, the same high, nervous voice asked for Capt. Foggarty and, when connected, began to complain once more that a policy bank was operating in the apartment below his.

"I'm a married man with wife and children." The thin voice was shaking. "It's nothing to me, but that's not the kind of thing kids should ought to have right in their faces where they live."

The man's nervousness irritated Foggarty. "Keep your hair down," he told him.

"What? I'm sorry, I didn't get you what you said. What? What?"

"I said to take it easy and give me a chance, will you."

The Captain made a note of the address of the bank and asked for the man's name and when he would be down to file a complaint.

"What are you trying to do?" The man's frightened voice rattled the telephone. "Are you trying to trick around with me?"

"Keep your hair down," Foggarty said. "What kind of tricks are you so scared about?"

In the silence of the office, the Captain had heard himself talking. The silence had been a mirror reflecting sound. The bullying contempt in his own harsh voice upset him. It meant sloppy police work. He lowered his tone steeply.

"We get these complaints all the time," he said, "and it's just a matter of formality to come down and show you're serious about it so we don't have so many wild goose chases to chase on our hands."

Before he had finished, Foggarty knew by the vacant stillness in the telephone that he was talking to nothing. "Hello," he said and waited a moment. "Hey, there, hello, Goddamnit!" He jiggled the hook.

The patrolman on the switchboard downstairs answered, "Your party hung up, Captain."

"Goddamnit," cried Foggarty, "what the hell kind of a way is this, to cut me off like this way."

"No sir," the patrolman said, "your party hung up. Your line is still connected, but he hung up. He done that before, a little while ago."

The patrolman's young, eager voice grated on Foggarty as much as the frightened voice had. The frightened voice meant work for him. The eager voice meant ambition.

"He sounded scared," the patrolman said, "like he thought maybe the call was going to be traced back if he hung on too long."

Foggarty was growing old in a young man's job. Pushy people alarmed him. "You pay attention to your work in the future instead of your imagination," he told the patrolman. "I want the right numbers out of you down there instead of imagination. I don't want to be cut off in the middle of an important conversation again and that's all I want out of you instead of imagination."

An emotion of violence formed in the patrolman's brain. "Yes sir," he said. "I can't help it if your party hung up." He hesitated, wondering whether to keep on trying to impress Capt. Foggarty with his alertness. Then he went on in a swift, sullen tone: "His voice didn't sound nigger to me, although he give a nigger address for home."

The Captain had not thought of that before. His mind became busy with the idea. The idea struggled with fear of "pushiness" for possession of his mind and, after a moment, fear won as fear always wins. "How did you get his address?" Foggarty shouted. "Are you listening in on my calls?"

"No sir. I wouldn't do that, Captain, sir. He give it to me when he called up the first time, before, when your line was busy, sir."

"I catch you listening in on your superior officer's calls and I'll burn you right off the force. Get me?"

"Yes sir. I didn't, sir. I never do, sir, Captain. That's not fair for you to say, sir, when I just told you."

"Never mind. That's all. And remember what I said." Foggarty hung up and sat a moment glaring at the telephone and thinking, "I'll push that pushy son of a bitch where he belongs."

The switchboard had become piled up with calls. When the patrolman had time, he thought: "Captain Fat Guts Foggarty, sitting up there with his fat all over his lap, trying to minimize my statements."

❧

The ambitious patrolman annoyed Foggarty into thinking about the tip on the bank. Policy banks were not in his province. If he had not been stirred to thought, he would not have done anything about the tip unless a formal complaint were filed with him. Then he would have forwarded it to Detective Captain Milletti. But the more he thought, the less able was he to ignore the possibilities involved in the tip.

The next morning, Friday, he assigned Detective Bernard F. Egan, third grade, to make an investigation. "It's a 974 violation," he told Egan, "but I want you to act independent. Keep away from uptown."

Egan was a man of slow reactions. When he stood at attention to receive orders, his mind was as stiff as his back and he never understood what he had been told until he had had time to go over it privately. But this time he understood immediately that Foggarty was trying to get Detective Captain Milletti into trouble. His eyes became alert and rose in his face as if on tiptoe. If somebody had to get Milletti into trouble, he didn't want to be the one.

There was too much risk. Egan's heavy face suddenly looked frail with worry. He had a habit of talking to himself and now he said silently, "Here's a man with a family," and meant himself.

Foggarty noticed the change in Egan and thought about it briefly. His thoughts complicated what he said next. "I want you to go through there," he said, "and find a man who lives there and don't talk nigger talk. I'm not interested in a man who don't talk nigger in the bank, unless there's nobody else. What I want to know is, there is a man living in the house not connected with the bank who don't talk nigger." He felt there was something wrong with what he had said. "You get me?" he asked.

"Yes sir, I'll take a census."

"All right, yes, well, all right. Whatever you do is your business. But find this suspect, defendant, I mean informant, who don't talk nigger and tab him so you can put your hands on him when I want him. Don't bring him in. Just make a report to me personally, an oral report, on whatever you're able to get on him. I want to know is he what he says he is."

"It's my kind of luck that I got all my life," thought Egan, "to get put in the middle." He meant in the middle of a fight between Foggarty and Milletti. The two were fighting for promotion and it was generally believed Milletti was the better bet to win. Milletti was younger and smarter than Foggarty and more likable and had more important connections. Now, when Foggarty lost, Egan would lose with him. After Milletti had won the promotion and was going around rearranging the department, Foggarty would look out for himself, but he wasn't the kind to look out for Egan, too. He would throw Egan to Milletti, maybe to save himself, which would be excusable, but then again maybe just because he was too scared to stand up for anything.

"It's all clear in my mind, sir," said Egan and his blue eyes flickered in his heavy, red face.

Foggarty noticed that Egan's nervousness had increased. He got up. "Come here a minute," he said. He walked to a corner of the room by the window and waited for Egan to follow him. He had decided to become confidential with Egan to quiet him. He spoke in a low tone, directly into Egan's ear, and pronounced his words in his throat so that his secretary would not hear. "I'll give you the whole thing," he said, "so you'll know what to do if something comes up."

Both men were facing the secretary, a young policeman, who lowered his head busily over an assignment sheet he was filling out in long hand. Foggarty and Egan rested blank looks on him. He felt restless under their glance, but they did not see him any more than they saw the furniture.

"This is for the hat only," Foggarty said, "and I'm trusting you with it because I think you know what to do with information."

I guess, thought Egan, he's tied everybody on the squad to him this way. I'm the newest so it's my turn to get on the spot and be where I'll just have to give him loyalty in self-defense.

"There's something going on in policy," said Foggarty, "and I think it will be handy for us to know what's there."

So if I lay down on the job, thought Egan, Foggarty puts me back in uniform tomorrow and if I don't lay down, then Milletti breaks me the first chance he gets. That's the way it is and a hell of a way it is to be, too. Egan tried to fix his eyes on the secretary's back. He couldn't. His eyes leaped from right to left, from edge to edge of the man. He saw the back of the man's right arm, then the back of the left arm and what was in between was just a blur. He fixed his glance on the man's spine and held it there for an instant and then his eyes began leaping again from right to left. I'm not cut out for this kind of politics, he thought. The thought sounded in his head like a cry. "A man does his job," he said to himself, "and that ought to be enough."

"Milletti knocked over a bank last week," said Foggarty, "first big bank he knocked over, and I hear it was a good bank. I hear it was the Minch bank. Minch has had a good okay up there three, four years that I know about."

"Is this the Joe Minch in Tucker's organization," asked Egan, "Guinea Minch?"

"No, but that's a point you got to consider. This is a fellow named Leo Minch. He's Joe's brother, older brother, I think, but the way I get it, he's got nothing to do with Tucker. He works independent. So that's the layout and what's going on is what I want to know."

"Yes sir."

"Do you follow me?"

"Yes sir."

"You see what it is, don't you? Here's a fellow with a good okay and Tucker has a handle on him. I don't think Tucker uses it, the way I get it and I think I got it straight, but there it is, he has the handle—Guinea Joe. So here's Guinea's brother and he gets his bank thrown in the street and then along comes somebody who wants another bank thrown in the street. You see? Maybe it's nothing. Maybe the raid on Guinea's brother is an argument or a shake-down or somebody's got a better okay, you know, something like that, nothing important."

If it's big he wants it for Hall, thought Egan. He's going to give the dope to the new boy and play with the new boy for promotion.

"Maybe," said Foggarty, "this phone tip is the same way, an argument, somebody sore at the bank, a thing like that, or this guy calling up is levelling and really has his kids living over the joint and don't like it. But the thing is, I don't know. You see? It might be big, maybe nothing. I don't know and I want to know, that's all."

"If it's big, then Hall will want to know, too," said Egan.

"What's Hall got to do with this?"

"I don't know. It's like I'm asking is the way I said it."

"Decker is still district attorney, isn't he?"

"As far as you can tell by me, he is."

"All right, you got your work and you do it and pay attention to your work and you won't have trouble."

That's what he's going to do, thought Egan. His own connections are all in the can from the last election and he's going to work in with this special prosecutor and the whole squad will be tied in with Hall and then, when Hall goes on his way, off somewhere to Albany or Wall Street or Washington, there we are, holding the bag. Why, the son of a bitch! What does he think he's putting us into?

"I want to tell you something to put you wise to yourself," said

Foggarty. "Decker is D.A. He is an elected man, elected by the people of the city of New York in the regular way. That's what you know and that's the way you act. Whatever Hall wants to know about things, he'll have to find out for himself. I've seen three or four of these guys come in as special prosecutor in my time and give a black eye to the department, saying they're not going to use us for investigation because we're in with the machine, can't use us, got to have their own investigators. All right, the hell with them. Leave them alone is my advice."

"We're here after they're gone," said Egan.

"That's right. Hall is okay as far as I'm concerned. I'm all for him and I hear he knows the prosecution business pretty good, but what he wants to know he'll have to find out for himself, except, of course, if he comes over here and asks us. Then we give him every cooperation."

"Yes sir."

Foggarty tried to pull his mind back to the policy bank. Hall had been plaguing him. If Hall were going to make a long time job of fighting the regular party, then it would be a good thing for Foggarty to throw in with him. But if Hall were going to stay only long enough to get himself something bigger, then a Foggarty tied to him would be out of luck hard. Just as Leo had felt that a man over fifty who lost his money was losing not merely money but the value of the remaining years of his life, so Foggarty felt now. Foggarty did not have many years left on the force. If he jumped to Hall and it was wrong or if he did not jump to Hall and that was wrong, he wouldn't have time to make up for the mistake. He put the decision off. I'll see what Egan finds out, he told himself, and if it's useful to Hall, then I'll think what to do. He realized he was only temporizing. I'll be saying the same thing a year from now, he thought, and two years from now, when it's too damn late to do a God damn thing.

"What are you worrying about Hall?" he cried to Egan. "You take your orders from me and that's all and, if you don't like it, I'll find somebody who does."

"It was just something that happened to occur in my mind, sir."

"Well, get it out of your mind, that's all, and think about what I'm telling you. There's this fellow who says he lives up there over the bank. He was scared when he called up and he didn't talk nigger. I want to know does he comes from inside the bank or outside. Just tab him. Don't do anything about him. If he's outside the bank, all right, that's what I'd like to know. Don't do anything about the bank either. Just find out if it's there and how many men you need to knock it over. You got that clear?"

"Yes sir."

Egan saluted and did an about-face. It looked rather spectacular in plain clothes. As he walked out of Foggarty's office, he said to himself, "I got him mad anyway a couple times. I should have spit him in the eye to cool him off."

⟡

To worry about a promotion was new for Egan. In eighteen years as a patrolman, he had taken the examination for a sergeancy twice and had failed twice. After that, he had felt the best he could hope for was a long life as a traffic cop, ending in a short one as a retired traffic cop.

It had not seemed to him a bad life. Egan was a large, broad, hard man, heavy on his feet. That made learning how to take care of his feet important. Next in importance was the loneliness of the job. There were things to do for the feet and for the loneliness and he did them and felt his life was all right, safe anyway, money coming in every two weeks for as long as he lived no matter what the hell happened to anybody else. So he should have been happy, but he wasn't. Has anyone ever seen a happy policeman?

The trouble was the loneliness involved in his business. During working hours on traffic duty, Patrolman Egan led a hermit's life. He stood in the middle of traffic eight hours a day, six days a week, and it was like living in a cave of air. He was not a sensitive man, but, as the cars brushed by him, filled with silent, expressionless people, the only sounds mechanical sounds, he felt as if he were not on the earth. Here, in his cave of air, the living noises were the suck of rubber, and the squeak and chatter of metal. The motors hushed and sniggered, hushed and sniggered with a pocketed uproar and blew sounds that were like the breathing of an iron thing. The sounds and the soundless people whisking by made Egan feel, occasionally, as if he were on a foreign planet where God had made man not of flesh, but of metal. And occasionally he felt that he himself was not a man at all, but was a bolt standing upright in a many-engined machine.

To pass the time in his loneliness, he played that game—standing still, listening to pocketed uproar, being the thing in a machine that was always not there when the other thing always struck, or being the wall along which pistons slid. The automobiles were the pistons and he was the wall. If the wall were between them, the pistons worked alongside each other smoothly. If the wall were not there, the pistons would smash themselves and each other. He thrust out his wall of a chest and watched stolidly, wall-like, as the cars slid by, so close sometimes the wind of their passing moved along his coat.

When Egan tired of playing wall, he talked aloud to himself. "Hup! Hup!" he shouted at the cars. He warned himself tenderly about standing so close to the traffic: "Mr. Egan, you *do* take too many chances earning a living." He commented on the cars and the people in them: "Looka! Looka-looka-looka what that greasy ginzo is doing!"

He could shout as loud as he wanted to and nobody could hear him because of the traffic. People could see his mouth open and his big red face strain with shouting, but they couldn't hear what he was saying or even whether he was saying anything. "It's a crazy way to have fun," he thought, "but it's fun all the same."

In a sudden lull in the traffic, Egan's shout would sound over the street and people would stare at him. Then he would look solemn and busy and tell himself: "Not me. Somebody else did it." When the traffic roar was in full swing again, he would grin. "Caught with my pants down that time," he would say aloud and, as the noise continued loud, he would yell: "Wow! Wow! Bernard Egan caught with his pants all the way down right out there in the middle of Gimbel's window."

When an expensive car drove by, he came to attention and saluted snappily. "Hah-ten-shun!" he shouted and slapped his heels together. Occasionally, one of the occupants, thinking he was being greeted, would wave and Egan would shake his finger slyly and say: "Ah-haah! Trying to suck up to the law, eh? What's on your conscience, Mr. Gotbucks?"

The regular passersby came to recognize Egan and, once in a while, Egan would catch one looking at him eagerly. It made him uncomfortable. He would lower his head. "No show today," he would shout into the ground. "Get your rain check on the way out." I am becoming a scandal, he thought. Then he added, I am also become a crazy lunatic. He was worried for a moment. What do I do after this? he asked himself. It's getting worse and worse all the time.

However, it worked out fine for Christmas. He got boxes of 10-cent cigars and bottles of whiskey, envelopes with $1 and $5 in them and ties from people he had shouted to and waved at during the year. Once, in a contest run by a tabloid newspaper to discover "New York's Most Cheerful Finest," 121 readers voted for him, and he won one of the $5 consolation prizes. A man on duty at Grand Central station won the $1,000 first prize. The traffic was heavier there, the loneliness greater.

"There's more of a steady trade at Grand Central with all them taxis," Egan explained to his wife. "The steady trade gets a chance to know a man's cheerfulness better."

Summers were always an ordeal for Egan. Before the mayor got around to allowing policemen to take off their coats, it was uncomfortable to move in the heat, and the languid, moist-aired city did not seem to make enough noise to hide his shouts. To save his feet from the winter's cold pavement and the summer's hot pavement, he had had a small wooden platform placed in the middle of the intersection between the car tracks. But, on very hot days, even the platform failed him and he would have to go to the curb and stand in the shadow of a building.

On one such day, Egan stood listlessly in the still hang of heat. He rested one foot on the curb and the other in the gutter, first the right foot on the curb, then the left foot, then the right foot, then the left foot, shifting his weight, then standing motionless and waiting for time to pass, and, when enough time passed, shifting his weight again. He could feel the time passing. It was like a length of rope going by. For a strange instant, he could feel himself growing older. It seemed the rope was being pulled out of him and unravelling him. Each minute, another stitch of flesh was unravelled and it was plain that finally there would be nothing left but bones and he would be dead and a skeleton. Patiently and listlessly, he watched himself grow older and waited for the cool of the shadow to soak into him. Heat oozed out his body as heavily as sweat. There's a real difference, in the heat, he thought, between if I hold my hand close to my body and away from my body.

Wisps of wind straggled through the building shadows. The wisps pushed and brushed at the heat of his body. He watched it happen. He watched time pass and himself grow older and watched the cool of the shadow soak into him and the heat shift away from the cool and stand out into the air and the wisps of air, small and frail as the broken straws of a broom, brush away the heat as if the heat were dust. Overhead, the traffic lights clicked. One click, a silence, then another click. Crosstown traffic moved. One click, a silence, then another click. North and south traffic moved.

The splintered crackling of his deserted platform thrust abruptly into his ears. His head lurched around so quickly he could still see the automobile riding over the platform between the car tracks.

"Hey!" he said.

The soundless, expressionless people in the car did not seem to have heard. The backs of their heads did not move. They drove on placidly.

Egan hadn't had time to see their faces. His attention had been caught by the wood of the platform as it twisted and splintered and flung up arms. When he had looked up, the car was past him and he could see only the back of a young head in the rear window.

"For Christ sakes," he shouted. "Hey!"

Egan blew his whistle. The car seemed to put on speed. The head in the rear window was plucked from sight by its owner. Egan jumped on the running board of a passing taxi. "Follow that there car!" he commanded and pointed with one hand.

There were two, three things he could paste on them firemen, he thought, destruction of property, leaving scene of accident, refusal to obey officer in pursuit of his duty, speeding, reckless driving. He blew his whistle again and again. Each time the sound shot through the air. People lifted their heads out of their own business to stare. Some came running from around the corner. Cars slowed down and a few confused ones halted. But the car that had run over Egan's platform increased its speed. It was now thrusting in and out of and through traffic wildly.

The anger drained out of Egan. For the first time it occurred to him he might have bulled his way into something serious. Here was a clash between opponents in business that could not be laughed off or talked away. Egan suddenly felt conspicuous standing on the running board of the taxi, clutching the post with one hand. The platform, he thought, hadn't cost anything in the first place. He reached back and loosened the gun in its holster on his service belt. Here it comes, he thought. He didn't really believe there would be shooting. He had never shot off his gun before while on duty. Here's the business, he told himself.

The car Egan was pursuing turned a corner. Its wheels whined. Then there was a huge, smashing crash.

"Contact!" said the taxi driver.

The man was trying to be funny, but his voice went along his throat like scratching. Egan looked at him. He hadn't noticed him before. The driver had not been a person, just something to use in business. Now he saw the driver was a man, a little one, with a thin, dark, yellow face.

Egan took out his gun. His hand felt nerveless. It was a small gun, but his hand had become so flabby it was hard to hold it. "When we go around the corner," he told the driver, "stop the car and get on the floor."

Egan hoped the man would keep the car between him and what-

ever lay around the corner. But this was an old-fashioned cab.
There was no front door on the right side. If the driver steered
the car so that it lay between Egan and whatever was around the
corner, then he himself would be exposed. He couldn't be expected
to take the bullets aimed at Egan. No, no one would expect him
to do that.

The taxi driver turned the corner with his eyes closed. Just as
he was about to step on the brakes, Egan yanked the steering wheel
out of the man's control and maneuvered the car so that it lay
diagonally across the street, its right side facing the scene of the
crash, its bulk between him and the crash.

Egan fell to one knee on the running board. The driver, his eyes
still closed, flung himself out from behind the wheel. The man's
head knocked against the post of the taximeter and he lay there,
crouched in a small space, his eyelids closed tightly around erratic
bursts of redness, his hand rubbing violently against his aching
head. He lay exactly in the path of the accident. If there had been
shooting, he would have been the first killed.

But there was no shooting. After a moment, Egan lifted his head
above the hood of the motor. He saw that the car he had been
chasing had turned too wide and had collapsed against an oncoming
street cleaning truck. Everything had happened so quickly, the three
members of the truck's crew on the front seat were still staring down
at the car that had squashed so suddenly against them. A man in
shirtsleeves, his head far back and his feet pumping awkwardly,
was running down the sidewalk.

"Arrest that man!" shouted Egan.

As he shouted, a second man crawled slowly from the car and
took a few steps and then slouched against the front fender. He
clung to the fender with both hands and looked at the thick, long
drops of blood that dripped from his face and splashed against the
car. A third man, who died later, was lumped unconscious in the
driver's seat. He had shattered the steering wheel and was nearly
impaled on the steering post. In the rear of the car lay a pile of
raw furs which, with the license plates, had been stolen a short
while before.

Egan moved swiftly now. He flung the injured man into the car and manacled him and his unconscious companion to the remains of the steering wheel. Then he began running after the fugitive. A large crowd had gathered. It parted for him. "Giddyap, Sherlock," someone called.

Egan began to blow his whistle again, running steadily and blowing, his gun in his free hand. He did not remember until much later that he had forgotten to release the safety catch. When he did remember, at home, in the evening, his heart vaulted violently.

A few hundred feet down the street, Egan caught up with the fugitive. The boy had run blindly into a bystander and had been knocked down. He was being held and trampled and kicked like an underdog when Egan arrived and rescued him.

The police commissioner personally promoted Egan to the rank of third grade detective for his heroism.

"It was just the luck," Egan told his wife, "that lay between you being married to a dead man and a promoted one."

The promotion brought with it a small increase in pay. Failure in business had instilled one kind of poison in Egan. Success had its own brand. Egan was afraid now his wife would spend his increase in advance and then, when he was broken back into uniform, he would have trouble paying it off. He felt sure he could not last as a detective.

"I walked into it," he told her, "and if I had known what it was, let me tell you, I would not have walked into it. That's a fact. I would have run the other way for my life."

His wife was nearly as large as he. She was a big, slow-moving woman, red-faced and gray-haired like her husband. "There were times before when I thought you was not the coward you looked," she said. She glanced at him speculatively and her eyes became bright and she smiled. "How do you suppose I felt, feeling my husband was fool enough to be a glory lover?"

He did not know how to take her words. His muscles had swelled at her first words. No doubt, he thought, she had added the rest to make him feel small. It was a mean, jealous thing to do.

"Would you feel better knowing you are married to a man without force?" He had almost said it. He caught the words in his head and held them there and did not utter them. It was not the thing to say now, he decided, when what he wanted was to make sure she would be careful with their new money.

So he did not ask her to explain her shy, proud remark and did not understand it and another drop of poison dropped into Egan and did its work on him and on his relationship with his wife and, through that, on her, too.

"You know what I thought about in the midst of loving the glory, when I was pulling out my gun?" he told her. "I thought the bullets cost me five cents apiece for each one and remembered how often I had walked on my feet three blocks and four blocks extra to save a penny or two cents on something in the stores. All those walks and now I was to pump the bullets like water."

"Yes, and I have walked further," she said. "How often do you buy anything, when I buy every day and walk further every day?"

He thought angrily of how she could sit down during the day and he must stand. "You must keep on walking," he told her. "You married a uniform and he will not be a detective long."

"Surely not, if you start thinking not." Her voice was sharp.

It was an effort to look at her, but he forced himself to do it. "You married what you married," he said, "for better or worse, as the priest told you. There's too much politics being a detective. I am not a politician, but just a cop."

"You mustn't talk like that," she said helplessly.

"What I say is the truth and you must be careful with the money as before."

He held a cigar in his hand. He had bought it in the first feeling of being flush. He looked at it with distaste. "This is my celebration cigar for escaping death," he said, "and if you want to buy a celebration cigar for yourself, that will be all right. But then the celebration is over."

"A cigar! I thought that's what I would get out of you, a cigar or maybe a nice new broom to hit you where you belong with."

Thus Egan had brooding to do over his new assignment from Detective Captain Foggarty.

❦

Egan did his brooding while drinking coffee in a cafeteria and while watching a movie on 42nd Street. It wasn't useful brooding. He knew his conclusion before even he began to travel toward it: demotion wasn't a tragedy; in a way it was a good thing for a man to find his level and remain there. But brooding passed the time.

He did not want to rush his assignment. If he finished the investigation today, the raid might be made the next day, Saturday, and then there would be a chance that the arraignment and paper work would carry over into his day off or, anyway, to late Saturday night. Saturday night was holiday time for him.

It was after one o'clock when Egan finally reached Edgecombe Avenue. The building at the address given was in a row of about half a dozen that looked alike. It had two steps to a vestibule, and then there were four more steps to a stone hall lined with lumpy tin doors, painted brown. A gray light from the day outside lay along the stone floor and darkened slowly to a band of gloom that hung from the ceiling. At the end of the hall, a staircase zigzagged once before disappearing from view.

The avenue rose over a small hill and Egan walked it in a leisurely manner. It was a residential street with stores at each end and none between. He believed a leisurely walk would make him less conspicuous. He wanted to look like a man strolling, but his disguise was not successful. Men built and dressed like Egan always look unexpected when strolling.

He passed Negro children bouncing balls and playing on stoops. There were Negro men sitting in parked cars or leaning against the fenders of cars. A big-bosomed woman, bulging out of her corset, stuffed so tightly into her corset that her legs stuck out and waggled like those of a tin toy, jounced along stiffly, a snort squashing from her wide nostrils at each step. Everybody looked at Egan curiously, but Egan believed they would look at any white man who came through as if he were a rent collector. He went toiling along through his stroll, stooping his head casually and leisurely over each forward step.

It was a gray day. Gray air stood down from a gray sky and gray light dripped through it in a slow, uncertain way, like rain. Skinny trees lined the slow-sloping hill. With their crooked boughs, they were like a row of sad, rickety children, their bodies bones and holes. Egan felt their loneliness and silence and he peopled each side of himself with children and began to talk to himself, sounding the words in his head. "See," he said, as if to children dragging from his hands, "all the trees is good for is for toothpicks."

He had been thinking of his own children, scattered at this moment through the city, the girl and the youngest boy on the way back to school now from lunch, the two older boys in high school where they could not get home for lunch. Because of his own melancholy, he had thought of them all as laughing and had seen the laughter in their child faces. Then he had thought of how they must all suffer because Foggarty, whom they had never seen, was scrapping for promotion with Milletti, of whom they had never heard, and because Hall, of whom they had read in the newspapers and heard over the radio, was in business too, and ambitious.

However, the children Egan imagined dangling from his hands were little ones. "The reason them trees is good for only toothpicks," he said to them silently, "is they didn't eat their oatmeal for breakfast all up. If they had et their oatmeal, they'd have leaves on them and their branches would be fat and juicy and they wouldn't be toothpicky at all."

The conversation got him painlessly to the corner. Now there was the problem of how to turn back without arousing suspicion. The talking in him stopped and he looked around and saw a diner across the street and went in. The place was steaming and even the smells seemed to steam in it. It was only sparsely filled.

Egan asked for cigarettes and the white counterman who handed over the pack said, "You from downtown?"

Although Egan was startled, he continued methodically to pick up his change. "From downtown where?" he asked. He did not realize that the composure he had fought so hard to maintain had given him away even more.

"I got a friend who works in the main office downtown," said the counterman, "and I thought maybe you knew him."

"Listen, there's six million people downtown and you thought maybe I knew him?"

"I mean in the main office, headquarters. Aren't you on the force?"

"Not me, brother!" Egan laughed nervously. "I'm a law-abiding man, maybe that's why you thought." He was pleased with what he had said. He turned in the doorway and boomed, "That's all, brother, just a law-abiding citizen."

"Guess you can't be on the cops then," said the counterman.

When Egan came out into the cold gray of the day, he became thoughtful again. There was nothing in the street for him to lounge against without giving himself away as a watcher. A bus line ran along Edgecombe Avenue. He decided his best disguise would be as a watcher, or spotter, for the bus company. "If I got cop written all over me," he told himself, "I'd better make out I'm a company cop."

He remained on the corner in plain view, looking up and down the avenue, mostly down where the building housing the bank was located. When a bus came along, he made notes in his memorandum book. He was pleased to see the bus drivers and conductors glance at him furtively as they passed and straighten out of slouched positions and become precise with their work. "On your toes, boys," he said to himself, "Bernard Francis Egan is cracking the whip."

A few moments after Egan had taken up his post, Murray walked into the apartment house, carrying a black tin lunchbox. The lunchbox gave him away. Without it, he might have seemed a canvasser or bill collector. "That's one of them," decided Egan. Almost on Murray's heels came Delilah with one of the Spanish women sorters who was carrying sandwiches and fruit, wrapped flat in a brown paper bag. "This is going to be easy pie," thought Egan. "The criminals carry lunch for burglar tools."

Delilah's beauty annoyed him. It seemed uppity to him. She

dressed soberly and tastefully in gray and brown and, except for the soft, beautifully brown color of her skin, looked like the kind of woman Egan would have felt humble before. Inside a white skin she would have been "real class" to him. The woman beside Delilah was telling a story and Delilah was listening with parted lips. Just as they turned into the building, Delilah cried, "But that's fantastic!" Her small, soft voice went like music along the quiet street.

"Miss Ritz putting the ritz on the fritz," thought Egan. "Fawncy that!" Her cultured air, too, seemed uppity to him. "Fawncy, fawncy," he thought, "fawncy how fawntastic it is, you fancy pants!"

This was not a natural enmity Egan felt for her. It was even true that brown was a color he liked. Yet his reaction to Delilah had been made to seem nearly instinctive by all the prodigious complex of emotions bred by the society in which he worked, and he never even argued with himself about it.

A bus came by and Egan put Delilah down in his book. "Female spick, short, fat, accompanied by female negress, tall, mocha-colored, fawncy!" The bus driver sat up straight behind the wheel. The conductor stood straight and unsmiling on the rear step. Egan scratched out "fawncy" and wrote "looks like mocha tart," and smiled.

When he looked up he saw Bauer standing a few doors down from the apartment house, staring at him. Bauer was standing as if shocked into motionlessness. Egan had no time to think about the man. He looked at him and then he heard footsteps bearing down on him rapidly from the other side and turned towards them. A short, chunky, black Negro woman was coming full tilt. "You the bus company, mister?" she asked, while still at a distance.

Egan felt like laughing. She seemed so intent on gaining him. "Are you?" She brought up short before him and it was as if a wind had stopped blowing.

"Yes ma'am," said Egan. "I sure am. Do you want to buy a bus?"

"I don't see what's for laughing." She tossed her head high. Her eyes were so bloodshot it was hard to see where they left off and skin began. "I am making a serious complaint and it's not for laughing as you think."

Egan noticed out of the corners of his eyes that Bauer was still poised in fright and was listening nervously. "I am not laughing," he said.

"My money is as good as anybody. My money has got the same color as your money."

"That's right, ma'am. Is that your complaint?"

"If you from the bus company, you got no call to act at me like that, laughing and fresh. I didn't do nothing to laugh at me like that just because you're so white."

Bauer had begun to take uncertain steps towards them.

"I'm not laughing, sister," said Egan. "I'm trying to listen to your complaint, but I ain't heard it yet. What's wrong with you? I'm willing to listen. That's the way we build our business, listening to what's wrong and then doing the right thing."

The woman began suddenly to look diffident. "I got misery in my legs," she said. "I use the bus all the time, mister. Even when I have to go a step, I give the bus the dime. I'm a good customer for the bus."

Bauer was standing very close, listening, his head drawn back, his eyes fluttered upward, his body trembling. "What do you want?" Egan asked him.

"Are you from the bus company?" Bauer's voice had a high-pitched quake in it.

"That's right," replied Egan harshly. "What do you want?"

"Who me?" Bauer's whole face seemed to flicker under the harsh voice. "Me? I use the bus, too, every day, twice a day, and the service . . . I want to tell you about it."

"Take your place in line for complaints. This lady here got here first and you can sound off after her." Egan turned to the woman with a polite smile.

"I live near the corner here," she began. "Right there is where I live." She pointed. "Where the bus stop when I'm going, that don't bother me so much. That's down the hill. I can't walk down the hill like everybody, but it's better for me than walking up the hill. But when I come back, the bus stop where I must walk up the hill to my house 'most the whole way. I just can't do it with the legs I got. Is that right, mister, that I should give the dime to ride two blocks and then I have to walk a whole block up the hill? It's not right with the legs I got."

Egan looked sympathetic. He had nothing to fear from this Negro woman as he did from Delilah. She was not cultured. She had not struggled against the weight of the white man's burden. She had allowed it to crush her.

"See, mister, there the bus stop, coming back, on that corner." She pointed down the hill and Egan and Bauer stared after her finger. "See that? I got a whole block up the hill to go with my legs. If I stay on the bus to where she stop next, it's 'way there, up the hill." She pointed again and again the two men stared. "It's 'most nearly two blocks back down the hill and, with the trouble in my legs, I just can't be going that far."

"The thing is, ma'am," said Egan, "you want us to move the bus stop. Is that it?"

"Sure. I told the driving man why he can't stop the bus on this corner instead of that and I won't have to take my legs up the hill. I'm not well in the legs, I told him that. I can't even stand long because the misery, no less than walk all that long way. You know what he say to me, that driving man I told it to him? You know what? 'Reggelations,' he say. Just like that. Then I told, why he can't stop on the two corners. He can stop the bus where the stop is and where I live. You know what he say, the driving man? He say, 'Reggelations.'" She looked at Egan and her head began to bobble angrily. "'Reggelations,' he say, 'not to stop where no stop is at.' He got no call to say that just because my skin is darker as his is."

"You shouldn't think that, ma'am," Egan told her. He knew if she had been an ailing white woman, the driver would have let her off at her house. "There's regulations that he has to live up to if he wants to hold his job. It's the public service commission. They tell us where to stop and where we can't stop. It's worked out very careful along the whole line for the benefit of all, including the people who don't even ride the bus, the traffic. They got to take the traffic into consideration, too. Believe me, sister, it would be a whole lot easier for you to move your apartment than move that bus stop."

"Oh no, we can't move. The folks that own the house is the boss where my husband works and they wouldn't care for us to move. Is it so hard for you, to pick up that little sign down there where it say 'bus stop' and carry it up the hill to here? My husband will do it when he come home at night and you can just sit and rest yourself, if it's too hard."

"You think that's all there is to it, the sign?" Egan laughed. "The public service commission. . . ."

"My money has got just the same color as your money. I'm a good customer for the bus, wherever I go, one or two blocks, and I give the dime every time."

"I'll tell you what I'll do," said Egan. "I'll try for you, being you're such a good customer. Now that's fair, isn't it? I'll try my best and I can't say more, can I? You give me your name and address and I'll bring the matter up before the public service commission, and you'll be hearing from them in a little while what they can do about it."

He marked her name and address in his book and then turned to Bauer. "Now what can I do for you?" he asked.

"Aaah, Christ!" Bauer lifted his hand and threw it down violently. "Talk to the bus company, talk to City Hall, for all the satisfaction you can get out of these big corporations."

"Is that the way you feel?"

"Yes, plenty, twice as much."

"Now that's no kind of talk for a young fellow like you." Egan noted with surprise that Bauer actually was young. He didn't seem to be over thirty. At first glance, he had appeared much older.

"Aaah, Christ!" Bauer lifted his hand again and again threw it down violently. "What the hell is the use," he said. He walked quickly down the block and into the apartment house where the bank was.

"He's right," the woman said. "He's talking the right talk." She walked slowly back to her home, shaking her head and muttering.

In the next half hour, several people went into the apartment house, but Egan found it more difficult to make up his mind about them. He was sure only of the criminals who carried burglar tools. A thermos bottle gave away Juice. The two Cubans brought their lunch in the brief case they had once used to carry music and Egan put them down, too, as suspects.

When Edgar arrived in Leo's big green roadster and bounced briefly across the pavement, carrying a mail sack, Egan knew there would be no more bank workers. The sack contained the day's policy slips. He looked at his watch. It was 2:40. It would be a good thing for the raid to know exactly when the evidence arrived.

Egan waited until Edgar drove away and then waited ten minutes more before going into the apartment house. The walk in was a ticklish moment, but he decided there was nothing he could do except just go in and let the people on the street think what they pleased about it. Once he got into the vestibule, he felt a little more secure.

A band of pearl-colored light ran along the tiled floor of the hall. It was nearly a yard high and then it began to fade into a band of brown that looked as if it had been laid on top with a brush. As he walked down the hall, a clutter of musky odors folded around him. He didn't like the feel of the people at his back, standing on the street and puzzling over why a bus spotter had gone into the house. "Start from the top and work down," he told himself. "That's the best." He wanted to get as far away from the street as possible.

The job ahead of him was going to be unpleasant. Standing in the open halls, without cover or explanation, leaning his ear against doors and listening for the sound of a policy bank in operation would not be a picnic. If he could think of a story to explain himself when caught, it would not be so bad. What the hell did a policy bank sound like anyway? Adding machines going, probably, and so forth, typewriters. No, no typewriters. Who would they be writing letters to? Well, anyway, a policy bank ought to sound like a lot of people sitting in a house without any housework sounds going on.

As he walked down the hall and the street's people receded further from his back, the fear that was driving him to start from the top of the house and work down diminished. He realized it would be better to work up. Then he would have a chance to talk his way out if caught listening at doors. He could say he had a friend and had forgotten in which apartment his friend lived.

"I didn't want to go knocking on all the doors," he heard himself say to his imagined discoverer, "disturbing everybody. I thought maybe I could hear his voice. Maybe you know where he lives?"

He heard his discoverer reply: "Who is that to whom you is referring?"

He stopped. "That's right," he thought, "got to get a name."

He returned to the row of bells in the vestibule and picked out a top-floor name and went back, thinking, "Simon Legree. The party to whom I is referring to that I am in search of is my very good friend, Simon Legree," and reached the stairs and said to himself sternly, "Got to stop fooling around now, Mr. Egan, and pay yourself attention to the business on hand." He shook his head and smiled. "That was no fooling around," he thought, but not in words. He never told himself in words what the feeling of loneliness did to him.

Then even thought vanished from Egan's head. He began to climb the stairs slowly, stepping with his toes, nervousness springing up in him and running like a wind through the hairs of his body. He had decided to begin on the second floor. The fear of the people in the street drove him that far. He was going to take the ground floor on his way out.

The sounds of apartment life boomed through the lumpy, brown, tin doors. There were hollow steps along a board floor, a smash of pans in a sink, hollow voices, the hollow slap of slippers. The sounds dropped into the hall like stones. Egan lingered briefly before each door. Then he came to one from which no sound emerged and he pressed his ear against it. As he listened, his eyes looked down the hall, gloomy here, gloomier than the ground floor, the band of pearl-colored light no thicker than a rug. His ears seemed to sink through the cold tin and to stretch deeply into emptiness.

A black, terrified face flickered down the hall. It had peeped from a crack in a doorway. Egan heard the door shut and heard the frantic rattle of a chain bolt fumbled into place. It was followed by a burst of footsteps.

Egan straightened up slowly. Woman face? Woman feet? Hard to tell. Couldn't tell. It was too dark. The feet had been running too fast. Egan's brain felt numb. It bulged in his head and would not work. It seemed that way to him because he was driving it so fast. He flung himself across the hall soundlessly on tiptoe. Four leaps, five leaps, his breath held in his throat. He began to press the bell.

He must stop whoever it was from telephoning for help. He didn't want to have radio cars come pouring down, frightening the people he was hunting. He must quiet the fear of whoever it was that had seen him. Even if the person had no telephone with which to give the alarm, he or she would come out later and talk fearfully to neighbors and word would get back to the bank.

Egan pressed the bell again and again and waited and pressed and waited. At last he heard a voice shout, "Who dere?" It was a man's voice. It had thrown the question at him like a ball, from a distance.

Egan thought of a man standing at the end of a dark hall, maybe holding something, maybe holding a knife, standing there frightened and ready to fight. Egan leaned his mouth close to the crack in the door and held his hands like a funnel around his lips. "I need your help," he said. His words bounded back from the door and crashed around his ears. Everybody in the house is going to hear me, he thought.

There was a long silence and then he heard the man's voice again, saying, "What you want?" still from a distance, still frightened and fight-ready.

"I need your help bad," said Egan. He knew Negroes always liked to be asked for help by white men. A panhandler had told him that. White panhandlers can always get a nickel out of a Negro.

Egan waited again, a long minute, and then steps sounded slowly down the hall and the voice said, "What you up to?"

"I can't talk through the door," said Egan. "I need your help in a private matter."

"Yeah," the man said. "That's what you think, man. That door stay shut just like she is and you get the hell away from there. I'll call the police. I sure will unlessen you clear out of here mighty God damn fast."

To Egan this wasn't a person behind the door. It wasn't a man into whose life he had intruded terrifyingly. It was just an opponent in business, a dangerous one. "Listen," he said. He could whisper now. The man was near the door. "I need your help very bad and it's private. I don't want the whole house to hear."

He knew he would have to think of something to disarm his opponent fast. "Open the door a minute," he whispered. "You can leave it on the chain. I can't get in, if that's what you're afraid of, if you leave it on the chain."

"I'm not afraid. You just clear out, that's all, unlessen you're looking for trouble. Who's afraid? I got something here to take care of you all right."

If that no-good black bastard has a gun on him, thought Egan, I'll throw him in jail and throw the key away. "I just need your help," he said. "I'm not wanting to hurt anybody. I just need your help bad."

The door opened an inch. Egan could see only darkness and behind it a dark wall. "All right," said the man, "now say what it is you want." His voice came from behind the door.

"I got slips," said Egan. "I didn't get there in time for them to pick up the slips account of a little piece, you know, to knock off, you know, and now I got to deliver the slips myself. I know the bank is in this house, but I don't know just which apartment."

The man came around from behind the door and stood where he could see Egan. He stood against the wall, as far from the door as possible. He was a tall Negro with wooly hair that looked greased. He had a bread knife in his hand. He looked Egan up and down importantly and with care.

"What you asking me?" The Negro shot the question like a cross-examiner, with an air of triumph, as if he believed he had said something clever that would trap the witness.

"I got to deliver the slips or they're no good," said Egan. "You know that. I got caught with the girl, delayed there a little bit. Well, you know, you know . . . I was in the middle right when it was time for me to deliver the slips to the regular place. Couldn't stop there."

"What you talking about?"

"What's the matter with you? Didn't you ever have a woman in your life?"

"Oh." The colored man sniggered. "I heard you making a noise with your mouth, but I couldn't tell what you were saying."

"That's the way it was. I was in the middle when it was time to turn in the policy slips and there's no man going to leave off then, take his tongue out of the honey right in the middle."

The Negro laughed delightedly. "No sirree," he said, "not me, not nobody there is."

"So that's the way it was," said Egan.

"That's the way it was. Wet inside and dry outside and wuhking away to rain. Ummmm . . . yeah man!"

Egan smiled and looked down. He felt a little excited himself. He did not want to show it before the Negro.

"Wuhk away, wuhk away, wuhk away. Heeyah, heeyah. Come on and rain. The hell with all them poor colored folks playing the numbers." The man's body shook up and down with delight. "Here's my port all cozy ahead," he said.

Christ, I started something, thought Egan. The man was speaking rapidly, chuckling and fluttering his hands, all disarmed now, the knife glinting up and down unheeded.

"Damn if I didn't nearly break my back trying to make it rain fast," said Egan. "I wanted to get my slips delivered on time for my clientele. But it's something that's hard to hurry up at my age. I didn't even take my shoes off. But I missed him anyway and I came on here because I know the bank is here, except I don't know just which apartment."

The Negro looked sly. "Ought to change the scenery," he said. "She always rains faster over new scenery."

"No, you'll find out yourself when you get older, it takes you more time. It's not bad that way. It's better that way. That's my sales talk where I pack my sausage. It's the only thing good there is about getting older."

"That's good, man. Hee-yah-yah. That sure is good to look ahead to."

"Listen, I got to find that bank fast. I got to get them slips in or they'll be no good."

"Apartment 46, that's where it is, the new one, just moved in last week. Two up and over in the corner there, just over that one there." The Negro pointed to an apartment door.

"Thanks, you been a big help." Egan started off hurriedly and went up the steps two at a time.

The colored man stared after him. He sniggered and then burst into a high laugh and closed the door slowly. "Hot damn it to hell," he cried.

Egan's mouth felt dirty. "What a way to make a living," he thought, "to have to talk like that to a nigger!" He spit suddenly.

XIII

In calling Foggarty, it had been Bauer's idea to raid Leo out of business. The moment Leo opened a new place, bang! there would be a raid and another raid and another and another until everybody would be afraid to bet with the bank and there would be no business left and Leo would have to let him go and work for the WPA, where he would not have to live in fear.

But everything this man did turned out unlucky for him. He had "no brains," as they say, meaning his brain was tormented, stunted, corrupted, distorted, goaded, palsied and altogether prevented from either functioning or developing. Even this simple plot of his to drive Leo out of business turned into a kind of comedy.

On Thursday, while Capt. Foggarty was thinking his way cautiously around the triangle of Milletti, the regular party machine and Hall, Bauer was sure there would be a raid and remained home. He telephoned that he was ill. By Friday, Bauer was sure there would never be a raid. The police would not come running when he whistled through the telephone. They were on Joe Minch's payroll.

So he came to work Friday and saw Egan and was sure Egan was a bus spotter and was sure he was not a bus spotter and was sure he was and was sure he wasn't until, at the end of the day, when he was sure for the last time and for all time that Egan was a bus spotter because the bank had not been raided that day, he was so exhausted he trembled as he walked to his coat. Leo thought he was still ill and told him to stay home Saturday.

"You got to take more care of yourself," said Leo worriedly. "If a man is sick, I don't ask him to kill himself."

So Bauer was at home Saturday and clung thinly to a hope that the raid would happen that day. Saturday was the day Egan reported to Foggarty that he had located the bank, but hadn't discovered the identity of the informant yet and would have to take a census of the house. Egan was convinced Bauer was the one who had tipped off the bank, but he needed an excuse to delay the raid until Monday. By Monday, all Bauer's hope had vanished. He went hopelessly to work.

A burly, black-haired detective named Badgley, a young man with a narrow forehead from which hung, between large ears, a long, full, rosy face, thick with hard fat, was assigned to make the raid with Egan.

The two men came up together from downtown Monday afternoon, after Edgar had delivered the policy slips to the bank and Leo had returned to his own office. They went up the stairs in silence and stood outside the door of apartment 46 a moment, listening. Then they took their badges—potsies, they called them—out of their pockets and fastened them to the lapels of their overcoats with horse-blanket safety pins.

Egan removed his gun from its holster and dropped it into the outside pocket of his overcoat. Badgley saw him do it. "You think so?" he whispered.

Egan smiled at him. He turned to the door and lowered his head and crossed himself swiftly and, almost as a continuation of the sign, knocked twice on the door.

Juice opened it. He was nearest. He had got up for a drink of water and was just passing the foyer when the knock came.

The moment the door began to open, Egan threw his weight against it. Juice was knocked backwards and Egan charged in with his hand in his coat pocket where his gun lay. He didn't take out the gun. He felt it might excite someone and make trouble.

Egan didn't waste time straightening himself out. He came in shoulder first, just as he had thrown himself against the door. He went past the backward reeling Juice like a burst of noise and was through the foyer and on the sorters before any of them had a chance to do more than look up.

"Nobody move." Egan shouted to keep his voice from shaking. "Keep your hands just where they're at."

Egan held his finger on the trigger of the gun in his pocket. He stood with his feet spread wide. Everybody sat still and looked at him. As the feeling of excitement fell off him, he slipped the safety catch of the gun back into place. He stood looking at the faces around the sorters' table and he could see the fright go out of all of them slowly.

Badgley was coming forward with Juice. "Boy oh boy," thought Egan, as he saw the massive man he had thrust aside with the door, "what I nearly mixed with!"

"Go back where you usually work," Badgley told Juice, "and sit down."

"I don't work here," said Juice.

"What do you do, live here? Go on and sit down like I told you before I sock you one."

Juice laughed. "You're some Hockshaw," he said. He went slowly, laughing and shaking his head, to an empty chair at the sorters' table.

Then suddenly a sound started at the far end of the room. It came with a scuffling rush. Egan looked away from Juice and saw a tall, awkward figure plunge open-mouthed around the table and towards the door. He shifted over a few steps and held out his arms and braced himself and waited and the man ran blindly into his arms. He caught Bauer as if he were fielding a football. Bauer hit him hard. Bauer's glasses jounced off his face and fell to the floor and Egan grunted.

"Whoaza baby," said Egan. He laughed a little bit at the unexpected, helpless fury in the lumpy body he held. Bauer was so thin, Egan could pin the man's two arms in back by throwing one arm over him. Egan held him that way, against his own middle. He became aware it was an embrace. He patted Bauer's shoulder with his free hand. "Whoaza baby there," he said. "Whoa up your kicking there."

When Egan had burst in, Bauer had been in the bookkeeper's room down a small hall in back of the sorters' room. He had stood a moment, rooted with terror. Then a thought had driven through his brain: it was good that he was there; now no one could suspect him of bringing on the raid. The thought had held him another moment. Then terror had smashed all thinking and he had screamed and run.

"Whoa up there, my baby," said Egan.

Bauer's body was shrill with panic. It rang against Egan. The man was flopping up and down, thrashing, hanging from Egan's arm, lifting his feet up high and slamming them against the floor, swinging and twisting and shaking and clawing with lunatic fury at Egan's chest and arms.

Badgley came in from the side and stood waiting. He held up his big fist and stared at the lunging figure with detachment. He crashed his fist into Bauer's ear as the man was in the middle of an upward wrench. Bauer plunged sideways. He acted as if he had been shot. His eyes rolled back. Badgley saw the whites flash and then Bauer's body flew away like a flung rag.

"I think you broke his ear," said Egan. Bauer was bent far over Egan's arm. Egan had to shift to keep from falling.

"I guess maybe I did," said Badgley. The sight of Egan getting his gun ready before the raid had frightened him. The fear was not out of him yet. He took Bauer out of Egan's arms and dragged him to a chair against the wall and flopped him into it. "Stay there," he said, "and you won't get hurt no more."

Bauer was thrown into the chair so hard, his head jounced. His eyes flew open and he sat staring glassily at Badgley for a moment. Then he lifted his two hands and pressed them against his ears. He bent a little forward. "I can't hear," he said. "I'm ringing."

"You'll be all right. Just stay still." Badgley stood over him, looking down at him, his hands in his pockets. He was relaxed a little. It was possible for him to become aware now that Bauer was not merely an opponent in business, but also a human being.

A trickle of blood came out of Bauer's ear and spread in a thread down the inside of his wrist. He didn't feel it for a moment. Then he pulled his hands away from his ears and looked at both of them and saw the blood on one and looked at Badgley and then at the blood again and then back at Badgley.

"Nobody told you to run, did they?" said Badgley.

"You deafed me." Bauer's voice crashed through the room.

Pie-Eye drew in his breath in a long hiss and Juice looked out the window and Murray stared at Badgley with a sneer and Mr. Middleton's hands shook as they rested on his belly. The two Cubans looked down at the floor and Delilah put two fingers against her lower lip and Miss Anderson clicked her tongue and the other women looked angry and frightened.

Bauer half rose from the chair, but Badgley pushed him down with one hand. "Sit down or I'll clunk your other ear," he said.

"What's the matter with my voice? I feel like I'm talking far away." Bauer sat stiffly on the edge of the chair and looked around wide-eyed. His voice was loud enough to echo in the silent room.

Egan had picked up Bauer's eyeglasses. They had not broken. He came to Badgley's side and looked at Bauer anxiously. "You'll be all right when your head clears," he said.

"My voice is broke. I'm bleeding."

"Just sit still and you won't get into any more trouble," Badgley told him.

Egan held out the eyeglasses, but Bauer did not reach for them. He touched Bauer's hands with them and Bauer took them without looking and stared at Egan with frightened eyes.

"You crippled me," he said. "I can't hear my voice." He put his hand to his throat and rubbed it.

Badgley went to the telephone and called for a prison van and a detail of policemen. Egan began making an inventory of the room and collecting evidence. Badgley helped.

"This is something you will be sorry as long as you live," shouted Bauer suddenly.

Badgley gave Bauer an angry glance. Bauer was straining forward in his chair. He still sat on the edge of it. He seemed afraid to get off.

"You bastards don't forget what I told you," he shouted. "You dirty rat son of a bitches, deafing a man who's trying to live by the law. That's what you are, bastards, sold your life out to gangsters."

Badgley made a move to go towards him, but Egan held his arm. "Let's get this stuff done," said Egan, "before the wagon comes."

"I'll make it my business to get you the rest of my life," said Bauer from the edge of his chair. "You'll get yours. Don't worry. You'll get yours or I'm a liar. I'll see to that myself, you whore rats, sold yourself to gangsters."

Badgley turned to Egan. "He's only working himself up to make trouble," he said.

"Oh, let him talk himself out." The talk of gangsters worried Egan. He didn't know what to do.

"He'll make trouble sure as hell, I'm telling you," said Badgley.

Egan looked at Bauer speculatively.

"Whores for gangsters," Bauer shouted at him. "Pimps for gangsters. Rat pimp bastards."

Egan went over to Bauer and stooped down and brought his face on a level with Bauer's. "Listen to me," he shouted into the man's face. "Shut up!"

Bauer drew back in fear.

"What's this about gangsters?" asked Egan.

"You shouldn't have deafed me." Bauer's voice was hesitant.

"What gangsters were you talking about we sold out to?"

Bauer realized suddenly that if he involved Joe Minch, he would have to be a witness against him. He knew from the movies and newspapers what happened to witnesses against gangsters. "You know yourself there's plenty gangsters," he said, "but you don't arrest them. No, only us."

Egan sighed with relief. Then this wasn't a big case! Foggarty wouldn't be tempted to give it to Hall and tie the whole squad to Hall. Egan straightened up and walked to the sorters' table and resumed gathering the evidence.

Bauer twisted his body and put his hand on the back of the chair and lowered his head onto his hand and, after a moment of silence, he began to cry.

❦

When the prisoners were taken downstairs, Juice got his foot on the back step of the police van all right and then he stopped and took down his foot and turned around. A street crowd had collected for the show. It had spilled over the sidewalk and around the van. Ordinarily, the police walked prisoners into a van one at a time, but Egan had been afraid of trouble from the crowd. He didn't want to leave his arrests in a bunch in the vestibule and take them out singly. Sometimes, in Harlem, when Negroes were arrested, people on rooftops threw bottles down at the police and others tried to fight the prisoners free. So Egan hustled his prisoners single file through the crowd.

When Juice stopped, the people in back dammed up against him. He had been near the head of the line. As he turned, Badgley, who was standing nearest, shoved him and said, "Hurry up, fat!"

"I got to talk to you." Juice's meaty white face was puckered earnestly.

"Talk inside."

Juice shook his head. "I can't," he said. His voice had to struggle to get through his throat. He began to walk towards the sidewalk. Bauer was just behind him and Juice walked into him blindly. Bauer gasped and fell away and then put his head down and ran around Juice and leaped into the prison van. He had not thought of Juice when telephoning for the raid. He had forgotten him entirely until this moment. Juice felt him go by and saw his clothes, but didn't see him. The man was not a man, but just cloth blowing past him.

Badgley ran back along the line to get ahead of Juice. He pulled out his gun. "Here," he said, "you get inside."

At sight of the gun, the crowd trampled itself to retreat. The line of prisoners shrank and bulged and shrank again and stood shrunken and quivering. Some men at the edge of the crowd bolted down the street. They ran wildly, with a rushing sound. Juice stopped short and looked at the gun. He opened his mouth wide and closed it.

"I ain't kidding, fatty," said Badgley. He pointed the gun steadily at Juice.

Juice opened his mouth again, but he couldn't speak. He closed it and opened it and kept opening and closing it. His throat swelled and jerked, but he couldn't utter a word.

"You get in that wagon," said Badgley, "or I'll shoot your guts out."

Juice put his hand to his forehead and rubbed. He opened his mouth wide again and then closed it and stamped his foot. Two policemen came up and took hold of him and turned him around and tried to haul him towards the van, but he dug his heels against the pavement and braced himself. They tugged hard at his unwieldy bulk and one of the policemen kicked at the calf of his leg.

Egan had been standing in the doorway of the apartment house, checking out the prisoners. He came pushing up.

"Get the others in first," he told Badgley and turned to the line of prisoners.

"Come on," he said, "come on, come on. Stop dragging your drawers." Delilah was nearest and he took her by her two arms and yanked her forward. She stumbled and almost fell on her face. "Come on you tramp," he said. "Hurry up, come on, hurry up. Hurry up. Hurry, hurry, hurry, up. Hup. Hup. Hup. Hupup."

Juice stood still. The two policemen held him and he stood with his heels shoved against the pavement. The line wound around him hastily and disappeared into the van.

"What's the matter with you?" asked Egan.

Mr. Middleton put his pink face out of the van. "If you'll let me tell you," he said.

"Keep where you belong," roared Badgley. He waved his gun and leaped on the step and shoved Middleton into the van and slammed the door.

"I can't ride there," said Juice.

"We haven't got no limousine at our disposal," Egan said.

"I'll go in the subway."

"What do you think this is, a party?"

"Please, I don't mind going. It's not that. If you'll just take me there in the subway or walk."

Egan removed the handcuffs from his service belt. "Hold out your right hand," he said.

"I had an accident," cried Juice, "and it makes me upset."

"Hold out your hand."

Juice put out his right hand and Egan fastened one cuff.

"I really can't, mister officer," cried Juice. "Honest to God, I get upset in a car."

"You should have thought of that before you broke the law," said Egan. He felt safer now that the handcuffs were on. "We've got no conveniences to treat you special. I got to do with you like what the law says, like with the others."

"It upsets me something terrible after the accident I had."

"We don't have no accidents," said Egan. "We drive careful."

Egan began to pull him towards the van by the handcuffs and Juice walked along slowly, like a led bull.

"I can't do it." Juice shook his head rapidly. "You'll see. I can't do it." He spoke rapidly. His small eyes were coated with worry and his forehead was wrinkled. "I can't do it no matter how I want. You'll see. I can't."

Badgley still held his gun. It had been an unnerving afternoon of business for him all around. He brought the barrel of the gun up high and then slammed the butt down on Juice's shoulders. "That'll help you," he said.

Juice stumbled forward under the blow and then pulled himself to a stop and turned his big, anxious face. "No it won't," he told Badgley. "You'll see. It won't. It's just that I can't no matter how much I want."

Egan led Juice to the front of the van, just behind the chauffeur, and locked the handcuffs around a ring in the wall. Juice had to sit twisted around, the top of his body toward the wall and the lower part facing into the van. A policeman was seated alongside him.

"I'm telling you," said Juice, "this is exactly the wrong thing for my condition."

"I got to take care you don't make trouble," explained Egan. "You know that."

Juice rattled the cuffs impatiently.

"It's the wrong thing," he said. "You'll see. I can't help it. It's wrong."

"I can't help it either," said Egan. He pulled the handcuffs to make sure they were tight. "Just try to behave yourself. We'll go slow and careful for you."

As soon as the door of the van was locked and the motor started, Juice stood up and turned his back. He crouched low over his locked hands. His big buttocks bulged in the air.

"That's some billboard," said the policeman sitting next to him.

Nor was he a callous man. He was young and so homely as to be appealing, red-headed with large, nearly pink freckles all over his flour-white face. It was just that all Juice meant to him at the moment was business.

The policeman laughed at his remark, but no one else did. All but Bauer looked at Juice with frightened eyes. Bauer sat at the far end, nearest the door, his head in his hands.

Juice put his face on his fastened wrists and rolled his face back and forth over his wrists. He was shuddering and gasping. His breath came in big, noisy quavers. When the van jerked into motion, he let out a short, wild howl. He rolled his face faster over his wrists and his whole body shuddered. He drew in his breath with shivering gulps and then let it howl out through his tightly shut teeth. It was a deep howl and it stretched down deep into those in the van.

"For Christ sakes," the young policeman said.

Mr. Middleton leaned towards him. "I think," he said, "if you release him, he'll be better."

"Who's going to hold down a big Polak like that?"

"I don't know what to do," said Mr. Middleton and settled back against the wall slowly, worried and shaking his head.

"Shut him up," shouted Bauer suddenly. He still kept his head in his hands and shouted through his hands.

"You guys certainly got lots of advice to give out," said the policeman. He had to speak loudly to make himself heard.

"Shut him up," shouted Bauer at the floor, "or I'll go crazy myself." The thought that he had done this to Juice was too much for him. "Shut him up! Shut him up! Shut him up or I'll kill myself!" Bauer didn't lift his head from his hands. With each shout, he dug his head deeper into his hands.

Delilah was sitting pressed against the wall of the van. Her head was high and her large, pain-stained eyes stared sightlessly at the jolting, creaking ceiling of the van. She was thinking of the schools she had been to and how hard she had worked to succeed in the schools and how hard her parents had worked to send her. Her brown face had become a thick yellow. She had her hands folded over her arms where they still hurt from Egan's grasp. Her chin quavered and she put her trembling lower lip between her teeth and held it there. "I will not feel sorry for myself," she told herself. "I will not, will not, will not, will not give them the satisfaction." The tears ran abruptly out of her eyes and fell down her face.

"What are you two guys trying to do, enjoy yourself?" said the policeman to Bauer and Juice. He sat back and crossed his legs and folded his arms over his chest. "Go ahead and play," he said.

The van, followed by a long line of curious auto drivers, howled down Edgecombe Avenue and down Seventh Avenue and into

Central Park. Bauer had begun to sob, and Mr. Middleton moved over next to him and tried to comfort him. Bauer didn't lift his head from his hands. "Let me alone," he said. "All I want is, let me alone." Bauer shook his head violently in his hands and twisted away as far as he could.

The howling kept on, across to Park Avenue and down Park Avenue. The policeman on the back step banged with his nightstick against the mesh of the door and Egan and Badgley, sitting up front with the driver, hammered against the rear wall with their fists.

"They're having a Polak party," announced the policeman next to Juice.

Juice was trying to pull himself loose from the handcuffs. He pulled and howled and pulled again. Between howls, his breath sucked and rattled in the air. He howled like an animal. The handcuffs broke the skin of his wrists, but he did not seem to notice. He pulled and howled and slumped exhausted against the bench and then forced himself up and pulled and howled again. As debris of the business game he didn't look human any more. His long, wet black hair had fallen over his face and his small eyes rolled in the mat of it, looking red as blood. He shook the whole van and then, finally, he slumped against the bench and his whole body went stiff. His legs kicked out under the bench opposite and he lay there sprawled for a moment, his body stiff and swollen looking. A deep breath blew into him and he held it endlessly and then he exploded it out. He took another deep breath and fainted.

The silence lasted a long time. The feeling of sickness lay in it like an echo. The sick feeling cleared slowly and Bauer turned his face towards Mr. Middleton. He still held his hands around it. "Is he dead?" he whispered through his fingers.

Mr. Middleton was startled. He had been so relieved at the silence he had not thought of that possibility. "Is he dead?" he called to the policeman at the far end.

The policeman looked at Juice. He saw the man was breathing slowly and heavily. "I hope so," he said.

Bauer shuddered and stuck his face deeper into his hands.

Juice was still unconscious when the van arrived at headquarters downtown. He was left in the van until an ambulance could come for him.

∼℮

Before being booked, the women were put into one room and the men into another and questioning began. Egan had told Foggarty someone in the bank had telephoned the tip for the raid; so they went through the women first, asking the women who ran the bank and if anyone had had trouble with him.

The Italian and Spanish women said "no spikka ingless." The others said they didn't know the place was a policy bank. They had just gone there to visit friends. The women were frightened. Nothing like this thing of being taken to headquarters and questioned like regular criminals had ever happened before in a policy arrest.

Foggarty noticed the tear stains on Delilah's face and decided she would be the easiest to break down. He ordered her into his office and took Egan with him. "You're a damn fool," he told her.

She had stood quietly, her face emotionless, her long, beautiful hands folded before her and hanging down her skirt like vines. Now she stirred, but she made no answer. A thought lay deep in her. She did not know what it was. It grew bigger and clearer and more disturbing and still she did not know what it was. It lay heavily on the tip of her brain.

"We've got enough on you to send you away for a long time," said Foggarty, "but we're ready to forget it if you tell us who runs the bank and if any of the men in the place is against him."

"I have never done anything wrong," she replied, forcing her voice to remain firm. "I am a graduate of Hunter College and I know the law and I know my rights under the law."

"You went to college and learned to be a fresh nigger, is that it?"

The words released the thought on the tip of her brain and she cringed. That's what the thought had been, a "good nigger" cringe. She forced it down in her violently.

"Of course," Delilah said. "That's why my mother and father

both got down on their knees and worked to send me to college, to be a fresh nigger who knows her rights."

"I don't care to hear your troubles," said Foggarty. "I'll take it for granted you got them. We all have. Answer my questions, that's all. I am not interested in what you were doing in the bank. All right, I'll stipulate you were visiting a friend or waiting for a street car, whatever you say. But you had better tell me what I want to know unless you feel like going away for a year for peddling your tail."

Her hands clasped more tightly as she cringed inside her, and her large eyes closed swiftly and opened. Again she forced the cringe down in her. The effort was exhausting. Her hands parted and swung listlessly and she stood listlessly, but she didn't say anything.

"You were known to have solicited," Foggarty said. "You're a known street walker."

"A real, regular mocha tart," said Egan.

"We've had an eye on you for a long time, sister," Foggarty told her, "and this is where we got you. We have a nigger stool for the vice squad who says you solicited him and he paid you a dollar and got a clap to prove it."

"I'll find a hundred more in Harlem with the clap from you," said Egan.

Delilah looked at Egan coldly. It was not a successful look. There was too much triumph in it. She could not express her contempt for her torturers confidently. It had to be triumphant contempt. "Are you, too, entrusted with the enforcement of the law," she asked Egan, "a man of your sort of quality, too?"

"That's the business I'm in."

"We all enforce the law," said Foggarty, "and we don't take nigger lip. If you want to be a fresh nigger, go ahead and see what happens."

It was unfair. She could not keep fighting down the cringes in her forever. "God will get you," she cried in a small, trembling voice. "God is watching you, the both of you."

Foggarty was a devout, that is a fearful, Catholic. It angered him to hear God mentioned by a Negro. "In the meantime," he said angrily, "you can watch me put down in the book that you were paid off in marked money. That's what happens to fresh niggers. They get paid off in marked money and Egan found the marked money hiding under your titties."

"It was a happy hunting ground," Egan said. He leaned forward and chucked Delilah under the chin. "Wasn't it, my little coal mine?" he asked.

Delilah's head snapped up. Her eyes flashed like dagger blades. Then her head sank to rest and she stood listlessly and looked at the two men listlessly.

∾

A little later a detective came into the room where the men were being held and wanted to know who Bauer was. Bauer had not been asked for his name yet and had thought of giving a false name. But Pie-Eye and Murray and Mr. Middleton and the two Cubans all glanced at him involuntarily and the detective said, "Come with me."

Bauer was taken to another room. A telephone was put in his hand and Foggarty, at the other end, asked him where he lived and whether he was married and how many children he had and how old they were and to say, "What are you trying to do, trick around with me?"

After that, he was taken into Foggarty's office. Badgley was there now, along with Egan and Foggarty turned to them and said, "This is our man."

"He give us the tip all right," said Egan.

Bauer stopped short. He saw Foggarty smiling at him in a friendly way, but the friendliness of the smile did not mean anything to him. All he thought of was that they were working for Guinea Joe Minch to find out who had tipped over the bank and to tell Guinea Joe Minch who had tipped over his bank.

"Sit down," Foggarty said cordially. "You gave us information and we appreciate it. We want to know about this argument you had with Leo Minch, what it's about, that's all."

Bauer walked to the chair slowly. He had felt himself break into pieces. He was all squeezed up inside and he thought he had to squeeze to hold himself together.

"What's happening there that you want to quit your job," asked Foggarty, "and what's going on that he won't let you? That's why you called me up after you run out on him, and said you quit. Wasn't that why?"

Bauer was a long time in working words through his throat. "I don't get what you're talking about," he said at last.

"What are you so worried about?" asked Foggarty. "Just take it easy. You're our friend, giving us this information. We'll be your friend."

Who ever heard of such a thing in a lifetime! thought Bauer. A man tries to live by the law and the law turns him over to gangsters to be killed. A thing like that! Did anybody ever hear of a thing like that in their whole life? "I was up there to ask for a job, that's all," he said. "I never phoned you in my life."

Foggarty looked at him a moment. He thought how easy it would be to break down a man like Bauer. He couldn't resist trying. "Who said anything about a phone?" he asked.

"Why you did. You did. You know you just did." Bauer was frightened. He couldn't remember now whether Foggarty had said the tip was telephoned.

"No I didn't. You see, we got you there right away. If you knew the information was phoned without my saying, then it's because you phoned. But that's all right. We appreciate your helping us."

"You said just a minute ago, that's why I called you up."

"Well, I'm glad to hear you're admitting you called me up."

"I didn't. You said. That's what you said. You think you can twist me up and make me say what I don't want to say. But you can't."

"Why don't you want to say? What makes you not want to say?"

"I didn't mean that. You know what I meant. I meant say what's not so, twist me up I meant, so I don't know what I'm saying and say whatever you say, what isn't so."

Foggarty laughed.

"You ought to hear yourself talk," Badgley said to Bauer.

"He's a regular goof," said Egan.

Bauer's frightened stare went slowly from one smiling face to the other.

"Now look," Foggarty said. "We know, we know, you can't kid us by stepping into a new lie every time you open your mouth. We know you want to quit Leo Minch and he isn't letting you and you called us up, me up, for that and all we want is a little more. Just why you're quitting and why Minch don't let you. Did one of the other banks offer you more money and Minch is afraid you will take some business away from him if you leave? Is that it?"

This was what Foggarty wanted to believe and strove to believe. If it were just that, if Tucker were not mixed up in it somewhere, then Foggarty would not have to make up his mind about Hall. He could just keep on thinking about Hall and thinking and thinking until it was too late to do anything and the decision had been made for him. Foggarty did not like to take chances. He was not a gambling man. He was a businessman.

Yes, thought Bauer, he wants to know a little more and a little more and then they tell Joe and then a little more and Joe is waiting for me, maybe when I get home, and a little more and a little more and a little more, up, up, up, up to me, shooting, shooting. In my back. He said he would kill me and he will. He's a killer and he'll kill me. "Who's this Minch you're talking about?" asked Bauer.

Foggarty thought how easy it would be to get Bauer to say yes, that was it, he had been offered a new job and Leo was afraid he'd lose business by letting him go, so there had been a fight. All he had to do to get Bauer to admit it was to have Badgley pull Bauer's head back by the hair and to have Egan rap him once with a billy over the Adam's apple and he'd admit it, all right, as soon as he could talk. And it would be good to hear someone tell him he was right in believing what he wanted to believe.

"I was up there looking for a job," said Bauer, "and that's the first time I was ever there in my life."

Foggarty made a gesture of impatience and scowled threateningly.

"I was waiting for someone to interview me for a job," said Bauer, "when these two men came in and deafed me. Broke my ear just like that, without thinking a minute what it means to me to be crippled the rest of my life. All right, that's my statement that I give out and will sign."

"I think," said Badgley, "I better go to work on the other ear."

Foggarty held up his hand. He had suddenly developed an active distaste for Bauer. "What the hell is the use," he said. "We know the story all right. Get him out of here before he wets his pants and spoils the paint on my chair."

Foggarty was afraid that if Bauer were forced to talk, he might not stick to his lie. He would tell the truth and Foggarty feared the truth and did not let himself speculate about it. If he had let himself think about it, he would have known Bauer could not be so frightened unless Guinea Joe were involved. But, if the Guinea were involved, Foggarty would have to make a decision right then, right there, and whatever he decided would affect the remaining years of his life, even the pension he would retire on. "Why should we do a lot of work to hear what we know already," he told himself and felt relieved and, because of his relief, decided he had done the right thing.

He waved Bauer out of his sight and out of his life.

XIV

THE COUNTERMAN in the diner across the street from the bank, who had asked Egan if he were a member of the police force, made money on the side as a collector for Leo. He took bets from his customers who wanted to play the numbers. As soon as he saw the police van, he telephoned his controller who telephoned Edgar in Leo's office.

Leo got Joe on the phone first and Joe said he couldn't believe it, it was impossible. Then Joe said not to worry and he would take care of everything because this was the combination's end of the business. "Just take it easy and go home," he told Leo. "You don't have to do a thing."

After that, Leo called Wheelock and Wheelock, too, said he couldn't believe it, it was impossible.

"After it's done, they can't do it, is that it?" cried Leo. "Well, damn it, the joke stinks. I'm on my way there now."

Leo thought he might be able to do business with the police. But Wheelock told him not to try or it would spoil everything and just to find out which squad had made the raid and to meet him in Joe's office in twenty minutes.

By the time Leo got to the bank, the police had gone. He went upstairs and found a patrolman guarding the empty bank. Leo didn't recognize him.

"Beg your pardon," he said, "wrong apartment I guess," and went downstairs and drove to Joe's office.

Wheelock was there. "The raid is a black eye for the whole combination," said Wheelock, "and I'll show you, Mr. Minch, how we're going to make a good thing out of it."

"All right, show," cried Leo. "That's what I want to see. How? How? Not to worry. That's all you say. I tell myself that for my dizziness. I get my brains knocked out and you tell me not to worry, you'll put them back, maybe."

Joe lifted his hand and started to say something. "Keep quiet," shouted Leo. "Let me talk for a minute, too." He turned back to Wheelock. "Is that what you're going to do, tell me not to worry and all the time the business gets blown up and my people go to jail? Why shouldn't I worry? I come in on the combination because you say you're big shots with the right of way and what happens the very first crack out of the box? Raid!"

Joe tried to interrupt again and Leo waved him down. "Shut up," said Leo. "Can't you shut your big mouth for one minute?"

Wheelock was pained by this display of bad manners. "You're a very excitable man, Mr. Minch," he said.

"Yes?" Leo wagged one finger in his face. "And let me tell you something. I didn't have a raid in four years in my business and the minute you start up with me, there's two. Two in two weeks. What kind of a thing is this? Two raids and 527 hits. Is this bad luck, or what should I think? First you tell me you're big shots with the right of way, flags on them, and then you tell me not to worry if your okay, you'll pardon me, stinks. Stinks! Plain stinks! Should I believe you? Answer me. Why should I believe you? Would you believe you in your place? I mean in my place. Your place, I mean. Answer me! Would you?"

"You've put your finger on it, Mr. Minch," Wheelock said calmly. "The way you feel is the way the whole policy market and the trade, too, feels. They're all watching us. Now we can show just what we can do and prove for everybody, the market and the trade, just how we can operate."

"All right, what can you do?"

"We're going to have the magistrate, whoever he is, throw out the case tonight, whatever it is. No postponements, no bail. The hearing tonight and bang! out it goes. And as soon as we can, maybe tomorrow, the detectives who made the raid, whoever they are, I don't care, or who's in back of them, I don't care, they'll be broken into uniform and pounding a beat."

"Can you do all this?"

"You'll see," cried Joe. "You'll see the kind of people you got working on your side and what kind of strength they got in them."

"I'm looking," said Leo.

Wheelock said he would take care of the court end and told Joe to see that the prisoners were brought in for arraignment as quickly as possible. Leo asked how Wheelock was going to get to the magistrate.

"I don't mind telling you," Henry replied, "if you really want to know. But I should think the less you know, the better you would like it."

"It's a trade secret?"

"Well, after all, that's one of the things we're selling to the combination and we don't like to give it away."

❧

They were all to meet at eight o'clock in Ruddy's bonding office alongside magistrate's court and go into court together. Leo went to his own office, but he couldn't stay there long. He was too worried about his employees. He thought Juice might have pulled over the whole patrol wagon and that Bauer, too, might have become excited and made trouble.

He went to the station house nearest the bank where the prisoners should have been booked. They weren't there. They hadn't been there. He went upstairs to Detective Captain Milletti's office. Milletti said the first he had heard of the raid was at four o'clock when the patrolman on the beat came in off tour.

"All I know is they came from downtown," he told Leo.

"Downtown where?"

"The main office. Foggarty's squad."

"What's this? Why there?"

"I don't know," said Milletti angrily. "I don't know a damn thing what the hell the whole thing is all about."

Leo drove downtown to police headquarters. But he just hung around. He didn't know Foggarty and was afraid to talk to him. He had thought he might see Joe, but Joe didn't seem to be around.

Then he called Wheelock's office. Wheelock wasn't there. The office didn't know where he was and didn't expect him back. After that, Leo drove uptown to Joe's office. Joe wasn't there either.

"Did you ever see two such people for getting lost all of a sudden?" he cried to himself.

He went back to his own office and called Wheelock again and called Joe and left word for Joe to call him back as soon as he came in. After that, he called Sylvia and said he wouldn't be home until late.

"When do you think you will be?" she asked.

"How do I know when? When I'll be there, I'll be there. Must you ask foolish questions to waste my time all the time?"

"What's the matter with you?" said Sylvia. "You never think of talking to me like a person any more."

He hung up angrily and sat fuming a long time.

Leo was at Ruddy's office at 7 o'clock to keep the 8 o'clock appointment. He waited impatiently. He sat and stood and walked up and down and leaned against a desk and looked out the window and went out into the hall and looked down the stairs and came back and watched the street from the window.

Ruddy was in and out of the office. "Are you having a fit for Christmas?" he asked.

"What do you mean?"

"I mean I can't work with you dancing on my head."

"I'm sorry," Leo said. "These people make an appointment and then they don't care what happens."

When Wheelock arrived, a few minutes before eight, Leo pounced on him. "They've been taken downtown," said Leo.

"I know. It's all right."

"They didn't used to do that before. Never. It's unheard of."

Wheelock smiled. He looked very confident and reassuring. "A main office squad made the raid," he said, "so they took them to the main office. That's routine."

"No, you can't get away with telling me that. It's not routine they should be treated like crooks, little people like that, working for a living."

"I don't see what difference it makes where they're taken."

"You don't see? What do you mean you don't see? The minute there's Tucker's name in it, they treat us like crooks. We got to suffer because Tucker's name is in it. That's what I see."

Wheelock smiled again. "You'll see something else in a little while," he said. "It won't be suffering."

Then Joe came in. He looked tired. He had his coat unbuttoned and his hat far back on his head. He said he had finally got all the prisoners together and they were downstairs in the pen, awaiting the hearing. Leo wanted to know what "finally" meant and

Wheelock explained that Juice had had to be gotten out of a hospital.

"He's all right," said Joe hastily, "just a little weak on the pins. I'll tell you something, it's harder to get a guy out of a hospital than out of jail. It took practically the mayor."

Then Leo wanted to know from Joe why his people had been taken downtown.

"That's not what's worrying me," Joe said. "That's simple. The main office, a Capt. Foggarty, may God cook his guts good, got the tip over the phone and the thing is, who gave him the tip? That's the worry. Who's the bastard that done it and what for?"

It came to Leo suddenly that Bauer had done it. He had been thinking that all afternoon, but he had not been aware of the thought. Bauer had done it Thursday, when he was home ill. No, not Thursday. Saturday, when Leo had told him to stay home.

"When did the tip come in?" asked Leo.

"They got it Thursday morning over the phone."

Yes, thought Leo, Bauer! But he had looked sick on Friday. No, only sick with fear that he would be found out. He had come in Friday only so that no one would suspect what he had done.

"I was told by the fellow who made the raid, this fellow, Egan, that it was just one of those things that come in over the phone," said Joe, "and Foggarty don't know who done it either."

Leo remained silent. There's going to be trouble, he thought. There's going to be terrible trouble if Joe finds out, God knows how much trouble. He didn't want to be responsible for it.

"Mr. Egan sounds quite obliging," said Wheelock.

"Yes, he's scared to death what's going to happen when we go to work and he's trying to be friendly. He's a nice fellow."

"Are they trying to find out who the tipster was?"

"I guess so," said Joe. "I don't know, you know how those things are."

Joe felt pretty sure a man named Ficco had telephoned Foggarty, either Ficco or one of the sorehead bankers. Ficco had worked in

beer for Tucker a long time and he had been pushed out recently
by the new people in the brewery. Joe had heard Ficco had got a
small organization together and was looking for something to do
with it.

"They think it might be someone in the bank," said Joe. "Anyway, Egan threw out a kind of a hint like that." Joe didn't believe
it. He knew if the tip came from Ficco the police wouldn't tell
him. They weren't sure what Ficco's connections were. He had
been an important man. Maybe he still was. Why should they
risk making him sore?

"No," cried Leo.

Wheelock looked at him sharply. "How do you know it's not
someone in the bank?" he asked.

"I know. Nobody in my bank would do this to me."

Joe became interested. He believed it was Ficco, but he would
have liked not to believe it. Ficco meant a lot of trouble. "Not
even this fellow, what's his name," he asked, "the one I had to
talk to?"

"No," said Leo, "not him, not anybody. They wouldn't do it to
me and I wouldn't believe it if you showed me on black and
white."

"I guess you're right." Joe wondered if he should tell Leo about
Ficco. He decided Leo was too excitable. Nothing could be gained
by telling him now. But he'd tell Wheelock all right. He'd let
Wheelock stew in it and give himself the needles over it. "They're
all crazy about my brother over there," he said to Wheelock. "I
saw it myself."

"That man's name was Bauer," said Wheelock.

"Bauer's worked for me more than two years," cried Leo. "I know
he wouldn't do a thing like that to me."

"Jews lived in Germany a thousand years."

"What's that got to do with it?"

"I don't trust Germans," said Wheelock. "They're mad dogs.
They go along quietly and then, all of a sudden, they go berserk,
crazy. They act like animals."

"Well, maybe. But Bauer is no Nazi. He's a clean-cut American boy born in this country and he wouldn't do a thing like that to me."

Leo had decided he would handle Bauer in his own way. It would be better with Joe out of it.

❧

Magistrate's court was crowded with people, with their worried faces and their small, worried sounds and with the smell of them and of their clothes and of disinfectant. The people looked strange and, also, sad and poor. They looked more like sweepings than like people. They crowded the benches nervously and the large room seemed to steam with them. The air was colored yellow by the electric lights and whispering rose through it like the sound of steaming.

Wheelock led the way down the aisle toward the railed-off enclosure before the magistrate's bench. Leo followed and Joe was in the rear. Someone in the crowd caught Joe's attention. The man was sitting with head averted. The back of his neck and the set of his head appeared familiar. Joe slowed his step and looked carefully, but the man did not turn his head and Joe could see only the side of his face. The side of his face did not look familiar.

When Joe reached the railing, Wheelock and Leo had already passed beyond it. "Attorney," he said. The attendant let him go by.

The enclosure was swarming with lawyers and uniformed attendants and policemen and detectives with badges pinned to their coats, all walking and talking quietly so as not to interfere with the case being heard—an assault and battery case. The complainant, an old Italian with a dark, gray moustache, was on the stand. His arm was bandaged and in a sling. The defendant, a young Italian, his eyes downcast, stood between two court attendants.

Wheelock was talking to the clerk at the table before the magistrate's bench and Leo had found a seat against the railing. He was crouched on the edge of it, leaning forward and looking around nervously, trying to see the magistrate. Judge Garrett was a small man. He sat scrunched in his chair so that it was hard to see him over the bench. All that could be seen was his thin, white hair and his pink forehead and the tops of his pince-nez.

Joe sat down beside Leo and suggested the bank should work out of his own apartment for the next few days anyway. He said he lived there all alone and there was plenty of room. He had decided that, if Ficco had really begun to operate against Tucker, then it would be safest to put the bank where it couldn't be found easily.

"But I've already rented another place on Edgecombe Avenue," said Leo. They spoke in low tones, putting their lips close against each other's ears.

"We'll use it later," said Joe. "I think we ought to duck our heads a little bit until we find out what happened here, I mean who's responsible for what happened, so we can tell what we're up against and do something about it."

Leo felt the sooner the bank was settled in a permanent place, the better for the business. He tried to think of a way to tell Joe that hiding the bank was a waste of effort. But he couldn't do it without bringing in Bauer. He remained silent.

"That's only sense, isn't it?" said Joe.

Leo did not answer.

Joe stood up and looked slowly and casually out over the courtroom. He wanted to get a good view of the man he had thought seemed familiar. The man was staring at him now. Joe saw all of his face. It wasn't anyone he knew. At least it wasn't anyone he could remember. No doubt, the free man in Germany had thought the same thing at seeing his first Nazi—this was someone vaguely familiar, but no, no one he knew, a stranger in his country.

"I'm going out for a smoke," Joe told his brother.

Wheelock had left the room. As Joe started out, he saw Egan come in from the side room where the defendants were held. Egan nodded and smiled and Joe went over to him.

"We're on next," said Egan. He spoke in the way Joe and Leo had and the way Foggarty had used when speaking to him con-

fidentially—a deep, muffled tone, dropped at close range into the
ear.

Egan had seen Wheelock go back to the clerk's office. He knew
Wheelock was Tucker's lawyer and he wanted to meet him. He
thought he might be able to help himself along by showing he
was friendly. He knew he couldn't throw the case. Even though
Foggarty had given up on Bauer and had given up on Hall,
he couldn't give up on Milletti. If there were an acquittal, the
damage done by going into Milletti's territory and grabbing off a
bank would rebound against Foggarty. So Egan couldn't go too
far with Tucker's people, but he wanted to do something for
them. He realized Tucker was in a position to harm him.

"I think," Egan said to Joe, "we got time to get ourselves a few
puffs if you want."

Joe said that was just where he had been heading, and Egan
told him he'd take him to a spot that was quieter than the hall.
He led the way down a corridor and through several rooms to the
clerk's office where Wheelock was talking to a man who stood
behind a wire partition.

It was a long room, deserted except for Wheelock and the clerk,
and it smelled cleaner than the courtroom. It smelled only from
dust and disinfectant. Egan kept looking at Wheelock and Joe
finally called Henry over and introduced him. The clerk went
back to his desk and the three were as if alone.

"The complaint is drawn the usual way," said Egan, " 'found with
policy slips.' " He looked at Joe and Wheelock, but he couldn't
read anything in their faces, and he realized abruptly they were
going to get him. They were going to beat Milletti to taking away
his job. Egan remained silent for a moment, looking away silently
and trying to think of what was best to say. He could feel the
sweat squash as he wrinkled his forehead and his hand shook a
little as he took the cigarette from his lips.

"With a wide open complaint like that," he said, "you can let
in anything you want, in or out, whatever is wanted." He thought
maybe he could fool them into making a bargain with him on

the case and then, when the case didn't come out as promised, it would be Badgley's fault or Foggarty's, not his.

Wheelock laughed. "That's the way you fellows respect the right of an accused to know what he is accused of. Yes, I know." He wagged a finger mockingly at Egan. "Always trying to get away with more than the law allows."

"It's not a usual case, Mr. Wheelock. But the complaint is drawn up usual."

"What's unusual about it?"

"You." Egan tried to smile. He saw Joe wink at Wheelock and Wheelock reply with a warning shake of his head. So, he thought, the two of them had a party all fixed up for him, cooked and waiting. "The instructions I got, too," he said. "They was in plain language to tie a rope around and hang them. That was the orders I was given to understand by the old man, by Foggarty of my office."

"You tied the rope around the wrong neck," said Joe.

Wheelock stepped forward hastily and pushed against Joe to keep him quiet. "I think we had better start back," he said. He threw his cigarette on the floor and stepped on it. While his head was lowered towards the butt, he turned his eyes sideways and glared at Joe. Joe accepted his glare indifferently.

Egan understood that, if they were going to get his job, it wouldn't be out of pique or for revenge. It would be for business reasons. They had to make an example of him for their customers and for the rest of the police department. So it was up to him to do business, too, and bargain his way out of the spot. But how? What did he have to bargain with? It was obvious they had the case taken care of. So there was nothing, nothing more to say, nothing more to do. Yet Egan wanted to hold them and talk to them more. The urge to hold them with him, talk to them some more, argue with them, show them he was a nice fellow maybe, make them sorry for him maybe, lifted from deep in him. But he knew that, too, was hopeless. What difference did it make how sorry they felt for him? Business was business. He stood hopelessly and couldn't think of anything except that, when they walked away, they would take his job with them in their pockets.

Wheelock was smiling a goodbye at him now and turning. Joe had already turned. Egan raised his hand to stop them. He saw Wheelock's face perk into a listening attitude. He saw Joe turn back to listen. Egan's mind felt numb. All he knew was that he had to keep them from walking away with his job in their pockets. He didn't know how he was going to do it. He didn't know what he was going to say. The words he found came from thoughts he did not know existed.

"I wonder," he said, "if you fellows have any idea who tipped over your bank." The half-question, half-observation hung in the air like the space between lightning and its thunder.

He knows who did it, thought Wheelock. He's going to tell us, and Joe will have something done about it and then Egan will know who did what was done and will have us where he wants us and what he will do with us, God only knows.

And Joe, too, was terrified. He knew if Egan gave them the name of the informant, then he would have to do something about it or have something done about it. And suddenly he knew, too, that he didn't want to do anything about it or want Tucker to do anything about it or want anybody connected with himself to do anything about it. If the thing were let slide, it might take care of itself or at least be settled without him having to make up his mind to settle it. But if it were known he knew who had done it, then he would be forced to act. All sorts of things would force him, and not the least powerful would be the necessity for having to be, as a matter of business, the kind of person those he dealt with in business believed him to be.

The three men stood staring at each other. For a moment, Joe and Egan looked enough alike to be brothers. They were both big men and now their faces were flushed and their eyes were bright with uneasiness and their mouths hung open. Wheelock seemed least affected. He looked merely thoughtful.

It's murder, thought Egan. His words had shaken him as much as if he had not heard them until they were spoken. It's murder with my own hands if I turn Bauer over to Joe, he told himself. And what would be the use? What would be gained? Only $425 a year extra for a million dollars' worth of headaches. Besides if he killed for Tucker, then Tucker would own him. Egan would have a hold on Tucker, but Tucker would have a hold on him, too, and Tucker was the stronger man. Egan had a policeman's notions about gangster connections. He felt Tucker had the power, not in himself, but in his connections, to bend Egan with his hold and own him. If Tucker had to break him back into uniform for the sake of his business, then what would stop Tucker from doing it if he owned him?

Joe had been half turned and he shifted now to face Egan squarely. "Well," he said harshly, "do you know who done it?"

Wheelock touched Joe's arm. His nimble legal mind had found a way out of the dilemma Egan's words had thrown him into. "I should think," he said, "that whoever gave the information doesn't concern us, only the people who own the bank, whoever they are." He looked brightly at Egan. "Why don't you find out who owns the bank and tell them, if you know?" he suggested.

"I don't know," said Egan. "I was just asking."

He was too shaken still to realize how glad he was that, although business had pushed him to the brink of murder, it had not pushed him over.

Joe leaped at Wheelock's way out. That's right, he thought with an emotion so intense it was like joy, we can't afford to admit to the police that we own the bank, not right to their faces anyway. "Yes," he said to Egan. "Tell the banker. Find him, why don't you, instead of bothering us."

Wheelock walked off and Joe followed him and then Egan went after Joe quickly and said, "You know yourself I got the complaint drawn the best I could."

Joe stopped. The fear in him had relaxed and he was beginning to feel sorry for Egan.

"Come on," cried Wheelock. "If we miss our place, we'll be put over to last."

Joe began to hurry after Wheelock again and Egan went along

with him, his head stooped forward, his face earnest and damp looking. I can't get down on my knees to them, he thought, and beg them with crying. "You know yourself," he said to Joe, "I done the best I could so that nobody should get hurt that don't have to."

Joe did not answer. No matter how sorry he felt for Egan, business remained business.

᙮

When they got back into the courtroom, Judge Garrett was still hearing the assault and battery case. Joe noticed that a space had opened on the bench alongside the youth he thought he had recognized and he went up the aisle and crowded himself into it.

"I got a kind of a feeling," he said, "that I think I know you from somewhere."

The lad had a thin, dark face, so pale it looked a little green. He was very small and young looking and his lips and nose and ears and eyes and hands and feet were shaped as if by an artist. He had a few long dark hairs at the edges of his upper lip and his green-tinted cheeks were so smooth, he did not seem to have begun to shave yet. He wore new patent leather shoes with high heels.

"I know you," he told Joe, "from your reputation. You was pointed out to me once in Boyle's."

"Where?"

"Boyle's, on 47th Street."

"Where is that on 47th Street?"

"A hundert and forty-seventh Street. You was shooting a game of pool with a short man with a belly on him. You gave him the 15 ball."

"Oh yes, that's right, a long time ago. Who said all this, did all this pointing?"

"Just fellows who was there. You're a prominent celebrity and they pointed you out for me to maybe get your autograph."

Joe laughed. But the boy continued to puzzle him. He had

thought if he heard him talk, he would be able to place him. He was sure now he had seen him somewhere and spoken to him, but it couldn't have been at Boyle's. He had been there only once. He wouldn't remember the boy just from seeing him in a crowd at a pool room. "Are you here on a case?" he asked.

"Sort of. One of the fellows I work with was picked up."

"Where do you work?"

"I'm with Koch." The boy saw the name didn't mean anything to Joe. "Barney Koch," he explained. "He makes book up there and I run for him. You might remember, in case you want to place a bet some time. I work the bars up there in that territory and Boyle's, places like that. If you're up there any time, I'll run into you."

Joe promised the boy his business if he ever got up that way. As he walked away, the boy looked after him stolidly. His beautifully moulded face was vacant and hung loosely. But, when he saw Joe take his place beside Leo, he sniggered. To hide it, he brought a handkerchief to his lips and then raised it to his nose and blew his nose loudly.

It's just, thought Joe, he must carry himself like someone I know. He had felt at first the boy might be one of Ficco's people, watching to see how the case came out, but the boy's story had been straight enough. If he had told it too willingly, that would be because he thought Joe gambled a lot and wanted the business. No, the kid just must carry himself like someone Joe knew. These kids were always imitating people they thought were big shots and, to tell the truth, some so-called big shots, too, were always imitating their pictures in the movies or in the papers.

Their case was called then and Joe stopped thinking about anything else.

The assistant district attorney began the hearing against Leo's bank by asking for a postponement. He said it was an important case, perhaps involving more than a misdemeanor, and he had had no time for preparation.

Wheelock argued briefly that the state had no case and that it would be an injustice to put his clients to the expense of getting bail. Judge Garrett ruled for the defense and, after that, Wheelock had nothing to do. The Judge did all the work for him.

Judge Garrett was finishing out his term on the bench. He was anxious that his son should be named to succeed him. This was the handle Ed Bunte had used, this and the fact that Garrett owed his job to Bunte.

Bunte had driven to the Judge's office in the late afternoon with Wheelock. He hadn't brought the case up at all until shortly before they left. Then he had said merely, "Wheelock has something coming up before you that is important to me."

"Who is it?" the Judge had asked.

"It's a policy case," Bunte had replied. "If you think you can take care of it without too much trouble, I'd be obliged."

One thing weighed with another in the Judge's mind. A Judge, just as everyone else on earth, must play the business game, too, and must play it for profit. In some cases a Judge's profit lay in doing his sworn duty. The public would reward him better than the other side or the reward offered by the other side for failing to do his duty was not great enough to be worth the disturbance to his conscience. However, this was obviously a minor case. Policy cases were always minor. The reward for failing to do his duty need not be minor, at least not to him. It was worth a tweak of his conscience.

"Well," the Judge had told Bunte, "if you make a point of it as a personal favor, if it's a matter where you personally are interested."

But Bunte had known he did not have to commit himself too much in so small a matter as this. "I'm not personally interested," he had said, "except I think I'd appreciate it as a favor to my young friend here."

"That's what I meant, Ed," Garrett had said.

It had been left at that.

Badgley was the first to take the stand. He told of entering the apartment "on information" and finding ten people sitting shoulder to shoulder around a table, each with a pile of policy slips before him, and six others in another room working over adding machines and ledger sheets with policy slips before them.

"One sought to escape and had to be prevented," he said.

The Judge questioned him closely about the position of the defendants' hands in relation to the policy slips. Badgley replied finally, "The best of my recollection is that some had been touching the slips and some had their hands on the table an inch or two away from the slips."

"What I want to know is," said the Judge, "to give me your best recollection on who was touching the slips and who was not touching the slips."

"My best recollection is that some was and some was not. Who in particular they was, I don't recollect, your Honor."

The Judge frowned. "Is this the way you ordinarily prepare cases?" he asked.

"I was occupied at the time elsewhere," said Badgley, "with the defendant who attempted to escape. I came over to the table later after Detective Egan had begun to inventoryize the evidence."

By this time, the assistant district attorney realized what was happening. He was a man who had been working in the office of the district attorney for nearly twenty years, almost since his admittance to the bar. He, too, was worried about Hall. He thought that if Hall succeeded in putting Decker out of office, then his own job would be in danger unless he made some kind of a record as a little more than a man who did as he was told. However, he couldn't go too far. Decker was still district attorney. There was always the chance he would be re-elected when his term was up.

Badgley's testimony had put it up to Egan to make the case good or bad. Egan sat stiffly in the witness chair. He looked directly ahead and answered questions in a loud voice that sounded through the whole courtroom. He answered precisely what he was asked and no more and, while he answered, his mind ran frantically from corner to corner of the trap in which he had been caught.

Foggarty was in one corner of the trap, Milletti in another, Tucker in a third and now there was the Judge, walling the trap, slamming it shut. He could make the case good all right by picking out five or six people and swearing they had had policy slips in their

hands and the others were only near the slips. That would make
Foggarty happy. But it would get the Judge sore and Tucker sore
and they were right here before him.

Wheelock would go after him. How did he remember these people? Had he taken their names and marked them down anywhere?
Why not?

"Not necessary," he heard himself answer.

He had begun to talk to himself in his loneliness, while listening
to and answering the Judge's questions.

Was his memory so good that he didn't have to mark down such
vital facts and yet he did have to mark down the names of the defendants on each envelope of policy slips? Was it? Was it? Answer!
Was it? If he had marked down the names, why hadn't he marked
under each one whether the accused had been in contact with the
slips or only adjacent to them? Why? Why? Answer, why!

He could see Wheelock hollering at him and the Judge hollering
because that would put the Judge in a trap and make the work
harder for him and could see Foggarty hollering tomorrow and
Milletti hollering later.

"The truth's best," Egan said to himself. "The truth never hurt
a man yet. Who has the truth ever hurt worse than lying?" He
sought to believe that in the way those afflicted by death seek to
believe in God. He turned desperately to truth. This was the morality he had been taught as a child. But it was also the morality that
had been invented before the game of marauding for profits had
grasped up the whole earth. Now this morality was no more use than
a sword to an admiral—good for swank, good for suicide, but for
what else? What use could morality be on an earth given over to
profit except to ornament a life or fill a grave? Yet morality lingered in man, perhaps to make a life of hunting and being hunted
less intolerable to his nature, and lingered in Egan, too, and now
he turned and clung to it.

When the time came, Egan said stolidly that he did not remember which defendants had been actually touching the slips and
which had been merely near them. For the sake of the record, the
Judge questioned him a long time on that point, but Egan stuck to

the truth. He turned his perspiring face to the Judge and said, "That's the best of my recollection, your Honor."

The Judge leaned forward, "You bring cases in here," he said angrily, "without the slightest indication that you have ever been trained to prepare a case."

"Your Honor," interrupted the prosecutor, feeling it was now his turn to decorate the record, "I submit, the preparation of the case is not the witness's concern."

The prosecutor perched gingerly on the floor and the Judge stared down at him.

"This man as I understand it," the Judge said, "and, if I am wrong I will permit you to correct me, this man was the arresting officer, one of the arresting officers. It was his duty, as far as I am able to discover, on seeing a crime in the course of commission, to assemble properly the evidence which led him to conclude, which indicated to him that a crime, a violation was going on there in the first place."

The prosecutor attempted to interrupt and the Judge said, "Just a minute, young man. The court is talking now.

"My impression is that the duty of an officer, as an officer of the court, is to assemble the evidence. I don't see any evidence here that can be called evidence properly, not one single, clean, hard question of fact, only a collection of assumptions and conclusions, instead of facts, and deductions, instead of facts."

"I submit, your Honor," the prosecutor turned directly to the court stenographer, "and I want to so state for the record that Detective Egan, acting on information, duly obtained a warrant and entered the premises. . . ."

"This is all repetition," said the Judge.

"I want it for the record."

"All right, you may have it."

Judge Garrett made a tent of his hands and touched them to his lips and stared unconcernedly at the prosecutor.

"Repeat that last part for me," said the prosecutor to the stenographer.

When he had picked up the thread, he began to speak in an in-

dignant voice that stilled the courtroom, ". . . the premises known
as Apartment 46 at 92-57 Edgecombe Avenue and found there the
sixteen defendants, each with a pile of policy slips before them,
what the defense stipulates is policy slips before him, some with
his hands in direct contact with the policy slips and none with their
hands further removed from the policy slips than two inches. That,
I submit, your Honor, is constructive possession in the meaning
of the law."

Judge Garrett took his hands down from his lips.

"Young man," he said and looked thoughtfully at the ceiling, "a
trial, as you know, is a search for truth. A hearing is a search for
facts, sweet, clean, hard facts that a jury can take hold of and decide what is the truth and what isn't the truth. I have heard no
facts here this evening, nothing that can be called a fact within the
four walls of the law."

"But your Honor . . ."

"Silence! Address the court when the court is finished talking.
The law on constructive possession is plain. Is it a fact that the defendant was in actual physical contact with the exhibit? That is
possession. Is it a fact that the defendant was in such proximity to
the exhibit and is there other proof that shows, beyond a reasonable
shadow of a doubt, that the defendant must at some time have had
possession, in the legal sense of that word, of the exhibit? Then, that
is constructive possession.

"Now, in this case, who is there to say that one of these defendants, I don't say all, but one of these defendants, was not up there
on a visit and was sitting at the table as a friend to keep a friend
company and not to work on the policy slips? Who is to say that
and who is to say who that one is?

"No, the law is plain. I have heard nothing this evening to make
me aware that a new interpretation of the law of constructive possession is in the throes of being born amidst us. Perhaps, young
man, we, all unbeknownst to ourselves, are witnessing the throes of
creation and your philosophy of constructive possession that is being created before the doubting eyes of the Philistine will prevail
some day. But, in the meantime, I am bound by higher courts and

by plainly marked precedents. I am the servant of my master, the law. The case is dismissed."

There was a small flurry of activity as papers were written on and stamped and the clerk began to call the next case. Wheelock thought the Judge had handled the matter fairly competently. He was glad the Judge had criticized Egan and Badgley. It would be a good excuse for whoever was given the job of demoting them. There would be no record to search there anyway.

Wheelock knew how that would work. Bunte would ask the party leader to do it and the leader would put the request for a transfer of Egan and Badgley to uniformed duty in with other requests from policemen who had gone to district leaders to get transferred to posts nearer their homes. They would all be sent in a batch to the police commissioner. Nobody would know, or at least would have to admit he knew, whether the requests for a transfer involved demotion or not. No consciences would be disturbed. The price of such transactions could be kept down.

The Judge suspected Bunte had something like that in mind. He called Egan before the bench. "If you bring any more cases into court without evidence," the Judge said, "this court will see to it that you are made to learn your duty before being entrusted with the performance of that duty. This court is fully aware that the probability is a policy bank was being operated in this apartment and is aware of the ancient precept of law that better that 100 guilty should go unpunished than one innocent be punished.

"You come here in such a way, with nothing to say, with no proper evidence except suspicions and conclusions without any probative force and tie the court's hands. I am giving you the benefit of a doubt, a very small doubt, in ascribing your conduct and that of your fellow officer to ignorance rather than a more sinister, wilful intent to obstruct justice. You understand what I'm saying?"

He thrust his soft, pink face forward and looked angrily at Egan. Egan stood stiffly at attention. He held his hat in his hand. His face was red and wet and his eyes were lined with blood. He didn't think anything or take in anything. His mind was as stiff as his back.

"I am saying," said the Judge, "that you are not corrupt, just dumb. But if another attempt is made by you to put this court in a similar position by bringing in people who are probably guilty and then failing to bring in the evidence against them, this court will bring the matter to your superior officers' attention for remedial action."

The prosecutor was putting some papers slowly and angrily into a folder. He shoved them into place with an indignant flourish and slapped the folder shut.

"He looks just like I wouldn't take him into the combination," said Leo to himself. He turned his head away quickly. He didn't want to see.

BOOK SIX

A GLEICHSCHALTUNG

XV

JOE WALKED out of the courtroom behind Wheelock. Leo had gone on ahead with his employees. Joe leaned forward on the way up the aisle and spoke over Wheelock's shoulder. "I think Ficco was back of it," he said.

Wheelock's face twisted around. He had heard of Ficco from Tucker, but had never met him. Joe saw Wheelock's face like a blink of white light and then he was lookng again at the back of Wheelock's head as Wheelock walked steadily out of the court-room.

They stopped in the corridor near the door, close against the wall.

"We're putting Leo's bank in my apartment for a few days until we make sure it was Ficco," Joe said.

"What about the other banks?"

"Ficco don't know anybody's with us yet. Nobody knows."

"But still . . ."

"I got only four rooms in my chateau. Maybe you can take care of the others in your places."

"They're just what I need. I'll hide them in the toilet."

Joe laughed. "I guess not," he said. "I guess you'd forget and pull the chain."

"The way I feel it would be on purpose."

Leo was at the far end of the hall, near the door leading to the street. His employees were huddled near him. He was giving them the address of Joe's apartment and telling each the best way to get there. They were arguing about subway expresses and locals and street cars and buses that gave transfers and Leo's head and tongue wagged earnestly. He looked like a shepherd trying to talk out his loneliness with his flock.

Wheelock stared at him and at the crowded corridor filled with people walking among knots of low-talking people. I deserve it, he thought. I've been heading for Ficco for a long time. He felt a wallop of fear. His hand went nervously into his coat pocket and pulled out cigarettes and chewing gum. He looked at them both for a moment. He decided on a cigarette. He intended to put the gum back into his pocket. Instead, he kept the gum and threw the cigarettes on the floor.

"Look at that," he said. The breath blew out of his nose in a snort. He turned to Joe. A smile had leaped to his face and his eyes were bright, but they were darting from side to side. He pointed to the pack of cigarettes on the floor. "I didn't want the gum," he said, "so I threw away the cigarettes."

He laughed and looked at the gum in his hand and then, abruptly, threw the gum away, too. He stared helplessly. "What am I doing?" he cried. "Can you figure it out? I'm all scattered." He looked at Joe helplessly and laughed helplessly and stooped and picked up the cigarettes and gum and put them into his pocket.

"You ought to chew cigars," said Joe slyly.

Wheelock did not notice Joe had attempted a joke. He reached into his vest pocket and pulled out a cigar and fiddled with it fretfully. "If it's Ficco," he said. He looked along the corridor and then looked down at his cigar. His fretfully fiddling had cracked the wrapper. He rolled the broken place against the inside of his lip and then tamped the cigar together carefully.

"I told Ben," Joe said. "He is asking around and we ought to know for sure pretty soon."

The small, greenish-faced boy came hurrying out of the courtroom. His high-heeled patent leather shoes clicked quickly and glittered against the stone floor. His narrow-brim hat was pulled down over his face and his coat collar was turned up. He went down the corridor and past Leo and out the door without looking at anybody, seeming not to want to be recognized. Joe decided the boy must have had bad luck with the Judge.

"If it's Ficco," said Wheelock and stopped again and put the cigar into his mouth.

"So what if it is?"

"It's what I didn't like in the first place."

"You mean that's what you were afraid of."

"Yes." Wheelock took the cigar out of his mouth and drew himself erect. "Scared to death."

"You'd better put that cigar away. You don't seem to be getting any fun out of it, the way I see."

Wheelock looked at the cigar as if he didn't know he had been holding it. Then he threw it on the floor.

"I'm scared, too," said Joe. "Tucker is scared. He is so scared he can't see out of his eyes. I'm not even telling Leo a word about this because I am afraid he will go crazy and do something crazy."

"Our army certainly needs to have its diapers changed."

"Yes, but in a way there's nothing much to worry about. There isn't anything to Ficco. I don't think he's got any backing or money or nothing. He's just a shooter, so what is there really to worry about?"

"Only getting shot," said Wheelock.

"That's not what you're worried about."

"No."

"You know you won't get shot. Somebody else might, but you won't."

"I know."

"The other thing can't be helped." Joe smiled. This was one thing he enjoyed telling a man like Wheelock. "If something happens to somebody," he said, "and it's all over the newspapers with all of us, with our pictures in there and so forth, well, that's what you let yourself in for in the first place when you started with us. That's part of the profit and loss in the business."

Wheelock began buttoning his coat. His face was flushed. His eyes danced and jerked from side to side. One cheek twitched suddenly. It twitched and flicked and kept on twitching and flicking. He twisted his mouth far to one side to stop it and drew in his breath noisily.

"You don't have to take it so hard," said Joe. "Maybe it's not

Ficco. Maybe it's one of the bankers we are freezing out trying to make a little stupid trouble for us."

"It's Ficco."

"How do you know?"

"I know because my luck has all run out."

"That's not the way to feel."

"That's the way I feel," said Wheelock, "and I'll tell you this to think about. When the newspapers go to work on us, we're going to have trouble with Bunte. I'm telling you. With Hall in there watching, Bunte is going to get clear of us once the newspapers pull us into the open and, when the protection goes, Tucker is going to get hard to manage, too. You haven't studied Tucker up close the way I have. I know. He's going to get fight-crazy and tough. It's all going to come out in him, the whole thing, bust out like pus, when he's pushed like that. That's what I think and then where will all of us be?"

Running for the rat holes, Joe thought. For a moment, he felt sorry for Wheelock. The man had been so poised and friendly. He had had an aroma of success. Then a single name dropped into Wheelock's ear had hit like a bullet. Joe lifted his hand to put it on Wheelock's shoulder to reassure him, but he let his hand fall and stood still and thought, "Me too."

"What I worked for, too," he thought, "all my life."

There was a bubbling and spewing in him, a hectic, frothy feeling in his head. All the layers of his mind were working at once as he thought of what lay ahead and of what it might bring Leo and himself and of how he had meant only good to Leo all his life and how it had never worked out and how the combination would not work out now, how the combination was the worst of all, the thing he had meant to be the best thing ever for Leo, so good as to wipe out the memory of everything else and make up for everything else, was the worst, the very worst of all.

Joe tried to speak. He found his throat choked up. He rasped it clear. "If there's a situation like this," he said, "the thing I've always found is good is not to think about it but just go ahead and do what you have to do."

"Some people can't stop thinking. I think all the time."
Joe's mind was so crammed with thoughts, he found it difficult
to choose words. "I mean not to worry," he said. "You think what
you have to do and do it and not to worry, not to look at the bad
side of it, at the wrong end. Well, I guess I'm not saying it right,
but what I mean is, the way it's been with me is . . . Well, look.
I'm in a business. So what? So I'm in a business and I do what I
have to do to stay in it. That's the law. Stay in business. Tend to
business. Everybody does it. That's the law for everybody. Well,
a situation comes up and you figure out what you got to do to stay
in business and you do it and it works out all right. And if it
don't work out all right, what's the difference? Maybe it's better
if it don't work out right, because that way you're licked and out
of business and maybe better off. I don't know. I don't know."
Joe felt he was talking too loud. He stopped and rubbed his
hand against his face. The thoughts in him were too many for him.
He couldn't assemble them or understand them. He had never
questioned the business game. Business was business and everybody
has to make a living unless he's born rich. He had never tried to
find out what business had done to him. Who says business does
something to a man? A man does something to it. That would
have been his attitude if he had ever bothered to adopt one. But
now, now, in this crisis, his mind was turning itself inside out for
him and he couldn't understand what lay in it. He said things he
couldn't understand and thought thoughts he couldn't understand.
As he rubbed his face, he looked suddenly like Leo. He had the
same sad, timid expression. It was the first time Wheelock had
noticed any resemblance between the two brothers and he opened
his mouth to remark on it.
"I don't know," said Joe abruptly. "All my life I've wanted to
get by the right way. When I was a kid, even when I was a kid
and didn't know better, I tried. That was my instinct, to try, to try
and all the time there was something in my way. Every step I took.
I want to get by like everybody else and they don't let me. Every
time there is always something coming up."
In the past, Joe could blame his "temperament" for some of his

failures and his rivals for others of his failures. But now he was confused. Now he thought his "temperament" was not something he had made all by himself. It was something that had been made for him. And if it had been made for him, who could he blame? What was there to blame? If not himself, then who? He did not understand his thought and it confused him.

"That's with everybody," said Wheelock.

"No, not like this. I start something and then something always comes up, from nowhere, from no place. You think Ficco is the first time it happened in my life that I was stopped? Why should it be that way? Why should I be something special like that? Do you know?"

"Really, everybody has the same thing. It's business, dog eat dog."

Joe didn't hear Wheelock. He was too rapt in the struggle to understand his own thoughts and in failure to understand. "No, I'm telling you, no!" he cried. "What's the reason? Can you tell me a single reason why every time I try to go ahead regular, something comes up to stop it, something from outside, from what people do to me, lawyers, businessmen, police, my own friends, my own brother, every time, every God damn time, like the whole world is against me wherever I go, in every state in the union, in Canada where I was, across the ocean, too, Paris, France? Why is it?"

"That's the profit system. Dog eat dog. Your loss is my profit. That's the way the world is. What do you want to do, change the world?"

"But why is it they don't let a man live? Why? Look at me. Am I special? Am I a rat to be chased and chased and chased, I got to bite back and chase me again and bite back and chase me again and chase and chase until they get me in a corner and I bite back and chase and chase. Is that my life, in the corner, out of the corner, bite, chase? Is that what life is?"

"Ssh, take it easy," said Wheelock. "Calm down. Everybody has the same thing."

"No, no, not the same. I want to get by like everybody else. So what? So I try something. It's good and I'm going good. But they don't let me! All right! I won't fight. I don't want to fight, get in trouble. Who enjoys trouble? I give it up and try something else and they don't let me there either. Wherever I go, they don't let me. Why? You're smart. Why? You got an education. Tell me why. Do you know why from books or somewhere, why a person trying to get by nice and ordinary, the regular way, should have to live like an animal with everything against him?"

Joe searched Wheelock's face. He saw nothing in it but concern over the loudness of his voice. "I'm going to take that son of a bitch Ficco," said Joe, "and pull his eyes out with my fingers, with these fingers!" He held his fingers out before him, curved like claws.

"I guess we need a drink," said Wheelock.

"Aaah!" Joe straightened his fingers and flung his hand downward in exasperation.

"It will do us both good," Wheelock said.

"That's all you think of all the time," said Joe. "I don't drink when there's work to do and you'd better do the same instead of sticking your head in whiskey like an ostrich."

"That's a fallacy about ostriches."

"Yes, sure, that's what your education taught you, nothing else. That's what you learned from your books."

"Well," smiled Wheelock, "ostriches really don't put their heads in the sand."

"I don't care what the hell they do and what you do." Joe walked swiftly down the corridor. As he passed Leo, he called out abruptly, "See you, tomorrow." He opened the door and was out and down the street before the door closed.

Wheelock followed. He had his hands in his pockets and he walked as if he were strolling, with a slight sway to his steps. He halted thoughtfully beside Leo. "Well, Mr. Minch, it worked out all right, didn't it?" he said.

Leo answered, but Wheelock didn't hear him. He was trying to fix his mind on whiskey. It was difficult.

"Good night," said Wheelock. He bowed and waved his hand

gravely, including all the people around Leo in his bow and wave. The whiskey was clearer in his mind now. Everything else was fading. "I'm going to think of all the whiskey there is in New York," he said to himself and smacked his lips noisily, noisily enough to drown all the other sounds in his ears. He saw rows of brown and black bottles behind bars. He thought of them standing silently, waiting for him, their shapes slick and cold and their insides still and warm and swarming.

He began to walk towards the bottles like a sick man looking for a place to lie down.

XVI

LEO WAS tired and hungry, but the problem Bauer had become could not be ignored and Leo forced himself to deal with it at once. His idea was, first, to show Bauer how wrong it had been to do what he had done, then how dangerous and, finally, when the man was all melted down, to forgive him, or, at least, put him on probation. But he did not want to spend much time. He told Bauer he would drive him across town from the courthouse to where he could get a subway home.

"I'm not going home," said Bauer.

"It must be nine, ten o'clock. Where then are you going so late?"

"Is there a law that you have to know what I'm doing when I'm not working, too?"

They had stopped on the sidewalk in front of the courthouse. Leo stared at Bauer until Bauer's eyes fell. He thought of what this man had done to his business and to his people and to his relationship with his people. He struggled to stick to his plan for handling Bauer. But he couldn't. The best he could do was keep his voice down.

"I'm just about at the end with you," he said.

"Fine," Bauer replied sullenly. "Now maybe you'll let me alone."

"I'm not going to fight with dirt like you. Get in my car."

Bauer did not move. He stood with head stooped sullenly.

"You're in trouble," said Leo. "You know that, don't you? You're in such terrible trouble that you don't know what trouble you're in. You know that, don't you? Get in my car and tell me where you're going."

Bauer did not lift his head. "I'm going to get rolls for coffee," he replied.

Leo's car was parked a short distance down the block. As they walked towards it, they passed a new Ford roadster in which sat the small, green-faced boy who was Barney Koch's runner. The boy put his head out the window. "Hey, Fred," he called, "do you want a lift?"

Bauer looked at him. He had trouble remembering him. "Oh, hello," he said slowly, trying to think of the boy's name.

"I'm going to your neighborhood," said the boy.

"Thanks." Bauer shook his head. Wally, that was it. Walter something from Boyle's. He waved his hand. "I've got a lift, Wally," he said and walked on with Leo.

Leo was curious, but he refrained from asking questions about the boy. He didn't want to make Bauer antagonistic again. "I know where there's a bakery near your subway," he said as they drove off, "where they have wonderful rolls that they make fresh in the evening. We'll go there."

"Do what you want," said Bauer. "What I want is never anything to you anyway."

Leo controlled himself with an effort. "They're your rolls," he pointed out.

The streets were black and cold. The lights sparkled frosty green in the dark air. Leo drove swiftly. He thought of Juice and Delilah with bruises on her arms and of Murray, who wanted to be a policeman, and of how he had given Bauer a job when Bauer had come to him and said his children were starving.

"I want to tell you plain," he said, his voice tight with the effort to control it, "that after what you did to me today and everybody, I'm through with you from now on."

"What do you mean?" cried Bauer. "What did I do?"

"I mean? You know what I mean. I'm through with you. From now on, you're a dog in the street to me and you better watch your step."

"That's all right with me." Bauer's voice was small. He twisted away from Leo and gripped the door handle with two hands. "I want to get out now," he said.

Leo realized he was handling Bauer wrong. It exasperated him even further. "We're not there yet," he said.

"You can't make me stay. I want to get out."

"You'll stay and you'll not get out."

"Let me out. Why don't you let me out?"

Leo steered the car abruptly to the curb and brought it to a sharp stop. "Get out if you want," he said.

Bauer looked at him uncertainly. He still gripped the door handle.

"Get out," said Leo. "Go ahead. Take care of your own troubles."

Bauer's breath sounded heavily through the silence. He sat twisted around, looking at Leo, his nostrils gaping and closing, flinging open and sucking in tight. "I don't know what you're talking," he said. His chin trembled and he turned his head away and looked straight before him.

"You don't know? That's a good one. You don't know nothing, do you, not nothing. Well, I know. I know what you did and I have a good mind not to help you. Get out. Go ahead. Get the hell out in the street where you belong. What are you waiting for?"

Bauer remained silent. He sat with lowered head. His hands had fallen from the door handle and they lay lifelessly across his legs.

Leo waited a moment and then put the car into gear and drove on. Just as he was about to tell Bauer that he was willing to help him if he only showed he was sorry for what he had done and would not do it again, he saw the bakery. "Here's where you get your rolls," he said.

The shop was a warm-looking brightly lit place with white light bouncing up from the white tile floor. Its window was empty. Only a gray wire basket of yellow rolls and a few brown breads remained on its white porcelain shelves inside. Two stout blonde women stood talking near the cash register at the rear of the store. Their plump, floury skins looked pink against their white uniforms.

Bauer opened the door of the car hastily and almost fell to the sidewalk. Leo looked at him startled. For a moment, he thought the man was going to run.

"I'll wait for you," he said. He had decided to drive Bauer home. He would start over again with the man and work him along as he had originally planned.

Bauer walked into the shop without answering or turning his head.

The glass front of the store was wide open to the street. Leo could see Bauer, looking tired and sullen as he talked to one of the shop women while the other went behind a partition in the rear of the store. He saw the tired face talk and the plump, floury pink face answer, smiling, and whisk to a counter for a paper bag and whisk to the basket of rolls while the sullen, tired face followed.

Leo began to fiddle with the cigarette lighter on the dashboard. It did not work all the time. He pushed it in and took it out and looked at it. It wasn't hot. Then something caught his eye and he saw that Bauer had slipped out of the store and was walking down the street, his thin body hunched close to the shadow of the building, the white paper bag of rolls hanging luminously from his hand.

"Hey," shouted Leo. He jammed his foot angrily against the starter. "Dumb, rotten dog," he mumbled.

Bauer had broken into a slow run, as if he didn't really want to run and felt there was no use running, but had to run nevertheless. Leo caught up with him in a moment and leaped out of the car and raced across the sidewalk and cut him off.

"Why you," he cried. Bauer looked at him mutely. Leo pushed him in the chest. His hand seemed to sink in. There was no fight to Bauer. He was all give. "What do you think you're doing?" cried Leo.

"Let me alone," whimpered Bauer.

"Do you know what you're doing?" Leo tore the bag of rolls

from Bauer's hand. He had thought suddenly of what Joe would do if he ever found out about Bauer and what Joe's act would mean to him and to his whole business and to his whole life. "You want to live, don't you?" he cried. He held the rolls to Bauer's face. "You want to eat these rolls, don't you?"

"Leave me alone," Bauer whimpered, "please."

The tone was different, but the words were the same Leo had spoken to Joe, and Leo knew it and the knowledge rose screaming in him. It was torture to have to do to Bauer what Joe had done to him. "I don't want to hear that! I don't want to hear another word like that from you!" He screamed with the pain in him and rage at the pain and stood shaking, his body lifting and thrusting with his words. He held the bag of rolls in the air and it shook in his shaking fist. "What you done to me today," he cried. Suddenly he slapped the bag of rolls across Bauer's face. He didn't hit hard and even then he pulled back the force of the blow, but the bag broke and the rolls spilled across the sidewalk.

Bauer seemed to become crazy for a moment. His face filled and bulged and boiled. He had raised his head high to escape the blow and the bag had struck against his chin. He stood now very tall, his head reared, and lifted both his fists into the air and stamped his foot. His eyeglasses quivered. He stamped his foot again and opened his mouth wide and a hoarse sound came from it. Then he turned and began to run. He stepped on a roll and leaped away from its soft, crushed body so violently he nearly fell. A wail broke from him and he ran faster, head down, his breath struggling from him in sobs.

Leo felt faint with fear. He watched Bauer and then looked down and stood staring at the scatter of yellow rolls. Bauer's broken breathing and the scraping noises of his feet as he ran on his toes sounded like the flurry of an animal plunging into hiding.

Bauer ran straight down the block, past Wally sitting in his car and did not see Wally. Leo did not notice Wally either. Neither knew he had been following them.

XVII

A CANDY store owner, coming out to collect pennies left on the news stand, saw Bauer running and looked at him curiously. His stare slowed Bauer to a hurried walk.

Bauer pulled out his handkerchief and buried his face in it and walked along blindly with long, hasty steps. "What's the good of running," he thought. "I can't get out of it."

It was a vast, enormously complicated thought. It had tossed up from deep in him. But he did not understand it. He believed he meant he was sure the police had told Leo and Leo would tell Joe.

He took off his glasses and wiped his eyes and face and blew his nose and put back his glasses, still going quickly with head lowered. His loud, rapid breathing came in sucks and bursts. He crossed a street head down, without looking to see if the way were clear, and went swiftly down stairs to the subway station.

"Whatever I struggle," he thought, "I hurt myself." The complexity of the thinking in him confused his language. "It hurts me if I do," he told himself, 'if I don't, if I do something, if I stand still. Whatever I do, I end up it hurts me."

He was pacing up and down the station platform. He became aware, as Egan had been aware and Leo and as most contestants in the business game at some time must become aware, that he had been made into an animal in a trap. To pace up and down like this made the thought too plain to Bauer. He went trembling to a bench and sat down. His hands fumbled nervously with his knees. He swayed back and forth slowly, with eyes closed, and rubbed his thighs. All he could think of was Joe and Joe knowing about him and Joe was a hard man, a man like a nail, and there was no use crying tears to him or crying blood to him or doing anything because there was nothing to do that would be any good.

He bent far forward. The thoughts went around and around in his head like noise. His forehead touched his knees and he felt a groan rise from deep in him. He stopped it in his mouth. He could taste it. It seemed to have been torn off from down inside him and to be warm and bleeding. His tongue and lips worked over the fleshy taste.

"Jesus Christ!" he said to himself. He lifted his head from his knees. His body was still folded over his thighs, but he pulled his head back and stared ahead of him without seeing anything.

A train came and stopped. There were people getting on and off. Some turned to stare at him. He looked like a drunk with a sick stomach.

"Help a man who is good, Jesus," said Bauer to himself.

A man chuckled and pointed at him and said, "There's one done his Christmas shopping early."

The prayer went out of Bauer. He had been praying with his mouth only. There was something in him that prevented him, no matter how he tried, from turning for help to his God. He heard the man laugh and pulled himself erect and sat still, looking straight ahead. The train went away and the people went away. Bauer sat still, thinking of nothing.

"What's this?" he thought suddenly. The thought was as abrupt as a cry. His mind had wandered away from his fear of Joe and had drowned in blankness. The abrupt thought, that, despite the emergency, he had not been paying any attention to it had brought Joe back to him. He clung to fear of Joe for a moment and then fear wandered away once more and he sat blankly.

"What kind of a way is this," he told himself. The fear sprang back into his mind. Then slowly blankness came like sea and rolled over it and washed it until no fear was left, only blankness, a long, profoundly moving, enthralling blankness.

"What kind of a way is this to sit here while I'm dying!" he cried to himself and felt fear again. Fear vaulted across his brain. It was gone in an instant and the blankness came rolling and washing in its wake. The blankness rolled and washed over the floor on which fear had vaulted and, in the end, it washed the floor of fear away. Then, again, only blankness remained.

❧

In the blankness lay the sum of Bauer. There lay the reasons for his doing what he had already done and the reasons for the awful thing that yet remained for him to do. It was blankness to him because it was too multitudinous to grasp as thought. So it became emotion. Each emotion was many things. There were many emotions and they all mingled into a single sea that rolled overwhelmingly and drowned even the thinking he might do.

To see into this blankness, it is necessary to understand Bauer far better than he understood himself. He did not, for instance, understand that each man is, of course, many things. Each man is what he thinks he is. Then he is, equally, what others think he is. And a man is also what he was and what he will be and, in a certain sense, he is, too, what he could be. And each of these separate creations stands in reciprocal relation to each of the others and to the total of all the others. That, in passing, is the parsing of man, but of greatest concern to Bauer is that man is two things: in the first place, he is what he actually is; and then, he is what he has been made into. One of the widest tragedies of individual man in the misshapen, modern world is that these two—what he is and what he has been made into—exist in him at the same time.

The man Bauer had been made into was, in a way, a tribute to the efficiency of the modern world. The modern world had left no inch of him unmarked. It had let no single plant grow straight out of the roots in his natural self. Bauer had become the modern world's creature, almost from the moment of his birth into insecurity to parents who themselves had been twisted out of their natural selves by insecurity.

As a child, Bauer's mind, like that of all children, had gone out to learning. It was a sort of love, full of need and full of reward. The desire to learn was the root. The reaching out for learning was the plant. Learning itself was the flower that might bloom on the plant. But no flower grew, nothing that might be called a flower, and the plant was wrenched out of shape because, by the time Bauer was of school age, insecurity had already done its work upon him. Insecurity breeds fear and fear is stronger than love. Some believe it may even be the strongest of all the forces in man.

There was nothing in school to help Bauer. Perhaps he was already beyond all but medical help. At any rate, he did not study to learn, he did not reach out to learn, but studied only because he feared his teachers and feared bringing bad marks home and feared to be thought stupid. Thus he studied without learning and was made stupid. And thus was this first great love of all mankind, love of learning, deformed in the boy Bauer had been deformed into and turned into something pathetic.

Now the pattern was formed and Bauer went along with it. He remained in school because he feared leaving a place to which he had become accustomed and face new problems. If he had clung to school until the end, until, say, he had acquired a profession, this might have been a great adventure for him, shaking enough to have broken the pattern. But perhaps it would not have been. Fear is tenacious. There are many who are trained, for example, as doctors or teachers and practice their professions without showing any signs of having learned it. Fear had shut out learning from them and they could not shut out fear. Anyway, there is no way to tell if the adventure would have broken the pattern of fear for Bauer. He did not undertake it and he was not so situated that it could be thrust upon him. He was afraid to go on from high school to college because it meant parting with the life he knew in the neighborhood he knew. Taking a job after finishing high school did not. He had become accustomed to working during summer vacations and after school hours.

Bauer was a man with a talent for mechanics. There he had another chance to break the pattern. Finding an expression for his talent might have saved him. But, among the people Bauer knew, a boy with a high school diploma was regarded as educated, and educated boys did not work with their hands. They went into offices, else why had they wasted so much time in school? Besides, office-workers were accorded more respect than those who worked with their hands.

Fear drove Bauer to do what was expected of him. Fear drove him to seek the respect of those around him. If he had ever had to set himself against these fears, his feeling of insecurity would have become uncontrollable.

So Bauer could not set himself against his fears. He sacrificed his natural talent and went into an office. There, he could not succeed. He could be merely adequate to his work. He was afraid to be ingenious—too much risk. He was afraid to assume responsibility—too much risk. He could do no more than exactly as he was told. Nor was the work compelling enough to a man of his natural talents to make him ingenious or authoritative despite himself. The result, altogether, was that Bauer not only sacrificed his personality (as it might have been expressed through his talent for mechanics) in order to control his sense of insecurity, but he sacrificed with it any chance he had had to find security in business.

The poison of insecurity was now in every pore of him. The love that entered him through Catherine had small chance from the start. It is true, he went out to her instantly. In another mind, or, as it is called, heart, Catherine might have become a great love. But fear drove Bauer away from her. He wanted her, so he was afraid he would be rebuffed. Then he was afraid to let himself want her because that would make his rebuff even more painful.

Catherine happened to Bauer at a time when it was expected of him to go out with girls. It was a rule he was afraid to disobey. This drove him back to Catherine, even after he had rejected her in his mind. His fear of failing to go with girls was not strong. It would not have been strong enough to make him go out simply with any girl. No, if Catherine had not been there, he might easily have remained withdrawn fearfully from women all his life. But Catherine was there and he loved her. Love was the root and it put out a plant. It made Bauer stand before her eyes and cling to her presence, even after he had rejected her in his mind. That was the plant. Fear fastened on it and made itself strong with it and shaped it, and finally all that the man Bauer had become could know was he had gone back to Catherine because it was expected of him.

And all the man Bauer had become could know was that he had

married Catherine because he was afraid of what she would think of him if he did not and afraid of what people would think of him and afraid, too, of what he would think of himself. Equally awful, this was all Catherine could see of the love her husband bore for her. She saw the ugly, flowerless, creeping plant, not the root, nor the root and plant.

The children came. He loved them. It is not natural to fail to love one's own children. But children added to his responsibilities. Responsibilities added to his insecurity. Insecurity strengthened his fear and so this love, too, became twisted unrecognizably.

What chance did any love have in this man? Leo had come to him with help, clumsily, it is true, but nevertheless in a moment of great need. Bauer's natural self went out to Leo, but the man Bauer had become did not permit it. And so it was with all the people he knew. His natural self loved them or was willing to be at peace with them. Fear forced him to love no one and nothing and did not allow him to live at peace with anyone. The best the business world permits the fearful man is an armed truce.

Yet love remained in Bauer. What one has become can govern, but cannot destroy what one is. Fear had twisted the plants of love into hate, but it could not dig out the roots. So another terror was added to Bauer. He was fastened by what his natural self loved to what was hated by the man he had become.

His natural self loved Catherine and his children. Fear had twisted his love into hate. The man he had become hated them. Yet Bauer could not leave them. The man Bauer had become needed to explain this puzzling situation to himself and explained it thus: if he left his family penniless, it would be a crime; he would have to hide from the law; he would be afraid of what his family would think of him for doing it; of what people would think of him; finally, of what he himself would think of himself for doing it.

There was nothing of love in any of this, yet, would there have been any of it if there had not been love? It never occurred to Bauer, as he had become, that these little fears of words in others' mouths and thoughts in others' minds were not strong enough in themselves to fasten him to his responsibilities unless they were strengthened by love, unless actually he loved what he believed he hated.

In the crisis that had come to Bauer, the proof of this became even plainer. Now the fear of staying with his family and facing what lay before him grew violent. Yet he did not run away. He had to run and he did not run. What else but love could make such an incidental emotion as fear of what Catherine and the children would think of him for running away from them and fear of what he would think of himself for running away, such a flabby-bodied, unreal emotion, such an echo of unheard blame, such a shadow of a black look, such a tickle in the brain, such a dewdrop among a heart's sweat, what else but love could make it powerful enough to hold him up to the face of death? No, it must have been love that was holding him in this crisis.

And it was truly crisis. Bauer's whole life had been flung into crisis. The first raid had set the crisis in motion. It had made Bauer think about his job. If he thought about his job, he must think about his fear of it. If he thought about his fear of his job, he must think of the stronger fear that had driven him to ask for such a job and take and work at such a job—fear of shirking his responsibilities to his family. If he thought of this fear of his family and its inordinate power—power enough to overthrow the whole pattern of yielding to convention on which his previous life had been formed—then he must know that he loved Catherine and his children and had only been made to feel hate for them.

The knowledge was in him. He had ignored or refused to understand it, so it had remained hidden in his mind. But the arrival of the police for the first raid had been a shattering experience, and everything in his mind had been jolted out of hiding. Now he had to think of it. He had to think of everything, of what he was and of what he had been made into, of his whole life and his whole career in it, for it was all of a piece.

The task was overwhelming. He could not sort out anything. Each emotion was a mingled thing, a root and its twisted plant, All the emotions, all the roots, and all the twisted plants had mingled into a matted sea-like mass and he could not untangle it.

Instead, the mass, under pressure of crisis, flung and crashed in his mind like nothing knowable, like a force.

His first instinct was to run. The frightened must run and Bauer, always frightened, always had run. But a different kind of running was required now. It was no longer a question of running out of a room or away from someone, for what he had to run away from was in himself. The man Bauer had been made into by environment had to run away from the mess that man had made of Bauer's whole life. But the man Bauer had become was fastened to the life from which he now had to run. He was fastened by his natural self and its instinct for survival and its love for Catherine and the children. These were indestructible except by death. They would be carried with him wherever on earth he ran. So it was no use merely to run from a situation or a series of situations. The man Bauer had been made into must run from life itself.

So, a will to self-destruction had sprung up in Bauer almost as the raiders sent by Joe had come into the bank. It had sprung up and begun to battle for expression against the things that opposed it. It was not an unequal battle. The urge to suicide is rarely successful. Many, if not most, alive in the modern world have fought it and survived in one way or another. Even sensitive adolescents, in the crisis of their adolescence when their selves are thrown open to them, fight it and all survive except those who are usually said to have "studied too much" or to have been "so much in love it became unwholesome," and are seldom said to have become frightened at what a world of business was making them into.

The weapon of the will to self-destruction is fear. It wars with an army of fears. The man Bauer had become had lived so long with fear, it was something he could turn to readily. But now he had to feel ultimate fear, the rare kind that comes to few, the kind that reduces a man's conscious mind to flesh fighting to survive. If Bauer could induce himself to fear life that much, then he could overthrow his natural self and escape to death.

The will in him had begun to seek out fear long before, when he sat in a chair in Leo's bank and became paralyzed by the thought of going with the police who had arrested him. It had accumulated more fear from having to go back to the job at which he had been arrested. But this was not yet enough. The will in him had pounced on Joe to get more fear. Bauer might have realized he could count on Leo to protect him from Joe, but he had not let himself realize it. He kept driving fear of Joe back into his mind every time his common sense told him he need not fear Leo's brother.

Nor was this enough. He was not sufficiently imaginative to make this fear real enough. He did not relinquish fear of Joe or fear of working in the bank, but he needed to make these fears stronger with other, greater, realer fears. And now, terribly, as he sat in the subway station, his mind began to reach out for them.

❧

The subway station's yellow gloom fell on Bauer as silently as dust. Another train came and stopped and went away. He watched it listlessly. "Where in the world have I got to turn?" he asked himself. Everybody has something to rest his head on, he thought, and where in the world can I put my head?

He began to think of what he had endured in the last two weeks, from the police, from working in the bank, from doing what he had done to Leo, from the police again and, finally, tonight, from Leo. It all went through his mind as emotion, a single, vast, vastly tangled emotion. "What was it for?" he asked himself. "Was it for me, that I should have what to eat? When a man's by himself, he can always get what to eat."

He thought of what he would do if he were by himself. He wouldn't have been in such a job in the first place, he decided. He would have been a different man. He would have had a different life altogether.

"A man with a wife and children that he suffers for like I suffer for," he told himself, "and with a father living who owes him that he brought him into the world, and yet he is alone, like a stone in the street." He thought suddenly of the rolls as he had seen them spilled across the street and of the one whose soft body had been crushed under his feet. "Step on him," he told himself. "Kick him.

Throw him. Break him to pieces. Who is there to care? Who is there to help? He's alone like a stone."

He began to cry again. He put his head down and wept tiredly into one hand. He heard another train come and stop and go away, but he didn't look up. He sat still, his warm, wet face lying in his wet hand. When the noise of the train's passing died down, he lifted his head and took out his handkerchief and wiped his face again and blew his nose and stood up and smoothed his clothes carefully and began to walk up and down the platform with quick, nervous steps. He went into the next train that came.

The train passed several stations before Bauer realized it was going downtown instead of uptown. His father was downtown. His home was uptown. It was no accident that Bauer, fighting fear with one part of him and seeking it with another, was on his way to his father. It was a simple, natural thing to do, but the evil will in him battled that, too, as it battled every inch of every way he took.

"I've gone so far to the old man," Bauer told himself, "I might as well go all the way. I haven't seen him or heard from him in so long." But, he thought, Catherine would be worried. He had not told her what was delaying him. How could he tell her? There was no telephone. Besides, what could he say to her. Go into a long, long story that he was arrested, why he was arrested, how he was arrested? What was the use?

Anyway, he shrugged, let her worry a little longer. It wouldn't hurt her to have to worry and go through a hundredth, a millionth of what he was going through for her. He thought of her putting her head into the dumbwaiter shaft and suddenly he could hear clearly in his head the wail of her cry for her upstairs friend: "Mrs. Allan, Mrs. Allan!" When she wailed like that, her plump face shuddered and folded around the wiry wail. He could see that happen now. He made himself see it.

"My husband didn't come home yet, I don't know what to think, he's never like this before. . . ." All this up the dumbwaiter shaft for the whole house to hear as the neighbors sat in their kitchens.

"And me not able to go out and see what's happened because who do I have to stay with the children?"

Love had brought Catherine into his mind, but the will to die had made her act in his mind as she was acting. Bauer, like all insecure people, was shy. To have his private life draped up and down and along a dumbwaiter shaft and hung from the ears of a whole tenement house was hideous to him. He must hate it. And, from this hate, he could draw fear because it is frightening to have to hate what one loves.

Mrs. Allan would come to help and Mrs. Bauer would go downstairs to the candy store and telephone the bank and there would be no answer and she would stand in the candy store, worried, and tell the candy store man she was so worried she didn't know what to do and he would say, go to Boyle's and if he's not there go to the police station and the police station would say, what's his description, and then his private life would be draped across the whole city.

"The hell with her!" he said to himself. His mind rebounded from the words, and then was forced back to more hate. "The women enjoy that kind of thing, anyway," he thought. "It makes them feel important. That's where they shine, with their 'come to me' and 'mama will kiss and make it better.'" And then he was forced to more and more hate, to a paroxysm of hate. "Yaaaah," he cried within himself, "who wants a kiss off that big, wet, smelly sink of a mouth of yours."

He squirmed. He felt the train rush along with him. The thought of death was closer to his conscious mind now. He buried his face deeper into his collar and the thought sank, shuddering, back into place. Still the train rushed along with him.

Bauer needed only a little help to remain alive. His central fear had become the insecurity attached to working in the bank. He needed only someone or something to take him out of that fear, either by helping him argue himself out of it, shaming him, coaxing him or loving him out of it, or, physically, by showing him how to go away from the bank. If he could find that, the crisis would pass. It would not be a cure. There might be another crisis at another time when something else happened to break his control over his insecurity. But, for the present the crisis would pass, his mind would return to its previous order, and the will to self-destruction would lose.

But who or what could do the friendly deed? Who, in Bauer's life, had the knowledge to tell him that, if he hid himself for a few days and moved his family to a new neighborhood, he would not ever have to work in a policy bank again? Who had the money to give him to hide? If he hid from Joe, his fear of Joe would become real. Who had enough control of Bauer and would stay with him in hiding and help conquer this fear?

Was there no one? Was there nothing in his life to shame or coax him from the fear enthralling him? A feeling of loneliness plucked at the flesh of his brain, as if with lips. His grave opened its mouth and breathed on him. His eyes went wide and he stared horrified into the darkness of his coat collar.

Slowly, tormentedly, he reached for a thought of Catherine. She came into his mind. His natural self had brought her. His perverted self wrenched at his thought of her. He thought again, almost tenderly, how worried she must be. Then he thought of how she would feel if he were dead. Tenderness struggled to cling to Bauer's mind. It struggled without strength against the gunning of the thought of death.

"Let her worry a while and think I'm dead," Bauer told himself and hung balanced for an infinitesimal moment on the edge of the phrase before tenderness vanished altogether and he could add, "and be disappointed when I come home."

He grinned suddenly and ferociously into the darkness of his coat collar. The grin did not seem to belong to his face. His face seemed to have split along a seam, and his teeth stuck through like split-off bones. He took the breath of his grave into his mouth, making it, for a moment, his own, and breathed it back into the train until the round-ceilinged, coffin-shaped, gloomy train seemed to him filled with it and seemed to him like a coffin in which he lay alive.

XVIII

BAUER GOT off the subway train at Grand Central station. He could see Broadway from there, or at least the reflection of it, red and crackling and leaping into the air like a bonfire. When he got to Broadway and looked uptown, he could see his father.

Even at a distance, Bauer's father looked tattered and old. The man had been a trolley car conductor for forty-two years and now, as a result of a "good" act by a benevolent company, he was a switchman. The switch he threw by hand could be thrown electrically by the motorman from the control boxes on the trolleys, but the company had made a job out of it for him because his pension of $7 a month had not been enough to live on.

It seemed a civilized thing to do. However, during the late afternoon and, when the theaters were emptying and filling at night, a Broadway motorman had plenty to think about besides throwing a switch. In fact, accidents had happened in the past to motormen too preoccupied to remember the switch. So the old man's job was not entirely a "good" act by a benevolent company, nor was it even so nearly good as it must seem at this point.

The elder Bauer had been one of the four men who had not gone out during the big railroad strike in New York. While he was scabbing, the company had used his life story in an advertisement to show how square it was with its employees and what lies the brotherhood, as the union was called, was telling.

The advertisement described how Bauer had come to the company as a young man and how he had married on money earned from the company and was sending his boy through high school on money he earned from the company and had had a good life as a railroad man serving the public and how, although his job was small, just a cog in a single one of 488,016 wheels, the company had given him a share of whatever wealth it had earned. He had kept the same job all his life, the advertisement had pointed out, but the company had kept step, not merely with the rising cost of living, but with their cog's rising expenses as a family man.

When the time came to give the old man the $7 pension he had earned in his loyal lifetime, it occurred to someone in the company —someone moved by the plight of the company's subordinate pensioners—that a reprint of the advertisement, perhaps by some company-baiting publication, would not read well.

So the job had been thought up and those who knew nothing about it believed it was a "good" act and those who knew something about it believed it was a "nearly good" act and those who knew something more about it believed it was an act that was only "a little bit good" and those who knew all about it believed the act wasn't good at all, but was, in fact, evil.

For, the elder Bauer was crippled with rheumatism after forty-two years on trolleys. He could not live long at a job that kept him outdoors at night. His salary for the job was paid out of his pension fund. Giving him the job was only giving him his pension fund in lumps instead of dribbling it over his normal life expectancy.

This was not premeditated murder. Businessmen do not premeditate murder, except under great stress. In normal circumstances, they merely protect their property. This act was merely a variant of a traditional benevolence in business: "Let's give the old man a break; he doesn't have long to live anyway." The fact that the idea of giving him a "break" might have been rejected if the "break" would prolong his life—what has that to do with murder?

Bauer went towards his father shyly. He had not seen the old man in several months and they had never been very close. The elder Bauer had spent his life with the railroad. He left the house long before six every morning, before his son woke up, and did not get home for supper until after seven, when his son was doing his home work for school.

The old man's job, at its best, after the brotherhood had won the strike despite him, had been from six in the morning until six at night, with two hours' swing in the afternoon for lunch. He lived too far from the car barns to get home during his swing. He hardly ever took a day off because the company did not like to put in-

experienced relief men on a run. An inexperienced relief man accumulated headways, which made the company lose fares to the
subway. When a regular man insisted on taking a day off every
week (at his own expense, of course, since all were paid by the
hour), he was given poorer and poorer runs and might end up
getting no run at all and having to take his chances on working
as a relief man.

It was nearly eleven o'clock now, but the theaters hadn't emptied
yet and people and automobiles were scattered sights on Broadway.
It was so quiet the lights could be heard clicking on and off and rat-
tling in the signs.

The old man was wearing thick rubbers against the cold and had
tied burlap bags around his thin legs over his trousers. He wore a
gray shawl under his hat. It came down over his ears and was
knotted below his chin. His old uniform coat, held together with
safety pins because the company had taken back his buttons with
his badge, was lumped over other shawls and sweaters.

He was a small, slouched man with a shaggy face. There were
tufts of hair on his short, wrinkled neck and in his ears, and his eyebrows hung over his eyes like old, frayed rags and he wore a big,
ragged moustache. He couldn't stand on his rheumatic feet long so
he brought a heavy wooden beer case to work with him and set it
down alongside the tracks and sat on it between trolleys. For safe-
keeping, he took it with him every night to the 30-cent room in
which he lived. It was the last piece of furniture he owned.

One end of the box was upholstered with rags. Black oilcloth had
been tacked over the rags. When he sat straight, his feet could rest
on the street. But it usually was painful for him to sit straight or walk
straight and he walked hunched over and sat with his legs drawn
up slightly. That was the way he was sitting now, his legs drawn
up and his body slouched. He was mumbling to himself and stirring
like an old bird.

When his son greeted him, the old man lifted his head suspiciously. "Well," he said, "there's Freddie."

He stretched out his hand and Bauer shook it. The hand was
covered with a heavy, leather mitten and, under the mitten, were

two pairs of woolen gloves. Bauer could feel the frail hand through all the gloves. It lay inside the wrappings like a dried bone. "What's he going to do when it gets really cold?" thought Bauer. He felt suddenly that the old man would not last out the winter. More loneliness came into his mind and more fear of loneliness.

"You're not putting on any weight," said the old man.

"What's there to get fat on in these hard times?"

The old man had heard of the depression, but he could not keep the thought of it in his mind. He had had hard times all his life and prosperity meant to him simply that times were no longer too hard for a man to accustom himself to them. Now he did not keep up with the newspapers and had no friends left alive to keep reminding him of the difficulties of the world. "That's right," he said. "There's no meat to the men nowadays. The big men are all gone."

The old man turned and looked up the tracks to see if a trolley were coming and, when he turned around again, he did not look at his son. He was thinking of a motorman named Edge who had brought four pig's knuckles and a loaf of bread in his lunch box every day for his swing. Edge was the greatest eating man of his day. "Why," he said aloud to his son, "the bones would make a pile you could hardly get a newspaper around, a real newspaper, not these writing paper newspapers they make nowadays."

Bauer was used to these sudden, inexplicable blurts from his father. He stood looking down at the old man. He towered above the hunched-over body. He wanted suddenly to touch his father, but he was afraid. His father looked so frail as he sat huddled inside his blue, thin skin. Bauer hardly heard what his father had said, but he thought suddenly the old man looked like a paper bag of bones and he felt that, if he were to touch him, the old skin would break and the bones would spill out.

This was loneliness indeed. His father was dying. He was losing the last connection that remained with his youth. And in the loneliness lay insecurity and in the insecurity lay fear.

"Father," said Bauer, "I've got something I'd like to tell you."

A trolley was coming and the old man darted a few paces up the track and threw the switch with a long iron bar. He waited until it passed so that he could set the switch back for the next car. The trolley banged by busily. From down on the street, close to it, it looked as big as the company itself and bright and teeming with noise, like the company, and, when it passed, it left behind air that felt smashed and smelled metallic.

When the old man returned to the box, his face was empty. It had no questioning look in it. He had forgotten what his son had said.

"Father," said Bauer, "I'd like to tell you, if you'd listen a minute, please."

"Yes, son? What is it now?"

Bauer stood thinking. How could he begin? Where? He couldn't pick words out of the emotion that blew up in him every time he thought of himself.

The two looked into each other's eyes for a moment. Bauer did not look at his father's eyes often. Ordinarily, only streaks of the old man's eyes could be seen through the fringes of his brows. But now the old man's eyes had widened with questioning. The fringe over them seemed to have parted, as if in wind. Bauer could see the mild, interested look swimming in his father's watery eyes and he leaned forward. His own eyes filled with tears. He looked away and blinked them dry and, when he turned back, the questioning look had vanished from his father's eyes. The old man was sitting hunched up in himself.

"I don't see or hear from you never," said Bauer. "You act like you don't know you have a son."

The old man looked up with fear. He sat looking up silently and fearfully. "I'm a very busy man," he said at last.

"You have your day off."

"No more. I give it up. Can't afford it."

"Why not? You used to take a day off once in a while after you became switchman. What's different now?"

"Can't afford it. They don't like it anyway when they have to put on a green relief man."

The old man felt suddenly his son knew his job was a charity job, thought up by the company to help him out and no substitute was used when he was absent. That was one of the reasons he didn't take a day off. He was afraid to remind the company by his absence that it could get along without a switchman. He thought of telling his son that and of telling him the rest of the truth, that, if his son were an old railroad man, he would be glad to visit him. But, as it was, there was nothing they could talk about. The old man had railroaded almost all the waking hours of his adult life. The company had shut him out from everything else in the world, even his family. Now that he had time for his family and the world, he was too gone in age to rouse himself to absorb anything new.

"I don't live any further away from you than you do from me," he said.

"Yes," his son cried, "but how can I bring the three children down all that way? Your room is too small for them all anyway."

The old man was silent. Bauer watched him and wondered what he was thinking about and then turned and looked at the sidewalk and the automobiles going by and the buildings with big, brightly lighted signs that made their walls glare like furnace walls.

"What's the use of this?" he asked himself, but he knew the use and he couldn't leave. He put his hands into his pockets and shuffled his feet slowly against the cold pavement.

Another trolley came and, as the old man hurried to the switchbox, the motorman shouted, "How much headway I got?"

"I don't know," said the old man. "I'm not supposed to know." He turned and looked petulantly at his son. "A railroad man can't pay attention to his job," he thought, "with people pestering him all the time."

His anger was a weak thing and did not last long. By the time he got back to his box, he was deep in thought of what he used to do with a headway and how sometimes he and his motorman would accumulate a headway on purpose. This was called "dragging the road." The more passengers on a car, the easier for a conductor to steal fares; the more behind schedule the car fell, the greater the number of passengers.

The old man saw his car bulging out the sides with passengers, people standing all over themselves, and himself at the back end, forgetting to register "the odd nickel" for the company and Woody, the motorman, at the front end, sweating like a bull to make up the headway he had deliberately created. Only no matter how Woody sweated, he never neglected to take time off for his entertainment, which was to let the air brake go sharp and sudden when a girl was passing so she would jump with fright and show her legs.

The old man cackled and looked gleefully into his son's face. "That was the man for the female leg," he said. Then he saw that he was looking into the face of his son and his laugh died and he glanced up the tracks.

Bauer was alarmed. It was as if a curtain had lifted and he could look into his father and see only darkness. "You ought to come up and see Maria once in a while anyway," he said. "She misses your moustache." Maria was his older daughter.

"My moustache?" The old man pulled carefully, first at one end and then at the other of the yellow-gray brush of hair. "Kids like it," he said. "When my boy was young, he did, too."

"Did I?" Bauer stepped forward eagerly. "When I was a little one?"

"Yepper. Watched me trim it every night of your life. You ought to remember that, you watched it enough."

"Was that the way I was? I can't remember a thing." Bauer laughed. His face seemed to shine. He remained bent greedily towards his father, his face turned so that his undamaged ear was nearest the old man's tottering voice.

"Stood in the toilet where the mirror was and watched. Reached to my knee then. That was, let me see, was 'long about, let me see . . ." His voice faded.

Bauer was afraid his father would lose the thread of what he was talking about and start on something else. "I was three," he said.

"No, guess not, guess along about six or seven, I guess."

Another car came and Bauer cursed at it a moment. The old man stood waiting patiently for the car to pass so that he could reset the switch. The car was held on the switch by a traffic light. Bauer's mind hung thwarted a moment and then it returned to a note it had sounded before. Bauer looked at his father and saw the shawls and sweater and padding on him and thought, "Winter is two, three

weeks off," and thought, "It's coming," and the feel of winter
passed through him, still and deathlike. "It's going to kill him," he
said to himself, "this winter sure." He felt lonely, and a part of him
fought the loneliness and made him think, "He'll be better off
dead." He thought of how empty the old man's life was, but didn't
wonder what had emptied it. Instead he thought how empty his
own life was and thought suddenly, "I wish I was dead; I'd be
better off, too," and felt an uproar of hate and pity and loneliness
and fear shake him and burst in him and run over him. He had
to fight to hold himself still.

"Father," he cried.

The car had passed and the old man had returned to his box.

"Yes, son? What is it now, son?" The old man's voice was patient. He had heard his son's words, but the wildness of the cry had
been muffled in the fog in his head. Nothing can be to an old man
except as he thinks it is.

What is the use! thought Bauer. He was about to turn and run
off when he suddenly remembered what his father had been saying.
"You were telling me, father," he said, "I was six or seven."

"When?"

"Just now." Bauer knew that, while his father could not concentrate, his memory was sound. "You remember," he said, "when I
was six or seven, you said, about trimming your moustache, how I
watched all the time."

"Oh that. I told you just now." The old man had thought out the
whole story while waiting to throw the switch and he believed he
had recited it.

"No, you didn't, father. Not now. No, you didn't. What was it?
Well, tell it over again, will you?"

"I told you. You wanted to trim your moustache and I gave you
the scissors. You didn't have a moustache to trim, but that's what
you wanted and you trimmed away and then you stuck your nose. A
drop of blood came out no bigger than the head of a pin."

"Would you believe it? I don't remember a single thing. Cried
like hell, I suppose."

"Let out a scream fit to split, threw the scissors on the floor and ran away."

"To mother? Was she in the house?"

"Under the bed. That's where you run all the time. Under the bed. Under the blankets. Behind the clothes in the closet. Behind the sofa. Every time, like clockwork. Under the stove, when we moved where the gas stove was."

Bauer straightened up. He looked disappointed. "Kids are like that," he said. "My kids, too." He began to think about himself again. He halted himself abruptly. A single thought about himself was like a match dropped on gasoline. There was a flare-up and a sense, inside him, of exploding. He looked at his father and saw the old man's face had gone dreamy again and that his mind had swung away to somewhere far. "That's a habit you should have broken me of," he told the old man harshly.

"What's that?" The old man looked at his son and, for a moment, hated him for having disturbed him.

"I say you should have broken me of the habit of running away and hiding. That's what I say."

"Well, what do you think? What do you think I did?" The hate went out of the old man's face and he looked proud. "Why do you suppose you're a big man now, high school graduate, holding down a big job in a big office? I helped. Made you over with my two hands. Walloped you into the shape of a man."

"You seem to think that was nice, don't you? Very nice. Damn nice to beat up a little kid like that."

"Well, I had to do like a father should. What else was there to do, boy? You ought to know that now. There was sissy in you and I had to wallop it out or you'd be ruined. That's what I told your mother, that you'd be ruined."

"Maybe that's what I am."

"No sir, I did the right thing. Every time you went under the bed I drug you out and walloped you. Every time you hid in the closet, I locked the door until you hollered to get out. Then I walloped you for hiding."

"You could of saved your muscle. You can't change what's a kid's nature. I see it in my own kids."

"Oh no, now don't say that. Let me tell you, you wouldn't be where you are today, with a job in an office, if I hadn't walloped you until, by God, there wasn't a thing anywhere, with hair or without, that you wouldn't stand up to, except maybe another walloping."

Bauer saw the facade of excitement and pride erected on the old man's face as a defense against the wrong he had committed. He didn't let himself see behind the facade to where the old man knew that what he had done was wrong.

"I don't understand how you live," cried Bauer.

"What's that?"

"I said," Bauer told him in a suddenly loud voice, "I don't understand how you live. You got a son and three grandchildren and a daughter-in-law in the world and you don't show that you know they're alive. Not the slightest interest."

The old man looked away. "I'm a very busy man," he said.

"Yes? Yes? Is that what you are?" He's a mummy, thought Bauer. He sits here all wrapped up in himself like he was bandages and anything can happen to his son or grandchildren and he don't care.

"The cars will stay on the tracks without you," he shouted out of his loneliness and hatred of loneliness and fear of loneliness and fear of hatred.

The old man hung his head sullenly. A car was coming a long way off and, although there was plenty of time, he went at once to the switch box. When he came back, he did not notice that his son had gone away and had disappeared among the crowds now coming out of the theaters. The old man's rheumatism had begun to pain him and he forgot that his son had been there and sat thinking about his rheumatism and wishing it was midnight when he could go to his room and lie in a warm bed.

❧

It was a few minutes before midnight when Bauer reached the street on which he lived. There was a drug store on the corner and Bauer stood before the avenue entrance and looked inside and saw a rosy, chubby, young pharmacy student mopping the floor.

Bauer couldn't bring himself to turn the corner into the street. He wanted to believe that Joe, or somebody from Joe, was waiting for him near his doorway. He could almost believe it now. His experience with his father, the feeling of death that came out of the old man, had set Bauer to working over his fear of Joe all the way uptown. He had even thought of making his way home over the rooftops and down a skylight, but he couldn't go that far, not yet. Instead he found it difficult to round the corner to his home and stood still, his face sunk into his collar, his gaze fastened on the young man working behind the door.

The pharmacy student had dark, blond, curly hair and wore it parted in the middle. The light seemed to spark against its wavy edges. His trouser legs were rolled up to his knees and the white flesh of his round, hairy legs glinted. To clear the floor for mopping, he had piled the short-backed, long-legged, imitation wood, soda-fountain stools on the imitation marble counter. He swung the mop huskily and cheerfully, with spacious, smooth strokes. To him this was the best part of a long day that began with school in the morning. His leg muscles bulged in rhythm. His body swayed in rhythm and his face hung down and his young, plump cheeks bellied and swung back and forth in rhythm with the mop. For a moment he looked like the whole race of man living in a cheerful rhythm of work. He was experiencing, briefly, the joy of a man doing work from which the mind could be shut out and, with the mind, the whole structure of business.

Bauer's head began to sway from side to side, too, in time with the mop. It was a hammocky rhythm that the two kept on either side of the door, the natural, unspoiled rhythm of work and life, and it brought both of them a hammocky comfort. Then suddenly Bauer stopped his swaying. The mop kept swishing, but Bauer's head held still. He had noticed the young man's eyes were not following the mop. They were not rolling in rhythm with the face, but were clinging to Bauer with fear.

"He thinks maybe I'm a stickup," thought Bauer, "spying out the possibilities." He remembered the professional phrase for it—casing a job. He had heard it in Boyle's. A thrill went through him. His mind could take many things from it, disappointment that the rhythm had been broken, contempt for the man who was afraid of him, fear of what the man thought.

The young man was working away from the door, back into the store, and the mop swooped and twirled, long and free, from left to right and right to left. But Bauer noticed the edges and corners were being neglected. The hard places were being skimped. The young man was afraid to spend time on them. He wanted to get away from Bauer and get back behind the counter at the rear of the store.

Bauer forced his face into a grin of contempt. The young man was going to duck behind the counter and put his head in a shelf and close his eyes and shake. Bauer could see the store's telephone on a shelf behind the rear counter. The man might grab it and call the police. Bauer stirred. The police would come in radio cars. They would chase him and catch him and take him along for questioning.

Bauer found himself abruptly around the corner, hurrying down the street on which he lived. He did not think of Joe until it was too late to make himself afraid. He was almost at his doorstep. He could see the street was empty except for some young men he recognized standing in front of the candy store next to his house and reading the headlines off the news stand.

He knew that, if there were going to be a killing, there would have to be a car for the getaway. The two cars parked on the street were familiar to him. Yet he peered carefully into the doorway of his house. There was a small, silent, shadowed vestibule with a night bulb burning weakly in the ceiling. Behind it, a staircase rose gloomily into black air. He thought of the three flights to his apartment with a yellow night bulb at each landing, throwing a shadow of light, and dark doors and corners along each hall in which a man could hide.

He tried to make himself think of a man hiding and waiting for him. But he couldn't. He could think only of his wife waiting upstairs for him. He couldn't face her, not yet. He turned around and walked across the street, his mind licking catlike at the newest fear it had captured.

"That druggist," he thought, "he'll be sweating for a year, worrying did I decide yes or no on the stickup." He felt like laughing. The thought had stirred the fear to activity. He sought to laugh it down. He went around the far corner with the laugh just below his mouth and walked down the block a little bit and into Boyle's, where Wally had been waiting for him all evening.

As Bauer opened the door to the pool room, a familiar smell came out and, if he had wanted to, he could have closed his eyes and still see what was before him and, when he fastened the door, the world was shut out and he felt safe. "This is more home to me than home," he thought. The feeling of safety came over him like warmed clothes. He felt suddenly like shouting, "I am here."

The owner-manager, Palumbo, was in the inside room, where the tables were, and he didn't know who had come in. "Closing up," he called.

"Be a pal, Palumbo," cried Bauer over the partition.

Palumbo recognized Bauer's voice and did not reply.

The room on which the front door opened had only one bulb burning and was filled with frail light. This was where the showcase was with the cigars and cigarettes, and there were two slot machines opposite it and a pinball game and a telephone booth. Over the pinball game was a large sign, bright in the light from a street lamp:

"When BABY *does* NEED A PAIR OF SHOES—
Don't get Stuck—
Try your Luck—
at the DARLING BABY SHOPPE!"

There seemed to be even less light in the inner room. The overhead bulbs had been turned off and green-shaded lights were burning over only two tables. They made white cones, swarming with dust, and in the shadow, on the edge of one cone, stood Palumbo. He stood with his coat and derby hat on and held the ball rack in one hand and the keys to the place in the other. He was jingling the keys impatiently.

At one table, a game was going on between two men and four others were watching. Eleven dollars had been bet on the result and all were watching intently and in silence. As a concession to Palumbo's desire to get home, the spectators had put on their hats and coats.

At the other table, Wally played alone. He had been playing his right hand against his left hand for more than an hour.

"I need a beer," Bauer announced.

Some of the men looked up and nodded a greeting, but the majority did not take their eyes off the game. Wally stopped playing. He racked his cue, in obedience to the sign on the wall, and walked towards Bauer with a smile on his face.

"It's all closed up," said Palumbo from the edge of darkness.

"I know where you can get one this hour," Wally said. "I need one myself."

Bauer remembered suddenly that the last time he had seen the boy was outside magistrate's court. He became embarrassed.

"I'll drive you there in my new roadster," said Wally.

"Well, thanks. I guess not."

Bauer didn't really want a beer. He wanted only to stay in Boyle's. He went around the table and stood alongside Palumbo and watched the game. Palumbo told him who had bet what and the score and, while he was talking, he noticed the blood in Bauer's ear and how the man's face looked so tired—it seemed to sink down into the air from his neck. Palumbo struggled with himself for a moment. His lips moved as if they were muttering and his shoulders began to shrug and stopped and began another shrug and stopped again.

"You can have some of that flat ale out of the keg," he said at last. He didn't wait for an answer. He put the ball rack on the table behind him and the keys in his pocket and went to the back of the room.

When Palumbo saw that Wally, too, had followed him, he said, "What do you want?"

"If you can spare it, the same pig sweat as for him." Wally pointed to Bauer.

"The place is closed up. You guys act like you got no home." Palumbo filled two glasses with ale and pocketed a dime from each and stood watching Bauer drink. "It don't look inflamed," he said, "but you better put some peroxide in there."

"Where?" asked Bauer.

"In the ear. What did you do, run into something? Here." He turned on a light overhead. "Give me a look at that." He took Bauer's face in two hands and twisted it sideways to the light. He felt the man's face go hot in his hands. "There's no sore there or nothing," he said. "It must be under the blood." He let go of Bauer's head and Bauer straightened up slowly.

"What does it look like?" Bauer asked. "I haven't had a chance yet to see it myself."

His voice began to tremble and he pressed his fingers to his lower lip to hold it steady. It was no good. His eyes became wet and he looked away and looked into Wally's face. Wally was watching him thoughtfully. There was a sympathetic look on the boy's face, but his eyes were thoughtful.

"It don't look bad," said Palumbo. "How the hell did you ever get one in there?"

"That boss of mine," said Bauer and stopped. The whole story came to his lips. He wanted to tell it to Palumbo. No, he thought, what's the use! "I want to quit to take up something else I got in prospect," he began again, "and my boss don't like it."

"Some boss." Palumbo reached up and turned off the light. He was tired and he wanted to go home. "Everybody gets so excited nowadays," he said. "There's no self-control around anywhere."

"You know him yourself," said Bauer. "He used to come in here. You remember, Leo Minch."

"Is he any relation to Guinea Joe Minch?" asked Wally.

Wally's question was ignored.

"Oh yes," said Palumbo, "some time ago. What happened he don't come here no more?"

"How should I know?" cried Bauer. "As far as I'm concerned I'm glad he don't."

"If he's any relation to Guinea Joe Minch," said Wally, "I'm glad, too." He looked anxiously at Bauer.

"I get along without him all right, you understand," said Palumbo. "But just the same I'd like to find out. Maybe he's sore about something or something like that. Do you think you can ask him?"

"No."

Palumbo stood thinking for a moment and then he said, "Well, okay, I'll tell you what you do. You put some hot water in there first and let it cook in there. Hold your head to one side and let the hot water cook a while until it's softened up the cake in there and then put in the peroxide." He turned to Wally. "You get back and finish your game and let me go home, will you," he said.

"I'm finished. I was just waiting for Freddy here anyway."

"For me?" Bauer's voice rose with surprise.

"Well, yes. I thought maybe you'd be along and I got an idea that might help you, if we can go somewhere where we can talk."

"You can talk your heads off until they finish the game and then I'm locking up," said Palumbo. He walked back to the table where the game was being played and asked in a loud voice, "What's the score now?" He could see the score on the markers overhead, but he wanted to hurry the men up.

"Help me what?" asked Bauer.

"Help you out. You want to spend a minute talking to me somewhere, in my new roadster?" Wally's face was eager. It had a small, pleading smile on it and it seemed sick with eagerness. He looked like a salesman talking to an important customer, or a Nazi proselytizing an Aryan. "Come on," he said. He put down his glass and started to walk away. Bauer didn't follow. He stared after the boy suspiciously. Wally turned. "Come on," he said, "this is a break for you."

"No. I'm going to finish my ale and then I'm going to go home." He had nothing to do with this loafer, he thought. How could this loafer help him?

Wally returned slowly. "If you'd only listen for a moment," he said in a low tone. "This is a situation that I know just the people who can take care of it for you."

"What situation? What are you talking about?"

Bauer finished the ale and put the glass on the counter and walked over to Palumbo. The position of Wally's mouth did not change as he watched Bauer go. It held the same small, smiling curl, but the eagerness had left his face and he looked as if he were thinking curses.

The game was nearing its climax. Bauer stood alongside Palumbo. He felt suddenly that he liked to be near the man and he liked the quiet of the room and the way the players walked into position for a shot, intently and softly, the boards of the floor rubbing together with a soft sound under the pressure of their feet. He liked the silence that came out of the spectators and the dark, warm feeling that filled the room and the hushed sounds of breathing and of the keys jingling in Palumbo's hand and the balls rubbing dimly and clicking and the murmur as a shot was made or a ball rolled into a difficult position. He stood among the silent sounds and, for a moment, lost himself in the game. Then he noticed that Wally had come out of the darkness in back and was standing beside him. The sight of the boy stirred him out of his quiet and he shifted restlessly.

"Goodnight, gentlemen," said Bauer. They all looked up, even the players. His voice had sounded so unexpected. "I wish you all the same luck."

A murmur of goodnight followed him as he walked out and also footsteps. When he opened the front door, he saw Wally was behind him.

"I'll walk your way a minute," the boy said.

Bauer held the door for him. Then he said, "What are you following me for? I'm going home."

"You certainly are a hard man to help," said Wally. "Is this Leo Minch you work for any relation to the Guinea?"

"Who's the Guinea?"

"Guinea Joe Minch."

"What do you want to know for?"

"I'm trying to help. What's the matter with you? I never seen a guy so hard to help before."

"I think you're trying to butt in," said Bauer, "and if I were you, I wouldn't. You got your little business, whatever you do, bookmaker or whatever it is, and if I were you I'd stick to it. That's my advice to you, if I were you."

"I like that, and me trying to help."

Bauer walked off and Wally stood a moment, undecided, and then went after him. The boy walked like a dancer. He made a cheerful appearance. He held his small, tight body stiff and walked from the knees down. His high-heeled, patent leather shoes caught the light and flashed through the air. But his face wasn't cheerful. It was slack with thought. His eyes floated in thought.

When Bauer turned the corner, he saw Wally at his elbow. "I thought I told you," Bauer said.

"Now don't be foolish."

"Don't tell me what to be. I'm telling you."

"I'm saying not to be foolish. I got the right people to talk to your boss and he won't give you no more trouble. He'll do what you say."

"What I say? Christ Almighty!"

"Don't get so excited. Don't talk so loud." Wally looked nervously over his shoulder.

"Who do you think you're talking to?" cried Bauer.

"He'll do whatever you say, whatever you want. I'm guaranteeing you."

"Why can't you let me alone!" Bauer stooped low and thrust his face towards Wally's face. "All of you," he cried, "hounding and pounding, hounding and pounding every minute. Let me alone, do you hear? Go to hell, all of you!"

Bauer saw Wally step back a little and shape his mouth into a frightened circle and then suddenly Wally blurred and Bauer realized tears had come into his eyes again. He ran across the street, his head down. He went at a half run all the way to his house and, as he turned in at the doorstep, he saw Wally at his elbow. He hadn't heard him. The boy had come like shadow.

"When you're up against a situation like this," said Wally, "you shouldn't act so foolish."

"It's my business. Who asked you?"

"What can you do by yourself? I know people and they'll be glad to put in a word for you."

"Yes, just like that."

"I don't get you. You talk as if we're up to something that's not for your good."

"No," said Bauer, "you're my friends. I don't know you except to see you now and then the last few months and these people of yours—who are they? I don't even know who they are, but they're all my friends all of a sudden, out to help me."

"Well, of course, it's only natural we got something in mind for ourselves, too."

"Yes, sure, it's natural for all of you. You all got something in your dirty mind."

"What do you expect? This isn't college boy stuff. I'll tell you what it is we got in mind, if you'd listen a minute. It's no secret, if you'd stop hollering at the top of your voice so everybody will wake up. There's people sleeping around here, for Christ sakes."

Bauer looked at him a moment and then started for the vestibule of his house.

"Wait a minute," said Wally. "We got a proposition for your boss and he don't want to even talk to us. He's like you. Now, wait a moment, will you please! That's all we want, for you to tell us a nice quiet place where he is so we can talk to him and put the proposition up to him. You do that for us and we'll put in a word for you and I guarantee he'll do what you say, whatever you want, quit or whatever it is."

Bauer held still, thinking. He had one foot in the vestibule and he stood looking at Wally and thinking of nothing, lost in blankness, struggling and slowly drowning in the overwhelming sea of blankness. Then he made a gesture of helplessness and walked into the vestibule.

Wally came after him. "What do you say?" he asked. "Is it a deal?"

"Where do you think you're going?" cried Bauer. "Get out of here!"

"Well, I want to know."

"This is my house and you get out. Get out, I'm telling you!"

"All you have to do is tell us somewhere where he'll be."

Bauer lifted up his hands pleadingly. His face looked broken. "I wish there was one place in the world," he said, "where I could go for one minute and there wouldn't be nobody there hounding and pounding me."

"That's what I say. I'll help you. My people will fix it for you so you can go anywhere you want. You'll be free and you can do what you like."

"No," said Bauer. "I won't do that. Never. You'll never get me to do that. Never. Never until I'm dead."

"Do what? What do you think you have to do?"

Bauer turned and walked into the house. He wanted to run from this new fear. It was the ultimate, unknowable fear the will in him had hunted and now, having found it, his first instinct was to run. He held himself back. He forced himself to take the steps up one at a time.

❧

Bauer's home was breathing with sleep when he came in. The entrance was through the kitchen and he stood in the full, quiet darkness, among the odors of food, and realized suddenly he was hungry. He hadn't eaten since lunch, before the raid, Monday, and it was Tuesday now, deep in the black morning of the second day of the second week of December, 1934.

He turned on the light and went to the window and took a bottle of milk off the fire escape and got some cake out of the breadbox. He drank from the bottle and finished all the milk and almost all the cake. His throat made loud sounds in the quiet as he gulped down the milk. He wiped his mouth with his sleeve. There were cake crumbs on his hand and he went to the sink to wash them off. He turned the hot water faucet and waited patiently for the water to become warm and, while he waited, he stared into the sink. Fear was alive in his brain. It was abroad there, roaming and roving, throwing off hate as a beast throws a smell. There were shreds of vegetables and orange pulp clinging to the drain. The orange pulp must have been there since the previous morning when the children had their orange juice.

"Look at that," he told himself. Then he said aloud, "Sloppy damn slut." He turned his head angrily in the direction of the bedroom and saw his wife sitting in a chair near the door.

She didn't say anything. She just looked at him.

He took a dish cloth from the corner of the sink in which it had been thrown, crumpled, and wiped the crumbs from the top of the washtub where he had been eating. There had been shreds clinging to the cloth and he washed them off angrily. Hate accumulated in him. Finally the hate was big enough to spill over through his mouth. "You want to know where I've been?" he said.

"I'm glad you're all right anyway."

"I been laying with other women rather than to come back to this dirty slop of a house." He pointed at the sink. "Look at this! You've been too lazy to lift a God damn finger to clean it since we moved here."

"I'm glad to know you had a good time while I was sitting here waiting."

Catherine got up and went into the bathroom in the corner of the kitchen. She was dressed for bed, with a nightgown under her cotton kimono.

Bauer rinsed out the milk bottle and put it under the sink. When Catherine came out of the bathroom, she passed him without a word. Her slippers slapped against the floor. As she reached the door to the children's room, she reminded him to turn out the lights and then walked on.

There was an early edition of the morning newspaper on the table. So, he thought, he had been right. She had gone downstairs looking for him. She had called in Mrs. Allan and had draped his private life all over all the ears in the whole house and the police would come around in a few days and tell her it was all right, her husband hadn't been killed or run away, he had just been arrested. And she would know. She would know he had been arrested once and once before that, too.

He hadn't told her of either raid. Let her know, he thought. Let her see what I have to go through to earn a living for her.

He wasn't going to tell her his business, but he didn't care if she found out. It was her fault, anyway. Would he have taken such a criminal's job in the first place if it hadn't been for her? She had hounded him into it, maybe not with words, but she was with the others all right, she and the children, hounding and pounding with the rest of them, and never giving him a minute's peace.

The thoughts lunged through Bauer's mind. Fear prowled and thrashed among the plants of love in Bauer like an animal fleeing through jungle. Just as the animal claws at the plants that hamper its flight and hates them and draws further fear from them and from its hate of them, so with the fear abroad in Bauer's brain.

He was trying to read the newspaper, but he couldn't take in the words or the pictures. His mind was too full of the struggle inside itself. Finally, he folded the newspaper and put it away out of the children's reach so he would have it in the morning and began to undress. He made his toilet in the kitchen and went naked through the children's room, carrying his shoes in one hand and his neatly folded clothes over his arm.

The three children were lying tumbled across their bed. He did not notice them. Maria, the eldest, was awake. She was lying big-eyed in the darkness. She had been awakened before by the noise over her father's absence and had cried and been comforted and gone back to sleep. She had been awakened again by his home-coming and had closed her eyes and had opened them again to see a white, naked figure edge slowly past her bed. She slept on the outside to keep the two younger ones from falling. She gulped with fear now and her hands pressed against her chest. She watched her father go and she turned over on her side and felt she was going to cry. She was afraid to cry. She put her thumb into her mouth and closed her eyes tightly and made small, wet sounds as she sucked.

When Bauer got into his room, he put away his clothes carefully. He was skillful with tools and he had built a tie rack and a shoe stand and had constructed a special kind of trouser press that he had thought occasionally of patenting. After he had stuffed trees into his shoes and got everything in its proper place, he stood a moment holding his pajamas, reluctant to get into his pajamas.

It occurred to him it was pleasant to be naked now. He didn't think so much when he was naked. He decided nakedness felt pleasant because his body must be feverish and the cold must feel good against it. He touched his side. The flesh was colder than the air. He put on his pajamas and shivered as the pajama coat came down his thin, bony chest and the feeling of pleasure went out of him and the feeling of thought stormed back in his head.

"I'm getting sick," he told himself.

He didn't care. He suddenly felt listless. His body drooped down tiredly from his neck and above it was his head, empty of thought, drowning in a swollen and teeming blankness. He stood that way a moment, looking at Catherine.

She was lying on her side facing him. He would have to climb over her to get into bed. The outer side had been hers since their first child had been born when she had wanted to get up to feed it without waking him. Even now, when he always went to bed later than she, the habit did not change.

It occurred to him suddenly that it might not be habit. It might be she did not want to sleep on the part of the bed where he had lain so long. He had never thought about it before. "She must hate me the way I hate her," he said to himself.

The idea did not rouse him from his listlessness. It was a small thing and then nothing in the teeming fullness in his head. He stood looking at her steadily. Her eyes were closed and her breathing was deep, but he didn't believe she was asleep. He thought she was pretending so she wouldn't have to talk to him.

"Don't hate me, Catherine," he said to himself suddenly and was surprised. The words jolted the fear lunging in him. This was a cry of love. But fear was jolted only momentarily. Fear lunged on and pounced upon the words and mouthed them so that he added, almost without pause, almost as if the thought had been a single, connected thing, ". . . after what I've been through for you to keep our home together."

The noise of his first cry and the shock of it still clung to his head and fear fought to explain it. He must have been thinking, he told himself, how he hated her, the sight of her and sound of her and the feel of her and even the sight of her handiwork and even the fact that she was alive and how she must hate him the same way. She must hate the fact that he was alive, too!

An intense feeling of loneliness came into Bauer, the kind that ordinarily only the very old can know. He sat down on the floor and rested his head against the mattress near Catherine's head. His feet felt cold. He stretched them and looked at them. Her arm was in the way. It bulged before him. It was thick and white in the darkness and he could feel the warmth rising from it more softly than breathing. He closed his eyes and shifted his body on the cold floor so that a chilled part of him could reach a place he had warmed.

The warmth of her came into his face. The sound of her breathing came into his ears. This was love again, the noise and feel of it, fastening him to her side while fear clawed at the fastening. He could feel her breathing in the ear nearest her, but he couldn't hear it there. He remembered the ear was broken. He was half deaf. He would have to see a doctor. But what good was a doctor?

A punch like that! It must have split the ear drum. He was crippled forever.

Inside, he felt as if he were crying, but the tears did not come into his eyes. It just seemed as if something inside him were shaking and crying in a broken, violent way. He sat there with closed eyes, feeling it and feeling, at the outer edge of himself, like clothes, like something his skin touched but could not grasp, the warmth of his wife and the sound of her breathing. It was as if he himself were all skin and had no hands to take what he pressed against. The awful feeling of being all skin started his eyes open. He saw that Catherine had lifted her head and was looking at him.

"What's the matter with you?" she asked.

"I feel sick."

She sat up and put her hand out and touched his forehead. "You're hot," she said. "You shouldn't be sitting on the floor in a draft like that. I'll call the doctor."

"I'm not medicine sick." He pulled himself to his feet.

"You feel like you got a fever," she said.

"No. That's all you think about. Stick a thermometer in! Drink tea! Call the doctor! Get your mind away from those things a minute. People can be sick other ways, too, if you know."

"Sit down. Here." She made room for him on the edge of the bed. "Sit here and tell me what's the matter."

"What's the use? It's a long story. It's such a long story it will take all night and what can you do about it?"

He came towards her slowly and sat down. Her body was bent around his. She could see the side of his face. Then he turned and looked into her eyes and, for a moment, he felt as if her eyes were enfolding him. "It's about the business," he said. "He's driving me crazy so I don't know what I'm doing sometimes."

"Mr. Minch?"

"Sometimes I think if he don't let me alone, I'll kill him. Honest to God! That's the way I feel. What can I do?"

"Who? What? Mr. Minch? You mean Mr. Minch? When was this? Was this today?"

"Today, yesterday, Saturday, Wednesday, what's the difference when! It's been going on for a long time. You know yourself, Catherine, I'm not a trouble-maker. I never made trouble in my life. I don't want trouble from anybody and I don't want to make trouble. Why only just now, downstairs, when I came up here, there was a man. . . . I could have . . . I had a chance. . . . A terrible thing . . . to do. But I'm telling you. They hound and pound and they push a man so far, so far . . . so far, that . . . that he gets to the end of what he can stand."

He sprang to his feet. Then he thrust his face down at her. "The end!" he cried. "I'm warning you."

"Freddie, what is it?" Catherine scrambled out of bed. "Tell me. I don't know the first thing what you're talking about."

She went close to him and pressed against him urgently and looked into his face. "Come to me and tell me your trouble," she pleaded.

He backed away from her. "You'll kiss it and make it better?"

"You can tell me, can't you?"

"No. How can I? What can you do?"

"Freddie, please." She went to him again and pressed against him again. He felt her breasts lying on his arms. There was a roar in his head and, for a moment, the feel of her went through him and seemed to hold him tight, away from the roar.

"Please tell me, Fred," she whispered.

"All right." His voice was hoarse. "All right."

He made a step back. Words crowded into his brain. He couldn't choose among them. He thought there were a thousand things he wanted to say. His breathing was so heavy he seemed to be gasping. "I'll tell you," he said. "All right. You asked to know. All right. I've got to go away and where am I going to get the money to do it?"

"Where go away?"

"Like a bum, on a freight train, without a dime!"

"Are you out of your mind?"

"No." He looked down at the floor. "That's what it is."

"But the children! How are they going to eat if you go away from your job?"

"That's what I been thinking about."

"Here!" she cried. "Lift your head. Stop mumbling. Talk to me. What have you been thinking about?"

He raised his head slowly. "That's what I was thinking, that if I quit my job I could get a relief job on the relief and maybe from there I could get a job in some business where I wouldn't have to be worried every minute I'm going to get shot in the back."

"Who's this to shoot?"

"At least, on relief, I would have time to pick up my head and look around. But no, no, I'm not a human being. I'm just a stone in the street, step on, push here, do this, stay there, without my asking, knowing, telling me, nothing, just push around. It stands to reason a man can quit a job when he wants to, doesn't it? But no, not with them. They wouldn't let me and now I got to go away. I can't get on relief if I go away. That's what I been thinking and that I got to go away and that's all there is to it. That's my final decision."

"You're going to leave us?"

"Yes," he said, quietly and firmly.

"All right. Go ahead. Run out on us."

"Don't say that. You've got to help me." He began shifting close to her. "I never asked you for a thing since we're married. I've always tried the best I could for you. But now this is something you just got to do for me."

"You're asking *me* to help *you* starve the children to death?"

"No, Catherine. Don't talk like that." He reached one hand out to her. He did not touch her. He held his hand timidly above her shoulder. "I'm a sick man inside," he said. "I'm so sick I don't know where I'm standing half the time or sitting lately. What are the children going to live on if I'm dead?" He let his hand fall lightly to her shoulder.

"It isn't right that you should run away like this," cried Catherine. "That's what you're doing all the time. Whatever trouble comes along, the first thing you think of is to run away."

He took his hand from her shoulder and let it fall to his side. "Don't you believe me," he asked, "when I tell you that I got to go away or I'll be killed?"

"You're running away. That's what I believe. Because you got something in your mind, I don't know what."

"Catherine, I'll be killed!"

"Who's going to kill you, that little Mr. Minch who kept you working all these years when everybody was being laid off and gave you a raise just last week for Thanksgiving?"

"I hate that man. He hates me. When I'm in the same room with him, I'm not responsible."

"You hate him, he hates you! Go chalk it on the sidewalk like the kids. Hate him, hates you. Do you think you're pulling daisies with your own children's lives? I'm not talking about myself. I don't care what happens to me any more than you do."

"I see there's no use talking to you."

"No. I know what's in your mind, to run away, just like you've been all your life."

"Correct," he said harshly and walked out of the bedroom towards the living room.

Catherine stood a moment, looking after her husband and thinking. Then she got into bed. She lay still a little while and got up and put on her slippers and opened the door to the children's room. They seemed to be sleeping. Maria's thumb was in her mouth. Catherine pulled it out and the child opened her eyes and her face quavered. Then she frowned.

"Go to sleep, darling," whispered Catherine. She put her hand over Maria's eyes. When she took her hand away, the child's eyes were closed. "Sleep," Catherine whispered. "Dream about going to a party in a new dress."

She stood looking at her daughter. Maria's thumb crept stealthily into her mouth and Catherine sighed. As the little, lonely, wet sounds of sucking began, Catherine went out of the room and closed the door and went into the living room.

Bauer was sitting in the easy chair by the window. There was a small bookcase in front of him. Most of the books in it were from correspondence courses for which he had subscribed in the days when he still had hopes of making a success in business. He had been wondering what his life would have been like had he finished the books. Different, altogether different, he decided. "A man like me needs teachers," he told himself, "to drive him and make him stick at something until he learns it."

Catherine turned on the light. He blinked and scowled at her. She blinked, too, and scowled and looked at him and did not see him clearly, but saw that he was scowling at her.

"I think we ought to talk about this like we should, not fighting," she said.

"What's the use of going over the whole thing all over again?"

"The use is, how can I help you if I don't know what's going on?"

"You can't help. What can you do? I never expected any help from you."

Catherine went to a chair opposite him and sat down. He looked away from her out the window.

"They got me so crazy down there," he said, "telling me I can't quit, they'll kill me if I quit, that I called up the police and there was a raid. They know it was me."

The breath blew out of her mouth. Her hand flew up and clapped over her lips.

"Yes," he said, "that's right. That's the whole thing in a nutshell. I'm in the nutshell waiting now, this minute, they should break me up."

There was a long silence. She didn't trust herself to speak. He kept looking out the window, guiltily, until he thought perhaps she had fainted or gone away. Then he looked at her.

"Why did you do such a thing?" she asked.

"I told you. I wanted to quit. I'm not the kind of a man who can live like a criminal."

"What's criminal? Everybody bets on numbers."

"There's a law," he shouted. "Did you ever hear? There's a law in the United States!"

"All right, sssh. Talk right, Fred."

"I am talking right. There was a raid, another raid, before the one that came today. I'm not a criminal. I'm not cut out for that, police to come in and grab me like a thief and beat me up. You know me. I'm a man who has to live honorable, by the law. They sent their killers after me to tell me I can't quit and I thought if I put Mr. Minch out of business, then I can quit."

"Who? That baldheaded man, what's his name, the other day?"

"He was one of them."

"He seemed very nice when he was here."

"Nice? That's the way those fellows are, I tell you. Nice! They're so nice, they shoot a man dead like you spit. They look nice, that's all, act nice. Oh, what's the difference! Don't you think I know what I'm talking about?"

"Well, let me know, too. I've got a right to know, too."

"Well, now you know. Mr. Minch knows. They all know what I did, and if I want to save my life I got to go away."

"What did Mr. Minch say?"

"When?"

"When he found out you called up for the police."

"What should he say? What's the difference?"

"Tell me, Fred. I want to know."

"He said he's through with me and watch my step. It's not what he said. I can tell the way he said it what he meant. He's a killer, that man, a killer, a real killer. He looks nice, too, acts nice, too, doesn't he? He's a killer I'm telling you."

"Is that all he said, just he's through with you and watch your step?"

"What else should he say? Does he have to draw a blueprint for the rest, where my grave will be? Yes, that's all, and come to work tomorrow in a new place that he give me the address."

"See." Her voice rang. "It's what I thought. He's just bawling you out. Do you think if he meant you harm he'd give you the address where to go to work?"

He looked at her helplessly. "Whatever I talk to you doesn't mean a thing," he said.

"Don't you understand? He tells you to come back to work. What does that mean?"

"In one ear, out of the ear. It doesn't mean anything to you, not a damn thing, and you don't know anything, if you're alive or what!"

"I know this. You've got a job and you've got three children and you got to keep that job."

"Something new! I'm hearing something new that I never thought of."

"I'll help you, Fred. I'll go down and see Mr. Minch and tell him."

"Yes, what'll you tell him?"

"I'll tell him what it means, the whole thing, why you did it and about the children. He's a good man. I don't care. He's a good man in his heart. Why should he punish you? What'll it get him to punish you? Only more trouble for himself. No, he's a good man. He'll see what I say."

"Yes? And his brother, Joe? There's a good man, too. Go cry to him."

"I will. I will. Who's his brother? Where is he?"

"Aaah, I saw in the first place there was no use talking to you." Bauer got up and went back into the bedroom. "At least I don't have to climb over her to get in," he thought. "That's the good I accomplished."

Catherine sat thinking for a few moments and then turned out the light and followed him into bed. But, when she tried to talk to him, he wouldn't answer. She tried again and again. She asked him to tell the whole story from the beginning. She said it wasn't clear to her. He refused. She began to ask him questions.

"I want to sleep," he said and turned his face to the wall.

She pleaded with him and he made believe he was snoring. He

concentrated so much on pretending he was asleep that his mind was cleared of all other thoughts and finally he did fall asleep.

რ

When Bauer opened his eyes, the darkness was still there, but it had been hollowed by dawn. His brain had grown fresh and sweet in his head. I must have been asleep, he thought, at least for a little while.

Catherine lay in back of him and he listened for her. He could not hear her. He decided she was holding herself still. She wouldn't be so quiet if she were asleep. He closed his eyes. He was afraid if she saw him awake, she would start talking to him again.

The bed was still. The house was still. The street was nearly soundless. It felt as if a wind were gentling through his head. The color of gray swarmed restlessly in the night's black, scooping it out until the darkness looked like a shadow on the gray.

She couldn't be asleep, he thought, or I'd hear the sound of her. He turned around to face her. Love won that much, but fear held on. He kept his eyes closed and sighed to make her think he was turning in his sleep.

His hand fell on the soft flesh of her side and remained there. She did not move. She must be awake, then. She must still be thinking and afraid. If she were asleep, she would have moved. No, she was awake and holding herself still so as not to disturb him!

But, sometimes, when he touched the children in their sleep, they remained still. . . . Sometimes they moved and sometimes they did not. Sometimes they could be heard breathing and sometimes they could not. Sometimes he had to watch their chests to see if they were breathing at all.

He thought suddenly of Erna, his second daughter. When she walked, her fat little legs moved like a giggle. Children slept so deep. They fell asleep the way smoke falls into air and their sleep was sweet and deep. Maybe Catherine was sleeping that way now. If he opened his eyes a crack, she would not be able to tell that they were open.

He could not feel her breath or her warmth. The blankets had lumped between them. Suddenly there was a fumbling along the blankets. He closed his eyes tightly. Her hand was moving. It came to rest on top of his. The skin was rough. Her hand had no weight. It had brushed along his hand like a leaf and it touched so lightly now he could feel the roughness of the skin. She must be supporting the weight of the hand herself so as not to awaken him. She was thinking and afraid and yet holding herself still because she wanted him to sleep! He opened his eyes and saw that she was looking at him.

"Go to sleep," she said.

He closed his eyes, peacefully. She withdrew her hand. He kept his eyes closed for a moment. Then he looked at her again. She was lying on her side, facing him. Her lips were open and touching the edge of his pillow and she was staring over his head at the wall.

He realized suddenly that he had to force himself to look at her and that he had not really looked at her in years. At 27, she still seemed young around the eyes. The girl of her was still there. It was bundled in the fat of her face. Why hadn't he been able to look at her? he asked himself. Because he hated her so much? Because he wanted to hurt her all the time? Because he thought she hated him?

His mind went all around and nibbled at the edges of the answer. How could it tell him that the man he had become was ashamed to look at her because of what he had done to her and to their love for each other? If it told him that, then he would have seen into himself and into his problem and he would have solved the problem. But he was on the edge. The forces of love and self-preservation had pushed him to the edge of the solution.

"Catherine," he said and stopped. The name had come mumbled through his sleepy throat and even that was turned into fear, a fear of sounding ridiculous. The fear was fought down. "I'm sorry for you," he said and this time the tone was clear, but his voice was so low the words rumbled.

"Try to sleep," she said. "That's what you need most."

He closed his eyes again and remained still, thinking about her.

Then he opened his eyes and said, "I know the trouble I give you."

"Sssh, sssh. Don't think about anything but sleeping." She felt if he slept well, then he would see everything differently.

"I want to tell you that I know. I can't help it. That's the man you married."

"Ssssh, sssh, sssssssh, Fred."

"You know I can't help it. It's the last thing I want, to give anybody trouble."

"I know, Fred. You're a good husband."

"I try, but it doesn't come out right. I have no luck."

She put her hand on his face and said, "Sssssh," and stroked his cheek, saying, "Sssh, sssh," as if he were a child.

"I try." His voice trembled. "You know that."

"You go to sleep, Fred."

"I do what's right. I'm not for other women or drinking or carry-on with rough stuff around, like other fellows."

"I know. Don't you think I appreciate the way you've been?"

"I come home regular and give you all my money regular every week and whatever I do, it's for the house, not for myself. You know that. There's never been any change in me."

"You're as good a husband as there is." She drew the blankets around his neck and patted them cozily.

"I do my work. There's never been any complaint about my work and about me, the way I act, here and in the office and wherever it is. And yet it doesn't come out right. What is it? I've tried all my life not to make one step out of the way, to do everything right so that everything should be like it ought to be and nothing comes out that way."

"It will, Fred. You'll see. You keep on doing the right thing and it comes out right."

"It didn't with me. What did I do wrong in my whole life? Nothing. I'm clean and look! Look what happened! See for yourself!"

"You'll see, Fred. That's the way it always works out. What's right is right. You'll see."

Yes, he thought, that's what she's good for, sleep and the bogey man will go away, God is good, the right will win. No help! No help! Just, God is good.

He did not think it angrily. The thought hung and swung deep in listlessness, the kind of listlessness a general must feel when, on the edge of victory, while gathering his troops for the final thrust, he sees more and more of those troops turn on him and begins to know the battle is lost and he is lost with it.

"One thing I regret," he said, after a while. "I'm sorry for the way I've been around here. But I couldn't help it the way my whole life was all . . . it was all, the whole thing I mean, I was doing the right thing and it was all going wrong. I don't know yet why. Honest to God, I don't know yet why."

"I'm telling you, Fred. You'll see. What's right is right and you do right and it comes out right, for the best."

"You must hate me, don't you, the way I've talked and acted around here."

"Oh, I don't. How can you say that?" She shifted close to him again and struggled to get her arm free of the blankets and around him.

"How can you help it, the way I've been!"

She got her arm under his neck and pressed his face against her. "I don't, I don't," she cried. "Don't you think I understand nothing, Fred? Honest, I don't."

"I can't bear it if you hate me."

"I don't! I don't! How can you think I do when I don't?"

He lay still. He could feel the bones of her legs against the bones of his legs and the large, wide, warm softness of her body against his body. In her shifting, the skirt of her nightgown had lifted and tangled above her hips and the naked warmth of her body poured out to him and swept over him and he lay listlessly in it.

"I didn't intend what I said about going away," he told her.

She didn't answer except to press his head more tightly.

"I wouldn't do a thing like that," he said. "I know it wouldn't be right."

He could feel her hand tremble where it held the back of his head. His listlessness frightened her.

"All my life," he said, "it's been that I'd rather suffer anything than do the wrong thing."

He tried to move his head so that he could speak more freely, but she forced him against her.

"I never had an idea that I'd go away," he told her. "I just said it."

"Mr. Minch won't do anything. He's a good man."

"That's what I have to rely on."

"He's a good man and he understands what you did. Maybe he's sore for a little while, but you'll see, he's good and he understands."

"If I didn't think the same thing . . . but I just said about going away because . . . I don't know. Maybe to make a play for sympathy."

"I know. You poor darling, you were worried."

Yes, he said to himself, he had known even before he had thought of going away that he could never go away and leave his family like that. He'd have to stand and face this thing like a man, not run away.

"I really don't know why I said it," he told her. "I just said it."

"I know, Fred."

They lay still for a long time. He put his leg between hers and the warmth of her rolled into his leg down through the bones. Her hand pressed his head into her neck and the flesh of her body flattened against his body.

"You mustn't say I hate you, Fred," she said. Her voice shook and she began to weep. "It's not so," she wept. "Never. I appreciate all you do and the way you are."

One of her tears fell against the side of his face and rolled coldly down his cheek. He shuddered. He wanted to draw away from her, but he compelled himself to lie still. Her tears fell slowly and rolled coldly down his cheek and caught against his lips. He tasted the salt. Then, suddenly, he forced his head upward. He wanted her tears to fall into his eyes.

It was nearly the last moment of love left to Bauer before his mind throttled itself in a snarl of fear.

XIX

THE BANK had been placed in a large apartment house on the edge of the fashionable part of Fifth Avenue. When Bauer went to work Tuesday he thought, this can't be, Leo must have given out the wrong address.

But there were others there—Murray and Delilah and Mr. Middleton—thinking it couldn't be, either, and they all went along together to the delivery entrance and found out they were expected and went up to the ninth floor and it was the right address all right. Joe opened the door for them.

"This way, please," said Joe. "I'll show you where you work."

Bauer had got in among the others to keep the curious eyes of the elevator man off his back and was shouldered along. He went with head lowered.

First there was a foyer. Leo was in there, seated at a telephone. Bauer could see his shoes. Then there was a living room filled with red, brocaded furniture and black teakwood tables and a dining room stuffed with heavy walnut. After that, came a swinging door with a small oval of glass in it and then they were in the kitchen. Adding machines had been placed on top of the washtubs and the bank's books were scattered over the stove and the drainboard of the sink.

"You work there, Bauer." Joe pointed to the stove. "We had the pilot light turned off for you, so you can't get burned." Joe pressed the button that operated the pilot light. No flame came out. "See?" he said. "You got nothing to worry."

Bauer lifted his head, but he couldn't meet Joe's eyes.

"The sorters in here," said Joe.

He led the sorters into a maid's room that opened off the kitchen. All the furniture had been moved out of it and piled into the hall to make room for two tables and chairs.

Bauer stood looking at the stove and listening to the sounds of jostling and laughter and scraping furniture and the cry of words from the maid's room. Then he thought of Joe being in there and how nobody had told him Joe would be there, waiting for him, when he came to work. His legs began to move. Delilah and Murray, their hats and coats off, coming towards the adding machines, were a blur to him. His legs seemed to him to be moving away from his body. He was carried at a half-run on tiptoe through the swinging door and along thick rugs. He saw thick rugs in streaks and then he saw Leo in the foyer. Leo was still at the telephone table. He was looking through his address book. Bauer stopped short and, as soon as he stopped, he began to tremble.

"Where are you going?" asked Leo.

Bauer shook his head to stop its trembling. He shook his hands up and down to stop the trembling of his body.

"Hang up your hat and coat," Leo told him.

Bauer kept shaking his head from side to side and shaking his hands up and down.

"Haven't I got enough trouble without you?" cried Leo.

"But Joe . . . You didn't say he would be here." Bauer's teeth were chattering. He could hear them faintly as if they were far below his head.

"Go hang up your coat. Do you think there's nothing on our minds except you? If I had my way I'd throw you out to hell with you."

"Please, did you . . . does he . . . I mean did you . . . does Joe . . . please, tell me, for God sakes!"

"If you make this much trouble for us any more," Leo held up a clenched hand with his thumb pressed against the tip of his index finger, "it will be the end and I'm telling you that."

They heard Joe coming and Bauer looked around and saw him and stooped his head.

"There's a place in the kitchen to hang up your stuff," said Joe.

Bauer stepped around him and hurried to the kitchen.

It was to be all snarl for him now and anything that happened was to be grabbed up by his mind and made into snarl. It turned out that what happened next was, Joe rang the doorbell.

After Bauer started back to the kitchen, Joe told Leo he was going downstairs for a minute. He didn't say why. He hadn't even told Leo yet Hall had probably put a tap on all their telephones. It hadn't been necessary. Leo didn't know Bunte. His telephone conversations couldn't be important to Hall.

Joe went a block to Madison Avenue to find a store with public telephones. It wasn't a dial phone. He gave the operator Wheelock's number and told Wheelock to meet him at nine o'clock that night at the corner of 47th Street and Madison Avenue. He said he would pick him up in his car.

"Make that a little later. I have an appointment," Wheelock said.

"I didn't fix the time. You know who did."

Wheelock did not have an appointment, but he resented the sound of command in Joe's voice. "I'll be there later," he said. "I can't break my appointment now."

"You can do what you want. I'll be there at nine and, if you're not there, that's up to you."

Joe hung up and went out into the store. He had to call Tucker and tell him he had made the appointment with Wheelock, but he wanted to make sure all the other booths were empty before giving the operator the number. Tucker had moved into hiding that morning.

There was a man in one of the booths. He seemed to be a salesman, but Joe bought cigarettes and looked through the telephone book until the man left.

When Joe got back to his apartment, he discovered he had forgotten his keys. He rang the bell.

It was a chime bell. The soft notes went through the house. Leo was in the maid's room with the sorters. He came hurrying out and across the kitchen and through the swinging door.

Bauer lifted his head from his books. He looked at the door as it swung and swished and swung shortly and swished and trembled to a stop. He dipped his well ear into the silence and sat trying to hear whether it was the police. He heard nothing but silence.

Then Leo returned. He went through the kitchen to the sorters without saying anything.

"It must have been nothing," thought Bauer. He went back to work slowly and, as he worked, he listened to the silence that lay outside the kitchen. "The place for the garbage here is better than what I got to live in," he said to himself.

He thought of the elevator men and doorman and porters who had stared as he came in. They must be wondering what was going on. Anybody who saw them going in or out of such a house or saw them through the window would wonder what was going on. "Are they crazy," he said to himself, "to pick a place like this? They'll be on to us in a minute, anybody who sees us."

Somebody who looked into the kitchen window would call up and complain. Maybe the doorman would complain or the elevator men or somebody he had not even noticed. The policeman on the beat. What would he think, seeing such people as himself and the others go in and out of such a house? "I can't work here," he thought. "It's not for me."

He gripped the books tightly to stop the trembling in his hands. He listened to the silence beyond the kitchen door and the silence in the courtyard beyond the window. "If I pull the shade," he told himself, "they'll wonder why. What's going on in a kitchen that you have to pull the shades?" He looked out the window at the silent houses and the silent windows and his ear strained to reach the silence beyond the kitchen door.

I can't, he thought. It's against nature! He had to go away somewhere. If it was pain that he had to stand up to or even being killed, he could do it. He could force himself and do it. Men had done it before for their family's sake and he could do it just as well as anybody. But not this. This was against nature, to sit still in a place where a man was going crazy.

No question about it. That's why Leo had put the bank in a place where it stuck out like an electric sign. To drive him insane. First,

Leo shoves money in his face and rubs it in his eyes so that he should think about and feel the garbage is thrown in a better place than he can afford to live. Then Leo lets him know, out cold, out plain, that if there was a raid, he would be blamed for it.

If the elevator man called up the police or the doorman or the lobby man or the hall porter or the fireman, they wouldn't be suspected. Nobody would be suspected because Leo would know Bauer had done it and there would be no questions or arguments. Bauer had done it. No question about it. Bauer had done it.

If the neighbor next door called up the police, he would be the one. If the people across the court called up, he would be the one. If the cop on the beat saw them going in and got to wondering and investigating and made a raid, Bauer would be the one. No questions, no arguments. No more another chance. Just shoot! Shoot! That's all.

No, he had to go away. He had to go away without telling Catherine. He had told her Joe was going to kill him. She hadn't believed him. She hadn't budged an inch. So what was the use of telling her the truth, that it was against nature, flesh could not do it, a man could not hold a job that was making him insane and sit still and do the job and watch himself go insane.

"It won't make you crazy to see your children starve to death?" she would say. "A man has to be a man. A family man has to stand anything and be a man for his family."

"Insane!" he cried to himself. "But really wild insane, with my hair sticking out and not to know what I'm doing!"

At ten o'clock that night, Wally came in to Boyle's. He saw Bauer and nodded to him, but he didn't go over. He stood around talking and walked from table to table to watch the games and see if he could get into one of them.

Somebody asked him for the prices on a fight and he said he wasn't running for Koch any more. They wanted to know what it was all about, whether he had made a killing on a horse and had too much money to work or had had an argument with Koch or what.

"Everything is very friendly between me and Barney," he said. "I'm just trying to improve myself and take a little flier at something I got in prospect to see how it works out."

Bauer didn't watch Wally, but the boy drifted back and forth before him, generally with a smile on his face and looking bright. Bauer sat against the wall in a wooden folding chair. He had come to Boyle's to think. He felt he could think better there than at home. He thought there must be some way to quit his job and get relief work and be free, some simple way somewhere, some easy thing to do if he could but think of it. Several times Wally came into his mind and each time he said to himself, "What can that kid do except talk with his big mouth!"

While he was thinking of this, searching for the way to quit, the simple, easy little way and winding up with Wally and rejecting Wally, he was debating what would happen if he did not find the way.

"I'll go away on a freight train," he thought, "and then I'll send for them. I'll tell Catherine that in the note I leave."

But where, in the whole United States, was there a job for a man alive in the year 1934? Nobody had the right to be alive that year. People from all over the country were coming to New York to get jobs and if there were no jobs in New York, how could he expect to find a job any other place? A picture came into his mind of himself as a bum, knocking on back doors hat in hand or searching in garbage pails when no one was looking.

Finally he went over to Wally. "That big mouth!" he thought. But he owed his family that much, to listen to the boy and to be able to say he had tried every single way there was to get rid of the job that was driving him insane, even such a hopeless way as listening to what a boy like Wally had to say. He told Wally he had decided he would like to hear more on what they had talked about last night before making up his mind one way or the other, yes or no or maybe.

"I'm trying to fix myself up with a game here," said Wally.

Bauer wandered off, disappointed. After a few minutes, Wally came over to him and said he guessed there wasn't any game around there for him anyway and took Bauer into his car.

As they drove along slowly, Bauer asked questions about the car, how many miles it made to the gallon and about its pickup and how fast it could go in second and whether it could take the hill at Fort George in high.

"I'll give you the handbook of instructions," said Wally, bored.

"Would you, please? I've never read one and I sort of, well, I thought if I ever got ten bucks together I'd buy a jalopy just to take it apart."

"In the meantime," said Wally, "what about our deal?"

"Well, I don't know."

"You don't know what?"

"I mean I don't remember exactly what you said last night. I was tired and had something on my mind and didn't listen much."

"It's nothing hard to understand. If you name us a place where we can put a proposition to Leo Minch, that's all. Then we'll put in a word for you."

"Is that all?"

"That's all."

"You said something else last night."

"I said a lot of things, but that was the proposition."

"No, I mean there was something else in the proposition, something more that you said."

"That was all," said Wally.

"I'm sure there was something else."

"Well, whatever it was, there's the proposition now. Take it or leave it lay."

Bauer was silent. The car rolled along slowly. It went up Southern Boulevard and across to a small park where automobiles stood every few feet along the dark roadways. There were couples in the cars. "What do you think of that," said Bauer, "in this cold weather!"

"I guess they keep it hot enough inside," Wally said. "Well, when are you going to make up your mind either way? I want to shoot some pool."

"What kind of a proposition have you got for Mr. Minch?"

"What's it to you? It's a proposition, a deal we want to make."

"Well, who is we? I mean I got to know something that I am dealing with."

"You're dealing with me."

"You? How are you going to talk to Mr. Minch and get him to let me quit? Do you think I'm crazy!"

"I'm working with Ficco."

"Oh." Bauer tried to think where he had heard the name before. It was familiar, but he couldn't place it. Something, somewhere, in the newspapers, people talking.

"Who's Ficco?" he cried. "What's Ficco? I got to know. I can't rush in blind like this and make a deal with people I never heard about and I don't know what they're doing."

"You never heard of Ficco?"

"I heard of him, yes, but I don't know where or what." Bauer had twisted around in his exasperation and he looked full at Wally and Wally took his eyes off the road and looked at Bauer. The boy's lips had curled into what could have been either a smile or a sneer. He didn't say anything. He looked at Bauer calmly and Bauer lowered his eyes and turned forward.

"You see what I mean," said Bauer. "I don't want to be like I'm in the frying pan into the fire. I got to see my way clear in this before I take a single step."

"You don't have to worry. You're dealing with me."

"Yes, but I don't know. I'm tied to one and then I break loose from him and I'm tied to Mr. Ficco. What's the use of that, getting myself into a spot where I have to do what Mr. Ficco says."

"Ficco will never know you're alive. You're dealing with me."

"You don't have to tell him about me?"

"Why should I? It's my deal that I'm making with you and I don't want anything out of you. You know that. You just get your boss to meet you somewhere private, not altogether private, that's not necessary, just in a quiet restaurant or some place like that, you can suit yourself. You don't even have to be there if you don't want."

"That's all?"

"That's all. Just call up, I'll give you the number, and tell whoever answers, you don't have to give in your name or your boss's
name, just say for Wally to be at such and such a place at such and
such a time, whatever you make up with your boss, but don't mention his name. Then we'll show up and do all the talking and when
the deal is made I'll put in your name and that's part of the deal.
There's no need to be there at all. We'll put our proposition to him
and he'll take it and part of the deal is he fires you."

"That's all?"

"What else? Call up, say where the appointment is and hang up.
You're a free man. Go to Miami for the winter."

"I want to go on relief work."

"Go wherever you want. That's your business. I don't even want
to know."

"You said something else last night, I'm sure, what you were going to do to Mr. Minch."

"Make him a proposition," said Wally.

"Something more." Bauer didn't look at Wally. He knew the boy
was gazing at him with the same ambiguous curl to his full, shapely
lips, but he stared straight ahead through the windshield.

"I didn't," Wally said at last, "but what's the difference! That's
what the deal is and now give it to me yes or no."

Bauer's head squirmed as if with pain. His eyes were wrinkled
almost shut. "I don't know," he said, "I don't know, no . . . no . . .
don't know."

"Okay. I'll take that for no. And now I'm going back to Boyle's
if you don't mind." Wally made a U-turn with Bauer looking carefully to right and left and out the rear window as the car backed up.

"There was some other point you mentioned last night," said
Bauer, "I'm positive."

"Maybe you thought I said something that I didn't."

That must be it, Bauer told himself. He had a sense of relief, a
welling up of unreasonable joy. Wally's story was straight. They
had a proposition for Mr. Minch. Mr. Minch wouldn't listen. That
was logical to anyone who knew Mr. Minch. And they were paying
him off for tricking Mr. Minch into listening. That was straight

enough and simple enough and, if he had got the impression last night there was anything more to it, it must have been because he was so excited, he was thinking so many things, he didn't know what he heard and what he thought. So what could he lose? If Mr. Minch didn't make the deal with Wally's people, all he would do was get sore at Bauer for tricking him into listening. Well, he couldn't get sorer than he was now.

"I'll give you the number to call up in case you change your mind," said Wally.

"All right." Bauer took out his memorandum book and a pencil and leaned forward to get the light from the dashboard.

"Put it on a page that you can tear out after you've used it," said Wally. "It's a private number and Ficco doesn't want it to get around."

"Sure." That was logical enough, too, and straight enough.

Wally stopped the car so that Bauer could write more legibly. Bauer supported the book on his knee and wet the pencil in his mouth and wrote down the number.

"This doesn't mean I've made up my mind yet," said Bauer.

"Suit yourself. If you decide no, there's no obligation, and if yes, just call up and leave word where I should be and when. Don't say your name or your boss's name and that will leave you out of it altogether. Just say for me to be. After all, what can you lose?"

"I've been thinking the same thing. I owe it to my family to try whatever I can." If it goes wrong, Bauer told himself, they're the ones to blame. Wife and kids, that's who. The whole thing is for them and whatever goes wrong, it's their responsibility. But what could go wrong?

"As I say," said Wally, "suit yourself."

"Not myself, my family."

"Whatever it is," said Wally.

❧

The weight of history that a man carries on his shoulders as he goes about his daily life is not a small weight, although Bauer was among the great majority in never being aware of it. He never thought of himself and of each other man on earth as living all day in the stream of history. To him, history was not what was happening to all people but something in school books. Historical events were made by "big shots" who got their names in the papers and lived in government buildings or tried to live there. While they were alive, they were boss and people paid attention to what they said. After they were dead, statues were made of them.

It was now Tuesday night of the second week in December, 1934, and an incident that will never be recorded in written history had occurred in the small life of a little man. The little man had a heritage of insecurity that had begun from the day of his birth to make him into a certain kind of infant. He was born in a world given over to business played as a game with profit as the goal and man staking his life on reaching it. There was no security in that for him. Whatever insecurity he was born into must be aggravated by such a way of life.

Finally, a crisis had come to him, an event of importance to few. A man, in an effort to save his brother's money, had had his brother's employees arrested on a misdemeanor charge, involving perhaps a small fine. Only one man in the group had been ripened sufficiently by the history of the modern world to react totally to the meaning of this event.

To this one man, the arrest became an event that could sum up and make tangible and so, understandable, and so, shattering, the tragedy of insecurity. Insecurity had made him into a certain kind of infant and had aggravated him into a certain kind of man. That man could see no way out of insecurity except death. The will to self-destruction was strong in him, but it needed fear to do its work, a paroxysm of ultimate fear. This alone would be adequate to compel its victim to destroy, first, whatever love was in him for the things in his life and for life and then destroy life itself. So, the little man began to invent enemies in order to inflame fear and stirred hate in himself in order to inflame fear and worked on fear, nursed it, fed it, sheltered it. Towards the end, fear was becoming strong enough to make everything that happened its food. A doorbell ringing, forgiveness by his friend and boss, the promise of a new chance to resume the old life, his wife, his children, his father, the society in which he existed, they all fed fear and became fearful.

At this moment, an inept, inadequate creature, a puny-minded impotent boy came to him and he listened. Instead of ignoring the boy or turning him into food for fear, instead of using this evil-looking, diseased-seeming youth as he had used all the others, he listened and made himself believe.

"Give me your problem," the boy said, "I will solve it. Do what I say and you will have no more worries. A better life will open to you. I will remove your enemies and whatever you hate. Let me be your leader. You will not regret it."

The little man listened and an extraordinary thing occurred in his mind. He had not believed his wife's words or his boss's words. He did not believe the boy's words but, remarkably, instead of striving immediately to distort them to aid his campaign for self-destruction, he began to strive to believe them.

Is this a miracle, an accident, a coincidence, a freak of thought, a work of a high power?

The little man asked questions of the boy he strove to accept as leader. But he asked questions with his mouth, not with his mind. His mind was throttled by the will to self-destruction and with it he could think only that he had nothing to lose by trying what the boy offered. If the boy who would be leader had come earlier, he would have been rejected. If he had come later, he would have been too late. A solution to the crisis would have been found without him. So the time of his arrival owed its importance, not to accident or coincidence, but to itself. The time was a vital element in the fact that the "leader" succeeded in becoming actually a leader.

The little man's wife had promised to solve his problem and had been refused. The little man's friend and employer had promised, too, and had proved he could solve it and had been refused, at first, and then ignored. For the little man did not want the solution they promised. He wanted death. Then this diseased-seeming, evil-looking "leader" had promised a solution and outlined his method.

Was he a miracle of persuasiveness? Did he have Divine aid? . . .
Then, where was the reason for his success?

If his method had held a logical hope of success, if, for example,
it included an end to insecurity, a way to do the world's work without the ruinous device of profit for a goal and, for those who cannot
reach the goal, death without burial, death that can be tasted and
suffered, then, no doubt, he, too, would have been rejected. He
would have been regarded as an enemy—an enemy of the will to die
—and would have been hated and turned into food for fear. But the
leader's solution lay within the framework of the little man's experience. It was not a cure for the disease of insecurity; it simply
responded to its symptoms. That prepared the little man to accept
the solution. And the leader's method had no logical hope of success. It was not an enemy of the will to die, but an ally. That made
the little man eager to accept it.

So the little man questioned the leader with his mouth, but not
with his mind. For his mind knew that the leader was lying to him
and was truthfully promising only death. The leader's lies helped
the little man conceal the unbearable truth from himself and the
little man had his own lies to help further. What can I lose? he told
himself. I owe it at least to try everything there is, he told himself,
so I can say fairly that I tried.

Now, you may ask, what have these rather shabby confusions in a
little man's inconsequential life to do with so great a thing as
history?

Well, the time was 1934. Already a nation of Germans, ripened by
history, as the little man had been, and then flung into economic
crisis, as the little man had been, had invented enemies, as he had,
and stirred hatreds and nursed and fueled and fanned fear and had
allowed itself to turn to a leader, a gross, gruesome, diseased-seeming
man—all as the little man had. The Germans' leader was one of
them. He had the will to death in him and he knew the way to
it. He knew how to delude himself into gratifying the will to death.
The leader meant Germany's death, but he promised Germany a
better life. Being put into power, he did not change. He invented

more enemies for his nation and stirred more hatreds and nursed and fueled and fanned more fears.

The nation of Germany asked questions with the mouth and not with the brain. Is living with fear and cohabitation with fear to multiply fear the better life? Is slavery for all the better life? Yes! Yes! cried the nation of Germany, for its brain was busy arranging its own destruction. Delusion was a help.

Then the life of Germany as a fruitful, dignified nation, or force on earth, and the life of Germans as members of the human race was bound in slavery, and fruitfulness, dignity and humanity were destroyed in the flames of fear. The nation of Germans, in a paroxysm of fear over what it had done, warmed itself in the fire and rattled joyfully the chains binding it to death and shouted jubilantly with their mouths and became a lunatic beast abroad in the world, a monstrous triumph of insecurity.

This thing called the Nazi idea, this promise of wholesale death, crept across the earth. It was a climax to the modern world and its business game. Wherever it found climax men, strong only in the will to self-destruction, it found victims. All of Tucker's people, and, of course, Tucker himself, were climax men of the modern world. Some were riper than others, but each was ripening. In each was the sum of the history of the modern world to date. Whatever history lay after 1934 would be, in large part, their doing. What they accepted or rejected, acted upon or failed to act upon would be the story of what came next on earth.

That was the weight of history upon Bauer's shoulders. He was the ripest of all the climax men and he swam drowning in the stream of history towards Ficco.

BOOK SEVEN

THE VICTIMS

XX

AT NINE o'clock this same Tuesday evening, Joe found Wheelock waiting where he had been told to wait, at 47th Street and Madison Avenue. As he drove up Joe saw the young lawyer before he reached the corner and opened the door while still moving and hardly had to stop at all. He drove off swiftly, leaving Wheelock to fumble the door shut, and turned sharply into 49th Street and stopped near Fifth Avenue. A small sedan came around the corner behind them, rubber whining, and then, at sight of Joe's parked car, slowed and loitered up the block.

"Look down here," said Joe. He stooped over and put his hand on the floor. His back was to the street. He saw Wheelock stare at him in surprise. "Get your God damn head down and don't argue," he said.

Wheelock crouched and lowered his head so that it was below the level of the side window and only the slope of his back was visible from the street. When the small sedan passed, the two men sat up.

"What's this about?" asked Wheelock.

"I don't know myself."

"What the . . ."

"I just wanted to find out is there somebody following us and you saw. There seems to be that we got a tail."

"Look here!"

"Your switchboard is tapped all right, I guess, or maybe not. Maybe . . ."

"I'm an attorney. I'm not running away from anybody."

"I couldn't get a look if the tail is from Ficco or it's some of Hall's football boys. Did you?"

"I won't take part in this," said Wheelock. "You've always tried to do this kind of thing to me. I won't stand for it."

"You know what our tail is doing up there, don't you? They're sitting around the corner and they're waiting for us to come out. That's cheese stuff. We're the mouse, but they're cheese, if you ask me, football boys, not Ficco's talent."

"Did you hear what I just told you?"

"I could of lost them long ago, the minute they passed us only I got an idea to do. You watch, you'll see, they're going to send a man to the corner to tell them if we try to back out to Madison Avenue."

"You can't back out. This is a one-way street," said Wheelock.

"I want to wait and try to spot him and see if he's from Hall or from Ficco."

They both stared through the windshield at the corner. If Hall had found out about their appointment, it could have been through a tap on Wheelock's switchboard. But if Ficco had found out, then either there was a steady tail on them or Ficco had somebody in with Tucker selling him information. Many people passed the corner. It was difficult to pick out one man and say he was loitering to watch their car.

"Maybe they're smart," said Joe, "and got a woman to help. Watch the women, too."

"I'm not going to stand for this fantastic hocus-pocus," cried Wheelock. "I'm an attorney and I'm not in this thing like everybody else. You seem to forget that."

Joe kept his eyes on the corner. He was excited and worried, but he sat quietly and smiled a little, as if he liked the excitement. Joe liked anything that made him stop thinking. "I don't know who you're trying to kid," he said, "yourself or what."

"I'm not kidding. Goddamnit, you listen to me! You tell me where Tucker is and I'll go to him myself, as an attorney to his client, not this fantastic way."

"Just a minute. Watch in back."

Joe put the car into reverse and stepped on the gas hard and the car plunged backward. He kept his eyes on the corner. He knew how to drive. He could keep a car in a straight line by touch. He saw a man on the opposite corner lift his hand as if in a signal and start hurrying across the street.

"I thought we'd smoke him out," said Joe.

He was figuring that when the sedan got the signal that he was backing up, it would turn down 50th Street and tear for Madison Avenue to pick him up. He drove backwards until he felt the sedan had rounded into 50th Street. Then he raced forward. The man on the corner of Fifth Avenue saw him come and began waving for a taxi. Joe smiled again. No taxi was going to keep up with him. He got a look at the man as he raced by. It wasn't anybody he recognized, but he seemed too well dressed to be from Ficco.

"Watch that cab he gets," said Joe.

"A yellow."

"Remember the license and watch it."

The light was with them at Fifth Avenue and Joe made a left turn downtown. If it had been against them, he would have turned right. But as it was, the light gave them their first break. The taxi the man had called was facing uptown. It had to make a U-turn and wait for the light. Joe figured the sedan would be on the corner of 50th and Madison now, watching to see which way he would go. They would be watching in back, too, and would know he hadn't gone uptown. But downtown was good at this hour and the east side was good, too. There wasn't so much traffic. A man had a chance to cut some corners.

Joe drove straight down Fifth Avenue. He was playing for a break in the lights to shake off the taxi. He wanted to reach a corner just as the light was changing. The light would stop the taxi, but he would make it and steal the next one and then turn, with two blocks' start on his pursuer. He drove without thinking, except to count the blocks as he passed them. He could tell by the muscles on the back of the neck of the driver ahead of him what the man was going to do, whether he was going to cut right or left or slow up. He could judge distances to inches without thinking about them.

"You know," he told Wheelock, "when I'm pepped up like this, I can drive better."

Wheelock was watching the taxi through the back window. "You've got a hell of a nerve treating me like this," he said.

"Why, I thought you college boys liked to play cops and robbers."

Joe got his break at 39th Street. He forced the light and the taxi was too far behind to do the same. There wasn't much cross traffic at 38th Street. Joe drove through the light there and made a right turn at 37th Street and another at 6th Avenue, going fast, and came up 38th Street at top speed and made a right turn into Fifth Avenue and went down Fifth Avenue to 36th Street where he made a left turn towards Madison Avenue. He drew up alongside the curb in the middle of the block. He turned off the lights and shut off the motor.

"I'll watch Madison. You watch Fifth," he said.

They watched for a few moments in silence. The New York night hummed around them excitedly and excitement hummed in them.

"I want to know why you're doing this to me," said Wheelock at last.

"I'm not doing anything to you."

"You've always been like that, refusing to understand that I'm the attorney for the combination and not a member."

"Ben is the one I take orders from," said Joe. "He told me to bring you up, he's got something to talk to you, and not to let anybody know where he is."

"Why didn't he tell me and I'd have come up by myself instead of this way?"

"That's the answer, isn't it. He don't trust you to keep a tail off you. You're still the boy with the college education to him."

Joe began driving again, turning corners and stopping and going slow and speeding up and doubling back, but heading generally northwest. He finally drove the car into a parking lot on 58th Street and said they would take the subway from there. They walked down a quiet, rather dark street to the subway and once Joe stopped and put his foot on a fire hydrant and untied and tied the shoelace. He wanted to see if anyone was following. No one was.

"I intend to make clear to you once and for all," began Wheelock.

"Listen," Joe interrupted. "I'm going to tell you something. I've got nothing against you. We're in this business together and that's as far as we go together. What's for the business I'm with you, but I can't bother my head if you got pride or whatever you got, ethics or what. If you want to be on the Supreme Court, I don't care as long as it doesn't interfere with the business. Now, you get my point?"

"I'm the attorney for the combination and nothing else, no single thing else."

"Please," said Joe, "buy a newspaper for yourself and write it up there. Here, here's three cents." He put his hand into his pocket and Wheelock turned from him angrily.

They took the west side subway and got off at 96th Street. On the walk from the station to Tucker's new apartment, Joe stopped twice to make sure they were not being followed.

XXI

TUCKER HAD been thinking about Ficco for several days. He knew the man had put some people together and didn't have any money or backing or anything, except just these people to feed. Tucker was watching to see how Ficco would do it. He was a little nervous that Ficco would think his former boss was alone now and had his hands tied and was soft and ripe for taking.

Then Tucker found out this was just what Ficco was thinking. He found it out Monday night late, a little after Judge Garrett had thrown out the case against Leo's bank. At that time a white policy banker named Gilliam came to Tucker's home to ask if he could buy protection and to arrange a price on it. According to Gilliam's story, the night before, Sunday night, he was walking his dog outside his house when two men came out of a car parked nearby and said they would like to talk to him.

"All right," he told them. "I'm listening."

Gilliam was a tall, heavy man with rank, curly gray hair and a small face that was sharp-featured and forward-thrusting. He had been a Ku Klux Klan businessman hoodlum in the South and he felt there wasn't anything he was afraid of and he carried a gun to show it. People generally thought the same thing of him. Nobody could imagine him hiding under the bed from anything.

The two men said they would rather talk to him in their car because it was more private. That was when Gilliam became afraid. He had been to the movies and he knew what this was. He started to whistle for his dog. He thought the dog would make a noise and confusion and he'd be able to get his gun out and scare the two men off, but they saw Gilliam's lips become round and, before he could whistle, they put their hands on his arms and led him into the car. They didn't pull him or force him. They just led him and Gilliam was so surprised at their touch and so frightened that he couldn't think of anything else to do except go with them. His dog stayed home.

Gilliam remembered that one of the men had worked for him some years before when he had held a part-ownership in a Harlem dance hall. The man had been a bouncer, but Gilliam couldn't think of his name.

Tucker asked for a description and decided the man must be Jazz Smitty, who was doorman at a night club on 52nd Street where Ficco's wife worked in the ladies' room.

Gilliam couldn't describe any of the others. He had been too excited to look at them. He thought there might have been four altogether, but he wasn't sure. There could have been five or six. He remembered it was a big car, a seven-passenger, and Tucker wondered where Ficco had got it. He decided maybe one of Ficco's people was chauffeuring for somebody, perhaps an undertaker, and had borrowed it.

After the car got going, the men questioned Gilliam about what Tucker and Joe Minch were doing in policy. They seemed to know about the combination, but they wanted to know who was in it and where the banks were. Gilliam couldn't tell them. He wasn't in the combination. His bank hadn't been hit very hard by 527 and

Joe hadn't even approached him yet. He told the men, the four or five or six of them, the truth, that what with Joe coming into the field just at the time when everybody went broke, the whole business was so upset he hadn't seen anybody and hadn't learned anything.

"I think," said the man Tucker had decided was Jazz, "we should take him some place where we can open his mouth for him."

"That's all I know," Gilliam said. "Honest! Honest! On my mother's honor."

They drove to the Harlem speedway, a dark, cold valley road with a strip of park land climbing a bluff on one side and a river on the other. Gilliam got down on his knees on the floor of the car and prayed on his mother's honor that he was telling the truth. Jazz said, how do we know you're not a son of a bitch, and Gilliam said no, on his mother's honor. Joe, Leo, Tucker—that was all he knew or had heard. He didn't even know where Leo's bank was now because Leo had had a raid the week before and had moved. He offered to tell them where Leo's office was and a man took down the address. But somebody else said, what good was that when they could find out where Leo lived the same way they had found out where Gilliam lived, by looking in the telephone book.

"I don't get it," said Jazz. "We know Leo is in the combination and what's the use wasting time looking for somebody else in it when he can tell us everything we need to know?"

Then this other fellow, the one who had said they could look in the phone book, said Leo was out. "I want that understood, up and down and inside out and every way there is," he said.

There was a little argument and he explained that anybody who was Joe's brother might be tough and there was no point making a lot of extra work and trouble for themselves when they could find somebody else in the combination easily enough.

Tucker decided this must be Ficco and asked how the man talked, whether he had a high voice with an accent. Gilliam said he could not remember whether the voice was high or low or had an accent. He was too excited to notice such things. He was thinking that the way they were talking in front of him, without caring whether he heard or not, they must be intending to kill him, so he wasn't clear on all that had been said or done.

He remembered they had asked him for the names and addresses of all the bankers he knew and had taken them down. The fellow who was doing the arguing with Jazz said they had to talk to these bankers sooner or later and one of them would be bound to be in the combination and give them the information they wanted. Anyway, he said, they had this kid hanging out in magistrate's court, waiting for Joe Minch or Wheelock or one of Wheelock's people to show an interest in a policy case and that would be a tip-off on a combination bank. That seemed to convince everybody Leo ought to be left out, although one of them said he'd like to get a pair of hands on him just for Joe's sake, just to pay Joe back.

"Business before pleasure," said this fellow who seemed to be the boss.

After that they told Gilliam they were putting a payroll on him for $300 a week. He argued with them a long time. He said his business couldn't stand paying any sum like that and they said maybe his business couldn't but his health could. He told Tucker he finally got them to agree to take $75 a week. Actually, he had consented to pay $150 a week, but he was figuring on saying that, as a matter of principle he'd rather pay Tucker the $75 to keep the others off.

Then the men went through Gilliam's pockets and found the gun and took that and found $60 and some change, about 62 or 63 cents change, and took that, as a down payment. The doorman in Jazz came out and he said they should leave Gilliam a dollar for taxi money to get home, but the other fellow—the one who seemed to be boss—said the hell with that, Gilliam could walk.

After a little kidding and coaxing, this fellow figured out Gilliam could get home by taking two trolleys and gave him a nickel for one and two cents for a transfer to the other. Then they threw him out in the middle of the speedway where he had to walk more than a mile to the trolley.

"The penny pinching is Ficco all right," thought Tucker.

Tucker wanted to know how Gilliam had found out his address, but Gilliam wouldn't tell him. Gilliam said maybe a hundred thousand people knew where Tucker lived and that wasn't important anyway. What was important was what Tucker was going to do about all this.

"Why should I do anything?" Tucker asked.

"It's your responsibility. We never had anything like that before you came."

"I didn't do it, you know," laughed Tucker.

"Maybe not, but . . . " Gilliam let his voice trail off.

"I think maybe you're forgetting who you're talking to," said Tucker.

"But look at it from my angle. I've been in this business eight years and there never was a single thing going on like that until you came into the picture."

Tucker had decided to get rid of Gilliam. He had thought, at first, of telling him, as a kind of sales argument, that if he were in the combination he would protect him. But he felt tired suddenly and angry and he didn't want to be bothered with the man. He got up. "I'm inclined to think you're forgetting yourself," he said. He hadn't raised his voice. He had just said it.

Gilliam stood up, too. He was taller even than Joe and he bulked high above Tucker. "I was just saying, Mr. Tucker," he said, "just sort of, you know, upset and kind of excited, you know how it is, with all these things going on."

"Okay, then. That's okay if that's the way it was." He walked towards the door and Gilliam got his hat and coat.

"You're not going to do anything about it?" asked Gilliam.

The fear in his voice irritated Tucker. He thought for an instant he would like to see Gilliam down on his knees before him, swearing on his mother's honor. Tucker knew he could do it by putting his hand into his pocket, but he decided it would be bad for business and no fun anyway and wondered at himself for having thought of it. "You talk to Joe," he said. "He's running the policy end for me and he can make his own decisions."

After Gilliam left, Edna came out of the bedroom and asked what the man had wanted. She was ready for bed. There was cold cream on her face and she was wearing the cotton gloves she used to keep her skin soft and white.

"Nothing," Tucker told her, "just something, nothing of any importance."

Edna had heard snatches of the conversation when the men had raised their voices and she was worried. "You don't want to tell me, do you?" she said.

"I'd tell you if it was anything interesting. But it's just some piece of . . . well, it's nothing, nothing at all."

She had some cotton in her hands to stuff into her ears to help her sleep and she fiddled with it and looked at him a long time. He was sitting on a couch and he put on his horn-rimmed eyeglasses and picked up a newspaper and began to read it.

"I used to admire that I never could read anything in your face," she said, "but sometimes it's a nuisance."

He put down the newspaper, startled. He thought she had gone away. He readjusted his glasses to settle the start in him. "I don't get you," he said.

"I mean, I've seen you go through a lot of things, but I never saw you change and that's a nuisance."

"I think you're getting sleepy and should go to bed."

"No!" she cried. "What did that man want, whoever he was?"

"Would you like it better if I made up some lie and told you? I'm too tired to think up something for you now."

She went out of the living room and into the bedroom. He took up the newspaper. He didn't read it. He just held it in front of him, but the expression on his face was as if he were reading it.

He was trying to figure a way through Ficco. The man must have decided Tucker didn't want to fight or couldn't afford to fight with Hall watching to get Bunte. If there were a fight, things might get more or less out into the open and Bunte might have to move more or less in the open, and Bunte couldn't afford that with Hall there watching. So, Ficco was getting ready to put a payroll on all the banks in the combination. That was why he wanted to know who was in the combination, so he wouldn't waste time with the wrong people. If Tucker wouldn't fight or couldn't fight, then the combination would go over to Ficco. Or Tucker would buy off Ficco with a piece of the combination. Anyway, the least he would get would be the payroll off the banks. If Tucker fought, then there was going to be a fight. Ficco was willing to play that way. He was hard up and couldn't lose. His people were hard up. They wouldn't have taken the $60 off Gilliam if they weren't really hard up for it.

"I think you're actually reading that newspaper," said Edna. She had come out of the bedroom and was standing under the arch to the living room, watching him.

Tucker's whole body twitched. "Christ," he said, "you scared the pants off me."

"Did I?" She laughed. Her gaze did not leave his face. "I don't think so. I don't think anything scares you."

He got up from the couch and walked away restlessly. "Well, don't do it again," he said. He pressed his hand against his chest. "Christ," he cried, "I can still feel it in my heart."

"No you can't." She came into the room. "You can't feel anything. I used to think it was all right, it was a fine thing that a man should be as tough as you."

"Tough? What do you mean tough? Where do you get that kind of ideas? I'm not tough."

"I mean, hard. I mean, like a rock, so that whatever happens you don't change. The world changes, but you don't change. Whatever happens to you, you don't change. You don't bend, not even with a muscle on your face."

"You're crazy. I change. What do you mean I don't change? I'm older. I got a pot on my belly and I'm more settled down, a real settled down man now."

"Well, think of that! So you had to bend down to God. That's too bad about you, having to give in to God and grow older like everybody else."

"I don't know what you're getting so sore about."

"I'm sore because you stand there with that face of yours and I can't tell what's happening. I know something is happening and don't you try to keep on fooling me."

Tucker laughed. "A real tiger, aren't you?" he said.

"Never mind."

"A regular bloodhound."

"Ben, stop it! You've got to tell me. I have a right to know."

"Sure you have, and I'd tell you if I could remember what he said. But it was something for Joe and I told the fellow not to bother me, to bother Joe and washed the whole thing out of my mind."

"You're not fooling me, Ben."

"I guess not."

"I've lived with you too long not to know."

"Well, if you can't go to sleep without knowing something, let me see if I can't think up a little bedtime story for you what he said." He tapped his fingers thoughtfully against his wrinkled forehead. "Let me see now," he said.

She stood looking at his heavy, placid face, wrinkled now playfully with thought. "I used to think it was wonderful that a man should be like a rock like you," she said, "but it certainly can be a God damn awful nuisance, I'm telling you."

He walked over to her and took both her hands in his and looked into her eyes and said. "You know, Edna, if it was anything important I'd tell you."

"Can't you let me make up my own mind whether it's important?"

"No!" He paused a moment, still looking into her eyes. Then he said, "I haven't thought it all out yet, what to do."

"Oh, you have to do something?"

"Maybe. Maybe not. I don't know. I haven't thought it out yet. I'll let you know as soon as I can. You know that. Don't I always?"

"Yes, Ben, you do, or, as far as I've ever been able to tell, you do."

"I always do, always."

She thought a moment, searching thoughtfully in his eyes. Then she kissed his cheek and brushed it with her white, cotton gloves.

"It's all right," he said. "I need some cold cream on my big, tough-guy face."

Edna laughed. "I didn't mean tough guy," she said.

"I know, I know."

"Don't stay up too late." She blew a kiss along her glove and waved and went back to the bedroom.

❧

Tucker went to bed a short while later. He knew what he had to do. He had to send Edna and the children to some place in the country so Ficco couldn't do anything about them and so they shouldn't know what was going on, if anything did go on. There was a chance Ficco would try to force Tucker into a deal or a concession through the children. There was also a chance that, if trouble developed, some of it might get into the newspapers and the children would read it.

It was all clear now to Tucker, but he had known he would have to do it the moment he had heard about Ficco. He hadn't been able to make up his mind until he began talking with Edna. Even then, he didn't know he had made up his mind until he had sat alone for a while and thought the whole thing out all over again, from Bunte's angle, and Hall's angle, and his own angle, and had reached the point where he was thinking of what was going to happen after he started fighting Ficco. He stopped thinking then and went back to the decision he had made previously and announced it to himself.

When Tucker went into the bedroom, Edna was asleep. He stood looking down at her. She lay in a mist-colored light and her face was fresh and still. He could make out the heaps of her large body under the blankets. He thought of how pink and white the skin was.

"Her skin rolls down her body like cream," he thought. The picture, vaguely, did not please him. Her skin was better than cream. It looked cool and it was warm. It was white, but it glowed and was firm and full. The thought of her skin crept along the length of him inside.

"Look how she sleeps," he said to himself. He couldn't hear her breathing. He had to look close to see her chest move. "She trusts me," he thought. "That's the wonderful kind of woman she is. She's worried, but she trusts me so much she can sleep like a baby."

He turned to his bed at the opposite wall of the room and, as he got into it, he thought suddenly of Ficco and murmured aloud, "I hope she's right." He was surprised at himself. He looked around hastily at Edna. She hadn't stirred. She lay still in the pale light.

It took a long time for Tucker to fall asleep. He kept thinking of Ficco and of what Edna had said, that he was a hard man and how he had always known she thought that of him and had always felt she admired that in him and how he would have to fight Ficco and didn't want to fight Ficco and how there had been many times when he had wanted to give in on something, but hadn't been able to because Edna would find out and he felt that what she liked in him was his toughness and how that was a lucky thing all around, for the business, anyway, for himself, too, not only for the business, but for himself, sure for himself. It had made him rich and it was going to make a dead wop out of Ficco, if Ficco didn't get wise to himself in time, and maybe a dead politician out of Bunte and maybe a governor out of Hall and maybe not. Maybe nothing like that. Maybe Ficco was going to get smart enough in time.

He did not know when he fell asleep. He knew only when he began to dream. He dreamed a shape was sitting on his legs. His legs moved restlessly and the shape came forward. He couldn't see anything about it except that it was a dark, heavy shape. He couldn't even see how it moved. It just moved. It moved slowly up his body and he stirred and his head rolled slowly on the pillow and a low moan broke from him.

"Eddie!" he said. This was his private name for his wife.

The shape was on his chest now and his body thrashed, his breast bulged, his head rolled on the pillow and then he dug his chin into his neck. "Eddie! Eddie!" His voice sounded strangled.

He saw that the shape had the shape of a head on top of it and that it was leaning forward slowly, as if to lay its face on his in tenderness. He threw his head far back. He dug it into the pillow, straining, and arched his chest.

The shape leaned slowly and came nearer and Tucker's head strained deeper and deeper back into the pillow to get away from it. At the last instant, he realized his mistake. He had exposed his neck. His backward straining had stretched his neck bare to the shape and had thrust it up towards it. The shape suddenly had teeth. The teeth surrounded Tucker's adam's apple and bit into it.

Tucker saw the flash of the teeth and, in the same moment, heard a vicious crunch, as of a man biting a hard apple. He sat straight up in bed. His eyes were open. He had broken out into a sweat. There was no sleep left in him, only a feeling of wildness.

He had not known the shape had a face. He had not seen a face. Was it because he hadn't looked? He could almost see the shape before him yet, sitting on his legs, the shape with its shape of a head and no face, because he couldn't look at the face, he could look only below where the face should be and above. He felt wrinkled with fear and his head lurched away from the vision before him and he glanced around the room.

His eyes felt full of darkness. It was a moment before he could see the room. It lay still in pale light. He saw the blankets had become tangled around one leg. That's what must have started me off, he decided. He pulled his leg free. He couldn't sleep now. He couldn't even remain in bed. He got up and put on his slippers and passed Edna without seeing her.

"That must have been Ficco I dreamed of," he told himself and knew it wasn't Ficco. If it had been Ficco, he would have been able to look into the man's face. He didn't know whom he had dreamed of. He didn't want to be aware that, if he had looked into the shape's face, he would have seen Edna. "I guess I must have figured out," he thought, "the wop was dead and haunting me."

He went into the bathroom to get a glass of water. He used the bathroom at the end of the hall instead of the one in the bedroom because, he thought, he didn't want to wake up Edna. Actually he wanted to get away from Edna and his dream of her. He drank deep, but the fear from the dream about Edna wouldn't stop in him. He still felt shaken. He stood in the darkness a moment, listening. He didn't know what he was listening for—something creeping, something coming towards him. He heard the electric icebox, far off in the kitchen, click and whir into a hum. He shook his head. "I'm getting to be a regular willy boy," he said to himself.

He wanted to try the doors to make sure they were locked, but he wouldn't let himself. He went into his daughter's room and straightened her blankets and stood looking at her, but he kept thinking that maybe the doors were unlocked and he really ought to go try them. He went into his son's room and fussed with the boy's covers and stood there a long time, fighting down the thought of the doors.

"Who's going to rob my house?" he thought. "That would make a hell of a story for the newspapers."

He went into the hall and stood there, again in the darkness, listening, and caught himself listening and went back into his bedroom. But he couldn't make himself get into bed. "Nobody can sleep after a dream like that," he decided.

He smoothed his blankets and moulded them to form a cave and he thought he would get his body chilled and slide into the cave of warmth within the blankets and then he would be able to sleep. He went into the kitchen and got a pencil and paper and wrote a note for the maid to keep the children home from school in the morning. He didn't have to turn on a light to write it. The pilot light from the stove was enough. He looked at the service door in the kitchen. It worked on a latch and it seemed to be shut tight. He wondered if the latch were open, but he wouldn't let himself try it. When he passed the front door on the way back to his bedroom, he looked at that, too, but he didn't try it. It seemed to be shut.

He didn't get into bed. He stood over it, thinking, and felt his body wasn't chilled enough yet and pulled a chair towards the window. He was about to sit in the chair when Edna spoke. The noise of the moving chair had awakened her.

"Ben," she said, "is that you, Ben?" Her voice was drowsy and unafraid.

"Yes, it's all right. Go to sleep."

She didn't answer. He had been facing her bed when pulling the chair and he stood that way now, trying to see her and see if she had fallen asleep again. He stayed that way a long time and he realized suddenly he wasn't afraid any more. The restlessness had died down in him. The sound of her voice had done it. He could think of his dream about Edna now and think only that it sure was some crazy dream to have and laugh at it. Edna's tough man was beginning even to feel sleepy.

"Can't you sleep, Ben?" she asked, drowsily.

He thought of telling her his dream and then felt like laughing. How could he make such a crazy thing sound as though it had happened, even if only in his head. "Oh no," he said. "I'm just going now."

She lay still, her eyes half closed. "Maybe," she said, "if I fix you a drink for a nightcap."

"That's all right. I'll be able to sleep now."

He slid into the cave of warmth under the blankets and the warmth stole over his chilled body and came up to his neck. He felt the warmth of his hiding place come and smiled. He had forgotten how the terror had drained out of him at the drowsy sound of Edna's voice and had forgotten even that she had spoken. His success in fighting back into hiding the knowledge that it was his love for Edna and his desire to be what he thought she wanted him to be that had made him tough was complete.

"This little cave was a good idea of mine," he thought and didn't think of anything else and was asleep in a few moments.

Edna got up before Ben. When she found out the children had been kept in the house by his orders, she came into the bedroom and woke him and he told her she had to go away with them. He had made up his mind.

"What is it?" She looked worried, but her voice was calm.

"It's nothing, just some wop bastard putting his nose in and you know how wops are. I don't want to take chances."

"I thought we were through with that kind of business."

"I thought so, too." Tucker shrugged. "Well, this wop is one of the reasons a man wants to stay young forever."

She flicked her head several times, as if she were trying to shake off something. "You've got to remember," she said, "that things are different nowadays, what with Hall and all."

"I know that."

"I know you know, but I thought I'd remind you."

"I'm taking everything into consideration," he said, "and you don't have to worry. I'm going to do everything I can to keep the whole thing quiet. You know that, make a settlement or something like that. Maybe that's the way it will turn out, but I don't want to take chances with the kids and leave temptation in his way or leave myself open to anything."

"You mean that . . . you mean he would . . . might . . . what a rat bastard that is!"

"I don't say that he would, but you know. . . . Anyway, I want to leave myself free and clear when the time comes to do something one way or the other and not be tied up."

They talked about where to go and he suggested the south. She said it was too far away, but he told her it was nice and warm there and safe, if she stayed out of Florida. Too many people in Florida knew her and word might get back where she was staying. They finally decided on Biloxi because no one they knew had ever heard of the town and he telephoned about trains. There was one leaving shortly after twelve o'clock. She got busy with packing, but he interrupted her and brought her back into the bedroom.

"Aren't you going to tell the kids it's a vacation or something?" he asked.

"What for?"

"What do you mean what for? What do you think they're going to think? They'll start guessing and maybe they'll guess the right thing."

"Don't you think they know already?"

"No they don't!"

"Yes they do. How long do you think you can keep your business a secret from them? They're not dumb."

"No! They don't know! How do you know they know?"

"I know all right."

"Well, I don't care," he said. "You go in and tell them this trip is for your health. You're sick. I don't give a damn what they know as long as they don't know I know they know and I can act before them like I should, like they got a right to expect from me."

McGuinness and the maid were told to make the trip also. McGuinness was sent for the car and money. Tucker would not let anybody else out of the house until it was time to leave. "You can buy anything you need down there or on the way," he told Edna.

"I'll come back as soon as the children are settled."

"You won't know where I'll be."

"But you said you were going to telephone me."

"Yes, but I won't tell you anything if you're going to act foolish. I think you ought to stay with the children."

Tucker said goodbye to them at the door to the apartment and then went into the living room to wait for Johnston.

Johnston had been sent out to rent a furnished apartment for Tucker somewhere in the neighborhood. Tucker didn't feel like traveling too far in daylight. He wasn't afraid to send his people out. He knew Ficco wouldn't bother them. Ficco would realize he couldn't force Tucker into a deal by grabbing off one of Tucker's men. Tucker would just tell Ficco to keep the man if he wanted him so much.

Tucker's people all understood that, too, but they never thought about it. They didn't think it peculiar or think anything at all about how Tucker was staying in hiding and sending them all over the city with their only protection themselves and the fact that getting them into trouble wouldn't do Ficco any good because Tucker wouldn't let himself be influenced by their troubles.

McGuinness was to drive the family down to the station and leave the car there and Johnston was to pick it up and come back and take Tucker to the new place.

"It's going to be a long wait in an empty house," thought Tucker, "more than an hour, maybe two or three hours."

As Tucker went away from the door and walked into the living room, the emptiness of the house rang in him and he listened to it. He thought of how he had stood listening in the darkness last night and shook his head and told himself, "I'm getting soft."

He knew he could look out the window and see Edna and the children get into the car and drive away, but he didn't go to the window. He kept thinking that he was getting soft and Joe was getting soft and Wheelock had never been hard and had never been able to discipline himself.

"They must be downstairs now," he thought.

He stared at the window from across the room and saw sky. He thought of them going through the lobby and going across the sidewalk and getting into the car and driving away. He felt the tug of the window, but he held himself back. He wanted to discipline himself. He wanted to find out if he had become too soft for what lay ahead.

He stood struggling against the tug of the window and finally he said to himself, "What kind of a damn fool am I, playing games with myself!" and went to the window and looked down. The car had gone. He looked at the empty street and felt the empty apartment at his back, and the feeling of emptiness sank in him and rang in him and filled him.

"I'm getting soft as teats," he thought.

XXII

THERE WERE two beds in the bedroom of Tucker's new apartment. They stood side by side and were separated only by a night table. On the table were a telephone and Tucker's gun.

During the conference that Tuesday night, Tucker sat on one bed and Wheelock and Joe sat facing him on the other. The beds were covered with lavender taffeta spreads and Tucker thought the spreads were nice and said he hated to louse them up, but he didn't want to talk in the front room because their voices would carry out into the hall.

They had to wait for Bunte. Johnston had been sent for him and they decided the old man must be getting very careful because it was taking him a long time to arrive.

Wheelock couldn't keep his eyes off the gun. He would say something and Tucker or Joe would answer and Wheelock would listen to the answer for a moment and then his glance would wander to the gun and bounce away from it. He would look at Joe and then back at the gun and look away hastily and see that Tucker was watching him. He would smile at Tucker and shrug a little and start listening once more. Then his glance would begin to wander again. He would look at the ceiling or around at the walls or at the lavender taffeta bed spreads or at the fingers of his hands. His glance would go from place to place and then stumble on the gun and leap away and start wandering again and come back to the gun again.

"I got one for you to carry, too," said Tucker.

"Why me?" Wheelock didn't look frightened, only suspicious.

Tucker felt a gun would give Wheelock a feeling of protection and would help the man pull himself together. "Ficco is smart," he told Wheelock, "but he thinks he's smarter than he is and, when a man thinks he's smarter than he is, you can't figure out what he's likely to do next. He's a Sunday thinker."

"No, sir," said Wheelock. "Not for me. Whoever heard of an attorney carrying a gun?"

"I think you ought to."

"Well, by God, I'm not going to! By God, I never heard of such a thing. What do you think I am?"

"I think you're a damn fool if you don't want to put something in your pocket that's going to make you feel better."

"Cut it out, will you please! I wouldn't know what to do with a gun."

"I don't know what to do with one either. I keep it on me, like a hot water bottle, to feel comfortable. I guess Joe's the only one around here who's handy with one of those things."

As soon as he had got to where he could, Tucker had hired whatever shooting was necessary. He now had the same distant feeling about guns that an industrialist has about the brass knuckles and tear gas shells he buys to deal with labor.

"Not me," said Joe. "I only used a rifle in the war." Joe had been one of those who hired the shooting for Tucker.

Wheelock smiled. He didn't believe either of them. "I guess I'll have to decline, Ben," he said. "A gun wouldn't be a hot water bottle for me, only a laxative."

Wheelock didn't look at the gun on the night table for a long time after that. He kept looking away from the gun and trying to discover what Tucker intended to do. Tucker told him he didn't know yet. He said he was still trying to find out and that there were two things he needed to know first: what Ficco was going to do; and how far it was possible to go to make him stop.

Johnston arrived first. He said Bunte had sent him up in the elevator and was using the stairs himself because he didn't want to be seen by the elevator operator.

"That's a fine how do you do!" cried Joe.

But Tucker said, why not, the man had a right to protect himself any way he saw fit.

It was a five-flights' walk. When Bunte arrived, he was puffing. Tucker sent Johnston downstairs to have a look around to see if anyone had spotted their arrival and was waiting to pick up Bunte's trail when he came out.

"Just walk around like you're out for your health," he said.

"Instead of Bunte's health," said Joe.

Tucker frowned at him and thought, "Now I got myself two nervous guys on my hands."

Bunte was a quiet, elderly man. He was of middle height and spare looking and had a long upper lip and large yellow teeth and a small, straight nose and gray eyes and thin, gray hair. He wore a gray suit under his blue overcoat. He kept his hat and coat on and sat on the edge of the bed alongside Tucker, his hands in his overcoat pockets. He looked earnest. Only the bottom button of his overcoat was fastened and the coat bulged wide and the thin body rose deep within it like a stick.

Tucker asked Bunte if Ficco had arranged any backing for himself and Bunte said he didn't think so.

"If he had, I would have heard of him," he explained, "and I never heard of the man until what you said."

Tucker told the story of how Ficco had picked up Gilliam and Bunte listened to the whole thing in silence.

"He made that second raid on my brother's bank, too," said Joe.

"Maybe," said Tucker. "Maybe that's right, to annoy us and so forth. So you see what he's up to, more or less. He's going to grab off somebody who knows who's in the combination. Then he's going to slap a payroll on all the banks he finds out about and, where he can't do that, he's going to tip them off and have the police throw them in the street. That must be why he picked Leo's bank for the raid, if he did. Yes, I guess he did. He knows he can't get a payroll out of Joe's brother. So he's going to bother us that way and bother the banks and, if we don't do something about it, then we're going to lose all the banks. They'll go over to him if we can't protect them."

"It can be fixed so it won't do him any good to tip off the banks," said Bunte.

"That's one of the things I want to know."

Bunte said, if there were some way the police could tell which were the combination's banks and controllers and collectors, he thought he could arrange that these people wouldn't be bothered. Wheelock figured out the way. They'd print some new business cards for Ruddy, the combination's bondsman, and anyone who had a card or any place where the card was tacked up belonged to the combination. Bunte said he could work it so that the card would be enough to keep off the police.

"All right," said Tucker, "but what about the rest?"

"Yes," said Joe, "what about those payrolls he's going to slap on our banks?"

"We can have the police pick up Ficco," suggested Bunte, "and put him away."

Wheelock was against that. "Gilliam is all he has done so far," he pointed out, "and that's quite a case for us to let get into court. You can't tell what will come out on the witness stand in a case like that."

"Not necessarily for Gilliam," said Bunte, "but for carrying a gun or whatever it is, whatever they can find."

"How are the police going to locate him?" asked Tucker.

"That oughtn't to be hard," Bunte replied, "with the help of your people and their own."

"And in the meantime, I got to sit here and wait and let Ficco work and maybe break down my policy setup or damage it anyway. I've put a lot of money into that business, my own money, just for good will and to build up the confidence there."

Bunte stood up, still looking earnest. "Well," he said, "if you want the help of the police on Ficco, let me know." He squeezed past Wheelock's knees and got out beyond the foot of the bed and stood there.

Tucker followed him slowly. "Is that your advice?" he asked. "It is."

"You think it's good advice?"

"I do, very good."

"I think it's lousy."

"Now take it easy, Ben," said Bunte and held up his hand and Wheelock sprang to his feet and cried, "Just a minute now, just a minute please."

"What do you mean, 'just a minute?'" said Tucker. "I've got pretty near $110,000 of my own money tied up in the business just for good will. I could have taken the banks over without a dime the way Ficco is trying if I had wanted, but I bought them because I wanted a business and these people to work for me and have confidence in me. If you think I'm going to sit here and wait for the police to catch up with Ficco while he goes around knocking down my good will that I bought, you're crazy. The hell with that. It's not my way of doing business."

"It's a sensible way," said Wheelock.

"Maybe I'm not sensible. Maybe I'm the kind of a sucker who thinks if he hired people to work for him and pays them to work for him, he can call on them for work."

Tucker glared at Bunte and Bunte buttoned his coat and pulled the collar straight and swung his hands back and forth a little to settle the coat around his shoulders.

"What do you want me to do," asked Bunte quietly, "put a cop in every one of your banks to keep Ficco off?"

"No," said Tucker.

"That wouldn't be very sensible, would it?"

"I didn't ask for that. What I want is to give the word to Ficco that if I hear any more out of him, I'll send over and see him."

"Then you do know where he is."

"No, but I can get word to him."

"Well, and then? And then, if he don't scare, what then?"

"Then," Tucker said, "I want to send over and see him."

The silence that came over the room was thick. Joe could be heard breathing. His mouth was slightly open and there was an intent look on his face. Wheelock was standing with his arms slightly raised. His head was tilted to one side and his face was puckered, as if with vexation, but his eyes were so bright there seemed to be tears in them. Tucker was facing Bunte sullenly and Bunte was looking thoughtful.

"Well, Ben," said Bunte, "I don't run your business, you know."

Tucker didn't answer.

"But I can tell you what I think, can't I?" asked Bunte.

"That's what I've been waiting for all evening," said Tucker, "what you really think."

"I think if you just take it easy and stay quiet, you won't hurt yourself."

"Hurt you, you mean."

"I mean that, too, hurt me and hurt you. If you get into the papers now, with Hall where he is . . . why the man has a blank check as far as jurisdiction goes. He can butt into anything he wants."

"Now it comes out," said Tucker. "Now we're getting the truth."

"Why, Ben, you knew that all the time."

"Yes, but I wanted to hear you say it, that you were afraid of him."

"Of course I'm afraid of him. Why not? There's a feeling for change in these hard times and Mr. Hall has put himself in the spot where he can ride along with it. The vote is hard up and restless and don't know what they want so they want to get even and anybody who tells them they're being robbed and will fix it, he's the hero. Mr. Hall's got a monopoly on that just now, that they think he can find out who's doing the robbing and can fix it. All we can do is wait until Mr. Hall gets himself jammed up doing nothing or does so much that he is handed a bigger little monopoly for himself."

"All of you? My people in my beer business, too, who are robbing my beer business from me, too?"

"Oh yes," said Bunte. "Everybody on our side of the street has to wait. For instance, I know where I can get enough on Mr. Hall, the way he's been prosecuting his cases, to have him disbarred or put in jail maybe. But what am I going to do with it? I could get people, the finest, highest class people in the city of New York to be witnesses in the case, but who would convict? Any jury or any bar association or newspaper would say, 'Mr. Hall, you are doing very fine work turning their own methods against these people. Mr. Hall, we're glad to know you realize you can't be honest hunting crooks.' They'd be afraid to say different. And if we come out in the open with a case against Mr. Hall, all we would do was convict ourselves. We would be the crooks for trying to protect crooks from prosecution. No, the way it works out, Mr. Hall can do anything because he's against us and we can do nothing because he's against us."

"That's the way it is when you're big and respectable and got a monopoly," said Wheelock.

Tucker didn't pay any attention to him. He remained looking at Bunte. "What I see is," he said, "I'm in the middle between you and Hall."

"Well," Bunte replied, "that's the situation, Ben. I thought you knew."

"I knew all right, but I wanted to hear you say it and hear what you can do about it."

"I can't do anything except play it careful. If you go ahead and get your name in the papers and smoke up all that old stuff, well, of course, naturally, I'll do all I can for you."

"You'd better."

"You don't have to say that, Ben."

"I just want there to be no mistake and you should hear it, that if Hall gets me I'm not the only one he's got."

"You don't have to say a thing like that to me, Ben. It's not a fair thing to say. All I'm trying to get you to do is to be careful like me."

"If I'm in trouble, you're in trouble. That's what I think is fair."

"I'm not going to fight with you," said Bunte.

"No. I know God damn well you're not and if you think I'm going to give up my business because a five-dollar wop killer says so and a college boy has his cock-eye on me, you're crazy." Tucker turned on Wheelock and Joe. "You hear that?" he cried.

They both looked startled, but didn't say anything. Bunte began to walk towards the door.

"Wait a minute," said Tucker. "Before you go, I want a pistol permit for Wheelock here."

Bunte turned in surprise.

"Yes," Tucker said. "I want to see if there's something you can do for the money I pay you."

"Right now, at this hour of the night?"

"Right now, right this minute. There's the telephone by the bed there." He pointed to it. "If you can't do anything for me, I don't know what the hell you're doing on my payroll."

"I don't want a gun," said Wheelock.

Tucker turned on him, his finger still pointing to the telephone on the night table. "Shut up," he said. "You keep out of this and keep your mouth shut."

Bunte stood calmly. He thought, if Tucker were going to become unmanageable, maybe the time had come to beat Hall to it and arrest him first. But he had known Tucker a long time and had worked with him for many years. He felt that, in the end, when the showdown came, Tucker would be manageable. He always had been and, besides, there would be time enough to beat Hall to the arrest when the showdown came. He would know about a showdown before Hall could.

"Wheelock will have to have his fingerprints taken," he said. "It would be better in the morning."

"I want it done right now," said Tucker.

"All right, Ben, but you're making a lot of fuss for nothing."

"It's not nothing to me."

"Be reasonable," said Wheelock. "I'm tired. I don't want to go all the way downtown to headquarters at this hour of the night."

"All right," Tucker said, "but I want to see it arranged for tomorrow right now, right on that telephone there, so I can be sure there will be no stalling."

The police commissioner's office was the only one with the power to authorize pistol permits. Bunte went to the telephone with a small smile on his face, like one humoring a stubborn child. "Is it clean?" he asked, pointing to the instrument.

"It's all right," said Tucker. "Nobody knows I'm here. They can't have a tap yet."

They all remained quiet when Bunte talked. He found out the commissioner wasn't home and he called a deputy commissioner and they all heard the man's voice come, small and scratchy, through the telephone. "It's for a very good friend of mine," said Bunte and spelled Wheelock's name.

"Is that Tucker's lawyer?" they heard the deputy say and Wheelock winced and looked around helplessly.

"I'm very anxious to oblige him," said Bunte.

Then they heard the deputy tell Bunte the name of the police officer who would take care of it tomorrow and say that Wheelock could come in any time after nine in the morning.

When Bunte had finished relating the conversation to Tucker, he smiled. "You know," he said in a quiet, friendly voice, "it's not a little thing that I'm doing in getting the police to watch out for Ruddy's cards."

Tucker looked embarrassed. "I guess that's right, Ed," he said.

"You're a little nervous, is that it, lost your head a little bit, is that it?"

"Well, you know how it is." Tucker smiled shyly.

After Bunte left, Joe wanted to know if Tucker thought Ficco was going to grab off Leo.

"I'm not a mind reader," Tucker told him.

"I want to know," cried Joe angrily. "Leo can't take care of himself so good and, if I tell him about Ficco, he's going to fly off the handle and Christ knows what he'll do."

"He'll do what he has to do, like everybody else."

"I don't think Leo is taking any more of a chance than the rest of us," said Wheelock.

"Yes," Tucker said. "You heard what Gilliam said, that Ficco give the word Leo was out. If he's going after one of us, I'm the one. Why should he bother with you fellows?"

"All right," said Joe, "why couldn't you say that in the first place instead of playing around and putting the needle in me?"

Joe left in a few moments, still nervous and angry, and only Wheelock remained with Tucker. Johnston had picked up Bunte downstairs and was driving him to where he could take a taxi safely.

"We're jammed up again, aren't we?" Tucker said to Wheelock.

"Yes, and I still don't know what you intend to do."

"It's a tough question, isn't it?" Tucker rubbed his chin and looked down at the floor and then back at Wheelock. "If I put shooters into the bank to keep Ficco off," he said, "then I got the shooters working for me all over again and we'll be where we were in the beginning, our hands all dirty all over again. Isn't that right?"

"That's right."

"And if I go after the son of a bitch, or just stand pat in front of the son of a bitch, there's going to be trouble and we'll be out in the open where the newspapers will see us and most of the trouble is going to come from Bunte. I know that guy. I know all them guys. Bunte'd kick me for a goal so fast that college boy, Hall, wouldn't have a chance to take his sweater off, no less get into the game."

"He would. So, what are you going to do?"

"I don't know yet," said Tucker, "but I got a hundred and eight or ten thousand dollars of my own money laying in the business for good will and I'll tell you this. I'll see Ficco and Hall and Bunte and the whole God damn bunch of them in hell first before I let that get hurt."

"Yourself, too?"

"What?"

"Yourself, too, in hell? You'll see that, too, yourself hurt, too?" Wheelock was smiling steadily and unpleasantly.

"No! That's my money. That's what I see. That's my money and there's going to be a return on it for me. That's what I see."

XXIII

Tucker told Wheelock to try not to be seen going out of the apartment house. So Henry asked the elevator man to get a taxi for him. He explained he had a cold and didn't want to wait outside.

He stood in the foyer until the cab drew up before the door and then hurried across the sidewalk, head down, his hat pulled over his face and his collar turned up. He told the driver to take him to his apartment on Central Park West. It was the nearest one.

As the cab moved along, Henry thought of himself running across the sidewalk. "Like a bandit," he thought, "with a mask over my face." It occurred to him it had been a dead giveaway to the elevator man about the new tenant in the house. Then he decided maybe it had not been. Maybe the man believed he had a cold and was bundling up against the night air. Henry laughed. He laughed aloud with a single, unhappy, nervous, breathy cry. "Now," he said to himself, "I've climbed up in the world to where I have to lie to prove I'm not a bandit with a mask on my face."

His west-side apartment smelled musty. He hadn't been there in a long time. His manservant was at his Park Avenue place and the couple he kept were at his apartment on 58th Street. He went into the kitchen and got some ice and put it in a glass and filled it almost to the top with scotch. He held up the glass and looked at it thoughtfully. "I guess the ice waters it enough," he told himself.

He drank the whiskey as if it were water, in consecutive swallows, without taking the glass from his lips. He put down the glass and stood still a moment, waiting for the effect of the drink. There was no effect.

"I really need brandy," he thought. "It tastes softer."

He went into the living room and got some brandy and looked at the label carefully. He didn't see what he was reading.

"I'll take brandy and gin and rye," he thought, "and bourbon and scotch and rum and sweet cream and ginger ale and put it in the same glass and drink it and blow up and bust and still I won't get my luck back." He poured the brandy into a highball glass. His hand shook and he poured more than he had intended. "My luck is all run out now for the rest of my life," he thought.

He drank the brandy as he had drunk the scotch, without taking the glass from his lips, and stood waiting a moment. He could hear himself breathe. His breath came through his nose slowly and evenly, with a small, tickling sound.

A muscle twitch had developed recently in his cheek alongside his mouth. It had come suddenly and it would go on for a few minutes and then stop. It started now, as he stood waiting for the brandy to take hold. He could feel it. It pulled the whole side of his mouth. He put his hand on it and felt it work under his fingers. He tried to hold it down. It kicked his fingers loose and slid under them. He laughed and poured another brandy, a larger one. "A real big one this time," he told himself, looking at it and running the tip of his tongue greedily along his lips. He drank it as he had drunk the others and then, once more, stood waiting. He held the bottle in one hand, the glass in the other. "I must have put down pretty near a pint now," he thought.

But he couldn't feel anything except the warm, oily taste of the brandy. The warm, oily taste filled his mouth and ran down his throat and ended in his chest. He poured another drink and set down the bottle and touched his hand gingerly to his chest. His chest was swarming with restlessness. The restlessness swarmed so thickly, he thought he would be able to feel it with his hand, but he couldn't. He felt only his heart, beating rapidly. The beat was so distinct, it made him feel he was holding his heart in his hand.

His cheek was still twitching. He took his drink and went to the mirror over the fireplace and watched his cheek work. The twitch felt worse than it looked. It was hardly more than a flicker, but it was steady. It would pull his mouth to one side and then stop and his mouth would flop back and then it would pull his mouth to one side again. He watched it, feeling like laughing to keep down the fear in him, and lifted his glass to his lips to see if the twitching would go on while he was drinking. It didn't.

"Well," he thought, "at least I've found the cure." He patted the glass. "Good lill-tle old cure," he said to himself and looked at the glass fondly.

The moment he had lowered the glass, the twitching had resumed. It was as though someone inside his cheek were kicking. "A regular floor show," he thought.

"Come on, baby," he said aloud, "swing that thing!"

His voice sounded loud and lonely in the apartment. He looked around startled. "If I don't get out of here," he told himself, "I'll be making faces at myself all night."

He finished his drink and went back to the table to put away the glass and poured another drink and got it down fast and stood waiting. There was no effect. "What I need," he thought, "is to hit myself over the head with the bottle if I want any good out of it."

He walked out of the apartment quickly. As he stood waiting for the elevator, he sighed. Then he remembered he had not turned out the lights. "Let them burn," he thought. "Let them be bright as bejesus. Let my money put light in a black place for once, instead of the opposite, instead of black in a light place."

Wheelock was afraid to go back into the lonely apartment.

Downstairs, Wheelock got another taxi and told the driver to take him to his downtown apartment. Midway, he changed his mind and told the driver to take him to Park Avenue. Then he said to take him to Broadway and 49th Street.

The driver turned and looked at him.

"Don't worry," Wheelock laughed. "We'll get somewhere yet." He sat back and put his feet on the folding seat. "The hell with him," he thought. "What do I care what he thinks or who he thinks or if he thinks what or why or who the hell he thinks he is anyway."

He had decided Broadway would take care of him. "A man can

get anything he wants there," he thought, "even a good night's sleep." Now, as he sat back relaxed, he remembered Doris suddenly. He hadn't thought of her since their strange hour together on Thanksgiving, nearly two weeks before. But he must have been thinking of her just now. "Beat It!" was playing a theater around the corner from 49th Street. No, he decided, what for? What did she have for him that he couldn't pick off any chorus line in town? There was plenty better than her. The telephone book was filled with better than her. That's why the telephone book was so big, there were so many better.

Henry got out of the cab at the corner of 49th Street and Broadway and stood a moment debating where to go and then went looking for Doris, thinking, as he walked, he was a damn fool, she was going to bore him to death, she was going to make him sick of himself, she was so hot for him, too easy to get, too young and she didn't have enough style and she was too dumb and vacant and unformed and empty-faced and had a body only a sick old man could like, a child's body, and she was too this and too that and one thing and another and besides he could fall down a subway stairs and land on something better. He thought all this as he kept walking towards Doris and laughed at himself for continuing to walk and was angry with himself and said to himself, "What's got into me? Am I crazy?" and thought, "Do I need her to make me more sick of myself than I am already?" and kept on walking.

He found Pop at the stage door and Pop said Miss Duvenal had left some time before with a crowd of girls from the show and that probably they were all at "The White Way Drugs" on Seventh Avenue. "They give two balls of ice cream with their chocolate floats," he explained, "so the girls always go there."

❧

The drug store was lit so brightly, it hurt Wheelock's eyes. It was a long, L-shaped store with tables at the rear around the foot of the L. A flutter of girl voices and girl steps came from the rear of the store, and Wheelock went towards the flutter slowly, blinking and squinting.

The girls appeared to be at home in the place. As Wheelock reached them, one girl found something new in lipstick at the counter and squealed and the others thronged around her and looked at what she held and squealed, too, and thrust their bodies towards the two young pharmacy clerks behind the counter. They all flirted with the two placidly grinning men and held a squeal competition and a body-thrusting competition and pouted and complained of the price of the lipstick and swished their skirts and giggled and pulled at each other and retreated with their eyes while thrusting up their bodies.

"They're practicing on the goofs," thought Wheelock. He stood on the edge of their excitement, hat in hand. He was pale. The edge of his hair stuck to his forehead while the rest of it was rumpled into a pile. The twitch was beginning again in his face. He noticed Doris pouting in the throng around the lipstick and put his hand to his cheek. The twitch kept on. It felt like a living thing.

Doris stopped pouting. She wandered back to her table, making seductive advances to the air with her body as she walked, and sat down and giggled aloud at herself and sucked up some chocolate milk through a straw and lifted her head to call something to one of the girls still at the counter and saw him. Wheelock forced his mouth into a wide smile of greeting. He wanted to halt the twitch in his cheek. She did not smile at him. She sat watching him without moving, her head a little raised, chocolated bubbles beading her lips. He came towards her slowly. He held his hat in his hand and held a smile on his tired face.

Doris had told the girls in the dressing room all about Wheelock. "I know that type," one of them had said, "and I wouldn't go too far if I were you." She had spoken earnestly and as if she knew more than she wanted to say. But then there were always girls who liked to appear to know more than they did.

"I didn't even drop a hint," Doris had replied. "I just sat there and he ran out and bought everything himself. I don't see what's wrong about that, if a man wants to do that."

"Yes, but the *man!* That's the point, *the man* who did it!"

It developed finally that Wheelock had been pointed out to her in a night club as a big shot gang lawyer. "I don't see what's wrong with being a lawyer," Doris had said. But she had been alarmed anyway. In movies, the gang lawyers always seemed to be just as much hoodlums as the gangsters.

So Doris sat motionless now, watching Wheelock, and not knowing what to do or say. A silence came over the girls as Henry made his way through them. He stopped before Doris.

"I just dropped in for a chocolate soda," he said, "and look what I find—a peach."

"Yes you did!"

Her voice annoyed him. There was a real simper in it and it was high and frail and dull and sounded like the echo of an empty remark. Wheelock looked around irritably at the other girls. One of them had sat down alongside Doris and the others were standing around, carefully avoiding noticing him.

"Let's get out of here and go somewhere," he said.

"I'm tired," Doris told him. "I've been out every night this week. I need to go home and sleep."

"It's only Tuesday."

She looked embarrassed. She had forgotten the date. "I'm not dressed at all," she said.

"We'll go somewhere where it will be all right to be naked."

"Oh, Mr. Wheelock!" Her face flushed. "Puh-leeze!"

He did not listen to her. He was trying to think of her naked. He tried to think of her legs naked and spread upon a sheet and of the soft, white belly and breasts he had seen during one of the numbers in the show, but he couldn't do it. The picture wouldn't stay in his mind any longer than the alcohol had. He couldn't think of anything or feel anything except the swarming in his chest.

"Come on!" he said. His voice was sharp and commanding. He heard its tone and forced himself to smile and forced himself to add slowly, "You're only wasting valuable time arguing."

She began to say something about this not being the way to make a date, but he put his hand into his pocket and pulled out a large roll of bills.

"Where's your check?" he asked.

Doris got up and drew her coat around her. He noticed it was the same cloth coat with cheap fur collar she had worn Thanksgiving. She gave him the check silently. Doris had never seen so much money before in a man's hand.

The girls called goodnight to her. One said, "Don't do anything I wouldn't do," and Doris replied, "I can't imagine what that would be, dearie," and another one, the one who had said Wheelock was a gang lawyer, called out in a brittle tone, "Don't take any wooden nickels." Doris didn't answer her.

Wheelock nodded and waved and smiled goodbye to all of them, but he hadn't really taken them in. They weren't people to him, just faces and shapes and sounds.

At first, they stood up at a bar and talked of where to go. Doris had a single glass of sherry. She conserved it while Henry drank scotch whiskey rapidly, sometimes straight, sometimes with water and said he would take her to a society place where society people went to hear a piano player sing dirty songs in a refined way. He told her the society people smacked their eyes over the piano player and Doris protested. She said she didn't believe real genuine society people acted that way.

"Look in the social register," he told her. "It's all there, the whole story. Marriage, divorce, marry to get divorced, divorce to get married, all there." Somebody had to rouse them up to do all this, he said, to go through all the same, fatiguing motions over and over again with the same people or reasonable facsimiles of the same people. The society women couldn't rouse their men either to marry them or divorce them and the society men couldn't rouse their women. "Too well bred," he explained, "too refined. Can't love 'em or leave 'em, only let 'em."

"You're making this up," said Doris. Then she added, "But go on please," and snuggled up to her glass of wine with a mock shiver of mock delight.

"Oh no," he said, "it's the exact truth, printed plain right there in the social register. I'll buy you a copy to look it up for yourself." But, he said, there was no use reading about it in a dry old, dull old book when they could go around the corner there, down the block there and see the whole thing lived out. The society people all dressed up very refined, powder on the jowls for the men and for the ladies a touch of perfume on the whatchamacallit, the lips of the breasts, and the ladies and the gentlemen acting very refined with each other while waiting for the piano player to come in and go to work on them. And a kind of, well . . . sort of nervous feeling in the whole bunch of them, like you see in fellows straightening their ties and buttoning their suit coats while waiting for the girls in the parlor of a you know, a . . . what do you call them back home?

"Well," said Doris brightly and bravely, "what do you call them?"

"I? I call them whorehouses."

"Oh," she looked confused. "I didn't know . . . I mean . . . but . . ."

"You see what happens?" he said unsmilingly. "I wanted to use an expression you wouldn't mind, but you wouldn't help me. I tried my best for you, but you wouldn't help me. Anyway, you get the picture. You see the picture. Of the fellows in the parlor setting their ties straight, buttoning up all the buttons on their suit coats while waiting for the girls to come in and wreck them. Wreck them! Yes, yes, wreck them, wreck them outside, and inside, too. Take their clothes off and pull their bones right out of their bodies. Reach tongues in their mouths and suck their brains out right through their mouths! That's what!"

"Goodness, is that what goes on?"

"Yes, that's what goes on. Sometimes. When it's good. For the minute that it's good."

There had been greedy elation in Henry's eyes as he talked, but now, looking at Doris, noticing her, the elation vanished and he said contemptuously, "Don't be brave with me. You're a child, you know, so why try to play you're a woman with me." He saw her effortful gaiety vanish and, before she could reply to him, he added gently, "Because you're my love song. Remember? My little love song, the one I can't understand."

He rested his hand on hers and then folded her hand softly in his. She looked at their entwined hands a moment and then, firmly and ostentatiously, wriggled free. He burst into laughter. Laughing, he leaned towards her, and, laughing, put his arm around her waist and, still laughing, squeezed her.

"You're wonderful," he cried. "You're very good for me, Doris, do you know?"

She loosened his grasp deliberately and moved away from him, smoothing her coat and straightening her hat. There was a contented look on her face. "You certainly are a very fast worker, Mr. Wheelock," she told him.

He was startled and then alarmed. He hadn't thought of his arm around her in that way. He laughed uncertainly. But he couldn't laugh the alarm away. He had squeezed her and it hadn't meant anything to him. He had felt the flesh of her body within her coat and his arm had been dead on it and his body had been dead alongside it. It wasn't right. It wasn't normal to be that way. A feeling of loneliness fell into him like a stone.

"What is this!" he cried. "What is the matter with me?"

Doris's whole face opened with fear.

"I mean," he said hastily, "you're the first one in years who threw me off the track once I started talking." She frightens so easily, he thought. She must be scared of me. She must have heard about me somewhere. No, what could she have heard? Where could she have heard? No, no, he was imagining things. He was imagining everything. He had worked up all this fear and restlessness in himself with his imagination. "Particularly," he went on, "when I was in the middle of a good story, good description, going good like that about society people whom I love, whom I adore and admire and respect and think of as the backbone of the nation, that part of the backbone the nation should sit down on if it wants to be comfort-

able. Because I'm communistic that way, a little communistic about
my love for the folks in society."

"Now you're off again."

"That's right, off. I'd tell you the story of how society people
made a communist out of me, but we were on another story, weren't
we, and I don't want to get all mixed up." He was delighted to
have hinted at the story of why he didn't like wealthy people of
position. He had once been ambitious to marry a woman of that
class, to help his career, but he had never met any he dared ask
and so he had never asked any woman to marry him. There was
a pleasurable thrill of danger for him in lifting the edge of so
revealing a truth about himself and he plunged on ardently, excited
words running from his mouth. "We were on the story of the piano
player that we're going to see when we get out of here, finish drinking here, society's darling piano player, and how the refined people,
the men with jewels in their check books and the women with
just a weenchy, exciting little dash of perfume on the lips of their
breasts, sit waiting for him to come on and sing to them, tickle
the ivories for them, tickle them with the ivories. How they sit
there with style, but, just the same, like the boys in the plush parlor
of the house of bad, the house there, the boys who come to be
wrecked there and straighten their ties because they are nervous
while waiting to be wrecked."

"I can't make up my mind if you're serious or what."

"I'm serious, dead serious. You'll see yourself how the society
people sit there waiting for him."

"Not me I won't."

"Yes you, you'll see for yourself, walk in and sit down and look
around and see for yourself."

Then he began to tell her, in a low, excited tone, not looking at
her, looking into his glass and at the bar and down at his feet and
at her feet and at her hands and at her wine glass, why the piano
player was thought to be so good. This fellow, he said, had a way
of curling his tongue around every dirty word he sang and licking
its double meanings, and a way of breathing over the spaces between

the words so that they, too, became hot. He made "love" sound like
a four-letter word. That was his art and it had made him rich and
admired by society. She would see the debutantes there, he said, the
widows and divorcees and their males, sitting there and listening
to him. They would pick at the tablecloths as he sang and then begin
to jump up and down a little bit in their chairs, the whole roomful
of them, and pick at the tablecloths harder and start grabbing up
the tablecloths in their fists and blurt, my, oh my, oh my, my, my,
oh, oh, oh you, oh hoo, hooooh, oooooooh, my . . . and gasp, and
cry out, MY, HOW WITTY! and sit back all relaxed.

Henry saw Doris looking at him aghast. She seemed shocked and
revolted at him for a moment. Then she frowned.

"Yes, that's right," he cried into her frown, "that's how good that
fellow's tongue is." He grinned at her abruptly. "And society
wouldn't be without him because he keeps them all from marrying
beneath them. When they have him to rouse them up, they can put
up with each other."

Doris's face wrinkled with disgust. "I'd rather go some place else
if you don't mind," she said.

He laughed. "Anything you say," he told her. "This is your evening. I'm going to be the fellow with the ruby. Remember I told
you about him? The fellow who gives the girl the ruby and wants
nothing back for himself because he is perverted, an awful, terrible,
wicked monster. That's me tonight. Wicked, a monster." He leered
at her mockingly. "A monster to make you goose-pimply because
I'm going to give you everything and not want nothing back from
you."

"How you go on. Just talking and talking, without making sense.
If that's all the bad there was in the world, to give without wanting
something in return, it would be all right. If everybody was Santa
Claus all the time, it would be Christmas every day, wouldn't it?"

"You think so?" he said. He looked at her mockingly. There was
a small smile on his face. "Yes," he said at last, "I think you really
think so. But that's only because you are a child. You don't know
yet that it's not simple to be bad. It's the hardest thing in the world.

I mean, to be really bad, real rotten bad. That takes a whole lifetime. It's not just something that you can go out and do, adultery,
stealing, murder. That's not bad."

"It'll do for a start."

"No, child," he cried suddenly. He looked distracted. He seemed
to be crying out to himself. "That's not bad. It's not really bad to
take another man's wife or life or spit in the face of your father.
Yes, even that, even to spit, from the bottom of your heart, in the
face of your father. Those things happen to anybody in a moment
when he gets himself in a situation, or a week or a month or a year
when a man is in a certain kind of situation that is too much for
him. Everybody has it in him and it's an accident when it comes
out. But real badness, real rotten badness, where you do something
that's against your whole nature, and that rots your whole nature
. . . it takes a lifetime."

He seemed not to realize any more she was before him. He was
fighting to keep tears out of his eyes. Doris looked at him a moment,
puzzled, and then looked away uncomfortably and thought, "He
must be sick, have a fever or something, the way he runs on in this
nonsense way."

Henry calmed himself with a violent effort. He saw Doris was
not looking at him. He grasped her shoulder. "Look," he said
eagerly, "look, look, look at me. We'll forget the society people in
the blue book. I'll take you to a middle-class place with fat, whole-
some people there, big, solid burgher people. That's where we'll go,
to this place, what's its name, where they got a $2 dinner and Leila
Orr singing."

"The Famous Palace."

"That's right. She's marvelous, isn't she?"

"I like her work very much."

"A child. A body like a child and a face and a voice like a child
and those skinny little arms of hers that she holds out."

"She's got a high-class musical instrument in her throat."

"Yes, yes, her voice goes out and runs along her arms. It's one of
those high, sleepy-child voices and she makes you sit there dreaming
and you wake up and think she's sitting in your lap."

"She knows how to project her personality. That's something. If you got that on the stage, projection, you got everything."

"Yes, yes! You think so? That's what she's got. The ability to sit in the whole audience's lap and dandle there and snuggle and coo and fondle there like a sleepy-eepy baby child. And then? Then? Because, you see, that's not enough. The middle class can go home and get that. They don't have to spend $2 for indigestion with their dinner to get that. Then, then, you know what? Then, she socks it in. Then, she gives it the business."

"Who? Leila Orr?"

"Yes, yes, I've seen her. Socks it in. Sings little girl songs with dirty meanings and licks up, slicks up the meanings with her little girl tongue. That's horrible, you know. That's real sewer stuff. She takes advantage of the whole idea of childhood to get people to take her on their laps and then, while she's cooing and snuggling eepy-eepy-beddie stuff, you suddenly realize she's socking it in, giving the business."

"You're crazy. You're absolutely a madman."

"No, no, and you know what's worse, more horrible? What the burghers do. They gurgle over her. They take her in their laps and make out to themselves they're enjoying her, that way, you know, the way good, middle-class people enjoy a likable child's talents, when what they're really enjoying is that she makes their glands wiggle. Yes, that's what they all feel, while they sit there saying, 'Ain't she cute!' They feel every single one of their glands wiggling."

"For God sakes, Mr. Wheelock! Please! Don't you ever think anything is nice?"

"What?"

"I know Leila's work. Isn't there anything nice to you in the world?"

"Nice? Oh yes. It's very nice, quite nice when the glands wiggle, all of them at once, like Toscanini playing an orchestra."

"That's not so. I've heard her many times. I know it's just not so and it's just that you can't believe anything is nice."

"No, I can't," he said.

She was silent.

"I can't," he told her. "That's a simple fact. There is nothing in the whole world, nothing on earth that anyone has done anywhere to anybody or to himself that is nice. It can't be in this world."

She remained silent.

"Did you hear what I said?" he cried. "Do you understand what I said?"

"I don't know what you're talking about," she replied in a low voice. "What are you trying to do here?"

"I? Trying to do?"

"Yes. What are you trying to do to me?"

"To you? To you? Nothing. You can rely on that. Nothing. Nothing at all. I'm going to give you everything and not ask anything from you."

"I think," she said, "I'm getting sleepy and would like to go home."

"Are you afraid of my kind of wickedness?"

"No, but it's late. It's after one o'clock."

He became contrite suddenly. "We'll go just to one place to see a floor show and that's all," he said.

"I think not." She made a move away from him.

He came close to her. "You must give me a chance," he entreated gently.

"Chance to do what?"

"Chance to be with you. We've just started together."

"But you're sick. You ought to go home, too."

"You're acute, aren't you, for all your . . . air . . . I mean, of innocence. But you overlooked one thing. I have no home, no, no home. So, let's just go to one floor show and that's all."

"Just one, then."

"I see you are like all women, and can't resist logic," he said and grinned at her, engagingly.

❧

Then Wheelock made an effort and succeeded in being charming. So there was one floor show and after that another, then a third, a fourth and a fifth. He took her to many hotels. He liked going through the lobbies with their late-night feel and feel of sleep and empty lounge chairs and empty writing tables and pale, quiet clerks. He liked passing the empty registry desks where he might buy a room for self and wife and liked loitering past the white, waiting registry cards and black, waiting pens and glancing at the clerks and glancing at Doris, who never seemed to look, and then, at the end, coming to the "spot"—a room, packed, loud, and smashing away the night.

The feel of night and bed came to the edge of the room, right up to the open door, and stood there. It couldn't go any farther. The drummer kept it off. He leaned close to his drum and grinned and beat fast, then faster and faster and faster and the feel of night stood on the edge of the drum sounds and waited. When the drummer stopped, the night and the quiet of bed came through the door and fell on the people and the people all looked as though they were about to go away to sleep. But, as soon as the drum sounds began, night and quiet fell back and nobody looked as if he were ready for bed, not even the drunken men who lay sleeping with their heads on the tables. Everybody suddenly looked like a drummer and leaned close to each other and grinned and beat against each other's ear drums with fast talk and faster and faster talk.

After a while, there were no more floor shows, only drinking—Wheelock drinking and Doris looking at people and making simple, scratchy comments on them and their clothes. Henry drank continually in the greedy, persistent way in which an invalid breathes. He soon ceased to dance with her. He was too tired to manage his legs. She thought the liquor was getting to him and pressed him to eat, but he refused to eat and did not seem drunk. Yet, drink as he would, tired as he was and unmanageable as his legs became, he remained restless. He transformed their night-long tour of the city's entertainment area into a run through a factory of sensations.

Nevertheless, he entertained and managed to please her. He allowed her to talk. He appeared interested in what she said. At times, he deliberately made comments of his own on people present and the clothes they wore, so that she might feel comfortable with him and giggle into his shoulder and poke at him with a swizzle stick and say he was really terrible.

Her delight in him was interrupted once in a taxicab when, unexpectedly, in an astonishingly youthful, desperate way, he grabbed at her. He sprang and grabbed like an animal in darkness. When she struggled, frightened by the unexpectedness of an approach that was actually an assault, he pushed her from him so abruptly her shoulder hit against the wall of the cab.

She was angry and he laughed at her. Then he said he was sorry, he had thought the cab was falling over. That was why he had grabbed her.

"I'd like to be friends with you," Doris said. "I like you very much. I think you're very nice and I'd like you to think that I'm nice, too."

"All right, nice," he said. "We'll be sisters together."

She took both his hands and folded them in her lap and covered them with her hands. "Now," she said anxiously, "isn't that better?"

"It's better than handcuffs," he told her.

He tried to free his hands, but she clung to them and, after a moment, he was quiet. His head sank against her shoulder. He closed his eyes and was still. She could feel him trembling alongside her and, slowly, become still. If he slept a little or ate a little, she thought, he wouldn't be so drunk and would act nicer and talk nicer because he really was nice even if he did talk so awful fresh sometimes and always about the same thing. Whatever he started to talk about or she started to talk about, it always came back to the same thing. But that was just because he was sick tonight, that's all, had a fever or something the way he was shaking inside and running so loose at the mouth sometimes, and he drank like that in order not to be sick and give her a good time, and the drinking made him nervous and talk coarse and always about the same thing.

She tried to get him to go home several times, but he refused.

❧

At the end, they came to a place where the band had gone home and there were only a few people left.

"Now we can get down to work," said Henry. He rubbed his hands and ordered a double brandy.

Doris took up a menu and said she was going to have something to eat. It was her second supper and, for the second time, she said she never had to worry about her figure.

"Eating takes too much time off from drinking," he told her.

She studied the menu carefully. Disappointingly, there were no prices on it. She knew that meant everything would be expensive, but she wanted to know just how expensive. "I think I'll have some nice clams and a nice steak sandwich rare," she said to the waiter.

"I'll have scotch to make the next brandy taste better."

"I'm sure you would feel better if you had a nice piece of steak, too," she told Henry. She puckered her lips. "Please, for my sake," she begged.

Henry stared somberly at her puckered lips. Then he roused himself and smiled. "You know what would make me feel better, don't you?" He shaped a woman in the air with his hands. "Feel betterer and betterer the betterer you feel," he said.

The waiter hovered over them a moment longer. Then he went away.

"Why do you always talk about the same thing? Why?" she cried.

"Why?" He was startled. "What else is there to talk about?"

"No, you always talk about it. Talk, talk, drive yourself to talk."

"Talk and not do?" He looked into her eyes. He mocked her with his smile. "Is that the complaint? Talk and not do?" His voice was gentle and mocking. She returned his gaze steadily. She seemed frightened, but determined, timid, but full of longing and he realized suddenly that, if he were to lean over now and kiss her, she would like it. She would sit straight and hold her lips straight, but she would like it and maybe, too, she would fall in love with him, really fall in love, and he would have that. For the first time in his life, he would have a girl really in love with him.

He looked away. The mocking smile disappeared and his face flushed slightly. "You know why I talk like that?" he said. "I'm diseased, not the way you think, not wounded by pleasure as they say . . ." the flutter of mockery in his mind ceased and he added in a low tone, ". . . but I mean, I got an abscess in my brain and it drips out of my mouth."

"What? Hey!" She jumped a little. "Oh," she said petulantly, "you're joking."

"No, I'm not." Mockery fluttered up in him again. He smiled. "It's a real abscess. I'm abscessed with you."

"For goodness sake, Henry, can't you be serious a minute!"

"Yes," he said. His smile vanished. He leaned across the table and took her face in his two hands. "Yes, I can," he said. "I can be serious." He held her face gently a moment and then he kissed her gently. Her lips were stiff against his. "I can be very serious," he said and kissed her gently again. Her lips remained stiff. Her body remained bent unyieldingly towards him and he took her lips between his. He held her lips loosely in his and felt them soften and thicken and grow warm and stir. It was life in his mouth. It was like kissing the flesh of her heart.

"No," she mumbled into his mouth. Her breath moved among the bones of his face. "Please, no." She put her hand on his chest and he released her abruptly and sat far back in his chair. His face was flushed again. His eyes were unsteady, but once more there was a mocking smile on his lips.

She looked at his mocking smile angrily. Then she turned her head away and lowered it into the menu. She believed tears would come into her eyes and she didn't want him to see them. Her face colored up into her hair. Her lower lip began to quiver and she clasped it between her teeth.

Henry stared fixedly at her lowered head. His mind had become blank. Then he struggled back to thought of her. He noticed a small fold in the nape of her neck. It was fuzzy with red gold hair. He put his finger against his lips and touched the fold. "Boo," he said, "I kissed you."

Her head darted up. The smile was still on his face, but it was soft now and she could see that his eyes were afloat in fatigue. He looked like a boy loving sexlessly, perhaps his mother, perhaps a nurse, because he felt sorry for her.

"Don't treat me like that," she cried intensely, "like I was nothing. You have no right. I know I'm nothing to you, but you're nothing to me, either, mister. Remember that."

"I can't believe it," he mocked at her. "I thought we were going to be sisters." Then, again, the flutter of mockery in his brain halted. "I treat you like that," he said, "because I'm afraid of you, to be too serious with you."

"Yes sure," she said, but the color in her large, grape-shaped eyes seemed to curl with pleasure.

"That's right, you're full of danger, beautiful and full of danger for me. You will take my life between your lips and I will love you. Why should I love you? Is there any reason to love anybody?"

"Some people think up reasons later. That's been done, to pass the time that way."

"Yes, later, to fool themselves. But don't, don't . . . not to talk about it. I will not be serious with you. No, no, tell me, why should I let myself fall in love with you. You're a girl now, beautiful eyes and so forth, beautiful so forths, and etcetera, too, I guess, have to guess, can't see through this damned table. And, if I love you, you won't be a girl any more. You'll be smoke in my mind."

"Now you're talking crazy again."

"No, no, I know what it is."

"I bet you do."

"Of course! Of course, I do. Your body will be in my clothes. Why should I allow it, when I pay so much for a proper fitting? Will you take my heart between your lips, too? Yes, my heart there and you yourself will go into my eyes and fall down in me and go along my blood and dance in my blood, ring bells in my blood. Then I will be really crazy."

"You certainly make a picture out of yourself."

"Yes, a pretty picture." He was mocking at her again. "Can you see it, in blue and green colors, with red, too? A man there with an abscess in his brain and smoke there, with his heart stuck like a meatball in a girl's lips and jingle-bells jing-a-link-a-linkeling in his blood and his clothes all bulging up from a strange body inside there and his mouth bleeding words that say nothing."

Doris closed her eyes and shivered mockingly. "You can frame it on a nuthouse wall," she said and laughed.

"Yes," he cried angrily. "This is the third or fifth or tenth time you said I was crazy. Maybe you're right. But now I'll stop the nutty stuff. We're down to business now, kid. Order me a bottle of brandy, whole quart bottle, while I go powder my nose."

"Well, it's true. You're the craziest man I ever heard of."

He stood up. "Oh cut it out, will you please, damn it," he said in a low, exasperated tone.

"You go on," she told him worriedly. "Go on and come back and you'll eat some food and you'll feel better." Her voice was tender with pleading.

When Henry returned, the brandy wasn't there. She hadn't ordered it. "I don't want any of your interfering or mothering," he said. "The hell with that." He called the waiter and ordered the brandy himself.

The waiter made a small ceremony of depositing the bottle before him and the plate of clams before her. Henry sat back and drank and watched Doris pick her way fastidiously among the clams.

"You look as if you're afraid to get your fork wet," he said.

"What's that?"

"I said I will not, refuse to, that's all, fall in love with you."

"I don't remember asking you to," she said and laughed and returned to the clams.

She seems to have memorized her table manners, he thought. But no, no, he thought, she was all right. He was the wrong one. He had tried to make himself want her and he couldn't, but that wasn't her fault. His fault. If the Queen of Sheba was brought in on black sheets right now, he would say to her, can you make me sleep, Queen, that's what I got to know, can you make me sleep? No, Doris was good enough, the best in the whole city, really beautiful, beautiful eyes anyway, and a nice little girl with legs you could wrap around you to make you cozy, and still he didn't want her. He had tried to lick himself into it. He had tried to drink enough to forget anything he wanted to forget. He had tried to make love to her. He had held her in his hands and had held her on his face. He had said the love words right out, feverish words to make himself feel feverish for her, strong, crazy words, hot and dirty words and had thought hot and dirty, demanding, commanding thoughts. But the words went cold in his mouth. The thought wouldn't stay hot in his mind and wouldn't demand or command. He had undressed her so often in his mind her skin must be all worn out by now and it was no good. He had fastened pictures of her naked in his mind. He had forced himself to snuffle into the pictures and had forced his eyes to rove like hands all over the pictures of all the flesh of her body. He had degraded himself like that, had stuffed swill into himself, had covered his mind with sewer-muck and still it was no good. Nothing was any good at all. He couldn't hold anything in his mind long enough to have an effect. That was the truth of it and it was time to admit it, give up and admit it. That other thing, the worry and the restlessness in his chest, burned up all the alcohol he poured on it and burned up all the pictures he thought of and if he had a harem to look at and music playing in his ears and if he was lying on a bed of girls, what would he see? Just Ficco! Just Tucker! Just Bunte and Hall and his own name all over the newspapers!

Henry closed his eyes. He didn't think of anything for a moment. He sat still. The restlessness ground in his chest. It swelled and swarmed and swelled, swarming, and swelled and swelled and then burst and bound squealing up through him and plunged like fingers into his brain. He opened his eyes. He half rose from the chair. "Doris," he cried, "help me!"

Doris was lifting a clam daintily from the plate. She held it in mid air, her mouth open.

He sat down. His eyes groped from side to side with embarrassment. His hands found the bottle and grasped it. "I mean with the brandy," he said, "I can't finish it all myself."

The outburst seemed to have come from so deep in him that Doris hesitated. "I hope you're not going to try," she said at last, absently. If he wants to tell me himself, all right, she decided, and put the clam into her mouth.

Henry felt suddenly the clam was alive. He felt Doris was holding its life between her teeth. When her teeth, restless now, moving restlessly now, ground down, the life of the clam spurted out and drenched her tongue and splashed her mouth and that was juice. That was the flavor of the clam. Oh, he thought, Oh, Oh, Oh, she's no good to me! So what's the use! Why keep this kid out all night torturing her? Better to send her home and stand up at a bar and drink until he fell down and, when he fell down, he would hire a waiter to pour liquor into him through a funnel until there wasn't any room any more and it was slopping out of his mouth and then he'd tell the waiter to kick him in the head until he was unconscious. That way he'd close his eyes all right and sleep all right and dream. Yes, dream! Of Ficco! Of Tucker! Of Bunte and Hall and his own name all over the newspapers!

The swarm of restlessness began again to bundle into a ball in his chest and swell. He leaned forward hastily. "You beautiful one," he said to Doris in a shaking voice and smiled hastily. "My eyes shiver when they go up your beautiful legs."

"I'm sure if you put that glass down and ate something."

"Don't your legs shiver a little bit when my eyes go up them?"

"Why don't you do at least one thing that's good for you," she said. "Here." She moved the bowl of crackers that had come with her clams. "Just take one of these in your mouth, for my sake, please. Don't eat it. Just suck on it, for God sakes."

He laughed and obligingly put his hand into the bowl, but he did not lift his hand out. A thought had struck him. It had thrust into his mind at last, the climax thought, the one he had been struggling against and leading up towards and fighting down since his first sight of Doris. "I've been doing things all my life that were good for me," he said. "Tonight is a holiday. I'm going to do everything that's bad for me and wind up dead."

"I must say you certainly are making a good try, the old college try."

"Yes, that's right, change the diet for the holiday. Nothing good, everything bad." He sniggered. "Badminton and so forth, go sleep in bad after a shower bad and like that, and mix buckwheat badder."

The words came out of him in a rush and the laughter rushed away from him. But he couldn't snigger away the thought in his head. He couldn't frighten it away with unreal talk of death. He couldn't mock it away. He couldn't stifle it with sewer-muck or transform it with passion. His life was at stake. He took his money from his pocket and held it over the table. "You see this?" he said. "It's supposed to be good for you, isn't it?"

"Well, I don't know, the way you throw it around."

"Never mind," he cried. "Money is supposed to be good for you, full of vitamins. That's what they say, good as blood." He thrust the money towards her. He had violated himself for money. Now she must. When she did, that would be defeat for him, since he had identified himself with her, and it would be the last defeat he would allow himself to suffer. After that, he would go home and sit alone a while, only a little while, tasting defeat, imagining pennilessness, tasting loneliness, and then, then . . . and, after that, his friends would say they couldn't understand it, he must have got drunk or something, melancholy or something, to kill himself like that when he was making so much money. "Take it!" he told her. "Maybe the money'll be gooder for you than for me."

She drew back from it.

"Take it! Take it!" he said. "That's what you want out of me, isn't it? You think you've got a sucker here, don't you? Take it. You're right. You've got the biggest sucker you ever saw here. Take it before I give it to the waiter."

"Put your money away," she said indignantly. "You have no respect for me at all, have you?"

"Take it!" he gripped the money tightly. He was not aware of his terrible peril, but a sense of it shook in him and his fist quivered and the money quivered with it. "There's a thousand, fifteen hundred dollars here, something, I don't know, about that, a lot, more than you ever had in your life. Here, if that's not enough, I've got more."

He dropped the bills alongside her plate of clams and fumbled inside his coat. He unclasped a safety pin and pulled out a manila envelope. He slit and ripped the envelope awkwardly, in a frenzy

of impatience, and took out ten new $1,000 bills. It was his escape
money. He had been keeping it on him a long time, ever since he
had begun to think that some day he might have to go away in a
hurry. He threw his escape money down on top of the other bills.

"Take it," he cried. "Don't be a damn fool. There's a fortune
here, your fortune. Don't pass it up because people are looking at
you. It's your fortune. Take this money and go out of here. Once
you go out of here, nobody will be looking at you and you'll be
rich."

The shock of astonishment had passed in Doris. Her mind was
speculating rapidly. She ought to take it and keep it for him until
he was sober, she thought. It wasn't safe with him in his condition.
But, she thought, if she did take it, what would he do then? Who
knows what kind of a scene he would make then? And, anyway,
how dare he, what must he think of her, how dare he, how dare he
throw money into her face like that! And, if she didn't take it,
what would he think of her then? Would she get more that way,
would it be better that way, would she get more than money that
way, would she get him that way? If she did take it, she would be
out of his life. That was certain. Whether he really allowed her to
keep the money or snatched it back from her as she took it, they
would be finished together forever.

"Don't pass it up," he cried, "because you think it's not nice to
take it, because people are looking at you and will think it's not
nice. Who are they to you? You never saw them before in your
life. Even if they're all your father, who are they to you? You're
yourself. They'll look at you for a moment as you walk out rich
and then you'll never see them again for the rest of your life and
you'll be rich. You'll have a fortune. Maybe it won't be nice for a
minute, one minute, that's all, the time it takes to get to the door
and out of their sight, that's all, and then, for the rest of your whole
life, you'll have the money. Nobody will care where you got it and
what you did to get it. What did you do? You picked it up, that's
all, and walked away, that's all. And even if you did worse, who will
care? Everybody will admire you and respect you for having it, the

whole world, everybody in the whole world, your father, everybody,
the whole, whole world. Take it! Take it, I tell you!"

Doris had her hand on the money, as if she thought it might
blow away or he might push it to the floor with one of his violent
gestures. "I've got a good mind to do it," she said, "and then you'll
be sorry."

"If you take it . . . if you take it . . . I'll love you forever! I mean
it. I won't bother you. I'll love you forever. Take it. Doris, how can
I tell you so you'll believe, so you'll see. This is your chance, the
moment of your life. Take it. Get wise a minute, Doris! This is the
moment of your life and it will never come again as long as you
ever live."

"You shouldn't be trusted with so much money," she said. She
half rose and leaned across the table and stuffed the bills into the
side pocket of his coat.

He sat stiffly, without moving, staring straight ahead without seeing her. Her hair was close to his face for a moment. It went
through his thoughts and he could smell it and smell the perfume
and powder of her and feel the breath of her mouth.

"You should have taken it," he said in a low, sad, tired tone.

She sat down and smoothed the tablecloth before her. "Now,"
she told him, "I'm going to insist you eat something, a nice piece
of steak or something nice that you like."

He sat looking at her. Suddenly he was at a loss for what to do
next. He had made himself naked. He wanted to hide from himself
and from her and he didn't know how to do it. A sense of acute
embarrassment rose to the top of the clutter of thoughts and emotions in him. He lowered his head slowly. What a cheap, theatrical
show he had made of himself, he thought. He leaned forward
slowly, with stooped head, as if toppling, and leaned forward more,
and more, until his stooped head touched the table and rested there
alongside the bowl of crackers. This is theatrical, too, he thought,
cheap and showy. Then he didn't think anything. All the thoughts
and emotions smothered in the noise they were making in his head.

Doris waited a moment. She put her hand on the back of his

neck and waited another moment. Then she leaned close to his ear.
"You ought to go home and sleep now," she whispered and shook
his neck gently.

He did not move. He was listening to the smothering noise of his
thoughts.

Doris took out her compact and patted powder on her face and
began to work over her lips carefully. She stole glances at him. He
lay still. He had begun to breathe quietly, as if asleep. She lit a
cigarette and reached over for his half-filled glass of brandy. She
wanted to know how it tasted. She had never been drunk. Would
she give away all her money, too, if she were drunk, her mad money,
too? She wet her lips with the brandy and shivered and put down
the glass hastily.

A smiling man came over to the table. He seemed to be the manager. "Has your friend passed out?" he asked.

Wheelock heard him, but he couldn't move. The crashed-in feeling in him was healing. He thought if he would stay where he
was a few moments longer, he would be whole again, as he had
been before. Before when? Before he had met Tucker? No, before
that. Before he had gone to school? Before that, too. Before he had
got into his father's hotel? No, no, before that. Before he had been
born? That was it. He would be whole as he had been before his
father . . . not his father, no, no, not his father . . . before the
world had fertilized the seed that was to be him, had pricked it,
stamped it and shaped it with the dollar sign!

"Oh no," Doris told the manager, "nothing like that. I don't think
so. He's just resting a little bit."

Her words went into Henry's ears and seemed to fall straight
down to his heart. How did she know? he asked himself. Where
had she, a dull girl, really—but maybe not, maybe not really dull—
because, look, look what an instinct for truth she had.

"If you need any help with him," the manager said, "we'll get
him home all right for you."

Henry straightened up slowly. His face was red and streaked
with white where it had rested against the table. There was a
small dent in his forehead from one of the crackers.

"Upsadaisy," said the manager. He put his hands under Wheelock's arms and lifted him to his feet and held him for a moment to keep him from tottering. "That'sababy, you're doing fine now." The manager turned to Doris. "It's that brandy," he said. "If I were you, I'd take him off it. A steady diet of that and, one of these days, you'll see him going right out of the picture."

Wheelock struggled free of the man's hands. "Let's get out of here," he said to Doris. "I know a better place."

"I think you should take me home now," she told him.

There were half a dozen people in the room. They all watched the bill being paid and watched Doris and Henry leave. It was very quiet. Their footsteps could be heard.

"I'm all right now," said Henry. "I'll be good."

He couldn't walk well. She held on to him. His arm seemed so thin and light to her. He was like a sleepy boy dragging along beside her. She felt she wanted to carry him and tuck him into bed.

They took a taxi to where she lived—a brownstone rooming house whose front door was a long flight of stairs up from the street. But when they got there, he wouldn't let her out of the cab. He put his feet on the folding seat and blocked the door.

So then they drove through the park. Dawn was beginning. Between the black sky and the black road, the darkness was frail. The stars had turned an intense white. The park's road was fenced in by brown earth and the bare trees looked green and soft and the air among their branches was coloring yellow. Henry fell asleep against Doris's shoulder and, when he woke up, they were at her home again. He felt as if he had slept a long time. She opened the cab door herself and climbed over his legs, laughing and determined. He followed her up the steps and into the vestibule.

"Whoa up there, mister," she said. She had the key in the lock, but she did not turn it. "Where do you think you're going?"

"Why, I think I'm going inside."

She laughed. "You think much too much, oh very much too much, for one bad little boy. Now say good night and go home and sleep."

"I can't."

"Haven't you got a home?"

"No, nothing, nothing at all. I can't sleep when I'm not with you. That sleep just now was the best I ever had in my life. It was as sweet as honey."

"That's nice to tell a girl, that her company puts you to sleep."

"Yes, I mean it. You don't know how good it is to be able to sleep."

She turned back to the door.

"Don't go away, Doris," he cried. "I beg it!"

"We can have dinner tonight if you want to or after the show, if you want."

"No, that's too late. You don't know, Doris." He put both his arms around her and rested his hands gently on her back and held his face close to hers. "Let me stay with you, please."

"Now please, Mr. Wheelock."

"I don't mean, you know, that way, with that, but just stay near you. Please, please, Doris." His lips touched her cheek. "Please, please," he murmured.

She pushed his arms down. "I think," she said softly, "you'd better go home before you spoil everything." She took his hand and squeezed it. "Good night," she smiled earnestly, "and I thank you for everything, for a really wonderful time, a very unusual evening."

He held on to her hand. For a moment, she was afraid. His face seemed to be full of pain and to be yearning away from pain. She couldn't tell what he was going to do or say.

"Doris," he cried, "will you do me a favor? I mean now. I mean marry me. Now, right now. We can take this taxi to Greenwich or Elkton or somewhere and be married right now."

"I don't think you know what you're saying." She pulled her hand free. "Go home and sleep it off before you get into more trouble."

"I know what I'm saying. What do you think I am? I mean it. Doris, if you do this for me, you'll be the best, greatest woman in the world. You don't know. Please, Doris. I'm not saying it good. I know this is not the place or time." He looked around him at the vestibule and then pressed against her. "It's got to be, got to be, has got to be," he cried. "I need you."

She moved away from him. "I don't know what to say." She was flustered. "This is such a surprise."

"I know what I'm doing. I'm not a boy. This has got to be, just got to be."

"Well . . . my goodness . . . well . . . you certainly are a funny fellow."

"Yes, I'm ha ha funny, funny as hell."

"No, I mean . . . well, anyway. . . . I can't do a thing like this."

"Why not?"

"Because I can't. I mean right now. Maybe later. I don't know. How should I know? You don't give a girl a chance."

"When you didn't take the money from me, I knew then, that was the time. You were the one I needed."

Her triumph over the money was in him like love. When she had triumphed over the same need that had undone him, it became his triumph, too, and he loved it and must cling to it.

"I'm not the kind of a girl like that," said Doris. "Marriage is very serious to me."

"What do you think it is to me? I've never been married before. You're the first I ever asked." He recalled, suddenly, why he had never asked anyone else before, but he brushed the recollection away from him.

"I don't know you at all," protested Doris, "except that you're very nice and you had a lot to drink and you talk like you had a lot to drink."

"You think I'm drunk? I'm drunk with you. You think I'm one of those Broadway boys who get drunk and wake up in bed married to tramps?"

"I don't know what to think. Now you say good night like a good

boy and go home and sleep and we'll see each other some more.
We'll see each other as much as you want."

Before he could reply, she kissed him hastily, so that her kiss
bumped his nose, and pushed him away and flung open the door
and ran inside and slammed the door behind her, locking it.

"Don't!" His voice was so intense, it was like a scream.

There was a curtain on the door. She pulled it aside at the edge
and laughed and blew him a kiss.

He threw himself against the door. "Please," he cried, "please,
Doris, please."

He remained flattened against the door. Her lips formed the
words, "naughty, naughty." She laughed again and waved and
blew another kiss and went away. He heard her go up the stairs.
Her feet went lightly, brightly, with a sound like happiness. He
clung to the door until long after the sound had ceased. He was
afraid to turn around and face the vestibule. Dawn had come and
put a gray feel and a gray smell in it. It was the smell and feel
and color of stone-like loneliness.

Then he began to listen to himself. He was listening for fear.
It surprised him to discover it had gone. There wasn't any restlessness in him any more, only triumph. Worry had stopped. Chaos
had stopped. He was tired, sweet tired, like a tired man lying in
bed. He realized he had felt that way a long time without knowing it, an hour maybe.

He walked down to the sidewalk slowly. The taxi was still
waiting for him. He looked up and down the street. His brain felt
fresh and slumbrous. There was no longer the sense in it of having
to talk and of having to tear pieces out of it as he talked. The
air was sweet in his nose. His bones were sweet tired. His mind
was sweet with sweet longing for bed.

"What do you think of that?" he said to himself. "Here's love.
It's come. It's love." He shook his head and laughed eagerly.

For many years now, he had been afraid that he was one of
those men who never fall in love.

XXIV

LATER THE same morning, Tucker got hold of Joe and told him he ought to go up to Windsor in Canada to find a place to keep the cash reserves of the combination's banks. He gave the name of a connection he had there from prohibition days.

His idea was, if Ficco did grab off one of the bankers and put the arm on him for a payroll, then the banker wouldn't have any money to give. Tucker said there would be no trouble about making an arrangement with his connection in Windsor so that the bankers could pay off their hits from day to day out of the money kept up there. It was clumsy and would cost something, but it was safe. Tucker's connection was one of the largest banks in Canada.

Joe decided Leo would have to be left to operate the old way. "I don't want to go into long explanations with him," he said.

"That guy," said Tucker, "we got to keep babying him all the time. When will he grow up?"

But Joe was stubborn and Tucker finally agreed that Leo should go along the same as before, but no others were to be left out of the plan. Tucker was sure Ficco wouldn't bother Leo. That was why he gave in to Joe.

Joe tried several times during the day to get Wheelock on the telephone to tell him what was happening, but he couldn't reach him. Wheelock's office didn't know where he was and the manservant at Park Avenue hadn't seen him and the couple at his downtown apartment said the same. The telephone at the Central Park West place did not answer.

Wheelock had left word with the couple that he wanted to sleep and was not to be disturbed by anyone for anything and that, if anyone disturbed him, the first thing he would do was fire the couple and then he would throw the telephone out the window.

In the early evening, Joe located Bunte. The old man said he had been to police headquarters with Wheelock all right and had got the pistol permit, but after that Wheelock had gone away somewhere, he didn't know where. He said he hoped it was a hospital because the boy sure looked as if he needed one, that or a cemetery, he was hung over so bad.

Joe stopped trying to find Wheelock then. He took the night train for Canada and slept with $192,000 in cash under his pillow.

Bauer had allowed himself Wednesday to "think it over." On Thursday afternoon, as soon as Leo arrived at the bank in Joe's apartment, Bauer went up to him and said, "I have something important to talk to you about tonight."

"I'm agreeable," Leo told him. "I don't know what time I'll be home, but, if you want, you can stay there and wait for me."

"Come here a minute," said Bauer. He walked out of the kitchen through the swinging door and into the dining room where there was privacy. "I'd rather," he said, "if you don't mind, some place where you eat supper so I can talk to you better, in a restaurant, you know. We can talk there."

"I'll tell you." Leo laughed. "These days I'm so busy I don't know if I'm eating or what." He had been about to ask Bauer what he wanted to talk about that could be so important and needed such complicated arrangements. But the thought of a restaurant stopped him. He felt it would be nice to eat in a restaurant for a change where he could get the things his wife refused to cook for him because they made him ill. "I always eat home," he said. "But, you know, Freddie, I'm glad to help you, even after what you did. If it's going to help you, I'll eat in a restaurant tonight." He thought of garlicky meats soaked in gravy. His mouth began to water. He hadn't had anything like that in a long time because of his high blood pressure.

"I don't want you to do me any favors," said Bauer. His eyes were lowered. "You eat home and maybe we can walk around the street and talk there in private. Only tell me when you'll be there, so I'll know when to come."

"It's all right. I don't mind. I'll eat in a restaurant for you. I'm glad to help you anything I can do."

"No," said Bauer. "I won't come."

Leo laughed and poked Bauer's side. "As a matter of fact," he told him, "I'm glad for an excuse to get away from my wife's cooking."

"If it's that way, all right. If you want it, all right, but you wanted it yourself. I didn't say it."

"Sure, sure," said Leo. "I want it."

XXV

THEIR APPOINTMENT was for nine o'clock at "The Romanian Eats," a basement restaurant on upper Lexington Avenue.

Bauer hadn't intended to be there, but he was there. He finished work at seven and went home for dinner. At that time, he didn't know whether he would show up at the restaurant at all. He didn't have to. All Wally had said he had to do was call Ficco's number, which he had done, and leave word for Wally, which he had done. Now he was finished and a free man and could go to Miami for the winter.

He didn't feel free. He couldn't eat his dinner. He felt he would be sick if he put the food into his mouth. His head hung over the plate motionless and the fork lay motionless in his hand.

"You act like you think it's poisoned," said Catherine.

"Maybe it is." He pushed away the plate and stood up. "I wouldn't put it past you."

Their relationship had gone back to exactly where it had been before.

"Where are you going?" she asked.

"I'm going out. O.U.T. Out!"

"But you haven't touched a thing."

He didn't answer. He left in silence, without even looking at her. Bauer headed for Boyle's. He felt weighted down. He didn't know why. "Maybe Mr. Minch won't show up," he thought suddenly. "Maybe the others won't show up."

He turned around and walked towards the subway. "It's not going to do any harm," he thought, "if I'm there to make sure nothing goes wrong."

If Mr. Minch showed up and the others didn't, he could talk to him about something, beg him once more to let him quit. If the others showed up and Mr. Minch didn't, he could tell them he was sorry, it hadn't worked out, no, it hadn't worked out, it wasn't his fault, there was nothing he could do, nothing further to do, it hadn't worked out.

He walked faster. The feeling in him of being weighted down had lightened. He walked with head up and arms swinging, like a man who had thought of an excuse for doing what he wanted to do.

A steep flight of wide iron stairs down from the street led to "The Romanian Eats." The restaurant's windows could not be seen easily from the sidewalk. Nevertheless, there was a small sign in one of them. The lettering was white on a blue card and spelled: "10 Course Dinner. Ten (10) Courses. Including Choice of Appetizer and Soup. 55¢."

Bread was one course, butter another, cole slaw a third.

The restaurant room was narrow and not very deep. Just inside the door was a cashier's desk with a boy about fourteen years old, sitting behind it and reading. He was the owner's son. Beyond the desk were white porcelain tables. The floor was tiled and sprinkled with sawdust and the wall was covered with tin which had been curled and lumped and fretted with rosettes and painted tan.

It was past the dinner hour when Bauer got there. The place was nearly empty. There were only the boy reading and one waiter and four customers. The boy was plump and sallow. He had horn-rimmed glasses. His thick, dark hair fell over his forehead as he read. He kept pushing it back with one hand. The waiter wore a black, shiny mohair coat with a gold stripe on its edges and across the cuffs of its sleeves. He had a shy, sick-looking face and his graying hair was thin. It lay flat on his head, slicked to one side. The color of his skull showed through his hair and made it look grayer than it was.

The waiter brought Bauer a basket of bread, a glass of water, a menu, a napkin, a knife and fork and spoons, all at the same time and dropped them on the table and began sorting them listlessly. He was saving the butter for later to keep Bauer from eating too much bread.

"All I want is to wait for a friend," Bauer told him.

The waiter didn't say anything. He took away the bread.

Bauer sat facing the door. He looked straight ahead at the steep flight of iron steps that led up to the street. He could see the edge of the sidewalk and people's legs moving along it. His fingers began to drum against the porcelain top of the table. His mouth suddenly felt like a hot hole in his hot face. He drank some water.

After a few moments, Bauer got up and went to the telephone booth at the back of the room. He wanted to have something to do. He looked through the directory. There wasn't anybody he could call up. He didn't know anyone well enough. He turned the pages and looked at the names. Each name a person, none he knew. Seven million people in the city of New York, eight million, and he had lived among them all his life and he knew no one. No one. At least, not well enough to call up and say hello, how are you feeling, I thought I'd like to know how you are feeling. And none knew him. Who really knew him? Who remembered what he had been and who knew who he was? He had been a child, a boy, a youth and a man—and who knew what he had been as each and who knew what he was now?

He looked around the room. Leo hadn't arrived yet. He went into the telephone booth. He felt, if he looked at the telephone, he might think of someone he could call. He stood still a long time, thinking. He didn't think of names. He didn't know what he was thinking about. He just stood and thought. When it occurred to him how he was standing there, he put a nickel in the slot and asked for information.

The nickel came back and a girl voice said, "Information."

He asked for the telephone number of Frederick E. Bauer and gave his address.

"One moment, please," the girl voice said.

He looked out the door and waited. He could see through the restaurant to the iron steps and the sidewalk above them, but he couldn't see the people's legs.

"I'm sorry, sir. There is no telephone listed for Frederick E. for eat Bauer at that address."

"There must be."

"I'm sorry, sir."

"Maybe it's in the name of Catherine Bauer."

"I'm sorry, sir, there is no telephone listed in the name of Bauer at that address. There are three Frederick Bauers listed, but none at that address."

"Well, don't bother. I'll find it some place else."

Bauer put the receiver on the hook, but he did not take his hand off it. He held the receiver a moment, waiting, looking into the mouthpiece of the telephone, and thinking. At last he shrugged.

"At least it didn't cost anything," he thought.

He went back to the table. The waiter had refilled the glass with water. He came forward as Bauer sat down and began fussing with the table setting. He held a damp, soiled napkin in one hand.

"He didn't show up yet?" The waiter smiled.

A small eddy of hate sucked its way clear of the current of loneliness in Bauer. "What's the matter?" he cried. "Are you in a hurry for the table?"

"Did I say that?"

"There's no one here. You're not losing anything letting me wait."

"I'm here to twelve o'clock anyway, so you think it makes a difference to me? I just thought maybe you want to order."

"What *is* this? A man can't wait in this place?"

"Wait, go ahead, wait. Who's stopping you? Wait, wait all you want, it's all right."

"Here." Bauer took a nickel out of his pocket and threw it across the table towards the waiter. "I'll pay you for the table, just to let me alone."

The waiter put one finger on the nickel and pushed it back. "That's not right, mister," he said. "You know that. I'll get you fresh water."

He went away and Bauer thought suddenly, "I could have passed the time with him instead of fighting with him like that." Yet, when the waiter returned with water, Bauer only stared at him sullenly, unable to take himself out of the position hate had forced him into.

The weather had turned warmer and when Leo came in, his hat was tilted back on his head. His overcoat flopped around him unbuttoned and his jacket and vest lay under it unbuttoned. He looked shaggy and undone. He could be looked into deep down, to his shirt and to where his belly curled over his belt like the lip of a wave. Lines pouched his sad, gray face, but he looked around with pleasure. He could tell by the smell that the food here was what he wanted.

Bauer went to meet him. "I've got a table here," he said. "I thought you'd never come."

"It's only five minutes after nine. I had so much trouble parking or I'd have been here on the dot. You can't park any more in the whole city anywhere. Everybody's got cars."

"It's ten o'clock you mean."

"No, no. That's right." Leo held out his watch. It was a quarter past nine. "So I'm a little late." He hung up his hat and coat on a rack near the table. "There's a car has got the parking space right in front of the restaurant. You'd think they'd keep it clear for customers instead of for young loafers, waiting, they got nothing else to do except make chip-chip at the girls passing." He sat down and took up the menu. "Did you eat already?" he asked.

The car was theirs. Bauer knew it. They had come. They were waiting. It was going to happen, then, really going to happen. He forced himself to say something. "What customers come here with cars?" he said.

The waiter was standing over them. He had brought another menu and the basket of bread and another setting for Leo.

"Is the chop chicken liver good?" asked Leo.

"Why not? I can recommend it the best. I ate it myself," replied the waiter.

"It's not fermented?"

"If it's fermented, we don't sell it here."

"If it's fermented," said Leo, "I'll push it in your face and you'll eat it again."

The waiter laughed. "It's not fermented," he said. "I'm not hungry but I'm willing you can push all you want."

Leo put down the menu and took his eyeglasses out of his vest pocket and polished the lenses with the paper napkin and put them on. "I like to see what I'm getting," he explained. He began to study the menu.

A man came quickly down the steps and stood in the doorway of the restaurant. The waiter turned around and looked at him to see if he were a customer, but the boy at the cashier's desk remained stooped over his book. The man was small and chunky and had the smooth rosy cheeks of a child. He had a large, round face and blue eyes and his eyes looked high in his head. He wore a mackinaw, black corduroy pants and a gray cap.

"It says noodle soup here, then mandel soup," said Leo. "Could you sneak for me a few mandels into the noodle soup?"

The waiter turned back to Leo. "Naturally," he said. "There's no law not."

The man looked around slowly from the doorway. His glance came to Bauer and to Leo's back and passed on without halting. He seemed to be studying the room. He looked at the door to the kitchen and at the other people in the restaurant.

Bauer watched him. No matter how he wanted to, he could not stop looking at him. Bauer's eyes seemed to have become fixed. He strove to move them and couldn't. Then, as the man retreated up the stairs, Bauer's eyes closed and he leaned forward. He had his elbows on the table and he put one hand to his forehead to keep himself from falling. The touch of his hand steadied him. It took away the feeling of faintness and he leaned back.

"I'll bring you the liver until you make up your mind about the rest," said the waiter and went towards the kitchen.

"Mr. Minch, I'm telling you. You've got to tell me yes, right away, I can quit. Right away." Bauer was leaning forward now. The words tumbled out of him.

"You'll eat first," said Leo, "and then we'll talk."

"No. I can't. You've got to tell me. Now. Right away. This minute!"

Leo shook his head with vexation. "I thought maybe you had something new you could tell me," he said, "that you would work hard to make up what you did and trust your Leo he would work out things for you as fast as he could. Eat something."

The waiter had come with the chopped chicken livers. Bauer looked up at him with mouth open. Then he turned sideways in his chair and lowered his head into the palms of his hands.

"You're going to cry here," said Leo, "and spoil my appetite?" He turned to the waiter. "Bring him a cup of coffee. Maybe he'll eat something later."

Bauer didn't move.

"It's on the expense account," Leo said to Bauer.

Bauer still sat with his head in his hands.

"Hey! You heard? I'll pay."

Bauer made no sign he had heard.

"Don't sit like that," cried Leo. "Sit up. How can I eat when you sit like that?"

Bauer remained motionless. Leo leaned over and poked his arm. Bauer shuddered away and buried his head more deeply in his hands.

"What's the matter with you?" asked Leo. He had become alarmed and he began to rise in his chair.

~

Then the men came. There were three of them. One stood in the doorway. They all held sawed-off shotguns.

"Freddie!" cried Leo. "What have you done?"

He stood half out of his chair, poised that way, his hands on the table, leaning far forward on his hands. His gray face had become yellow. He had taken one look at the man in the doorway and the two coming towards him and then turned back to Bauer. Bauer did not lift his head from his hands.

"Freddie!" screamed Leo. "What have you done to me!" He did not look at Bauer now. As he screamed, he looked at the two young men with guns.

"Just take it easy, pop," said the rosy-cheeked man, "and nobody will get hurt."

Leo fell down into his chair. He fell so hard, his head snapped. The yellowed skin of his face began to blotch with red. One hand rose feebly toward his chest and then fell feebly. He seemed to be trying to talk. His mouth was open and his throat was working slowly, but he didn't say anything. He didn't make a sound except with his breathing. The breath blew through his nose in slow, exhausted blasts.

"You're coming with us, pop," said the rosy-cheeked man. "Come on, stand up."

Leo sat still, tilted to one side on the chair. His eyes closed and flopped open slowly and closed again. His mouth didn't move, but his throat kept working. He looked as if he were swallowing.

"Come on," said the rosy-cheeked man, "hurry up."

The waiter was standing fixed in a space between the kitchen and the two men with guns. He held a plate of soup in one hand and the damp, soiled napkin in the other. One of the diners had leaped up and was pressed flat against the wall, as if he were trying to dig into it. Two men and a woman sat rooted in their chairs. The men stared motionless at the woman and the woman's body was drawn taut, her head far back, her eyes closed tight and her hands clapped on her mouth. The boy had disappeared behind the cashier's desk. His book remained open on the desk. No sound came from him.

"Stand up and walk." The rosy-cheeked man waved his gun. "Come on, come on!" he cried. He pushed Leo's shoulder with the gun. "Get up there or you'll get it," he said.

The push toppled Leo slowly off the chair to the floor. He seemed to fall sluggishly. He lay on his side, his legs curled up in a sitting position.

The rosy-cheeked man jumped back in surprise. He hit the table and the table slid back and jostled Bauer. Bauer sprang to his feet. His chair grated behind him.

"You wanted it!" shouted Bauer. He shouted with his mouth wide open. It was hard to make out the words.

He looked around wildly for Leo and saw him lying on the floor and thrust his face down towards him. "You wanted it yourself!" he shouted. His voice came inhumanly through his wide open mouth. He stepped past Leo and, suddenly, he began to totter. He tottered a step and two steps and stood still and then folded up. His knees bent under him. He fell to his knees and doubled up his body so that his head lay on his knees. He closed his eyes.

The rosy-cheeked man saw Bauer settle and then turned to his companion. "Give me a hand with this," he said and indicated Leo.

The third man came forward out of the doorway and lifted his gun and stood silently, facing the others in the restaurant. The rosy-cheeked one stepped over Leo and put his gun on the floor. Leo's sphincter muscle had relaxed.

"This is a regular wop circus," said the gunman. He put his hands under Leo's shoulders. "You take his legs," he directed his companion.

The other gunman was a blond boy with sandy eyelashes and freckles on his pale face. He wrinkled his nose and looked away and seized Leo's legs.

Leo's head felt bursting. It seemed as though hot glass were thrusting and twisting through it. He saw and knew everything that was going on. Except for the pain in his head, he felt full of comfort. There was a warm, lazy feeling through his body, below his head. He knew he was on the floor, but he couldn't care about it. He kept thinking this was funny and he ought to want to get up, but all he wanted was not to move. The floor didn't feel cold and the sawdust, matted with dirt, was soft and the laziness seemed to drip through his body like sludge.

It took him a long time to want to do anything about the pain in his head. It was a splintering pain. It burned and dug and cut and shattered. He lay still in the lazy, drowsy sludge of his body and felt the pain and thought he ought to try to ease it. It wasn't natural not to try to ease it and yet he couldn't want to.

Finally, he decided to lift his hands and press them against his head. It was a decision. He thought of doing it. Then he thought he would do it and, at last, he tried to do it. One of his hands wouldn't move.

It just wouldn't move. He thought he must be lying on it. He couldn't feel it. He reached for it with his free hand and found it and grasped it and lifted it. It lifted all right. It was just numb from lying on, that was all. When he lifted the hand, something seemed to drop down inside it from the tips of his fingers, a thick, soft, warm, wet something, filled, as light is filled, with sparkles, with other things, little things, a horde of little things that jittered and prickled. It was a funny thing to feel, nice and funny. He lifted his hand higher and there was a smash against his cheekbone. The pain of it shot through the pain in his head.

"Keep your hands down," said the rosy-cheeked man.

He had hit Leo with the heel of his palm.

Then, Leo felt himself being lifted into the air. He thought his cheekbone was broken. He tried to lift his hand to feel it, but he couldn't. His hand just wouldn't move. He couldn't even find the

hand with his other hand. He couldn't see it the way they were
carrying him and he couldn't tell where it was. He thought maybe
the arm had fallen off. He found he couldn't care about that either.

The gunman grunted as he lifted Leo's shoulders. He took a step
backward and knocked against Bauer. He almost dropped Leo
in fear. He looked around and saw Bauer's folded body.

"Get the hell out of the way," he said.

Bauer rocked slowly from side to side. He didn't seem to hear.

"Come on, you dumb bastard! Move!"

The gunman kicked back and kicked Bauer's head. His shoe
made a thick, clicking sound against Bauer's skull and Bauer
twisted to one side and then scrambled and clawed to his feet. He
looked like a dog, scrambling along the floor, his knees and fingers
scratching against the slippery surface, his breath grunting and
snuffling.

When he got erect, he began to scream. He screamed at the top
of his voice with his mouth wide open. He stood tall, his whole
body twanging as if plucked, and screamed again and again and
then began to run. He was facing the door and he ran straight
for it, on his toes, screaming like an animal.

The gunman near the door was frightened. He stepped aside
to let him pass. Bauer ran headlong into the steps. His foot
smashed into the steps and his body crashed down and he lay
there, spread out, the rims of his crushed glasses sticking deep into
his eyebrows.

The two gunmen carried Leo past him. Bauer was moaning.
The sounds slopped out of his mouth. The third gunman scooped
up the weapons on the floor and backed out of the restaurant. A
car was waiting, with back door open and motor running. Wally
was in the front seat, leaning far over the side, looking at Bauer.

"Kill him," he cried and pointed to Bauer.

The two gunmen stuffed Leo into the back of the car. They
threw him in and stepped over him. Wally turned to them.

"He's crazy," he said. His hand flung out towards Bauer. "Don't
you see he's crazy? He'll make trouble for us."

A policeman around the corner had heard Bauer's screams. He

had been standing in a doorway and, when he first heard the screams, he started running towards them. As he reached the corner, he hesitated. He came around the corner slowly and saw the car standing there and the two men carrying Leo up the steps. There were people on the street. They weren't looking at the policeman. They were looking at the car and at the two men and at Leo, lying with doubled-up legs between them. The policeman turned and ducked around the corner and ran all the way down the block to a far corner where there was a call box through which he could summon help.

The third gunman came backing up the steps, two guns held loosely under one arm, a third in his other hand. Wally sprang out of the car.

"Kill him," he shouted, "he knows me."

The gunman turned around and saw Wally on the sidewalk pointing down at Bauer.

"Can't you see he'll tell everything he knows?" cried Wally.

The gunman walked quickly towards the car and, as he passed, Wally snatched a gun from under the man's arms and went down the steps to Bauer. Deep, low moans slopped out of Bauer's open mouth. Wally put the muzzle against Bauer's ear and closed his eyes and pressed the trigger and blew off Bauer's head.

The recoil threw Wally backwards a little. His eyes came open. For a moment he saw what was left of Bauer bound away from him and flop like a tail against the steps. Then he sprinted to the car and leaped on the running board as the car began to move.

He pitched face forward through the open door into the front seat. The car was going fast around a corner. Wally clung with his fingers to the upholstery for a long time and then slowly heaved his body inside and closed the door.

His stomach was sick. He didn't think of anything or see anything except the streets rushing towards him through the windshield. Then suddenly he thought of the memorandum book where Bauer had written down Ficco's telephone number.

That little thing! Maybe Bauer had it on him. Maybe he hadn't torn out the page as he had been told to do. Maybe he had forgotten to tear it out or didn't want to and the page was still there and the police would find it.

That little thing! It had been so good up to now and that little thing! Everything else was perfect. Bauer hadn't said anything about Leo when he had called up. The job was done at the restaurant, not at Leo's office or at his home. As far as Ficco could know, there was no way for Wally to have guessed that the combination banker he had grabbed was Guinea Joe Minch's brother.

Wally knew Ficco didn't want Leo, but he hadn't been told why. He thought Ficco was afraid to snatch Leo because Leo was a big shot. Well, this kid Wally hadn't been afraid. This kid had grabbed him off and it was a big thing to do and he wouldn't be the mob's errand boy any more. He'd be important in the mob.

Except for that little thing, that one little God damn thing!

The rosy-cheeked man was in the back seat with his feet on Leo. There was no other place for his feet. "You know," he said to Wally, "you're just a crazy lunatic."

"No," cried Wally. "You saw yourself how he was. He would have told anything he was asked."

"You're crazy for blood, that's what you are," said the rosy-cheeked man.

The word blood did it. Wally felt his whole stomach billow into his mouth and lunged towards the side of the car and leaned out and vomited, his sick, green-faced, shapely head leaning far over the side.

The woman in the restaurant had fainted at the sound of the gun. The policeman was turning from the call box and going slowly and nervously towards his duty. The waiter stood still with head turned from the sight in the doorway. He was afraid to move. The boy behind the cashier's desk squirmed harder against the floor.

"You ought to get your head blown off, too," said the rosy-cheeked man to Wally. "It's no good to you anyway."

Wally sat back weakly. "No," he said, "he'd have made trouble."

"What trouble? Who'd have taken us into court? The combination couldn't afford to take us into court. We had nothing to worry about. There was no case, don't you know that, you looney punk, no case at all until you, you dumb bastard, made it."

When the police searched Bauer's body, they found the memorandum book, but the page with Ficco's number on it had been torn out. Bauer had been a methodical man. He had wanted to do exactly as he was told so that, if anything went wrong, he wouldn't be blamed.

XXVI

LATE THE same night, Thursday, while he was on his way to get some coffee after taking Doris home, Wheelock bought an early edition of a tabloid newspaper. He did not read tabloids regularly, but he liked them when he was tired.

A gossip column in the paper had an item about him under a heading of: "Town Snoop's Scoops." The item read: *"OOH, Gs!* —A Broadwayward lawyer handed thousands of bucks across a night club table to a chorus filly the other moaning. Good moaning to you, ma'am? Ah, but no! The filly whinnied neigh-nay and the legaliteweight passed out from surprise (and soda?)."

Wheelock laughed. Nevertheless, the item made him lose his taste for the paper. He had felt like reading that kind of news, but not about himself. He gave the paper to a bus boy and drank his coffee and thought about the item. He decided the fellow must have got it from a waiter. The idea made him nervous. He hadn't been aware before that night club waiters knew him and his profession.

A man came through the restaurant with other newspapers and

Wheelock bought one. He picked a more conservative newspaper this time and got a late edition. He glanced casually over the front page before turning inside and thought he saw the name Minch. His glance was moving too rapidly to stop. When he looked back, he couldn't find the name any more. He didn't remember in which column he had seen it or whether it was in a headline or small type. He looked over the page quickly and decided he must have imagined the name in type and was about to turn the page when he saw the headline:

"GANGSTERS SLAY ONE AND KIDNAP ANOTHER"

It was a one-column headline, halfway down the page. The name Minch was in the body of the story:

"An overcoat identified as belonging to the kidnapped man had been left behind. In one of its pockets, police discovered a license bearing the name Leo Minch and the address 96-402 East Prospect Boulevard, Bronx. A Leo Minch of the same address, who could not be located immediately, has a record of a previous arrest in connection with bootlegging activities for Ben Tucker, a notorious gangster, at one time widely powerful as 'The Beer Baron.'

"Police stated that, after abandoning bootlegging, Minch became involved in the policy, or numbers, racket in Harlem. Minch's brother, known as 'Guinea Joe,' because of his taste in clothes, is also believed to have been a member of the Tucker gang, but is not known to have been active since repeal."

The story went on to relate:

". . . papers in the pockets of the man shot dead while fleeing identified him as Frederick E. Bauer, but there was no clue to his address. Eyewitnesses declared that Bauer had been eating with the kidnapped man when gunmen entered. He screamed and made a break for safety. A gangster, stationed on the sidewalk as lookout, shot him in the head and killed him instantaneously.

"Patrolman H. T. Wessel was attracted by the gunshot and ran to the scene, but the gangsters drove off with their living victim before he could arrive."

Wheelock held on to himself. He read the item over several times. The police and the newspaper reporter did not seem to be sure it was Leo who had been kidnapped, but Wheelock was sure. The name Bauer had a familiar sound to him, but he couldn't place it right away.

A man at a nearby table had bought a late edition of a tabloid. He was holding it so Wheelock could read the front page headline:

"BEN TUCKER MISSING
AS GANG WAR FLARES
1 DEAD; 1 KIDNAPPED"

This paper had been willing to take a chance on the kidnapped man's being Leo Minch and Leo Minch's being one of Tucker's people. It had sent a reporter to Tucker's home. The reporter had discovered that Tucker and his family had gone away. The paper wasn't worried about implications where a man like Tucker was concerned.

Wheelock held his coffee cup in two hands and sipped quietly. He knew he had to see Tucker right away, but he wanted to come prepared to argue with him about what to do next.

He tried to figure out what Tucker was likely to want to do, but he couldn't. He couldn't even decide what he wanted Tucker to do. Stay out of trouble. That was all he could think of and there didn't seem to be any way to do it. However they moved, there would be trouble and there would be trouble if they didn't move at all.

Wheelock became irritated at his inability to decide anything. "It's my decision," he told himself. "It's for me to decide about myself, not Tucker." After all, he could quit policy. He wasn't forced to stay. If he gave up the policy business, he would have to give up Tucker. If he gave up Tucker, he wouldn't have anything. With an office overhead like his, he would be bankrupt in a few months. The whole thing depended on Tucker and Tucker's people. But, if he didn't let go of Tucker, he would be dragged all over all the newspapers as a gang lawyer, a mouthpiece, and maybe, with a man like Hall in there gunning for blood, any blood, end his career in jail.

Wheelock thought about it for a long time, about what other clients he could get and about moving into a smaller office and letting his assistants go and starting all over again. He not only would have to start all over again in another field of law, but he would have to start with the label fastened on him: "Tucker's mouthpiece."

Tucker's mouthpiece! Who would call him such an incredible thing? Why, he wasn't at all any such thing as a mouthpiece. But there was no way to shake off the label now.

He realized suddenly there wasn't any decision for him to make. He was in too deep with Tucker. Even if he wanted to, he couldn't get out. Too many in the policy business knew him as Tucker's negotiator, not as Tucker's attorney, but negotiator, a man with authority to say yes or no, this one stays in business, this one goes out. Tucker would have to decide what to do next, and what Tucker decided would have to go for the both of them and for all of Tucker's people.

So what was Tucker going to decide? What? What? Fight. That's right, fight. Tucker was one tough damn baby. No $5 killer was going to scare him and no college boy was going to scare him with his cock-eyes and no Wheelock with his name hung out in the newspapers on headlines like dirty drawers. Nothing was going to scare that baby.

"What the hell!" Wheelock told himself. "I asked for it. I stepped into it when I was over twenty-one and in my right mind." He began to quaver. His lawyer mind leaped far ahead. A picture came clearly. He was facing Hall's cross-examination in a courtroom.

"You negotiated all these mergers on orders from the gangster Tucker, Beer Baron Tucker, didn't you? You and the gangster known as Guinea Joe Minch and the gangster known as Leo Minch, isn't that right?"

That was right.

"They treated you as one of them, didn't they? These gangsters, the Beer Baron, Guinea Joe, they gave you orders and you took orders from these gangsters and did what these gangsters said, didn't you?"

Yes sir, yes sir, right sir.

"You were a member of the gang, weren't you? You were a gangster, weren't you, a gangster along with the Beer Baron and Guinea Joe and the other killers, this Leo, and the other rats, human scum, weren't you? You were a killer along with them, weren't you?"

I object. On what grounds? The question calls for a conclusion from the witness. Sour! Sour! That was sour! You could see how sour it was by the jury's curled face. I want to make a statement for the record. Then he could make a statement proving legally he was not a member of the gang. He was its attorney. Sour! Sour! How juries loved legalistic proof.

"If you leave aside legal technicalities, you were a gangster, weren't you, with Beer Baron Tucker who has a record as a convicted criminal, with Guinea Joe Minch, a convicted criminal, with Leo Minch, who has a record of an arrest as a bootlegger? Isn't that so? Tell the truth. You're under oath now. You've sworn on the Bible of God. Remember your oath and tell me, isn't that true?"

Wheelock held himself rigid. He made his mind blank and sat staring over his lifted cup of coffee. He became aware of the weight of the gun Johnston had given him earlier in the day. It was in an outside pocket of his suit coat.

"Yes," he thought, "I'm a gangster with a gun in my pocket."

He waited for himself to be afraid. He had said it and it was true. He thought he would fly apart, jump up, throw away the cup of coffee, run out of the restaurant, and run through the streets to a train. What train? Any train. No, not the train. They might be waiting for him at the train. Hitch hike. Catch a ride. Stand on a road and thumb a way out of town in a truck, in the rear of a truck, hiding under bags as the bridge was crossed.

Wheelock saw his own white, frightened face under the bags and felt like laughing. There was no one to hide from. Tucker hadn't done anything yet. He probably didn't even know about Leo yet.

It occurred to Henry he had not become afraid. He was still holding the coffee steadily. He put down the cup and touched his hand to his heart. It was beating faster than usual, but that was just from excitement and maybe feeling sorry for Leo. Leo had been a sad, irritable man, but there had been something nice about him.

Henry let go his breath in a long sigh. He was sorry for Leo, that's all, and a little excited, that's all, from wondering what Tucker would do.

That much Doris had done for him already. She had taken him out of crisis and had halted the course of self-examination in him.

Wheelock found Tucker walking around his apartment in socks, trousers and undershirt. The air was clouded with the smell of liquor and smoke. There were nearly a dozen ash trays around the living room, all filled with ashes and burnt matches and cigar and. cigarette butts. Ashes had spilled over to the furniture on which the trays lay and stood on the wood like bald dirt. Two empty and three partly filled whiskey bottles were on a table among an array of empty soda bottles and a large bowl in which chips of ice cubes floated in water. Tucker seemed to be alone.

"You had quite a party here," said Henry.

"Plenty. I'm just going to bed." Tucker spoke languidly. His eyelids drooped in his drawn face. "This party has been going on since this morning," he said. "I'm just going to take a bath and a shave to feel clean for bed and I'll sleep all right. Believe me, I'll sleep."

Wheelock smiled. "That means you got something on your conscience," he said.

"What does?"

"The shave and bath."

"Does it?" Tucker looked at Wheelock steadily. "To who?"

"That's what they say, the doctors say, the psychologists."

"It's a handy thing to know. What's on your mind? I'm glad you came because I got something you ought to hear, but first, what's on your mind?"

Wheelock held out the newspaper.

Tucker did not take it. "I saw it," he said.

"That's what's on my mind."

"Yes, well, sit down." Tucker glanced around the room. "Christ," he said, "it looks like the parlor in a two-dollar house."

Wheelock chose an easy chair and sat far back in it and crossed his knees. He looked relaxed and comfortable, as if he had settled down to hear something entertaining, but the twitch had begun in his cheek.

Tucker went to the table at the side of the room and looked for clean glasses. There weren't any. He dipped two used glasses into the bowl of melted ice and swished the water around before throwing it on the rug. Then he poured whiskey into the glasses. "There's no more soda," he said.

Wheelock didn't answer and Tucker gave him his drink and sat down near him. He sat on the edge of his chair, leaning toward Wheelock.

"I'll tell you what I've been doing all day," said Tucker. "I was going to tell you tomorrow, but I'm glad you came now on account of this." He pointed to the newspaper. "I'll have to move faster on account of this." He took a small drink. He held the whiskey in his mouth and rolled it around before swallowing it. "I've drunk so much today I don't taste it any more," he said. "I never talked so much in my life. I started talking seven o'clock this morning and I haven't closed my mouth on a bite of food yet, except a sandwich. What time is it now, two, three o'clock?"

Wheelock held out his wrist watch.

"I can't see it," said Tucker. "I haven't got my glasses."

"It's 4:20. Who did all the listening?"

"Well, I want to tell you about that."

"That's what I'm waiting for."

Tucker looked at him for a moment and Wheelock met his gaze calmly and held it and fought it until Tucker gave in and shifted his eyes. "Say," said Tucker, "I'm getting cold." He rose and took another drink and put down the glass and rubbed his naked arms. "Just wait a minute," he said. "I'll throw something over me." He went into the bedroom.

Wheelock sat waiting. He did not change his position. The air in the room was thick and warm. Tucker had just been making an excuse to get something in the bedroom. What was he planning to say that he needed a gun? Wheelock asked himself the question calmly, but his mind plunged and bounded like a rabbit through a horde of memories of Tucker and impressions of Tucker's character and memories of gangster movies and stories. He found himself trusting the movies more than his own knowledge of Tucker, but he held himself still. He sat rigidly, far back in the chair, his knees crossed, one leg swinging gently, and felt his hands tremble. He could feel the tremors go into the glass and it seemed to him the glass, too, trembled faintly.

Tucker returned wearing a jacket over his undershirt. The gun was concealed in an outside pocket. "They turn the heat off too soon in this place," he said.

Wheelock smiled to stop the twitching in his cheek. Because of the smile, he cocked his head slyly and, because of the sly cock to his head, he said, "As a matter of fact, I was going to ask you to open a window it's so hot here."

Tucker didn't say anything for what seemed a long time. His face looked heavy and he stared with half-shut eyes. "You're like my wife," he said, finally. "If I say hot, she says cold."

"You know it's stuffy here."

"I say it's cold now. That's what I say and I don't remember getting married to you."

Wheelock gave in to his uneasiness. He uncrossed his legs and leaned forward and clasped his hands and looked up at Tucker. "I'm not going to fight with you, Ben," he said. "I think too much of you for that. I want you to know that I value our contacts together very much and that I admire you all the way down the line and I think I have learned more from you than from anybody I have ever met."

Tucker was embarrassed. "It sounds like I'm getting buried," he said. He picked up his drink and finished it in a swallow and sat down. "I'll tell you what I've got figured out," he said. "Now listen. I'm going to put all my cards on the table for you because that's the way we've always worked together." He grinned. "I mean, after we got started good anyway. I'm going to do what Bunte says and lay low and let the cops work for us."

"The cops?"

"That's right. I decided last night, I mean the night before, you know, the night before this thing Ficco did with Leo, go off his head like that. Let the cops do the work and then I'll come back."

"I don't know. Jesus, Ben . . . what . . . I mean . . . well, Christ . . . I don't know."

Tucker held up his hand. "Just a minute," he said. "Now hold your horses a minute until I'm finished."

"Maybe you've said enough, going away and leaving us here by ourselves like that."

"Now don't get excited."

"What do you mean not?"

"I said not. Just take it easy and not get excited. Hold your horses. Keep your shirt on and let me say what I got in mind. This thing Ficco did tonight, last night, you know, to Leo, well, that just shows you how right I was. Look at it this way. As far as the policy people know, I'm not here since Monday. I went away. You don't know where, a vacation somewhere, with my family. I'll be back soon.

"All right. If I'm here, what'll the bankers do? They'll come running to me for protection and I'll have to do something for them or where is my good will? And if I'm not here, I'm away somewhere on my vacation, you don't know where, I don't have to do nothing and you don't have to do nothing, just say, 'wait till Ben comes back and he'll fix it,' and, in the meantime, the cops will get Ficco and everything will be all right."

"Wonderful all right," said Wheelock. "We'll lose the policy business." He was sitting deep in his chair and frowning. His face looked dark.

"No," said Tucker. "Why should we? You and Joe can stall things along and Johnston. I got Johnston in there while Joe is away. You can stall things along, saying, when Ben comes back, everything will be taken care of and, in the meantime, the cops will get Ficco. We don't have to do nothing about that. The heat's on him now, now that there's been killing. This man, whatever his name is, this friend of Leo's, that done it for us and Bunte will get Ficco turned up as soon as he sticks his nose out anywhere."

"Frederick E. Bauer."

"That's right, so now the heat is on. You see, the thing is, time is with us and I don't want to be pushed in this. That's the thing. If I move in this against Ficco, anything I do, that's just what Hall is waiting for and he gets me and Bunte and he'll get you, too. I don't want that."

"You've got it worked out just right for everything to go in the ash can."

"Talk sense," cried Tucker. "You're supposed to be sensible. Talk like it. What do you want me to do? Go out looking for Ficco? The papers are waiting for it already. You saw the headline. That's just what they're waiting for. You want me to put shooters in all the banks that it's cost me a fortune to get rid of? You want all our names in the papers with the pictures that look like they took them while we was robbing a safe? You want that? I don't. I'll be God damned to hell if I want it. I've been through it and I know. They print something nice what you did in the newspapers and the people say, 'Well, for Christ sakes, even a guy like that has a time in his life when he acts like a human being.'"

Tucker got restlessly to his feet. "No," he said, "no sir, not for me. Think it over. Don't say anything for a minute. Just think about it, what they'll do to you, the newspapers, even if Hall don't get you."

"I've been thinking about it tnree years."

"Don't say anything. Think about it, that's all, some more."

Tucker went to the table and poured another drink for himself. He looked around and saw that Wheelock's glass was still full.

"So that's what you needed the gun for," said Wheelock.

"What gun?"

"The gun in your pocket."

Tucker took out the gun. He held it in the palm of his hand and looked at it a moment. "Yes," he said. "You've been getting pretty temperamental lately, as far as I'm concerned."

"You didn't need a thing like that for me."

"I guess not. It was just an idea of mine that, if you knew I had it on me, you'd sit and listen to what I had to say without making a fuss, getting upset or something like that, flying off the handle."

"I wouldn't make trouble for you, you know that."

"I know, but I knew you'd figure I had it on me and I wanted you to sit quiet and listen. That was the idea." Tucker put the gun into his pocket. He sat down near Wheelock. He held his drink on his knee.

"You see," he said, "I'm right. I saw this thing coming, not Leo maybe, but something like it and I wanted to be away and out of it so my hand wouldn't be forced. That's why I had the people up here today, all day, since seven o'clock in the morning, yesterday morning, people from so far back you never even heard of them, beer people and restaurant people and taxi people and bakery people and all the people from away 'way back, getting money out of them. They don't give up so easy, let me tell you. My throat feels like a stove pipe, like it's got soot in it."

Tucker took a drink and Wheelock did, too. Henry didn't want it, but he felt he couldn't keep smiling all the time to stop the twitch in his cheek.

"I don't want you to get the wrong impression, Ben," said Wheelock, "and think I believe you're trying to run out on us. But I want to know because I'm not going to stay in policy if you're not there. What's all that money for?"

"I'm not sore. That's a fair question and I'll tell you. I need to take care of myself. It's not you, but the other people in it with you and the other people around. I saw what happened to Mottersen when he got knocked off. He had maybe a million dollars cash put out in safe deposit boxes with his friends, in his friends' names on account of income tax and so forth, and when he goes, his friends grab up all the money and there's Mottersen's wife and two little kids without a dime to rub together. They're starving to death."

"You don't expect Ficco to come after you, do you?"

"No, but I figure ahead. Always figure ahead, that's my experience in life. I got this money of mine, some of it, in safe deposit boxes with my friends and they want it. If I take it out, then they'll want it back. If I take my money with me and borrow money from them all I can, the damn little they'll hand out, then what? You see? You get it? They'll have an interest in me coming back instead of an interest in me staying away.

"Also—I'm going to tell you the whole thing. I don't hold nothing back. I told you I'd show my whole hand. Also, if they decide it's cheaper to throw Ben in the street than let him come back when he can, then Ben has the money to take care of himself and his family, wife and two children. That's reasonable, isn't it? There's nothing dirty about that, is there? I even got a paper out of Bunte, down in black on white, that he promises to send me so much a week out of beer. That little thing will keep Bunte in line for you if he decides he knows better than what you tell him."

"In line for you, too."

"Sure for me, too. What's wrong with that?"

"I didn't say anything was wrong. I just said, for you, too."

"All right. Well, that's the layout. I'm leaving tomorrow, today I mean, when I get up, but as far as you're concerned, I've been gone since Monday. I'll send you a wire when I locate somewhere. Just the address and phone number and no signature so you'll know it's from me. You can call me from day to day from a booth."

"That's all?"

"That's all."

"Nothing about Joe?"

"What about Joe?"

"Did you tell him about his brother? Are you going to be gone when he comes back?"

"I didn't tell him," said Tucker, "and I'm going to be gone."

"You figure that's right?"

"Yes."

"You're going to let me do it?"

"Do what? What the hell are you talking about?"

"Handle him."

"He can handle himself. He's a big boy."

"Well, that's what I mean. You want him to handle himself?"

"Talk up. Talk up. What are you talking about?"

"You know. You know damn good and well what I'm talking about."

Tucker looked down. He saw the glass in his hand. He tilted the glass to one side and watched the liquor seem to slant and held it that way a long time. His hand was rock steady. "That's how it is," he said in a low tone. "Joe will have to handle himself."

"That's crazy, Ben. You know it's crazy."

"No, it isn't. I know Joe better than you ever will and I'll tell you what you're going to do, too. You're going to stay away from him for a couple of days or a week, hole up somewhere where he can't find you until he settles down. Let Johnston be there when Joe comes back. Johnston will keep the bankers in line and he don't know nothing. That's all he knows, keep them in line, and you'll be back in a few days and I'm away somewhere and will be back when Ficco is picked up. That's what he knows and was told to do, stall the bankers along."

"It's dirty," cried Wheelock. "It's crazy and dirty."

"And, if necessary, if Ficco comes out and tries to put a payroll on any of the banks, well, give him a few dollars until the cops catch up with him. That's what Johnston knows and that's all."

"But Joe, Ben! Joe! Joe! It's dirty, I'm telling you, real low and dirty, plain low dirty."

Tucker sat still. The whole upper half of his face seemed to have sunk into the lower half and the lower half was clamped around it. His lower lip stuck out thoughtfully. He remained that way a moment, thinking. Then he said, "I don't want to argue. I'm tired."

"That's nice. You're. . . ."

"I said not to argue. Did you hear what I said? Not to argue. Just keep away from him and he'll settle himself one way or the other. If he comes back in with us, all right. The place is waiting for him. I'm not closing him out. If he doesn't . . . well, let him alone and see what happens."

"You can't do it. There's a limit."

"I can't think of anything else for him."

"Ben, think a minute what he'll do."

"I know what he'll do. He'll be sensible and stay in the business and do what's right; or, he'll lose his head and go after Ficco and be out of the business. That's what he'll do."

"I've known you a long time," said Wheelock, "but I've never seen you do a thing like this, that's not right the way this is."

"It's right all right. It's the only thing to do. The only thing to do is always right."

"No. No. You know that as well as I."

"All right, go ahead, tell me what I know."

"Joe's been with you all these years and turned over his brother to the combination and now there's his brother and the combination sits there without moving and tells Joe to go to hell. For Christ sake, Ben! You're not pushing checkers on a board here. That's a crime to a person you're doing. A real crime. A real low, dirty, criminal thing to do."

"Don't get so excited." Tucker waved one hand slowly up and down. "Don't talk so loud. There's nothing we can do for Leo now. By this time he's either told Ficco all he knows or he's too bad off for us to help him. They got sore and lost their heads and he's too bad off."

"That's not the point."

"What do you want me to do, be college boys and get even? We're not playing kid games. If Joe wants to get even, that's got nothing to do with the business and it would be a real crime, my idea of a crime, to let him drag the business and everybody in it into getting even for him."

"You're not talking sense. You're talking plain dirt."

"It's sense! I'm telling you it's sense!" Tucker's voice was so high and so filled with pleading it almost broke.

"It's not sense to do nothing about Leo," said Wheelock. "Who's going to trust you? You put down $110,000 for good will, and now who's going to have any faith in you if you do nothing about Leo? You're thinking crazy, real dirty crazy."

"Oh, don't talk like a child, like the rest of them. That's the way all the others think, shooting off all over the place, dumping stiffs on doorsteps to keep up their credit and good will and reputation so people should go on thinking they really are what the people think they are and what some of them themselves think they are with the God damn brains they got around here in this business. I've seen it and seen what happens. No, this is sense. I've got enough of that kind of credit and reputation now and anybody thinks not, let them put it up to me right straight where I can't duck it and then we'll see. No, I'm right. I'm away. I don't know nothing. When I come back, the war starts. That's what they'll think. And, when the cops get Ficco, I'll come back and they'll think, if I'd of been here, I'd of gotten him. That's real sense."

"And Joe? What will Joe think?"

"If he cools off, he'll see we did what's right for the business."

"And if he doesn't cool off?"

"That's his worry."

"I won't stand for it," cried Wheelock. He got up and took a few steps away from Tucker. His face was flushed and his eyes moved wildly. "There's a limit to what a man will do for business," he said.

"I didn't know you liked Joe so much." Tucker looked at him calmly. "I always thought you two didn't get on so well."

"I don't care. That's not important. There's some place a man has to stop, Ben. He can't give himself away, his whole self, everything for business. There has to be a place, Ben!"

"Well, this is not the place." Tucker finished his drink and pulled himself heavily to his feet and walked slowly to the table and poured another drink. He didn't lift the glass from the table. He left it there and turned to face Wheelock. "What am I doing that's

so wrong?" he said. "I'm not a young man any more. I have a family
to think of and I have to take into account how many years left I
got to live it down when I make a mistake. I don't see what I'm
doing is so wrong, so terrible. What about any corporation when a
man becomes a liability to them?"

"Ben," cried Wheelock, "you know that's not the point."

He was standing and facing Tucker. His fists were slightly
clenched and raised toward his chest. He realized suddenly he had
made a stand for something he wanted to believe and had made it
where it couldn't be defended. He didn't know why, wily as he was,
quick-minded as he was, he hadn't seen to the end of his argument
before he began it, to where his argument was reduced to nothing.
He didn't let himself become aware of the reason for the blindness
that had fallen over his mind and had made it fumble in argument
where it was trained to go most quickly. For, if he had, then he
would have known he wanted assurance that there was no place for
a man to draw a line in business and say he will go this far and no
further. And, if he knew that, then he would have known he had
given his whole self to business and would have started on the way
of Bauer.

"Why not?" said Tucker. "Why isn't it the point? The corporation throws him out. They say, get the hell out. They don't wait
even if he's not a liability exactly. If the corporation can get somebody who's better for the job or who's cheaper, then the hell with
him, out he goes and the hell with his family and his feelings and
he can starve to death or kill himself for all they care."

"But," said Wheelock and stopped. He didn't know what to say.
He knew Tucker was wrong and the reason lay just below the surface of his mind, but it didn't come up. He couldn't let it come up.

"No," said Tucker. "What's the but? I'm not doing that to Joe. I
say, if he acts sensible, all right, the place in the business is open for
him. And if he doesn't, I'm sorry. I can't let the business be pulled
down by him. There's too much at stake, too much for me and for
you and for all the people in it. The whole thing will get broken up
if we let Joe tell us what to do.

"No, no, if I was younger or the times was different, there wasn't this fellow Hall and people didn't care so much, they weren't poor and they weren't looking for things to get sore at as long as you didn't bother them personally . . . but, Jesus Christ! Look at the people I got to think of beside Joe and Leo or myself or you, what you want. There's more than 6,000 people working for me in policy alone."

"Not me," said Wheelock, "not what I want. You're the boss and, if you say throw Joe out on his own, that's you doing it, not me."

"Yes, it's me. I'm the boss and I'm doing it. What you have to do is hole up somewhere for a few days until Joe settles this thing for himself one way or the other and that's all."

"All right, you're the head man. What you say goes."

Tucker looked at him for a moment. Then he turned away, back to the table where the whiskey stood. "Maybe it won't be bad," he said. "Joe is a good boy. He's got sense. I'm sure he'll see it right." He talked with his back to Wheelock and his gaze fastened on the whiskey.

XXVII

WHEN WHEELOCK left, it was daylight and Tucker was shaving. Henry had waited to see if he would really do it and Tucker was doing it all right. His hands were steady and he looked into the mirror carefully and steadily, as if he didn't have anything else on his mind and maybe even was enjoying the shave. That was the last Henry saw of Tucker, standing before the mirror and scraping at his upper lip, his whole face pulled out of shape and his tired, blood-browned eyes staring intently.

Henry went to his west side apartment and packed some clothes. He worked hastily, going rapidly from closet to valise, from bureau to valise, from bathroom to valise, so rapidly his suit fluttered. He remembered suddenly a $50 bill he had left in the dresser drawer a long time ago. It was under the amber velvet lining of a small leather box in which he kept collar buttons and studs and tie pins and collar pins. He had noticed once the lining was loose and, on impulse, had slid the bill under it.

"Like a squirrel hiding nuts," he thought as he pocketed the money and tried to think where he had hidden other money. He remembered putting money in the watch pockets of trousers and taking it out. He had folded a bill under the moistener in his cigar humidor once while fiddling around with nothing to do. But that was in the Park Avenue place. He felt sure there were other places, but he couldn't remember them. "The nut has been hiding plenty of squirrels," he told himself.

He picked up his valise and walked towards the door and realized he hadn't decided where to go and stood holding the valise. He tried to think of a place to go, but he wasn't able to concentrate. He kept trying to remember where he had hidden money and then he thought he ought to call his office and explain he would be away for a few days. He'd have to wait until nine o'clock for that. He looked at the grandfather clock in the foyer. It was kept wound by the day worker who did the cleaning. It showed 8:26. He went into the living room and sat down. He sat on the edge of the sofa, his hat and coat on, and stared expressionlessly at the valise at his feet.

The silence was all around him. It had the feeling of loneliness. Sounds hung in it and became part of the silence, just as people become part of a man's loneliness. The sounds were of the clock and the city stirring to work and the blood going through his head with a far-off roar.

He could have opened the blinds and let in daylight, but he didn't. He sat in sallow darkness. He could have gone to the window and watched the cars and the buses and the men stepping along the sidewalk to the subway snappily, as if on the way to success instead of to business. But he didn't. He sat looking at the valise. At least, he could have opened the window and let some air in to blow out the stale, unlived-in smell, but he didn't. The smell was strangling. It hit his nose and choked his throat and clotted around his face, but he couldn't bring himself to do anything about it. He sat waiting—for nine o'clock, he told himself.

At last he didn't hear anything but the clock in the foyer. The pendulum went back and forth, forth and back, back and forth, forth to tick, back to tock. It rapped the air and tacked the air, tick-tack, tack-tick, tick-tack, tock-tick, tick-tock, tick-tock, tock-tock, tock-tock, tack-tock. A change there, a small change there.

A pendulum going back and forth was a falling object. That was from Physics 1, Prof. Fahne, short and slight as a jockey, but sedate. A falling object, prevented from falling, swung back and forth— something like that. He had known it better when he was in school. Funny how those things one slaved to fix in the mind and fixed in the mind went away. Gravitation in there. Gravity made the pendulum swing back and forth because the pendulum was being held up, instead of allowed to fall. Back and forth, here to there, place to place—that was falling, going down. A man running from room to room, from place to place, was falling, going down. Down, down, daown, daow—wen!

Wheelock sat still. His glance clung to the saddle-leather valise standing sturdily in the sallow darkness. The sounds of the clock marched across the room steadily and marched into his ears in single file. There was a whir and a single soft bong and another whir and another single, soft bong. Eight-thirty.

He sat without moving, leaning forward a little, head stooped, and thought of Tucker shaving. That was a hard man, a real tough man, with horn-lined guts and a brain of brass flesh. To shave like that! With all the things he had on his mind and yet to stand there and shave!

Maybe that wasn't so tough. The psychologists did not know everything. Maybe it wasn't because his conscience was bothering him. Maybe it was just show. If he were really tough, he wouldn't give up the business and ruin it just to run away from Joe like that. That's what he was doing, running away, not for the business. Hell, he was killing the business and running away for himself. No, if he were really tough, he'd get Joe on the phone at Windsor and back

Joe into a corner and fight him down and make him listen to reason. That would be really tough and what Tucker was doing was running away, flying like everybody else, going from place to place, falling down. Scared. He just looked tough, but inside he was as soft as a pussy cat asleep . . . in cream.

Wheelock thought suddenly of Doris. The image of the soft cat had brought her into his mind. But he had been thinking of her all the time. She had been among the layers of his thoughts. He had been thinking that what Tucker had to hold him up and force him to act tough and steady and patient was Edna. He had Doris. If it had not been for Doris, he might have had a breakdown. He might not even be alive. He might have killed himself.

He felt that now. All night his mind had been running around and around the edge of its own destruction, teetering, scrambling back, plunging forward, gripped to the edge, always gripped to the edge. If it had gone over into what lay beneath his mind, then he would have been dead now or about to be dead, opening the window, standing on the ledge. Else, why had he come to this apartment and not the others? Because there were no servants to face? Because it was the nearest to Tucker? Maybe. But maybe, too, because it was the highest of the three and a jump from the window here would be the surest!

Henry got up and stood restlessly a moment and went into the foyer and looked at the clock. It was 8:33. He went back into the living room and turned on the radio. But, before a broadcast could start, he shut it off. He stood over the radio and thought of Tucker shaving with steady hands. Not a tremor in the man! Not a thought in his face, nothing, only a look of contentment, as if he liked the idea of shaving.

Edna was holding him up all right. She was doing that for Tucker. If a woman goes away for a while, she does not leave a man, not entirely, not so that his whole character changes and falls apart and does something he would not do otherwise, runs out on his business.

It wasn't smart to run out that way. It just wasn't smart. No matter how scared Tucker was or how guilty he felt about Leo, he shouldn't throw Joe out like that. Nobody had expected Ficco to take Leo, not even Joe. Joe had been there himself and had heard what Ficco was going to do and not even he had believed Ficco would take Leo.

All right, thought Wheelock, tell him that, not run out on him. Tell him Ficco's crazy, a Sunday thinker. Nobody could predict him. The whole thing was an accident, couldn't be helped, one of those things, and Joe, you hear, you be sensible, that's all. That's what Tucker should do instead of running out like this because he was afraid to look Joe in the face.

Henry debated for a moment going to Windsor himself, but he decided against it. He and Joe didn't get along. He had never been able to handle Joe. Joe brushed him off like a fly. No, it would have to be Tucker. He went to the telephone and called Tucker's apartment.

∾

Tucker was lying in bed, the telephone on the night table alongside him. He was bathed and shaved and his wet hair was neatly combed. He had been lying still with open eyes long before the telephone began to ring. He was trying to sleep, but his eyes wouldn't remain closed.

He listened to the telephone for a little while. Then he turned on his side and pulled the blankets over his head. It didn't shut out the noise. He put his head under the pillow and pressed the pillow down with his hands. He could still hear the noise. He lay still listening to it. It was like a nail being hammered with slow blows into his ears.

"Edna should see me now," he thought suddenly and went stiff for an instant while the telephone kept nailing its sound into his ears. Then he sat up and took the receiver off the hook and laid it carefully, mouth down, on the table.

Another sound came out of the telephone now. He could hear a series of buzzes drone against the table. He adjusted the pillow and lay back and closed his eyes. His eyes wouldn't stay closed. He listened to the telephone. It was silent. Then a scratchy girl voice came through the receiver and was smothered against the table. The words were smothered but not the feeble, struggling, angry, scratching sounds of her voice.

He knew what it was. Whoever had been calling him had complained. At first there was no answer. Then there was a busy signal. Must be something wrong there. Telephone out of order there. Receiver knocked off the hook, something wrong there. The girl was trying to find out. She'd send a man around to find out.

Tucker got out of bed and began to dress. He didn't want to see the telephone man or see the police or see anybody. The police would want to question him to find out what he knew about the killing of his man. He'd take a taxi to the ferry and take the ferry to New Jersey and take another taxi somewhere else. Short hauls, that was it. Then no hack driver would remember him. Short hauls to Newark and then he'd take a train, somewhere, somewhere. He didn't know where. Not to Edna. That would bring danger down on her and the children.

He knew there was no danger now for Edna. He knew Ficco was just as frightened as he and just as much in hiding. He just didn't want Edna to see him all soft and scared. He felt, if he went to Edna, just being with her would make him do something tough that would get him into trouble.

Tucker thought all that and didn't know he thought it and didn't want to know he thought it. Instead, he told himself, "That would be a hell of a thing, to bring all this down on Edna and the kids."

When Wheelock put down the telephone after complaining to the operator, he decided either Tucker had left or would have left before he could get there. He found he didn't want to do anything about it. He called his office. The girl voice that answered had the fresh ring of morning in it and sounded sharply in his ears. He didn't know who it was.

"This is Wheelock," he said.

He noticed the voice's abrupt slide into a kind of deference and fear for the "Oh, yes sir," and thought it must be one of the file clerks. He told her to tell Mr. Baker and Miss Locke he would be away for a little while, perhaps a week. Mr. Baker was his chief assistant. Miss Locke was his secretary.

Wheelock knew he would want to keep in touch with his office and with Bunte and Johnston by telephone. Johnston would need advice on the things that came up in the policy business and in running whatever was left of Leo's bank. He decided he would not leave town, but would go to a hotel somewhere and register under a false name and just stay in his room and do his work over the telephone. The best place to hide is in a big city. Somebody had told him that, somebody long ago, Joe. That's right, Joe. Or no, maybe not. Maybe it was somebody else. Anyway, it was true. And suddenly he thought it was true, too, that he had been training all his life to be a fugitive, picking up information and storing it away and not forgetting it.

Henry took up his valise and went out of the apartment without a backward look. He slammed the door. The sound smashed into silence and the closing door blew a gust of wind over him and in the wind was loneliness. All the loneliness in the apartment had blown out with the wind and sound of the closing door and it fell on his clothes and on the back of his head and swept around and covered his face and fell down along him and sank into him.

XXVIII

Wheelock got downstairs and walked slowly to the corner, feeling his loneliness and trying to decide on a hotel. He thought of hotels uptown and downtown and in Brooklyn and of hotel rooms he had been in and of how the bedsprings sounded when he had sat on them in the silence and how the dresser drawer sounded when he had pulled it out in the silence and how his voice had sounded when he had talked into the telephone in the silence. The loneliness was on his clothes and on his face and under his clothes. It was skin for his skin and it was within his body, too.

He got into a taxicab and gave the driver the address of Doris's apartment. He felt he'd be able to pick a hotel after talking to her.

When he rang, the landlady opened the downstairs door. She was a mousy-looking bag of a woman, her face plump and seamed, her fat slumped down from her chest and fallen over her middle. She opened the door inside the vestibule to a crack and held the neck of her robe closed with her hands.

"Is my wife in?" he asked.

"Your wife?"

"Doris Duvenal. That's her name, stage name she works under."

She looked at the taxi going away and looked at Wheelock and then at his expensive valise. "Why, yes, I guess so."

She opened the door wider and Wheelock stepped in.

"I didn't know Miss Duvenal was married," she said.

"Well," Henry smiled, "you know how it is on the stage."

She started up the stairs ahead of him.

"I'd like to surprise her if you don't mind," he said. "You know, this whole thing is a surprise, dropping in on her like this, and I'd like to surprise her by myself."

He kept his voice low. The whole house seemed to be asleep. The landlady halted and looked at him doubtfully.

"Just tell me which apartment it is," he whispered and smiled.

"There's somebody shares it with her."

"Yes, I know. She wrote me. But there are two rooms, she said, I remember she said, so it will be all right, won't it, even if they are in bed."

His friendly, quite charming, boyish smile was an unusual experience for her.

"I mean," she said, ". . . but you see . . . I don't know . . . you see, I mean, you know . . . I don't know."

Wheelock put on his most ingratiating smile. He let it stay for a moment and thought, "I hope she feels it in her pants."

"I could show you our marriage license," he said, "but it's in here."

He lifted the valise. "I keep it with me always, wherever I go, for good luck."

"Oh, you know I didn't mean anything like that!"

"Of course."

"But we have to be careful, what with all kinds of people. You'd be surprised at the things people can think up to do."

"It's all right. I'm really glad it happened because it makes me feel my wife is in such safe hands."

"I must say I don't butt in, but . . ."

"She's one flight up, isn't she?"

"That's right, in C."

The stairs were carpeted, but they creaked. It was an old, narrow, dark house. There was an apartment at the landing—A. Wheelock turned right down the hall, trailing his free hand along the thick, round, oak bannister. He went on his toes, but the hall floor creaked, too.

Apartment C was near the end of the hall. There was no bell. He knocked. No answer came and he knocked again. He was afraid to knock loudly. He tried the door. The door opened and he walked in and closed it softly and went to the middle of the room. He was in a sitting room. He found he was holding his breath. He let it go nervously and put down his valise.

"Doris," he said.

At one end of the room was a doorway screened with a brightly striped curtain. He faced it.

"Doris," he repeated. His voice didn't sound clear. He couldn't hold it steady.

There was a long silence. He didn't go closer to the doorway. He stood still facing it. "Doris," he said, "are you asleep?" His voice still quavered and he put his hand to his chest.

"Who's there?"

It was Doris's voice. Even in the confusion of sleep and fear, it had a simper in it. Everything inside that he had been holding up let go. He had forgotten about her voice.

"It's me," said Henry, his voice full and quiet, "your wandering boy." He looked around the room. The room had a dark, walnut table and a lumpy sofa and two worn easy chairs and cheap lamps and a blue picture on the wall in a gilt frame.

"So this is my pleasance," he thought. He knew now he had not ever intended to go to a hotel. He took off his hat and coat and threw them on a chair. He wanted to do that before Doris came into the room. If she saw him do it, she might become angry.

Doris brushed back her hair hastily and hastily wiped her face dry of cold cream and flung her bathrobe around her and then took it off and borrowed her roommate's because it looked better. The roommate was a girl from the show. She watched Doris wide-eyed, but Doris didn't say anything to her and dressed as if she were muttering under her breath and came into the sitting room, looking worried and frightened, her pink mules clacking.

"What's the matter?" she cried. She flew, her grape-like eyes swelling with alarm, to Henry.

Wheelock pointed to the doorway and Doris shook her head. She thought he meant he wanted to go in there.

"She's gone?" he asked.

"No. What's happened?"

Doris had whispered. Henry took her hand and led her to the far corner of the room. He put her against the wall and leaned close to her and looked into her face. "I'm in trouble," he said in a low tone. "You have to help me." His voice shook and he swayed and lowered his head until it touched her shoulder. He was very tired.

She didn't move except to turn her head slightly towards him. Her body was stiff. Her hands remained at her sides. "Why?" she said. "What is this?"

"It's nothing, except, that is . . ." He lifted his head and looked at her. "I'll tell you the truth. There's a man wants to make trouble for me and, if I stay away from him for a few days, I'll be all right."

"But who?" she cried. She put her hands on his shoulders. "I mean, a hotel. Why here? Why not a hotel somewhere?" She shook him a little bit and his body yielded to her touch without resistance. It was slack under her hands.

"I can't stay without you," he said.

"No, now listen. You can't stay here, simply can't."

"Please, I must. I can't be without you. That's the truth. I'll go crazy alone. You've got to help me."

"But, how can it be? No! How can it be?"

"I must. I must, please, Doris."

"You can't. My roommate."

"Please." He put his face close against hers and his whisper went along her face like breathing. "We'll tell her to go to a hotel for a few days. I'll give her the money, any money she wants."

"But it's impossible!"

"Doris, please."

"No, this is impossible!"

"Doris, you've got to help me. I want to marry you. I must, don't you see? Don't you see what will happen to me if you turn against me, too? You're all I've got left."

She tried to get out of the corner and he put his hands against the wall, fencing her in without touching her. "No," she said, "we're not married or anything. No!"

"I want to get married."

"No."

"You say no? You mean no? You, too?" Anguish rose and rolled and fell and rolled under the skin of his face.

"What's the matter?" she said. "Is it really bad?"

The tears came into his eyes. He looked away from her, ashamed. He pressed his chin against his shoulder and bit his lips.

"This man," she said, "is he bad? Will he . . . I mean, hurt you?"

"Pretty bad." He looked into her eyes for a moment. The tears were trailing down his face and his chin was twisting and his lower lip curled and quivered.

"Don't, darling," she said. She put her arms around his neck. He had lowered his head and she pressed him into her and his head went against her chest. He smelled warmth and the dry smell of sleep. His head began to roll slowly from side to side and she put one hand on it. It rolled under her hand.

"Ssssh," she whispered, "it's all right, all right, dear, all better now."

She saw her roommate standing in the doorway, the curtain pushed to one side. Doris frowned and shook her head and the roommate went silently back to the bedroom.

Doris led Henry to the couch, whispering, "Sssh," and, "it's all right," and "there, there," and, "please, darling."

❧

The roommate was sent to a hotel. Henry wanted to give her $100 for expenses, but Doris insisted $20 would be enough. When Doris heard Henry had identified himself to the landlady as her husband, she laughed.

"You've got your nerve," she said. But it made it easier to explain why he was staying and the other girl was moving out.

Wheelock slept all day and into the evening, almost until Doris came home from the theater. When he woke up, it was a little before eleven o'clock. He dressed and found a gas stove and icebox in a corner of the sitting room under a green drape. He made eggs and bacon and coffee for himself and Doris and found he was hungry and made more eggs and bacon and ate more bread and drank more coffee.

"I've never had a better meal in my life," he said.

"If you could only sew, I'd marry you." It was Doris's idea of a joke and Henry laughed willingly.

They cleaned the dishes together in the bathroom sink. She washed and he dried. He told her it was a hell of a place to wash dishes and she said it was all the place there was, this wasn't a housekeeping apartment. The landlady had put in a stove and icebox only because they had asked her to on account of the strange hours they kept, being in show business.

He was silent after that for a while and then he said, "I feel real married."

"Well, we're not." Her voice was too emphatic. It sounded frightened. She lowered her head and scrubbed at a dish.

He wondered if she had had some idea that he would continue to sleep in the living room. That was the way it happened in the movies. She must be thinking that. It happened that way in the movies and was always so cute that way and so exciting. Only she knew it wasn't going to happen that way here. Her voice showed she was thinking of the movies, but knew what to expect and was waiting for it to happen, and didn't know which she'd like better, the movie way or the real way. So she must have had a man before, one, two, not many. It couldn't have been many. She was so young. But at least one. Some country boy, maybe, with overalls to unhinge and drop, a general store squirt, or the fellow from the gas station or the local bus driver or somebody, in a barn or behind a barn or in the grass, or on the back seat of an auto, somewhere . . . maybe just to find out what it was like and if it was as good as they made it seem by wanting it so much.

Henry felt sorry for her. He felt her youth and eagerness and fear and laughed suddenly. He draped the dish towel over the edge of the bathtub and went over to her and turned her around and put his arms around her. "You know we're going to be married soon, Mrs. Wheelock," he said.

"Go away. I smell from dish water."

"It's a wonderful smell."

She tried to push him away, but he wouldn't let her and she tried to break his hold and he wouldn't let her.

"It's the smell of marriage," he said, laughing.

She struggled. Her body wriggled against his and he stopped laughing.

"Doris," he said.

She stopped struggling and looked at him and he pressed her close and kissed her. It was a long kiss. His lips moved over her mouth and moulded her lips. He led her towards the bedroom, still holding her, still kissing her.

"I've got my apron on," she said.

Her voice was muffled by his mouth and went into his mouth and sounded in his head.

"I'll take it off," he told her.

XXIX

The next day was Saturday and Doris had a matinee to give as well as an evening performance. Wheelock began telephoning. The only telephone in the house was downstairs in the hall where anyone might overhear, so he used a public phone in a drug store on the corner. He called Johnston twice to give him instructions on matters that had come up in the policy business and found out, the second time, that Joe had been there.

"How did he act?" he asked.

"What do you expect?" Johnston said.

"Can you talk now?"

"Yes, sure, there's nobody here."

"Well, how did he act? What did he do? What did he want to know?"

"He wanted to know where Ben was."

"Did you tell him?"

"How could I? I don't know where he is myself."

"What else? Tell me the whole thing, how he came in and what he said, what you said, how he looked, the whole thing, what he said he was going to do and so forth, the whole story."

"Well," said Johnston, "he came in and he looked like hell. I told him what Ben had said about going away to lay low, that's all. That's the whole thing. And I was to stall everybody off and run the works until you and him come back. That's all. And he was to help with the stalling off. That's all."

"Then he went away?"

"Not for a while. The whole thing lasted quite a bit of time. What did you expect?"

"Tell me the whole thing. That's what I want to know."

"Well, Joe wanted to know if we had heard from Ficco, anything like that, you know, about his brother, if we got some word that we have to pay Ficco something to get Leo back and like that. Well, nothing like that has come in and I told him."

"What else?"

"Well, that's all, I guess. He was sore, naturally. What do you expect? He thought I was holding out on him and knew where Ben was or you was, but I convinced him I didn't."

"How? How did you do it?"

"I showed him my bald head."

"What do you mean?"

"That's what I mean. I pointed to my bald head and he decided he couldn't go to work on an old man like me."

Wheelock was silent and Johnston waited a moment.

"He knows me a long time," Johnston said then, "and knows when I'm telling the truth and it is the truth. I don't know where Ben is or you and you'd better not tell me."

"He's not there now?"

"Who?"

"Joe."

"No, nobody's here, I told you."

"Did he say what he wants me for or Ben?"

"Yes, he did say. He thinks if Ficco is going to get word to someone he wants dough to let go of what he's got, you know . . ."

"All right. Leo. Say it. To let go of Leo. Say it!"

"Yes, that's the one I mean. Well, Joe figures Ficco will get word to Ben or to you, nobody else. Who else should he get word to, me?"

That's the thing, thought Wheelock. Of course! That was the thing, the little thing, they had forgotten! No, they had thought about it. Ficco hadn't snatched Leo for money, but for information. Why not for money? Why hadn't he grabbed him for money, a mad, wild dog like that!

"Listen," said Wheelock, "when Joe comes back, you tell him . . ."

"The hell I will. I won't tell him nothing. He's in a nervous condition and he's got a gun and he's very nervous."

"Tell him this."

"No, I won't. If you got anything to tell him, tell him yourself.

I haven't heard a word from you. I don't know nothing and I don't want to know nothing. That's the way I feel."

"All right," Henry said, "that's the best, I guess."

"I don't care if it's the best or not. That's what I'm going to do."

After that, Henry felt he had to walk around the block. The restlessness had come back into him. But he was afraid to go into the street. He kept thinking Joe would happen by and see him. "There are a thousand streets in this town," he argued with himself and added, "No, my luck's all run out." He remained in the drug store from which he was telephoning and drank some coffee and then called Bunte.

Bunte said the police had got on to the fact that the killing and kidnapping were connected with the policy business and he had given them the lead on Ficco. He hadn't said anything about Tucker. He had just told of Ficco's attempt to extort money from Gilliam. The police, said Bunte, were pretty sure Leo was dead. A woman who had been in the restaurant at the time said she had seen them beat Leo's brains out with a gun butt, but the police didn't believe her. They didn't think the gunmen would carry off a stiff. But they had decided pretty much, from what the waiter in the place said and from what Leo's wife said about his blood pressure, that Leo had had a stroke. They wouldn't get him a doctor so the chances were pretty good Leo was dead by now.

Then Henry called his office. He knew that, although it was late Saturday afternoon now, Baker would be there and his secretary, Miss Locke, too. Baker was ambitious and a hard worker, no clock watcher and the aging, unmarried Miss Locke, Henry suspected, found life dull outside the office.

Wheelock talked to Baker for a while. Everything seemed to be going all right. "I could go to Europe and you'd never miss me," he said.

Baker denied that and then Henry asked to be switched to Miss Locke. He wanted to find out what was in his mail. She told him. Her voice seemed dry and quiet. There wasn't anything important in the mail.

"Well," he said, "I'll keep in touch."

"Just a minute," said Miss Locke. "Mr. Minch has been waiting here to talk to you all afternoon."

Henry didn't say anything. His hand pulled the receiver from his ear and he stood a moment, holding the receiver in the air, thinking, thinking so fast he didn't know what he was thinking about. Then, slowly, he put the receiver on the hook and pulled it down to make sure the connection was cut off, and stood pulling the receiver down and staring at the blank, dead telephone.

He knew why Miss Locke had done it. She had been making a play for him all these years. Why, the woman was as old as he was, two, three years older. But she had been hoping. Even though he had never even looked at her, she had hoped. And now she had read the newspapers about Tucker being missing and had put things together and had decided there was no use hoping and had given him the needle on purpose. And now Joe knew he was in town and hiding from him. He would ask and they would tell him it had not been a long distance call.

"By God," he cried to himself, "do I have to get killed because an old maid bitch is in heat!"

When Henry got back to Doris's apartment, he was shaking.

❧

Doris and Henry had all day Sunday together. It was a long day. There were breakfast and the big Sunday papers for the early afternoon, just after they got up, and then nothing. He couldn't talk to her. The simper in her voice became more and more irritating. There was nothing to say to her. All she knew was what she had learned in Sunday school.

"Go down to Hall," she said, "and make a clean breast of the whole thing and you'll be out of it, you'll see. You'll be out of it and Hall won't do anything, you'll see."

That's all she knew. Confession was good for the soul. Be honest. Obey the law. Keep to the right. Cross only at crossings. Curb your dog. What did she know about Hall? How did she know he wanted to get out of it, this thing that was his business and that still had a future, if they could just lay low long enough and let the cops get Ficco and let Hall make his career out of Ficco.

"Hall will appreciate it if you help him, you'll see," she said.

It occurred to neither of them to question the morality of selling Bunte and Tucker and Joe Minch to Hall for a profit. Doris thought of going down to Hall only as an atonement to society and felt, mystically, that this mystical thing known in her mind as society would reward repentance. Henry knew better. He had a much more realistic appreciation of what Hall represented. But he had become so completely a man of business that it did not occur to him to defend himself on moral grounds, on the grounds that it simply was not right to sell the lives of human beings, any human beings, for a profit. And if he had thought of it, he could not have made such a defense ring true. Instead, he attacked Doris's naïvete.

Sure, he told himself as she spoke, put your hand out when making a turn. Stop clear of the crosswalk. Honor thy father and mother. Do not talk to the operator while car is in motion. Ask for transfer when paying fare. Spit in your handkerchief. Throw waste in the basket. Love thy neighbor if he's not a catholic or a jew or a seventh-day adventist or a nigger or a greaser or a ginzo or a hunkie or a bohunk or a frog or a spick or a limey or a heinie or a mick or a chink or a jap or a dutchman or a squarehead or a mockie or a slicked-up greaseball from the Argentine, or if he don't scratch himself too loud, or if to love him doesn't cost anything.

"I'm going to bed," he said. He forced himself to smile at her. "I'm still not slept out altogether." He thought, if he slept, it would pass more time. That girl is boring me to death, he told himself. He got into bed and lay still and closed his eyes, but sleep would not come.

Maybe, he thought, when he woke up it would be late at night and she'd be ready for bed and the whole day would be gone. But there would be more days. He couldn't spend the rest of his life in bed. "No!" he told himself, "the hell with that!"

He was through being a heel. There would be more days and

they would be married and they were going to have a whole lifetime together. "I've been a heel long enough and now I'm finished,"
he said to himself. "I'm going to start being decent for a change.
That I promise myself. And I'll stay decent. That I promise, too."

He had taken her as if she were medicine waiting on a shelf
for him and now he couldn't put her away. Even when it was all
over, he told himself, and he didn't need medicine any more, he
couldn't put her back on a shelf because she wasn't medicine, she
was a human being and he was going to be fair to her. If she
wanted him, she could have him. He was going to stick to her as
long as she stuck to him and be kind to her and decent to her
and not hint by one word or act that he didn't want her to stick
to him. That was final.

Wheelock got up and walked into the sitting room. Doris was
on the couch, darning some stockings. He sat down beside her.

"I want to tell you," he said, and knew before the words had
formed in his mind that he could not cure himself of being a "heel."
Even now he was going to try to get rid of her. But gracefully!
Not so she should know! At least, so she should not know!—"if
there's trouble, it's not going to be something you can blow away
with your mouth."

"I know." She put down her sewing. "You told me."

"If Joe finds where I am, it's not going to be something that
will last a minute or two or an hour or a day, the trouble, I mean.
It may be one of those always things."

"How can he find you?"

"I don't know." He thought of Joe going from place to place.
He wouldn't sleep. No, Joe wouldn't sleep. "I'm just saying," he
said, "and I want to be fair to you and warn you to look out for
yourself."

"He won't find you. He can't."

"If you don't look out, that's what I got worrying me, if you
don't, you'll be ruined with me."

"You're my husband now, practically, for better or worse."

"No," he cried. "Darling, now please be sensible. If you get all this notoriety, you're through on the stage. You know that. Let's talk facts."

"I love you." She leaned over and kissed him. "That's a fact, mister."

He remained still and thoughtful under her kiss. He realized suddenly he had never once told her he loved her. He would have to eventually, but as yet he could say fairly and honestly he had never lied to her. "I feel terrible," he said, "walking in here like this and dragging you into it, right out of your sleep in fact. It wasn't fair. I want to be fair to you. If he finds me, something will happen, may happen. I don't know. But we've got to look ahead."

"It was fair. I love you. All's fair in love or war."

"I know, dear. I know that. But, listen to me now. Something may happen, it may not, but something may, to break up my whole business and career, I don't know what, maybe go to jail and the notoriety and all will ruin you. Who'll give you a job? Just burlesque time for a few weeks. That's all you'll be able to get. 'Wheelock's Moll! See her dance! Adults only!'"

She looked at him archly. "I'm beginning to think, mister, that you're trying to get rid of me already."

"Darling," he cried. "Don't say that." He flung his arms around her and held her tightly.

"It's just," he said at last, "we have to act sensibly. I don't want to ruin you. I'm not going to ruin you and you listen to me because I'm the head of the family now."

They talked a long time about it. He told her he thought he ought to go to a hotel somewhere and she said he wouldn't be any safer there and he would be so lonely and he said he wouldn't. Then he told her he would be lonely, but he wanted to be fair to her and she said it was her right now to protect him and they argued and finally she promised him she would take care of herself. If trouble came, she would run out on him as soon as she saw it was the real thing, the serious trouble.

"I'll be a fair weather pal," she said. "I swear. I never heard of you until your trouble is over. But then I heard of you the rest of my life."

She went downstairs to buy something in the delicatessen for supper, smoked turkey, she said, and when she had gone, he looked at the papers scattered on the floor. But he didn't feel like reading them. He glanced at his watch. It was 7:30.

"Well," he thought, "it passed some time anyway."

He decided he would work on Doris some more about being fair to her and going to a hotel and hiding there. And then, when the trouble was over, if the trouble ever did get over, if Joe ever did settle down and Ficco ever did get caught and they could put the business together again, he'd marry her. Yes, he would! That was definite. If she wanted him, he'd marry her. He was through being a heel now for the rest of his life.

XXX

THE KNOCK on the door came a little after ten o'clock. The dishes had been washed and put away. Wheelock had begun again to talk about being fair to Doris and going to a hotel and she was saying again that, if there were any trouble, she would be sure to run out on it and stay away until it was all over.

When the knock came, Henry was standing in the middle of the living room in his shirt sleeves. He looked at Doris and looked at the door and felt the floor press against his feet. He was in his socks. He would have to put on his shoes before he could run.

"Who is it?" asked Doris.

"Exterminator." It wasn't Joe's voice, but neither was it the voice of any man. No one spoke normally in that tone. Doris and Henry stared at each other.

Run, thought Henry, hide, hide in the bathroom, in the closet, under the bed, out the window, down the fire escape, taking his shoes with him, coat, hat, money! No, how could he leave Doris to face Joe?

"Open the door, please," he said to Doris. He was surprised at his voice. It sounded so small and quiet.

Doris went to the door. She kept it locked now. She unlocked it. Before she could do more, Joe burst it wide open. The door knocked Doris to one side and Joe came in shoulder first, bulling through the air. He saw Doris first and pushed her so hard with one hand it was almost as if he had hit her. Then he faced Wheelock. He held a revolver and he pointed it.

"Now, you son of a bitch," he said, "now!" He was breathing heavily.

Henry looked at the gun. He didn't see anything but the gun. He thought if he could say something, some little something surprising, it would startle Joe and snap him out of it and quiet him.

"Now what?" Henry tried to keep his voice calm and questioning, but it shook a little. "What's the matter, Joe?"

Joe's gaze wavered towards Doris and then sprang back to Wheelock. "I had an idea," he said, "that a son of a bitch like you would hide in a hole with hair on it. That's what gave you away."

"Cut it out," said Wheelock angrily.

"Cut it out?" Joe took a step forward. "I'll cut your heart out, you double-crossing rat bastard. Rat bastard, rat son of a bitch, double-crossing, sneaky, God damn rat son of a bitch bastard, I'll cut your throat out." His voice rose into a scream. "Where's my brother? Where's Tucker? What's that son of a bitch done for my brother? I'm going to kill him, too, that's what I'm going to do."

"Sit down," said Wheelock. "Take your hat and coat off. I've got a lot to tell you."

"You're God damn right you have, you son of a bitch."

"You don't need that thing you're holding. Put it away."

"I'll decide whether I need it," said Joe. He took another step forward. "You're not going to decide anything for me any more. You, you son of a bitch, you're through with me. I'd kill you for a nickel. I'd kill you just as fast as I'd spit a rat out of my mouth, you son of a bitch."

Joe's left hand, the hand that did not hold the gun, was clenching and unclenching along his trouser leg. He lifted it suddenly and rubbed it across his chin. He hadn't shaved in two days. He had been too busy hunting Tucker and Wheelock. He had known Wheelock played Broadway and he had hunted along Broadway and had found out about Doris and had got Doris's address a few minutes before. He had come rushing, without thinking, to find out.

To find out what had been done for his brother? He knew nothing had been done. If Ficco asked for money, Tucker would tell him to keep Leo. To find out what had been done about the business? He knew. Johnston had told him and he knew that Tucker had figured out the right way—to stall, to play for time, until Ficco was caught and then move back and try to put the business back into line again. He knew this and knew it was right, it was business, and had gone hunting anyway, up and down Broadway, getting people into corners, waiters, night club managers, girls, telling them if they didn't come through for him, he'd remember it and, when he got time, they'd be sorry he remembered it, until finally he had found out and had come rushing. He had to rush and he had to hunt to get away from what he knew and didn't want to know—that nothing had been done and that doing nothing was the smart, right, only way, the business way. And now, maybe, hunting and rushing was not enough and he would have to kill to get away from what he knew and did not want to know.

Henry heard the rasp of Joe's hand against the stubble of whiskers on his chin. Joe's eyes looked drowned in blood. He was shivering and, when he didn't talk, he seemed to have to struggle to catch his breath. His whole chest lifted and fell and his whole face opened to take in air.

"You look as if you need something to eat," Henry said, "and a bath. Why don't you go in and take a shower and we'll fix you something while you're bathing."

Wheelock felt surer now. He smiled friendlily. Joe hadn't done anything. He had just talked. That meant he wasn't going to do anything. He was just looking for a place to work himself out, that was all. He had had Friday and Saturday and Sunday to figure it and he knew they had done what was right for the business, for him, too, because it was his business, too, and he'd stay quiet, too, like the rest of them until it blew over. He was just looking for a place to scream himself out and curse himself out and cry himself out and work himself out of what he felt because of Leo and what he felt because of what he had to do for the business, his business, too, more his business than Wheelock's now that Leo was out.

"While you eat, we can talk," said Henry.

Doris hadn't moved from where she had been flung. The door still stood open behind Joe. She had come up against a chair and she was standing there now with white face and open mouth. She was afraid to move. She thought a step by her or a loud breath would set off the gun.

"That's just like a son of a bitch like you," said Joe. "You want me to bathe myself when my brother is dying three days and you want me to take a shower and sit here with you and some tramp you picked up while my brother is dying." His voice quavered and struggled with it and struggled with himself. "You didn't want him," he cried. "No, you and Ben didn't want him, not good enough for you, you didn't want him from the first, you bastards, son of a bitchen bastards. Nobody wanted him. Not you, not you. Never. Not you."

Joe put his empty hand before his eyes, not quite touching his forehead. His chin was wrinkled up and quivering and the tears were hot in his eyes and dripped thickly down his face.

"From the beginning," he mumbled and meant to say something about how Wheelock had objected to trying to save Leo's money at the beginning of the formation of the combination three weeks before. But he thought suddenly of how he had been the favorite child and Leo had been the ignored one and how Leo had always helped him and how he had thought the combination was going to pay Leo back for everything, for running out of the home Leo had made for him, for running away from the cigar store Leo had bought for him, for ruining Leo's garage business, for

everything, for hating Leo sometimes, yes, hating him, hating Leo
enough to want to pull him down and kick him down and have
him lying at his feet and be sorry for him again as he had been
when they were children.

"Leo," cried Joe. His voice broke in his throat and seemed to fall
out of his mouth in pieces. "Leo, Leo, God forgive me, oh my Leo!"

He had tried for Leo. The combination! That was to be the
thing to make up for all. Anybody who said he had forced Leo
into the combination, not to make his brother rich, but to pull
his brother down and have his brother lying at his feet where
he could be sorry for him . . . he'd kill anybody who said that.
And yet . . . and yet . . . what had he thought of for three days?
What were the only thoughts plain in his mind? That Tucker
and Wheelock had done the right thing for the business. And,
with Leo out, Leo's bank would be his. Yes, that, too, had been
plain in his mind, fixed there, unconquerably there as dirt is unconquerably fixed on earth.

"Joe, please." Henry came forward slowly with one hand outstretched. "Joe, please, don't do that." He rested his hand on Joe's
shoulder and Joe threw it off.

"Naaaah," said Joe, "you bastard!" He hit Wheelock in the
chest with the side of the gun. "Don't touch me!" he shouted.
"Don't put your dirty, lousy rat hands on me!"

The blow was a hard one. Wheelock fell backward against the
table and spun around and clung to the table to keep from falling
to the floor. As he clung, his eyes closed with pain and, even as
the echo of Joe's words sounded in his head, he heard a small
noise flutter swiftly along the hall and down the stairs. He
straightened up and turned around slowly. "I just wanted to talk
to you, Joe," he said.

Henry looked for Doris. She was gone. His chest hurt him. He
thought perhaps a bone in it had been broken, but he couldn't
take his eyes off the spot where Doris had been. Then, slowly,
he shifted his gaze to the door. It still swung open.

He wondered why people hadn't come when they heard Joe

screaming and cursing like that. There must not be anybody to hear. It was Sunday night. The whole house must be empty, except for the landlady. The landlady must have let Joe in and then gone downstairs to her apartment in the basement. Wheelock stood figuring this out slowly and looking at the open door. He could see the hall and the stairwell and the blank, dark wall beyond.

"I don't want to talk to you," said Joe. "I want to know where Tucker is and I want to know what you know, that's all. God damn it, where's Ficco? Has he sent word? Do you know where Ficco is, that's what I want to know!"

"Can I sit down? You hurt me." Henry held his hand to his chest. "I think you broke a rib."

If Joe would stop hollering like that, he thought, then he could decide what to do, whether to tell Joe Doris was gone and they were both in danger. Had she run away? Was she doing what he had told her to do and taking care of herself? If only that were true! If only, if only! He had to think. If it were true, it would be dangerous to tell Joe. It would give him another run-out to think of and might set off his gun. And if it weren't true, it would be dangerous not to tell him because then it would mean she had gone for help, for the police. If only Joe would stop for a minute and let him sit down for a minute and think for a minute and figure out what she was up to and how she planned to work it to keep herself out of trouble.

"I should have broken your head," said Joe. "The dirty thing you done to me with my brother deserves no consideration."

"I didn't do it."

Henry knew Joe realized it had not been his responsibility, but he wanted to argue about nothing and think of Doris and whether she had run away. His chest still hurt him. His head was swollen and heavy and he knew it was going to be a long night of telling Joe what Joe already knew and letting Joe scream and work himself up and maybe hit him and work himself up and up and up until finally he was worked out and ready to stay quiet for the business.

"You know," he said, "none of us is really responsible. There was nothing to do anyway. He went, you know, painlessly, bing, like that!" He snapped his fingers. "I wish I could go like that when the time comes."

"What? What are you saying to me?" Joe's voice sounded high and far off.

"Well, Joe, I'm trying my best to say. Did he have high blood pressure?"

"What? Tell me! What? Who? Tell me! WHAT?"

"That's what I mean," said Wheelock. "He had a stroke at the time and there was no pain, no feeling or nothing. The best way, Joe, the very, very best way there is to go."

"Leo!" The name grunted out of Joe. "I knew it, Leo," he cried. He lifted his head high and shouted over Wheelock's head. "Leo! Leo! I knew it all the time!"

Henry looked away. It was too painful to watch Joe's face. "That's right, Joe," he said. "There's no pain, you know, no pain at all. The witnesses saw him get the stroke, the people there at the time, and when you get it, there's no, well, you know, no pain, the best way to go I guess, the best way, Joe, and that's a fact. It's merciful to go that way. I'm telling you the truth."

"You and Ben, you knew about this, my brother dying there, when maybe a doctor would help him, dying there and you did nothing, you and Ben?"

"What could we do?"

Wheelock saw Joe coming towards him. He took a step backwards. Joe's face was unrecognizable. He was a big man and he had cried big tears and the tears stood out on his face in yellow streaks and balls and, under them, his face looked black.

"Where's Ficco?" cried Joe.

"I don't know."

"Tell me!"

For each step forward Joe took, Henry retreated one.

"Honest," said Henry, "I don't know. I wish I knew. Joe! You hear me, Joe? I wish I knew!"

"Tell me! Where's Ficco? Tell me! Where the hell is he? I'll kill him myself. That's for nobody else. Tell me. That's for me. I'll chew his guts out with my teeth. Tell me, you son of a bitch! Tell me! Tell me or I'll murder you!"

Joe lifted his gun up and for a moment Wheelock wasn't sure any more. He thought Joe might shoot. Then Joe threw the gun on the floor. It landed with a thud and bounced and bumped and slithered and Wheelock was sure again. It wasn't death that faced him, only a beating, a bad beating, maybe bones broken, maybe a rupture. He had the physical courage to face that.

"Tell me, you lousy little shyster bastard. Tell me!" cried Joe. He lunged towards Wheelock and grabbed him and shook him. He was powerful. He lifted Wheelock right off his feet and threw him down as if he were a rag. Wheelock stumbled and Joe grabbed him again and shook him again.

"You tell me or I'll kill you," he said. "I'll break every bone in your body and kill you. I mean it!"

"Joe! I don't know! Stop this!"

"No."

"You know I don't know. If I knew, the police would be there. Stop this, I'm telling you! Stop it!"

"No! No!"

Joe hit him. He hit Wheelock as hard as he could with his fist, high on the side of his face, and Wheelock went backwards and lunged and tottered and pulled himself erect.

"Joe!" he whispered. "For God sakes! The door!"

Joe didn't hear. He was coming towards him again, blindly. Wheelock tried to get away.

"The door is open!" Henry said another time and ducked. He was afraid to speak loud. He thought someone might hear and come.

Henry hadn't ducked in time. Joe's blow came down on the side of his face again. The whole inside of Wheelock's head seemed to bounce away from the blow and smash. He fell to his knees and Joe hit him again, on his mouth, and kicked him and hit him again and again until he toppled over and lay flat. Then Joe began to kick him and stamp on him, on his body and his hands and legs and, when the police came in, they found him trampling Wheelock.

~∽

The police came in with drawn guns. There were two men in plainclothes and two in uniform. One of the plainclothesmen ran across the room and stuck his gun into Joe's middle.

Joe seemed surprised. His eyes were glazed and his mouth open. He backed away slowly, staring at the gun, and the other plainclothesman came alongside of him and hit him on the head with the butt of his gun. Joe crouched and spun and pitched forward. His body crashed against the floor.

Doris flung herself down beside Wheelock and lifted his head. "Are you all right?" she cried.

He heard her. He opened his eyes. "Yes," he said. "All right. I don't know yet. Maybe."

He tried to get to his feet. She helped him. He couldn't straighten out. His side hurt and his chest hurt and his back hurt and his arms and legs and head felt broken. He felt broken and bleeding inside. He went, all stooped over, to the couch and sank into it.

"It took so long to get them," said Doris, "that's why. Just rest. Rest and you'll be all right. I told them, 'Hurry.' I said, 'Hurry, hurry, it's Joe Minch!'" Henry moved his hand slowly and covered his face. "Oh darling, darling, I think you're hurt. Rest. Sit back and rest. If they had come sooner, but the policeman wouldn't come. I told him, 'It's Joe Minch, you must hurry, he has a gun,' but he wouldn't come until the radio cars came." He groaned. "Oh, you're hurt. I know you're hurt. I'll get you a cold towel."

Wheelock hadn't heard what she had said. He kept wishing she would stop talking. He was glad when she went away. He didn't have to smile at her any more and could close his eyes and groan to himself.

"That's the Guinea all right," Henry heard one of the plainclothesmen say. Then he leaned far back and closed his eyes and moaned softly. He was flat on his back. The couch felt deep around him. The flesh of his body trembled all over.

Doris wrapped a cold towel around Henry's head and wiped the blood off his mouth and from the side of his face with a wet handkerchief and sat crying and whimpering tenderly over him. The shock of the cold cleared his mind and he pushed her away and pulled on the back of the couch to sit up. He had to think. This was a moment when he had to do the right thing, think up something fast. His whole future, all the rest of his life, depended on what happened next.

He watched the police. They were taking a long time. They were in no hurry to make up their minds about this. They were sniffing around all over. It wasn't a simple assault case, not just a fight. No, no, this was Joe Minch. If it was Joe Minch in a fight, then it might have something to do with his brother, with homicide and kidnapping. Must have. Must have. No, they wouldn't be in a hurry to bundle up Joe and go away. They'd sniff and poke and see what they could find. They didn't know Wheelock, but they wouldn't be in a hurry to let him go. He was the injured party. It was plain. He hadn't committed the assault. He was the plaintiff. But, homicide! Kidnapping! They'd hold him a long while until they made sure.

Henry thought abruptly of the gun in his coat in the bedroom. Still there! With the permit for it in his wallet in the inside pocket!

That did it. There it was. The whole thing smashed. Hall was working on the homicide and kidnapping. He would learn about this and about the permit. That permit would give him the lead. He would track it down to the deputy commissioner who had issued it and the deputy would tell everything.

Sure, why not? Save his skin. Everybody telling to save his skin. Bunte had called him up, sure, late at night, said it was a friend of his, sure, Tucker's lawyer, do Tucker a favor, sure, anxious to oblige Tucker, personal favor for Bunte. Bunte always doing favors for Tucker. Sure, sure, late at night, just before the killing. Tucker must have been expecting the killing. Bunte must have been expecting the killing.

There it was, the whole case for Hall, the beginning of it, any-way, something to get his teeth into, something with which to put subpoenas to work for him and get at Wheelock's files and with Joe Minch in jail and Wheelock in jail and Tucker a fugitive and Johnston in jail, there was the case, the whole case, and the whole thing smashed up. The end. Finished! He was finished and done with and better off dead.

The police were still in the sitting room. Henry watched them. They were picking up things and looking into things and poking around and one was still bending over the unconscious form of Joe and putting handcuffs on him and going through his pockets. Henry felt he must have been lying on the couch and thinking only for an instant. The police had just come in and he had thought all these things in a fraction of a second.

Doris was alongside him. She had her arm around him. "Please lie down," she said. "Lie still and you'll be all right. The doctor is coming."

He looked at her. He had forgotten about her. She was in the smash-up, too! Why hadn't she let him alone! The damn fool! Oh, the God damn dumb jackass bitch of a fool! Why hadn't she let him take his beating as he had been prepared to do instead of bitching up her life and his life this way! Did God ever make a fool like that before in His life!

Henry heard a man call from the bedroom. The man must have been in there all the time, looking around.

"Oh, Pete," the man said, "can you come here a minute?"

A plainclothesman, talking in low tones to one of the police-men, turned and walked slowly towards the bedroom. Henry knew the gun and permit had been found. The plainclothesman went slowly, looking from side to side as he walked, to see if he could find anything. Henry watched him and held his breath.

When the man got past the brightly striped curtain in the door-way and the curtain fell back into place behind him, Henry grabbed up Doris's hand and stuffed it into his mouth to keep from screaming.

AN EPILOGUE

XXXI

As was pointed out at the outset, there is no proper ending to this story.

An ending requires a conclusion or a resolution. Leo and Bauer were dead, but their lives had not been concluded or resolved by death, merely interrupted. Joe could not decide whether he had forced Leo into the combination to make his brother wealthy or to strip his brother of power over him, but he did decide—having nothing to help him, having not so much even as Bauer had had—he did not want to live any longer. He hung himself from the bunk hook in his cell with a strip of mattress cover while awaiting trial. His death, too, was merely an interruption of his life.

The state sought to contrive a conclusion for the story, but it could not. How could it, when the bulk of its energies were devoted to perpetuating itself and, for that, it needs must conceal from itself and its citizens what its way of life was doing. Yet, the state staged a great trial and conducted an expensive, patient and talented search for "truth" and this was the "truth" with which it emerged—that Bunte, Wheelock and Johnston belonged in jail for contriving and operating a lottery.

Nor did Wheelock arrive at any conclusion about himself or resolve his life in any way. Instead, he prolonged its blunderings. His violent distaste for the corruption in him made him insist on making an end to it, by becoming "virtuous." So he corrupted his life all the more by being "loyal" to Doris and by marrying her after he got out of prison, thus corrupting her life, too.

Tucker, too, thought himself out in a limited way. He did not understand why his love for Edna and her love for him should have made him "tough," why "toughness" should have restored him to society, in the first place, and then made him an enemy of society and then, finally, should have placed the whole structure of his life in danger. But, although he did not understand why, he realized it was so and wrote Edna, sending her the keys for a safe deposit box in which $160,000 in cash lay. After that, he disappeared and neither Edna nor the children nor any of his other people ever heard more from him.

But there is no end in any of this and no ending either. Sylvia, for instance, was left comfortably well off and she bloomed into a new kind of life. She rejected all her brother's advice as to how she should invest the money Leo had left and went into the real estate business herself and managed to become crafty at it. She occupied her evenings with competent bridge.

Catherine Bauer got the relief checks her husband had lost his life striving for. A whole volume would be required to describe what the sense of guilt her husband bequeathed to her did to the balance of her life and the children's life. Egan remained on traffic duty until he reached retirement age. Milletti won his promotion and Foggarty got his pension as soon thereafter as he could.

The policy combination remained and thrived, resisting, for no mysterious reason, all its people's disasters. Ficco bossed the combination for a while, but other, smarter men took it from him and he is now working for them.

Wally is Ficco's chauffeur. It is felt he cannot be trusted with anything important. Perhaps that is the conclusion.

The End

IRA WOLFERT (1908–) won international recognition for his work as a journalist while publishing three major novels and a variety of nonfiction books. His second novel, *An Act of Love,* was a bestseller in 1949 and was reissued in revised form by Simon and Schuster in 1950.

ANGUS CAMERON was an editor at Little, Brown until he was blacklisted in 1951. After running his own dissenting publishing house for seven years, he joined the staff of Alfred A. Knopf, where he was senior editor and vice president until 1981.

ALAN FILREIS, a professor of English and director of the writing program at the University of Pennsylvania, is the author of *Modernism from Right to Left* and *Wallace Stevens and the Actual World*.